THE EARLY JOURNALS
AND LETTERS OF
FANNY BURNEY

1. Mrs Elizabeth Allen Burney. From a portrait by an unknown artist, before 1763.

THE EARLY JOURNALS
AND LETTERS OF
FANNY BURNEY

VOLUME II · 1774–1777

Edited by
LARS E. TROIDE

McGill-Queen's University Press
Montreal & Kingston · London · Buffalo

© Lars E. Troide 1990
First published in 1990 by Oxford University Press
Published simultaneously in Canada and the United States 1990 by
McGill-Queen's University Press
ISBN vol. 2   0-7735-0539-3
Legal deposit second quarter 1990
Bibliothèque nationale du Québec

This book has been published with the help of a grant from the Canadian
Federation for the Humanities, using funds provided by the Social Sciences
and Humanities Research Council of Canada.

Canadian Cataloguing in Publication Data
Burney, Fanny, 1752–1840
The early journals and letters of Fanny Burney

Contents: v. 1. 1768–1773. – v. 2. 1774–1777.
ISBN 0-7735-0538-5 (v. 1) –
ISBN 0-7735-0539-3 (v. 2)

1. Burney, Fanny, 1752–1840—Correspondence.
2. Burney, Fanny, 1752–1840—Diaries.   3. Novelists,
English—18th century—Correspondence.   4. Novelists,
English—18th century—Diaries.   I. Troide, Lars E.
(Lars Eleon), 1942–   .   II. Title.

PR3316.A4Z48 1988   823'.6   C86-094863-3

To Joyce Hemlow and the Memory of
Patricia Hawkins

ACKNOWLEDGEMENTS

This volume is dedicated to Dr Joyce Hemlow, Greenshields Professor Emerita of English, McGill University, the architect of modern Burney studies; and to the memory of Mrs Patricia Hawkins, who for twenty-five years served as Dr Hemlow's loyal and conscientious secretary and editorial assistant.

To many of the institutions and individuals acknowledged in Volume i, such as McGill University, the British Library, and Mrs Althea Douglas, who 'floated off' the paste-overs on the manuscripts in the Berg Collection (see *EJL* i, pp. x, xxix–xxx), I will continue to owe a large debt of gratitude for the duration of the edition.

For assistance with the present volume I am especially indebted to the Social Sciences and Humanities Research Council of Canada, which provided continued funding of the research. Permissions to publish the manuscripts in their care or possession have been granted by Dr Lola Szladits, Curator of the Berg Collection, the New York Public Library; the British Library (for the Barrett materials); the Pierpont Morgan Library, New York; John R. G. Comyn, Esq.; and Professor Margaret Doody, Princeton University. Illustrations have been obtained from the British Library; Sotheby's, London; Dr Raymond Paul Martin, Montreal; and Dr Szladits.

Fanny Burney's text in this volume was originally transcribed from the manuscripts by Mr Marc Cassini. Dr James Neil Waddell of Bishop's Stortford College deciphered the obliterated passages in the text. Additional help with transcribing, indexing, and research problems came from my McGill graduate student assistants, Mrs Jacqueline Reid-Walsh and Mr Stewart Cooke; Mr (now Dr) Cooke has since become my full-time research assistant.

Some of the original annotations for this volume were generated by students in my graduate seminar on eighteenth-century editing: Messrs Paul Murphy, Christopher Coy, and Stewart Cooke; Father James T. Peck, SJ; Ms Irene Aguzzi;

Mrs Susan Charters; Ms Mary Radcliffe; and Mrs Jean Mason-Parkinson. Other help with specific problems is acknowledged in the appropriate footnotes.

CONTENTS

LIST OF ILLUSTRATIONS   x

INTRODUCTION   xi

SHORT TITLES AND ABBREVIATIONS   xviii

EARLY JOURNALS AND LETTERS OF FANNY   I
BURNEY from 7 February 1774 to *post* 11 November
1777, Numbers 13–47

APPENDICES
1. Fanny Burney's First Letter to Thomas Lowndes   291
2. A Letter of Mrs Elizabeth Allen Burney to Fanny
Burney   292
3. Fanny Burney's Letter to Esther Burney, July 1770   295

INDEX   297

LIST OF ILLUSTRATIONS

1. Mrs Elizabeth Allen Burney. From a portrait   *Frontispiece*
   by an unknown artist, before 1763.

   ·By permission of Dr Raymond Paul Martin

2. The Orange Street Chapel, St Martin's   53
   Street, formerly the Burney family residence.
   From an engraving executed by Charles John
   Smith and published by William Pickering,
   Chancery Lane, London, in 1837.

3. Antonio Sacchini. From a portrait by Sir   69
   Joshua Reynolds, 1775.

   By permission of Sotheby's, London

4. Fanny Burney's letter to Thomas Lowndes,   218
   post 17 January 1777, showing her disguised
   hand.

   Reproduced from the manuscript in the British Library

5. Barborne Lodge, Worcestershire. From a   234
   drawing by Clement Francis.

   *By permission of the Henry W. and Albert A. Berg Collection,
   the New York Public Library, Astor, Lenox, and Tilden
   Foundations*

INTRODUCTION

THIS volume brings us to the eve of Fanny Burney's sudden fame as the author of *Evelina*.

The novel may have been gestating in her mind from· as early as 1767, when she burned its predecessor, 'The History of Caroline Evelyn', Evelina's mother (see *EJL* i, p. xv). In January 1776 her father, Dr Burney, published the first volume of his *General History of Music*. Fanny, freed temporarily from her labours as amanuensis, found the time needed to complete, in secret, the writing of the first two volumes of her work. In December of that year she wrote, anonymously and in a feigned hand, to the publisher Thomas Lowndes and subsequently sent him the fair copy of volume i (conveyed by her brother Charles, disguised preposterously as 'Mr King'). Volume ii followed in January 1777. Lowndes liked both volumes but refused to publish until the novel was complete. Fanny was able to send him the third and final volume by September, and after a temporary falling-out over the price Lowndes was willing to pay (20 guineas, whereas Fanny thought 30 guineas a minimum), the novel was set to be published early in 1778 (see pp. 212–88, *passim*).

Fanny later destroyed '*in totality*' her journal for 1776, on the grounds that it was '*upon Family matters or anecdotes*' (p. 199). It was probably fairly brief, in any event, because of her preoccupation with *Evelina*. (Some letters from that year are preserved.) The fullest year in the present volume is 1775, which is almost as long as the other three years combined. It contains, among other things, Fanny's lengthy accounts of some of the Sunday evening musical parties in St Martin's Street, whence the Burney family had moved from Queen Square in October 1774. She composed parallel accounts of these evenings in her journals and in letters to Samuel ('Daddy') Crisp, who in his self-imposed isolation at Chessington, Surrey, craved the entertainment they afforded. Since Fanny's two versions of a given evening substantially overlap, the longer or (when both are the same length) earlier version is offered, with additional details from the other in the notes.

xii *Introduction*

This volume shows the continuing development of Fanny's acute powers of observation and description. Her shrewd insights into character are exemplified in the many portraits which suggest types of human virtues and follies. Thus, in the journal for 1774 the callow impropriety of the young traveller, Richard Twiss, is balanced by the quaint humanity and good nature of the Moravian James Hutton. These portraits are followed by a scathing depiction of the minor writer, George Keate, who, 'attentive to his own Applause', holds court to a circle of fawning old spinster sisters whom he visits in Great Russell Street (pp. 34–6). In 1775 we are introduced to the great soprano, Lucrezia Agujari, who is the type of the operatic prima donna and whose rivalry with Caterina Gabrielli is vividly presented. Other, minor characters who appear or reappear in a moralizing or satirical light include, for example, Mrs Burney's old friend Dr King (the Prelate as Pompous Fool), Dr and Mrs ('Brilly') Wall of Gloucester (Good-Humoured Eccentricity Wed to Heartless Narcissism), and the ineffably silly Miss Waldron of Hartlebury.

Among the most memorable figures in this volume is a trio of exotics who visit the Burneys in St Martin's Street. The first of these, Omai, was the first Tahitian ever brought to England. He arrived in July 1774 on board the *Adventure*, James Burney's ship. Fanny's brother had befriended the 'Otaheitan', and in November Omai made his initial appearance in St Martin's Street. The day after his visit Fanny wrote a long and enthusiastic account to Daddy Crisp. In her eyes, as in the opinion of most of the English public, Omai, with his lively intelligence and seemingly natural gentility, appeared to be living confirmation of the myth of the 'Noble Savage'. She concludes her report with a disparaging comparison of Lord Chesterfield's natural son to Omai: Philip Stanhope, 'having all the care, expence, labour & benefit of the best Education that any man can receive,—proved after it all a meer *pedantic Booby*' (pp. 62–3).

The second 'exotic' to visit the Burneys was James 'Abyssinian' Bruce, the famous explorer who had recently returned from Abyssinia. Bruce was an imposing man in every respect. Enormously tall (he stood six foot four) and broad in proportion, he displayed a commensurate pride and hauteur that most observers found daunting. His haughtiness was no doubt increased by the open scepticism the British public manifested towards some of the tales he had brought back from Abyssinia, such as his claim that the natives there ate raw flesh. Fanny paints a vivid picture of his pride, but also shows him to have a sense of humour once he unbends a little, besides an unexpected (and strong) susceptibility to the charms of music. She concludes that 'It is a pity that a man who seems to have some generous feelings, that break out by starts, & who certainly is a man of Learning & of Humour, should be thus run away with by Pride' (p. 87).

The third exotic visitor was Prince Alekseĭ Orlov of Russia. Like Bruce he was a huge man, weighing some 300 pounds. Unlike Bruce, he was a murderer, having led the group of officers who assassinated Czar Peter III in 1762, permitting Peter's wife Catherine to ascend the throne. Fanny discounts his role in the assassination as mere rumour ('He is *said* to have seized the Emperor') but asserts (it 'is *known*') that he became Catherine the Great's lover, thus confusing him with his brother Grigoriĭ (p. 169). Diamond-encrusted, sensual, ribald, larger-than-life, Orlov emerges from Fanny's pages as the stereotypical Russian barbarian, in striking contrast to the polished urbanity of another Russian, Mr Poggenpohl, whom the Burneys had met in 1772 (and who satirized this stereotype in a delightful interplay with Fanny's ten-year-old stepsister Bessy; see *EJL* i. 194–6).

Yet a fourth 'exotic' might be added to the list above. This was Dr Samuel Johnson, who, with Mrs Hester Thrale and her daughter Queeney, made his first visit to St Martin's Street in March 1777. Fanny's portrait of Dr Johnson in her letter to Daddy Crisp is worthy of a Boswell. Her description of his bizarre appearance and mannerisms ('he is almost bent double. His mouth is ⌐in perpetual motion,⌐ ... he has a strange method of frequently twirling his Fingers, & twisting his Hands;—his Body is in continual agitation, *see sawing* up & down', etc.) and reporting of his characteristic conversation ('"There is not," said Dr. Johnson, "much of the spirit of *Fabulosity* in this Fable"') are equal to anything in the *Life of*

Johnson, published 14 years later (see pp. 225, 227).[1] They
show the hand of a fully mature artist, who was even then
finishing the novel that would soon make her famous.

It has long been observed that Fanny's journals, at their
best, often read like a novel. This novelistic quality is perhaps
most graphically evident in the passages of May–June 1775
where she describes, in suitably melodramatic manner, her
rebuff of the hapless suitor Thomas Barlow. In this episode
Fanny really comes centre stage herself for the first time in
the journals. Barlow is a boarder in Hoxton with a Mrs
O'Connor, an old friend of Fanny's Grandmother Burney.
Fanny first meets him one evening, accompanied by Mrs
O'Connor and her deaf-mute daughter Miss Dickenson, at the
home of Charles Rousseau Burney and Fanny's sister Hetty.
Their meeting may have been contrived by Mrs O'Connor
and Grandmother Burney, who is also present (along with
Fanny's Aunts Nanny and Becky). In any case, at the parting
of the company Mr Barlow surprises Fanny with a 'most
ardent salute' and soon after sends her an 'ardorous' letter
which amounts to a declaration (pp. 117–18).

Fanny's family and relations almost immediately join
ranks behind Mr Barlow. Unfortunately, though Barlow is
young, handsome, well-to-do, ⌐"civil"¬, 'good tempered', 'sensible', ⌐"bears an excellent"¬ character', and 'has a great desire
to please', Fanny finds his language 'stiff & uncommon', he
has 'no elegance of manners', and 'niether, though he may be
very worthy, is he at all agreeable' (p. 116). Until this point in
her life Fanny has virtually always yielded to the wishes of
her parents and elders. Now, though, confronted with the
prospect of being pressured into a marriage of convenience to
a man she does not love and who, she feels, would bore her to
death, Fanny shows a resolution to resist, which holds firm
even when Mr Crisp urges her to consider Barlow seriously.
Finally, however, her resolution almost turns to desperation
when her father speaks to her '*in favour* of Mr Barlow!' (p.
146). Knowing herself incapable of resisting 'not merely my
Father's *persuasion*, but even his *Advice*' (p. 146), Fanny

---

[1] In 1790 Boswell tried, unsuccessfully, to obtain from Fanny Johnson's letters to
her for inclusion in the *Life* (*DL* iv. 432–3).

instinctively resorts to the last tactic of a totally dependent daughter. She tearfully throws herself on his mercy, appealing to his paternal love:

'O Sir!—' cried I—'*I* wish for Nothing!—only let me Live with you!—'—'My life!' cried he, kissing me kindly, 'Thee shalt live with me for ever, if Thee wilt! Thou canst not think I meant to get rid of thee?'

'I could not, Sir! I could not!' cried I, [I could not out-live] such a thought—' I saw his dear Eyes full of Tears! a mark of his tenderness which I shall never forget! (p. 147)

Fanny's tactic succeeds. Dr Burney wants to settle Fanny in a comfortable marriage, but is convinced at last that *this* union would make her miserable.

Prior to this climactic scene Fanny has had what she hopes is her final interview with Mr Barlow. Fanny's report of the interview, with its artful blend of skilful narrative and convincingly recollected dialogue, is as finished as any scene in *Evelina* (and perhaps even more compelling since it is a distillation of real life). Fanny, her heart unmoved, stands adamant against the increasingly desperate arguments of Barlow, which range from protestations of his own worth and sincerity to an abstract consideration of the unnaturalness of the single state. When Barlow returns for yet another interview, Fanny forces herself to be extremely cold to him, which finally persuades him that his suit is hopeless.

Fanny's account of Barlow's suit is of course a slanted one meant to highlight dramatically the danger to her own happiness which it presented. It is not possible to read the episode, though, without feeling some sympathy for Barlow. However contrived the match may have originally been, it seems fairly evident, from his behaviour both during the courtship and after his repulse (as reported by Mrs O'Connor), that Barlow actually fell in love with Fanny. All in all, we are left with the picture of a young, well-meaning, but inexperienced suitor, who 'fell' for a young lady who possessed the intelligence and vivacity that he himself so conspicuously lacked.[2]

---

[2] See Samuel Crisp's defence of Barlow in his letter to Fanny, 8 May 1775, pp. 121–4.

One last character remains to be mentioned in this Introduction. That is Mrs Elizabeth Allen Burney, Fanny's stepmother. The frontispiece to this volume is a portrait (by an unknown artist) of Mrs Burney, painted when she was still married to her first husband, Stephen Allen (d. 1763), a wealthy grain merchant of King's Lynn. It is one of a matched pair of portraits of her and her husband which were recently discovered at New Orleans and acquired by Dr Raymond Paul Martin of Montreal. In the mid-nineteenth century they belonged to William Maxey Allen (1792–1865), son of Stephen Allen, Fanny's stepbrother. It is not known how they came to New Orleans. The portrait of Mrs Burney (then Allen) shows her when she reigned as one of the beauties of Lynn. Aside from the frontispiece, a letter of hers which is included as Appendix 2, and passing mentions in the text, she is conspicuous in this volume by her relative absence. A number of obliterated passages that have been deciphered contain unflattering references to her. In one of these Fanny calls her '*Mrs. Bramble*' (p. 177). (The Burney children also called her 'Precious', 'La Dama', etc.) It can be safely assumed that other unflattering references, and perhaps extended portraits, have been destroyed. A sense of Mrs Burney's eccentric character, of her domineering and abusive personality, may be obtained, at least in part, from the letter in Appendix 2. By the period covered in this volume Mrs Burney had largely alienated the Burney children.[3] The mutual hostility probably originated in jealousy over Dr Burney, who none the less seems to have always maintained affectionate relations with both his wife and his children. Mrs Burney's relationships with her children by Mr Allen were, to all appearances, no better than with the Doctor's children, as is indicated by all three of the Allen children eloping. According to all evidence the second Mrs Burney was a profoundly unhappy and neurotic woman whose main consolation was her marriage to a man who, despite her faults, seems to have genuinely loved her. Her absence from this volume lends the Burney household an air of tranquillity which tends to belie the real situation.

[3] In a letter to Crisp in 1776 Fanny alludes to her unfeeling treatment of Charlotte (p. 208).

EDITORIAL SYMBOLS AND ABBREVIATIONS

| | A break in the manuscript pages
⟨ ⟩ | Uncertain readings
[ ] | Text or information supplied by the editor; also insertions or substitutions by Madame d'Arblay, identified as such by a footnote
⌐ ¬ | Matter overscored by Madame d'Arblay but recovered
[xxxxx *3 lines*] | Matter overscored by Madame d'Arblay, *not* recovered
[xxxxx *2 words*]

The head-notes use or reproduce the following bibliographic abbreviations and signs:

AJ   Autograph journal
AJLS   Autograph journal letter signed
AL   Autograph letter
ALS   Autograph letter signed
Early Diary Manuscripts of the Early Diary (Juvenile Journals) of Fanny Burney in the Berg Collection, New York Public Library
pmks   Postmarks, of which only the essential are abstracted, e.g., 23 IV
⚹   Madame d'Arblay's symbol for manuscripts 'Examined & Amalgamated with others'; also, for manuscripts released for publication in a second category of interest
※ ✖   Other symbols of Madame d'Arblay for manuscripts in a second category of interest

The reader is also referred to the editorial principles outlined in *EJL* i, pp. xxix–xxxiii.

SHORT TITLES AND ABBREVIATIONS

PERSONS

CB	Charles Burney (Mus. Doc.), 1726–1814
CB Jr.	Charles Burney (DD), 1757–1817
EAB	Elizabeth (Allen) Burney, 1728–96
EB } EBB }	Esther Burney, 1749–1832 after 1770 Esther (Burney) Burney
FB } FBA }	Frances Burney, 1752–1840 after 1793 Madame d'Arblay
JB	James Burney (Rear-Admiral), 1750–1821
MA } MAR }	Maria Allen, 1751–1820 after 1772 Maria (Allen) Rishton
SC	Samuel Crisp, c.1707–83
SEB } SBP }	Susanna Elizabeth Burney, 1755–1800 after 1782 Mrs Phillips

WORKS, COLLECTIONS, ETC.

Standard encyclopedias, biographical dictionaries, peerages, armorials, baronetages, knightages, school and university lists, medical registers, lists of clergy, town and city directories, court registers, army and navy lists, road guides, almanacs, and catalogues of all kinds have been used but will not be cited unless for a particular reason. Most frequently consulted were the many editions of Burke, Lodge, and Debrett. In all works London is assumed to be the place of publication unless otherwise indicated.

Abbott	John Lawrence Abbott, *John Hawkesworth: Eighteenth-Century Man of Letters*, Madison, Wisconsin, 1982.
Add. MSS	Additional Manuscripts, British Library.
AL	Great Britain, War Office, *A List of the General and Field Officers as They Rank in the Army*, 1740–1841.
Alumni Cantab.	John Venn and J. A. Venn, *Alumni Cantabrigienses*, 10 vols., Cambridge, 1922–54.
Alumni Oxon.	Joseph Foster, *Alumni Oxonienses*, 8 vols., 1887–92.
AR	*The Annual Register, or a View of the History, Politics, and Literature ...*, 1758– .

Barrett	The Barrett Collection of Burney Papers, British Library, 43 vols., Egerton 3690–3708.
Berg	The Henry W. and Albert A. Berg Collection, New York Public Library.
Bibl. Nat. Cat.	*Catalogue générale des livres imprimés de la Bibliothèque nationale*, Paris, 1897– .
BL	The British Library.
BL Cat.	Catalogue of Printed Books in the British Library.
Boswell Papers	*Private Papers of James Boswell from Malahide Castle in the Collection of Lt.–Colonel R. H. Isham*, ed. Geoffrey Scott and F. A. Pottle, 18 vols., New York, 1928–34.
BUCEM	*The British Union-Catalogue of Early Music*, ed. Elizabeth B. Schnapper, 2 vols., 1957.
CB *Mem.*	*Memoirs of Dr Charles Burney 1726–1769*, ed. Slava Klima, Garry Bowers, and Kerry S. Grant, Lincoln, Nebraska, 1988.
CCR	*The Court and City Register.*
CJ	*Journals of the House of Commons.*
Commem.	Charles Burney, *An Account of the Musical Performances . . . in Commemoration of Handel*, 1785.
Comyn	The Collection of John R. G. Comyn.
Daily Adv.	*The Daily Advertiser*, 1731–95.
Delany Corr.	*The Autobiography and Correspondence of Mary Granville, Mrs Delany: with Interesting Reminiscences of King George the Third and Queen Charlotte*, ed. Lady Llanover, 6 vols., 1861–2.
Dennistoun	James Dennistoun, *Memoirs of Sir Robert Strange, Knt., . . . and of his brother-in-law Andrew Lumisden*, 2 vols., 1855.
DL	*Diary and Letters of Madame d'Arblay (1778–1840)*, ed. Austin Dobson, 6 vols., 1904–5.
DNB	*Dictionary of National Biography.*
DSB	*Dictionary of Scientific Biography*, ed. C. C. Gillispie, 16 vols., New York, 1970–80.
ED	*The Early Diary of Frances Burney, 1768–1778*, ed. Annie Raine Ellis, 2 vols., 1913.
EDD	*The English Dialect Dictionary*, ed. J. Wright, 6 vols., 1898–1905.

EJL	*The Early Journals and Letters of Fanny Burney*, ed. Lars E. Troide, Oxford, Kingston, and Montreal, 1988– .
Essex	Essex County Record Office, Chelmsford, England.
Garrick, *Letters*	*The Letters of David Garrick*, ed. David M. Little and George M. Kahrl, 3 vols., Cambridge, Massachusetts, 1963.
Gazley	John G. Gazley, *The Life of Arthur Young, 1741–1820*, Philadelphia, 1973.
GEC, *Baronetage*	George Edward Cokayne, *The Complete Baronetage*, 6 vols., Exeter, 1900–9.
GEC, *Peerage*	George Edward Cokayne, *The Complete Peerage*, rev. by Vicary Gibbs *et al.*, 13 vols., 1910–59.
German Tour	Charles Burney, *The Present State of Music in Germany, the Netherlands, and United Provinces*, 2 vols., 1773; 2nd corrected edn., 1775.
GLRO	The Greater London Record Office.
GM	*The Gentleman's Magazine*, 1731–1880.
HFB	Joyce Hemlow, *The History of Fanny Burney*, Oxford, 1958.
Highfill	Philip H. Highfill, Jr., Kalman A. Burnim, and Edward A. Langhans, *A Biographical Dictionary of Actors, Actresses, Musicians, Dancers, Managers and Other Stage Personnel in London, 1660–1800*, Carbondale, Illinois, 1973– .
Hist. Mus.	Charles Burney, *A General History of Music, from the Earliest Ages to the Present Period*, 4 vols., 1776–89.
HMC	Historical Manuscipts Commission.
Houghton	Houghton Library, Harvard University, Cambridge, Massachusetts.
Hyde	The Hyde Collection, Four Oaks Farm, Somerville, New Jersey.
IGI	International Genealogical Index (formerly the Mormon Computer Index).
Italian Tour	Charles Burney, *The Present State of Music in France and Italy*, 1771; 2nd corrected edn., 1773.
JL	*The Journals and Letters of Fanny Burney (Madame d'Arblay), 1791–1840*, ed. Joyce Hemlow *et al.*, 12 vols., Oxford, 1972–84.

Johnson, *Letters*   *The Letters of Samuel Johnson, with Mrs Thrale's Genuine Letters to Him*, ed. R. W. Chapman, 3 vols., Oxford, 1952.

Lib.   Leigh and Sotheby, *A Catalogue of the Miscellaneous Library of the Late Charles Burney*, 9 June 1814, priced copy in the Yale University Library.

Life   *Boswell's Life of Johnson*, ed. George Birkbeck Hill, rev. by L. F. Powell, 6 vols., Oxford, 1934–64.

LJ   *Journals of the House of Lords*.

Lonsdale   Roger Lonsdale, *Dr Charles Burney: A Literary Biography*, Oxford, 1965.

LS 1, 2, [etc.]   *The London Stage 1660–1800*, Parts 1 to 5 in 11 vols., Carbondale, Illinois, 1960–8. References are to volume and page in each part.

Manwaring   G. E. Manwaring, *My Friend the Admiral: The Life, Letters, and Journals of Rear-Admiral James Burney, F. R. S.*, 1931.

Maxted   Ian Maxted, *The London Book Trades, 1775–1800: A Preliminary Checklist of Members*, Folkestone, Kent, 1977.

Mem.   *Memoirs of Doctor Burney, Arranged from His Own Manuscripts, from Family Papers, and from Personal Recollections*, by his daughter, Madame d'Arblay, 3 vols., 1832.

Mercer   Charles Burney, *A General History of Music*, ed. Frank Mercer, 2 vols., 1935.

MI   Memorial Inscription(s).

Mus. Lib.   White, *A Catalogue of the ... Collection of Music ... of the Late Charles Burney*, 8 August 1814, priced copy in the Music Division of the Library of Congress.

Namier   Sir Lewis Namier and John Brooke, *The House of Commons, 1754–1790*, 3 vols., 1964.

Nat. Union Cat.   *The National Union Catalogue, Pre-1956 Imprints*.

NBG   *Nouvelle biographie générale*, ed. Jean-Chrétien-Ferdinand Hoefer, 46 vols., Paris, 1852–66.

NCBEL   *The New Cambridge Bibliography of English Literature*, ed. George Watson and Ian Willison, 5 vols., Cambridge, 1969–77.

New Grove   *The New Grove Dictionary of Music and Musicians*, ed. Stanley Sadie, 20 vols., 1980.

Nichols, *Lit. Anec.*	John Nichols, *Literary Anecdotes of the Eight-eenth Century*, 9 vols., 1812–15.
Nichols, *Lit. Ill.*	John Nichols, *Illustrations of the Literary History of the Eighteenth Century*, 8 vols., 1817–58.
OCD	*The Oxford Classical Dictionary*, ed. N. G. L. Hammond and H. H. Scullard, 2nd edn., Oxford, 1970.
OED	*Oxford English Dictionary.*
Osborn	The James Marshall and Marie-Louise Osborn Collection, Yale University Library, New Haven, Connecticut.
PCC	Prerogative Court of Canterbury.
PML	The Pierpont Morgan Library, New York.
PRO	Public Record Office, London.
Rees	*The Cyclopaedia; or, Universal Dictionary of Arts, Sciences, and Literature*, ed. Abraham Rees, 45 vols., 1802–20. CB contributed the musical articles in this work.
RHI	The Royal Household Index, the Queen's Archives, Windsor Castle.
Rylands	The John Rylands University Library of Manchester, England.
Scholes	Percy A. Scholes, *The Great Dr Burney*, 2 vols., 1948.
Scots Peerage	*The Scots Peerage*, ed. Sir James Balfour Paul, 9 vols., Edinburgh, 1904–14.
Sedgwick	Romney Sedgwick, *The House of Commons, 1715–1754*, 2 vols., 1970.
Singh	Prince Frederick Duleep Singh, *Portraits in Norfolk Houses*, 2 vols., Norwich, 1928.
SND	*The Scottish National Dictionary*, ed. W. Grant and D. D. Murison, 10 vols., Edinburgh, 1931–76.
Stone	George Winchester Stone, Jr. and George M. Kahrl, *David Garrick: A Critical Biography*, Carbondale, Illinois, 1979.
Survey of London	London County Council, *The Survey of London*, 1900– .
Thieme	Ulrich Thieme and Felix Becker, *Allgemeines Lexikon der bildenden Künstler von der Antike bis zur Gegenwart*, 37 vols., Leipzig, 1907–50.
Thraliana	*Thraliana: The Diary of Mrs. Hester Lynch Thrale (later Mrs. Piozzi), 1776–1809*, ed.

Katharine C. Balderston, 2nd edn., 2 vols.,
Oxford, 1951.

Tours *Dr Burney's Musical Tours in Europe*, ed. Percy
A. Scholes, 2 vols., 1959.

Vict. Co. Hist. *The Victoria History of the Counties of England*
[with name of county].

Wheatley Henry B. Wheatley and Peter Cunningham,
*London Past and Present: Its History, Associations,
and Traditions*, 3 vols., 1891.

'Worcester Mem.' 'Memoranda of the Burney Family, 1603–
1845', typescript of a family chronicle in the
Osborn Collection, Yale University Library.
The MS is untraced.

Young, *Autobiography* *The Autobiography of Arthur Young*, ed. M.
Betham-Edwards, 1898.

YW *The Yale Edition of Horace Walpole's Correspondence*, ed. W. S. Lewis *et al.*, 48 vols., New
Haven, 1937–83.

13   [Queen Square]
                                                7 February [1774]

To Samuel Crisp

ALS (Barrett), 7 February 1774
Double sheet 4to, 4 pp., *pmk* 7 FE wafer
Addressed: Samuel Crisp Esqr | At Mrs Hamilton's | Chesington, near
Kingston | upon Thames | Surry   .
Annotated (by FBA): ✠ 1774 Feb. 7th N° 5. 2

                                                       7th Feb^y

Did You draw me into a Correspondence, my dear Daddy,
with no other view than that of mortifying me by this entire
breach of it?[1]—I take it for granted that you were heartily
tired, & repented of your scheme: though I allow this to be
very natural, I cannot forbear noticing that it seems of
necessity for men to be capricious & fickle, even about trifles.
However, I acknowledge that if I had had any *Head*, I must
have foreseen this blow—but as I *never had none*,[2] it has almost
stunned me. Yet I will frankly own, that even while I received
your letters, they appeared to me too flattering to last long.—

But, if by any chance, I have been so unfortunate as
to offend you,—though I can hardly suppose it—I intreat
you, my dear Sir, not to punish me with *silent* resentment. I
would rather receive from you the severest lecture you could
pen, because while I might flatter myself with even meriting
[your notice,][3] I should indulge hopes of regaining your
kindness,—& if you will so far favour me, I will gladly kiss the
Rod.

But if, after all, I have only wearied you, do not think me so
weak as to wish to teaze you into writing—I could not forbear
sending this remonstrance, but will not trouble you again,

---

[1] SC's latest extant letter to FB is dated 1 Jan. [1774] (Barrett). FB no doubt
replied to this soon (it is missing), and was awaiting SC's response. See the next
letter.
[2] This intentional solecism is perhaps a humorous echo of Kitty Cooke's
ungrammatical speech.
[3] Inserted by FBA for a tear in the corner of the page.

unless you should again desire it.—which I only fear you should *now* do, out of Compliment, or compassion—however, I will not further pester you, but only subscribe myself,

My dear daddy
Your ever affectionate
& obliged
Frances Burney.

If you *should write*, I conjure you to let it be with *frankness*.

I4

Queen Square,
9 February [1774]

To Samuel Crisp

AL (Barrett), 9 February 1774
Single sheet folio (fragment), 2 pp.
Annotated (by FBA): ✳ 1774 9th Feby 3

Feby 9th
Queen Square

My dearest Sir,
    The sight of Your Hand, once again Directed to *me*, really made me *Jump*[4]—I am a thousand times more comfortable, too, in knowing that you wrote before my foolish scrawl could reach you, for which I now beg your pardon—though I can only urge in my excuse, that the readiness of your first answers, quite spoiled me. I cannot imagine how you can contrive to laugh with so much *gravity*, as when you are pleased to speak of my letters—however, though my swallow is not quite so deep as you apprehend, yet while I can at any rate procure *Answers*, I niether can or [*sic*] will forbear writing.
    I dare not—perhaps indeed *can* not—pursue your [*MS cut*] equal to such |

[*bottom of page cut away*]

---

⁴ SC's letter is missing.

Coquetry, I must acknowledge, is almost universal—& I know fewer Girls exempt from *that* passion, than from any other. It seems irresistable—I was going to add something of Vanity & love of pleasure—but there is no sort of occasion to make concessions to *you*, who are so little inclined to over rate our merits—I will therefore only say, that though I readily allow you a *general* superiority over us in most other particulars, yet in constancy, Gratitude & Virtue, I regard you as unworthy all competition or comparison. The flights & failings of Women are oftener from some defect in the *Head* than the *Heart*, which is just reversed by you—so that where we are *Weak*, you are *Wicked*—Now which is least justifiable?

[*bottom of page cut away*]

15   JOURNAL 1774

AJ (Early Diary, vii, paginated 409–[66], 475–85, foliated 1–27, 33–38, Berg), Journal for 1774.

Originally a cahier of large double sheets sewn. Now 24 single sheets and 6 double sheets 4to, 72 pp., with a cover *dated 1774 and numbered 7*. A journal letter to SEB in Sept. has been inserted at that point and numbered continuously with the Journal for 1774.

In her 'List' for 1774 (see *EJL* i, p. xxx) FBA names four persons not in the extant journal: the composer John Stanley and his wife; Jane Barsanti; and 'Mr. Hoole'. FB and her family no doubt attended Barsanti's benefit at Covent Garden on 23 April (*LS 4* iii. 1805); CB Jr. listed this and other performances by Barsanti in 1773–4 on several MS leaves preserved in the BL (BL Add. MSS. 39302, fos. 175–177), and, in a verse letter to FB, 3 May 1774 (Osborn), praises her in the roles of Maria (in Arthur Murphy's *The Citizen*) and Lady Brumpton (in Sir Richard Steele's *The Funeral*), both first played by her at her benefit. 'Mr. Hoole' was probably John Hoole (1727–1803), translator of Tasso and Ariosto and friend of Dr Johnson. FBA mentions him (*Mem.* i. 294) as often visiting the Burneys in St Martin's Street.

The top of the first page has been cut away.

February 20th

What will become of the World if my annals are thus irregular! Almost two months have ⌐⟨already⟩ passed, & I

have not ⟨yet⟩⁊ Record⸀ed⸀⁊[5] one anecdote! I am really
shocked for Posterity!—But for my Pen, all the Adventures of
this Noble family might sink to oblivion! I am amazed when I
consider the greatness of my Importance, the dignity of my
Task, & the Novelty of my pursuit! I ⸀shall⸀ be the 8th
Wonder of the World, if the World had not already, & too pre-
maturely, Nominated so many Persons to that Honour! ǀ

[*The bottom of the page and the top of the next page have been cut away. The
'sufferer' in the first paragraph following is probably CB, possibly afflicted by
a recurrence of his chronic rheumatism.*]

⸀he rather minds, it is true, [*half a line cut away*] confined at
Home, but he still suffers great pain [a]t Times.

By the way, I have been extremely Ill myself, too,—but it is
not worth mentioning, for I find that it did not terrify fatally
any of my unfeeling Lovers, who have all been callous enough
to survive my Illness.

As to the rest of the Family I shall speak of them as
occasions offer.

And as to the Rest of the World—according to the manner
of their presenting themselves to my memory.⸀

[*The bottom of the page has been cut away. Judging by FBA's 'List', missing
portions of 1774 before the following contained mentions of CB, the Stanleys,
and Arthur Young and his wife.*]

[Thursday Mama took us with her to Miss Reid, the
celebrated Paintress, to meet Mrs Brooke, the celebrated
Authoress.][6] Miss Reid is shrewd & clever, where she has any
opportunity given her to make it known; but she is so very
Deaf, that it is a fatigue to attempt her. She is most
exceedingly ugly, & of a very melancholy, or rather discontented, humour.

Mrs Brooke is very short & fat, & squints, but has the art
of shewing Agreeable Ugliness. She is very well bred, &

[5] Obliterated and partly written over.
[6] Inserted by FBA. For Mrs Brooke see *EJL* i. Miss Reid was Catherine Read
(1723–78), fashionable painter in crayons and oils, who lived at this time in Welbeck
St. Miss Read also executed miniatures and painted a miniature of FB's stepmother
(EAB), which CB later bequeathed to his daughter Sarah Harriet Burney. See
Thieme; D. Foskett, *A Dictionary of British Miniature Painters* (1972), i. 462; A. Graves,
The Royal Academy of Arts . . . Contributors . . . 1769 to 1904 (1905–6), vi. 243; *idem, The
Society of Artists of Great Britain 1760–1791: The Free Society of Artists 1761–1783 . . .*
(1907), pp. 208–9; Scholes, ii. 271.

expresses herself with much modesty, upon all subjects.—
which in an *Authoress*, a Woman of *known* understanding, is
extremely pleasing.

The rest of the party, consisted of Miss Beatson,[7] a niece of
Miss Reid's, Mr Strange,[8] & Dr. Shebbeare.[9] Miss Beatson is
a ⌈Girl [xxxxx *3 words*]⌉ not absolutely handsome, yet
infinitely attractive; she is sensible, smart, quick & comical: &
has not only an understanding which seems already to be
mature, but a most astonishing genius for Drawing, though
never taught. She Groupes Figures of Children, in the most
ingenious, playful & beautiful variety of attitudes & Employments, in a manner surpassing all credibility, but what ˡ the
Eye itself attains. In truth she is a very wonderful Girl.[10]

Dr. Shebbeare, who was once put actually in the Pillory for
a libel,[11] is well know for political & other writings; he
absolutely ruined our Evening, for he is the most morose,
rude, gross, & ill mannered man I was ever in Company with.
He aims perpetually at Wit, though he constantly stops short
at rudeness—he reminded me of Swift's Lines

> Thinks raillery consists in railing,
> Will tell Aloud your greatest failing.[12]

---

[7] Helena Beatson (1762–1839), daughter of Robert Beatson, of Kilrie, Fifeshire,
who m. (1777) Charles Oakeley (1751–1826), cr. (1790) Bt.; governor of Madras,
1790–4. Miss Beatson was a precocious artist who exhibited sketches at the Royal
Society of Artists in 1771, aged 8, and was an honorary exhibitor, aged 11, at the Royal
Academy in 1774. Horace Walpole called the sketches of 1771 'wonderfull' (MS note
in Walpole's copy of the exhibition catalogue of the Royal Society of Artists, 26 April
1771, items 309 and 310, cited in Walpole's *Miscellany 1786–1795*, ed. L. Troide (New
Haven, 1978), p. 37 n. 3). Her aunt took her to India in 1775, where she married
Oakeley and abandoned her art. See ibid.; Graves, *Royal Academy*, i. 152; *idem, Society
of Artists*, p. 27; E. Waterhouse, *The Dictionary of British 18th Century Painters in Oils and
Crayons* (1981), p. 44.
[8] In 1745 Miss Read painted the future Mrs Strange 'as a maiden in a blue snood,
pressing a white rose to her heart' (*ED* i. 283 n. 1).
[9] John Shebbeare (1709–88), political writer. Shebbeare had formerly practised
medicine and claimed to have obtained a medical degree at Paris; hence the 'Dr'.
[10] Wonderful, but also conceited, spoiled, and ungrateful, as FB suggests later. See
below, pp. 70–1, 205.
[11] In 1758, after publication of his 6th *Letter to the People of England* (1757), in which
he claimed 'that the present grandeur of France, and calamities of this nation, are
owing to the influence of Hanover on the councils of England'.
[12] Altered from *The Furniture of a Woman's Mind* (1727), ll. 19–20.

For he did to the utmost of his power, *cut up* every body, on their most favourite subject: though what most ⌈attracted⌉ his spleen, was *Woman*, to whom he professes a fixed aversion, & next to her, his greatest disgust is against the *Scotch*—& these two subjects he wore thread bare.—though indeed, they were pretty much fatigued before he attacked them; & all ⌈his⌉ *satire* which he levelled at them, consisted of trite & hackneyed abuse. The only novelty which they owed to him, was from the extraordinary coarseness of Language he made use of. ¦ But I shall recollect as much of the conversation as I can, & make the parties speak for themselves. I will begin with Mᵣ Strange's Entrance, which was soon after our's.

After his Compliments were paid to the *Fair Sex*—he turned to the *Growler*—

'Well, Dr. Shebbeare, & how do *you* do?'

Dr. Shebbeare ... Do? why, as you see, pestered by a parcel of Women.'

Mʳˢ Brooke ... *Women* & the *Scotch* always fare ill with Dr. Shebbeare.'

Dr. Shebbeare ... Because they are the two greatest evils upon Earth. The *best* Woman that ever I knew is not to be compared to the *Worst* man. And as to the Scotch!—there is but *one* thing in which they are clever, & can excell the English;—& that is, they can use both Hands at once to scratch themselves—the English never think of using more than one.'

Miss Reid ... Ay, Dr. you only abuse us, because you are sorry that you are not ⌈my⌉ Countryman.

Dr. Shebbeare ... What, *Envy*? hay? Why it's true enough that they get every thing into their own Hands, & when once they come, they take care never to return—no, no!'

Miss Reid ... You was saying, Mʳˢ Brooke, that you did not know till I told you, that Dr. Burney had a Wife;—what do you then think of seeing these Grown Up Daughters [FB and SEB]?'

Mʳˢ Brooke ... Why, I don't know how, but I own I was never more surprised than when I heard that Dr. Burney was married.'

Dr. Shebbeare ... what, I suppose you did not take him for

a Fool?—All men, who marry, are so; but above all, God help him who takes a Widow!'

Mr Strange . . . This is a strange man, Mrs Burney,—but nobody ever minds him.'

Dr. Shebbeare . . . I don't wonder that Dr. Burney went abroad!—all my amazement is at his ever coming Home! Unless, indeed, he left his understanding behind him: which I suppose was the Case.'

Mrs Brooke . . . I am sure that does not appear from his Tour—I never received more pleasure than from Reading his account of what he saw & did abroad—'

Dr. Shebbeare . . . I hate Authors! but I suppose one Wit must hate another.'

Mrs Brooke . . . Those few Authors that *I* know, give me great reason *not* to hate them.—quite the contrary—Dr Johnson, Dr. Armstrong—and I won't say *what* I think of Dr. Burney;—but for Dr. Armstrong I have a very particular regard. I have known him more than 20 years.'

Dr. Shebbeare. What, I suppose you like him for his Intrigues?'

Mrs Brooke . . . Indeed, I never heard he had any.'

Dr. Shebbeare . . . What, I suppose you had too many yourself to keep his in your memory?

Mrs Brooke . . . O, Women you know, Dr., never have Intrigues. I wish Dr. Burney was here,—I am sure he would be our Champion.'

Dr. Shebbeare . . . What, do you suppose he'd speak against himself? I know but too well what it is to be married! I think I have been Yoked for 1 & forty years; & I have wished my Wife[13] under Ground any Time since.'

Mama . . . And if she were, you'd marry in a Week!

Dr. Shebbeare . . . I wish I was tried!

Mr Strange . . . Why this is a sad man, Mrs Burney, I think we must toss him in a Blanket.'

Dr. Shebbeare . . . Ay, with all my Heart! but speak for

---

[13] Susannah Cornhigh (d. 1779), m. (6 Apr. 1733), at Abbotsham, Devon, John Shebbeare (*GM* xlix (1779), 615; IGI). Shebbeare did not remarry after her death.

yourself (to Mrs Brooke) do you suppose your Husband was not long since tired of you?'

Mrs Brooke ... O—as to that—that is not a fair Question;—I don't ask you if you're tired of *your* Wife.'

Dr. Shebbeare ... And if you did, I'd tell you.'

Miss Beatson ... Then *I* ask you;—pray, Dr. Shebbeare *are* you tired of your Wife?'

Dr. Shebbeare ... I did not say I'd tell *you*.'

Mama ... I wish that Mrs Strange was here—she'd fight our Battles admirably.'

Mr Strange ... Why do you never Come to see her, Dr.?'—

Dr. Shebbeare ... Because she has so much Tongue, that I expect she'll talk herself to Death, & I don't chuse to be Accessary. [To Mrs Brooke.] "Who are you to have for a singer next year?

Mrs Brooke ... Rauzini[14] a most excellent performer.

Dr. Shebbeare ... Ay, it's your Interest to say so.

Mrs Brooke ... Well, I sha'n't Talk to *you*, but I know Dr. Burney's opinion of him."[15]

Mr Strange ... What do you think of the Bookseller's Bill,[16] & the state of Literary Property, Dr.?' |

Dr. Shebbeare ... Why I don't think at all About it. I have done with Books! I have not written a Line these 20 years—though indeed, I wasted a Pint of Ink last Week.'[17]

Mama ... Then I am sure you must have *spilt* it, Dr.'

Dr. Shebbeare ... I never knew a Bookseller who was not a

---

[14] Venanzio Rauzzini (1746–1810), Italian soprano castrato singer, composer, and harpsichordist. In Nov. he made his London début as both singer and composer in the pasticcio *Armida*. See *New Grove*; below, *passim*.

[15] Mrs Brooke and her husband were joint managers of the Opera with the Yateses. For CB's high opinion of Rauzzini, see below, p. 55.

[16] A petition presented to the House of Commons by Alderman Harley, on 28 Feb., on behalf of the booksellers of London, asking for relief from an adverse decision by the Lords (on 22 Feb.) which ruled, in effect, that no publisher could purchase an exclusive copyright forever from an author. The petition passed the Commons in May but was thrown out by the Lords on 2 June. See *GM* xliv (1774), 137, 188; *YW* xxviii. 135 n. 9; Horace Walpole, *Last Journals*, ed. A. F. Steuart (1910), i. 352.

[17] Shebbeare is facetiously dismissing all his writings since *Lydia* (see below). He had received a pension from the government in 1764, and from that time on was a staunch propagandist for the Court.

scoundrel; I was cheated plaguly [*sic*] about Lydia[18] & the Rascal who sold the Marriage Act[19] promised to share the profits,—yet though I know there have been 6 Editions, he always Calls it the first.

Miss Reid ... pray, Dr. have you seen Nelly's last Drawing? She has made *me* Dance a minuet!'

Dr. Shebbeare ... Well said, Nelly! I'll make Thee immortal for that! I'll write thy Life.'

Mrs Brooke ... She'll make *herself* immortal, by her Works.'

As to Susy & I, we never presumed to open our Lips for fear of being affronted! but when we were coming away, Dr. Shebbeare Called out to us 'here—mind what *I* say—be sure you never marry!'

You are right, thought I, there could not be a greater antidote to that state than thinking of you—Miss Reid was, I suppose, some what scandalised at this man's Conversation, as it happened at her House, & therefore before we took leave, she said—'Now I must tell you that Dr. Shebbeare has only been Jesting—he thinks as we do, all the Time.—'

'This it is, Cried he, to have a friend to lie for one!'

What a strange fancy it was, for such a man as this to Write Novels! However— I am tired of Writing—& so adieu sweet Doctor Shebbeare—

March 17th

The spring is generally fertile in new Acquaintances. My Father received the following Note last Week—

I cannot find the Note but it was from Mr Twiss,[20] a

---

[18] *Lydia; or, Filial Piety* (1755), a novel by Shebbeare. His publisher was John Scott, bookseller, printer, and publisher at the Black Swan, Paternoster Row, *c.*1748–76. For the 2nd edn. (1769) he turned to Thomas Davies (*c.*1712–85), the bookseller, author, and friend of Dr Johnson (Maxted).

[19] *The Marriage Act*, another novel by Shebbeare, was published in 1754 by James Hodges (d. 1774), cr. (1758) Kt., who also published the 2nd edn. (retitled *Matrimony*) the following year. For the 3rd edn. (1766) Shebbeare switched to Thomas Lowndes (the future publisher of *Evelina*; see below) and John Knox (d. 1790). See Maxted; H. R. Plomer, G. H. Bushnell, and E. R. McC. Dix, *A Dictionary of the Printers and Booksellers ... from 1726 to 1775* (1932), pp. 127–8; *GM* xliv (1774), 542.

[20] Richard Twiss (1747–1821), miscellaneous writer. Possessed of an ample fortune, he devoted himself to extensive travelling. In 1772 he journeyed to Spain and Portugal, returning the following year. In 1775 he published an account of his *Travels through Portugal and Spain, in 1772 and 1773*.

Gentleman just returned from a Tour in Spain;—⌜or at least, in Spain he has travelled, recently or not—⌝ & he writes ardently to know my dear Father, & converse with him on Spanish music.[21]

My Father was much pleased with this Note, & soon after waited upon Mr Twiss, who ⌜made him a⌝ present ⌜of⌝ many scarse National Airs, & made an appointment to Drink Tea here on Sunday.[22] Being at present a *Candidate* to be a member of the Royal Society, he requested my Father to sign his *Certificate*, which he very readily agreed ⌜to, & found that it had already several very Creditable Names to it.⌝[23]

On Sunday [20 March] he came, at 5 O'Clock, & was shewn into the study, where he was *Cabinetted* with my Father till 7—when he ⌜came⌝ into the Parlour to Tea.

He is very Tall & thin; there is something very odd in him—I pretend not to even sketch his Character, not being able to form any precise idea of it: but it would be strange if there was *not* some peculiarity about him, when it is considered that he has spent more than a third of his Life, in Rambling about foreign Countries, & that he is still a young man, & has not seen England since 17, till within a few months.[24] He has Travelled entirely at his own pleasure, & without even a Tutor; he has not only been all over Europe, except the North, but ⌜even⌝ over great part of Africa. He speaks Spanish, Italian, French, German (& I suppose of course Greek & Latin) with great ease & fluency.

As my Father has never ⌜been in⌝ Spain or Portugal, & as Mr Twiss has always been very curious concerning musical matters, ⌜he gave him⌝ a Collection of Spanish Queries, relative to this subject, which I copied for ⌜that purpose.⌝[25]

---

[21] FB has left the bottom of the page blank, presumably in the hope of finding Twiss's note and copying it in later. The note is missing.

[22] CB visited Twiss on Sunday, 13 Mar. The next day Twiss wrote to thank him for his visit, begged 'leave to send to him, four Tonadillas, five Seguldillas, a few Portuguese airs, the Neapolitan Tarantella, & Romanella; & the venetian Furlana', and expressed his impatience 'for Sunday to have the pleasure of the D^rs instructive Conversation ...' (Twiss to CB, 14 Mar. 1774, Osborn).

[23] Twiss was elected FRS on 9 June. He withdrew from the Society in 1794 (*The Record of the Royal Society of London*, 4th edn. (1940), p. 425).

[24] Twiss had actually returned to England in 1770, where he remained until 1772.

[25] In his letter to CB, 14 Mar., Twiss adds: 'If the D^r has found his Copy of

While he was Drinking Tea, he turned suddenly to my Father, & asked him, in Italian, *which* of us two, (Susy ⌜&⌝ me) played the Harpsichord so well? My Father told him that the *player* [EBB] was not here—'*e maritata?*' demanded Mr Twiss. 'Si, e maritata,' answered my Father. As I know enough of Italian to understand any common & easy Conversation, I could not help rather *simpering*, which I suppose he observed, for he turned again to my Father 'Credo che questa signorina intende l'Italiano?—

However, as my Father ⌜said⌝ that we ⌜did⌝ play *a little*, & for our own Diversion, ⌜he⌝ was very earnest with him to speak to us for that purpose—but thank Heaven in vain. Soon after, he said something to my Father, which by the direction of his Eyes, concerned us, in a whisper—to which he answered, '*No*—' & then the other said aloud 'And do both the young Ladies sing, likewise, Sir?'

No—no—No! from all Quarters. |

He talked a great deal about Spain, which, as being least known, my Father was most curious to hear of. Among other Things, he said that the married Ladies were very *easy of access*, but that the single, who, indeed, seldom left a Convent till the Day of their marriage, were kept very rigidly retired, & that it was *Death* to touch them, even by the little Finger! He said that *no* ⌜Women⌝[26] were to be seen Walking, but that they appeared openly at the Theatres, w[h]ere they sat, however, generally in the Darkest part, but without Veils; and that they had *Glow Worms*, strung into beautiful shapes, for Ornaments to their Hair, & for stomachers, which had a most striking effect.

This Tale made Mrs Allen immediately his Enemy—the moment he was gone, she railed most violently at the *lies of Travellers.*—Mama, too, did not believe a Word of it, arguing upon the short life of Glow Worms, when once they were

---

Queries relative to Spanish Music, Mr T. will be glad to see them'. Also in the Osborn Collection is an undated note of Twiss to CB with pencil drawings of stringed instruments he had seen in a painting near Pavia and a bas-relief in Toro. CB planned to use the information from Twiss and others in a chapter on 'National Music' in *Hist. Mus.* He was finally forced to omit this chapter for lack of space (see Lonsdale, p. 338).

[26] Altered to 'Ladies' by FBA.

taken in Hand. For my part, I stood up ⌐for his⌐ Advocate, &
urged the unfairness of Judging of animals, any more than
men, only by those of our own Country[27] ⌐[xxxxx *1–2 words*]
that there is something⌐ |

[*A leaf or leaves have been cut away. The following passage concerns CB's
negotiations with Felice de Giardini to purchase from him plates engraved by
Francesco Bartolozzi, after drawings by G. B. Cipriani, to illustrate* Hist.
Mus.]

⌐The truth of this is by no means disputable, as Cipriani[28] &
himself[29] are particular friends; however, my Father very
candidly said that *he* had no right to avail himself of the
friendship of Cipriani for Giardini, nor should have thought of
it, had not Giardini made him make a promise; however, that
now that these plates had answered their full purpose for
Giardini, & were become some what common, it was by no
means just to pay the original price for them, but that
nevertheless, he would give 60 Guineas for them, which is 10
for each, there being six. Mr. Twiss undertook the Commission of speaking of this offer to Giardini, & of letting my
Father know the Event.⌐

March 30th

I have a most extraordinary Evening to give Account of.
Last ⌐Sunday⌐ [27 March] we had a second Visit from the
Spanish Traveller, M[r] Twiss.—

Mrs. Young Drank Tea with us. Her Husband is infinitely

---

[27] Twiss notes in his *Travels through Portugal and Spain* (p. 281) that after the plays or
operas at Cadiz were ended (which was usually about half past eleven), it was
customary to walk in the *alameda*, or mall. There he 'observed several ladies, who had
fixed glow-worms by threads to their hair, which had a luminous and pleasing effect'.
[28] Giovanni Battista Cipriani (1727–85), RA (1768), painter, draughtsman, and
engraver. A native of Florence, he came to England in 1755. Many of his drawings
were engraved by his friend and fellow Florentine Francesco Bartolozzi (1727–1815),
who had settled in England in 1764. CB eventually agreed to purchase from Giardini
6 ornamental plates, engraved by Bartolozzi from designs by Cipriani, for £120.
These plates, on classical subjects, had originally been used for tickets to the
Bach–Abel subscription concerts; Giardini presumably used them to grace some of
his own compositions. CB inserted 3 in the 1st vol. (1776) of his *Hist. Mus.* (the
frontispiece and facing pp. 275 and 326) and the remaining 3 in the later vols.
Richard Twiss's *Travels through Portugal and Spain* contains a print of 'Our Lady of the
Fish' by Cipriani and Bartolozzi. See also *Hist. Mus.* i. 517; Thieme; Scholes, ii. 335;
Lonsdale, p. 493 and nn. 1–3; below, p. 25.
[29] Presumably Giardini.

better, which I ⌜do⌝ much rejoice at. Dr. Shepherd also *assisted*
at that *Warm* Collation. Mᵣ Twiss did not come till late, & was
shewn into the study ⌜where, as I have since heard, he told
Father that he had not yet been able to get any answer from
Giardini.⌝

When they had finished their private Conversation, my
Father brought Mᵣ Twiss into the Parlour, & invited him to
stay supper; which from him, in his present hurry, is no small
Favour.

The discourse, till supper, was entirely in Parties. Mᵣˢ
Young, Mᵣˢ Allen and Mama talked upon fashions, which is
an ever agreeable subject to Mᵣˢ Young & constantly
introduced by her; Dr. Shepherd, Mᵣ Twiss & my Father
conversed upon foreign Countries, & Susy and I sat very *snug*
together, amused either by ourselves or them, as we chose.

Dr. Shepherd is going abroad himself in a short time, as
Tutor to a young man of the name of Hatton.[30] He has never
yet been farther than the Netherlands, though he has *intended*
to Travel I believe for thirty years of the 50 he has lived;[31] but
a certain *timidity* seems to have restrained him. Giardini
relates that when he was on the Continent, being obliged to
wear a sword, which his Cloth prevents his being burthened
with here, he was so extreamly aukward, from want of
Practice, that the first Day he Walked out, the sword got
between his Legs, & fairly tript him Up—*Over*—or *down*—I
don't know which is best to say. He is prodigiously Tall &
stout, & must have made a most ludicrous appearance. He
enquired many particulars concerning Mᵣ Twiss's Travels,
with a kind of painful eagerness; & whenever he related any
disasters, the poor Doctor seemed in an agony, as if the same
Dangers were immediately to become his own.[32]

Mᵣ Twiss has certainly Travelled upon a sensible Plan, as
he has carraid [*sic*] with him 12 curious Questions, to be asked
wherever he went; & he has made his stay at the Towns he

[30] Probably John Emilius Daniel Edward Finch Hatton (1755–1841), 2nd son of
the Hon. Edward Finch Hatton (?1697–1771), MP, and grandson of the 7th E. of
Winchilsea and 2nd E. of Nottingham. See Nichols, *Lit. Ill.* vi. 677.
[31] Shepherd was 52 or 53.
[32] Much like Fielding's Abraham Adams.

visited always according to the Entertainment he received. He has written 4 Quarto Volumes of observations and Descriptions, during his peregrinations. He intends to publish his Tour through Spain and Portugal, as being the countries of which there is the least known.—He is going soon to Danemark & Russia.[33] His curiosity seems insatiable. And I think his fortune too ought to be inexhaustible.

When supper appeared, Mr Twiss desired to sit by the Young Ladies—& making me take a place next to Mrs Allen, seated himself by me—⌐& my Father placed himself after him.⌐

Dr. Shepherd still kept the Conversation upon Travelling. Mr Twiss spoke very highly of the Spanish ladies, who, ⌐he said,⌐ he fully intended hereafter to Visit again. He said that the Bull Fights, which he much admired, were still in high Vogue at Madrid. 'It is curious to observe,' said he, with a *sly* kind of seriousness,—'that the *ladies* are very fond of assisting upon these Festivals,—& They, who scream at a Frog, & faint at a spider, will, with all imaginable courtesie, fling Nuts upon the Ground, to make the Cavaliers stumble; & whenever they are in danger, they Clap their Hands, & call out *Bravo*, Torre! *Bravo, Torre!*[34]

However, he did confess that there *were* ladies in Spain, who were never seen at the Bull fights; which for the Honour of my sex, I rejoiced to hear. It seems amazing to me, that this barbarous Diversion should not be exploded.

When Naples was mentioned, he was pleased to make Confession that he left it in disgrace; that is, that he was obliged to *run away*—! as these sort of avowals, immediately imply a *love affair*, & wear a strong air of Vanity, my Father, who *smoaked* him, putting on a look of ⌐ mortification, said—'Well—*I* was told, that when I arrived at Naples, if I did but shew myself upon the Piazza ⌐della⌐ [*space left blank*] I should be sure to receive 3 or 4 Billet doux in a few moments;

---

[33] He apparently did not make this trip.

[34] Properly *Toro*; FB seems influenced by the name of Signor Torre, the pyrotechnist (see *EJL* i. 267). The remarkable accuracy of FB's memory for dialogue is confirmed by the almost identical wording in Twiss's published account of the ladies at bullfights (*Travels through Portugal and Spain*, p. 289).

accordingly, as soon as I got there, I Dressed myself to the best advantage, & immediately went to the Piazza:—but to no purpose!—& though I Walked there every morning I stayed, the Devil a Billet doux did I ever meet with!'

Every body ⌐hollow'd,⌐ Mʳˢ Young ⌐in particular, &⌐ cried out, looking full at Mʳ Twiss—'Well, Dr. Burney, when you go next, you must put a mask on!—'

I don't know whether Mʳ Twiss felt the reproof my Father meant to Convey, or not; but he fought off the Billets doux, & declared that he had not had any. 'But why should you run away, then? cried Dr. Shepherd, who is dullness itself.

'O Sir,' answered Mʳ Twiss—'the *ladies* are concerned!— but another Time, Dr. Burney,—when we are alone—'

'The *ladies?*' cried Dr. Shepherd,—but how could the *ladies* drive you away? I should have supposed *they* would have *kept* you?'—

⌐'Lord!⌐ Dr. Shepherd—⌐for God's sake!⌐—' cried Mʳˢ Young,—who shewed as ⌐much⌐ too much quickness, as the Doctor did too much dullness.

'But, Dr. Burney,' said Mʳ Twiss, 'was you never Accosted by *una bella Ragazza?*' then turning to me, | 'you know what a *Ragazza*, is, Ma'am?'

'Sir?—'

'A *signorina?*'

I stammered out something like niether yes or no, because the Question rather frightened me, lest he should conclude that in understanding *that*, I knew much *more*; but I believe he had already drawn his Conclusions, from my foolish *simpering* before, upon his first Visit, for he began such an attack in Italian,[35] that my Head was almost turned—yet it so happened, all he said being of the *easy style*, that I understood every Word—though it is wholly out of my power to *Write* in that Language.—finding me silent he said, in English— —'Why what Objection can you have to speaking to me in Italian? [xxxxx *3–4 words*]

'A very obvious one,' answered I, 'because it is not in my power.'

'Mais, vous avez la bonté de me parler en françois,' cried

---

[35] FBA has added 'of preposterous compliments'.

he—⌐determined to *sift* me⌐—but I again Assured him of my inability;—for I was quite ashamed of this Address ⌐before so many people,⌐ all of them listening.

He turned then to my Father—'*Questa signora ai troppo modesta*—' |

My Father, all kindness, had seemed to pity my embarrassment,—'Poor Fanny! cried he, 'she has not had such an attack ⌐the Lord knows when!⌐—this is as bad as a Bull fight to *her*!'—

'I hope not, Sir! cried Mr Twiss, rather hurt—& then turning to me—'Do you go to the masquerade advertised for Monday the 11th of April?'[36]

'No, Sir.' Though I have some expectation of going, with my mother, to *see* masks: but I thought it most *fitting* not to confess that.

'Have you ever been to one?'—continued he—

'I was—at a private one'[37]—⌐said I—ashamed to own the others, to this so very curious Enquirer.⌐

'And what Character did you Honour with supporting—'

'O none! I did not venture to *try* one.—'

He then went on with some high flown, Complimentary *Guesses* at what I ⌐wore.⌐

'Did I tell you, Dr. Burney, how horridly I was served about the *Fandango*?—I went to Hammersmith, to find a Dancer, & found an Old Woman!—I was never so mad!'

'Well,' said my Father, 'if I see a Spaniard at the next masquerade, I shall know who it is!—'

'Why no;' answered he,—'I am not determined—sometimes I think of a High lander.' |

'O, I know you'll be *snug*,'[38] said my Father, Laughing.

'But if you see a *Fandango* Danced—' cried I—

'O Ma'am, cried he eagerly, 'will you Dance it with me?——& give me leave to give you Lessons?—'

'No, Sir:—I should require too many!—'

'O no, Ma'am—I can easily teach you.—but, upon my Word, the Fandango, like the Allemande, requires *sentiment* to

---

[36] At Carlisle House (see *Daily Adv.*, 11 Apr.).

[37] At Mr Lalauze's in 1770 (see *EJL* i. 97–107). The public masquerades FB attended are not mentioned in her extant journals.

[38] Quiet, inconspicuous; used ironically, of course.

Dance it well—without an Agreeable Partner, it would be impossible—for I find myself so animated by it,—it gives me such feelings!—I do declare that I could not for the Universe Dance the Fandango with an old Woman!—[39]

'No, Sir,' cried Mrs Allen, angrily, 'and I suppose that an Old Woman could not Dance it with *you!*'

When supper was removed, Mr Twiss again attacked me in Italian—

'Credo che e innamorata, perche non mangiate—'

'O no! answered I,—⌐but I seldom Eat much supper.'¬

'É il Lingua d'Amore—' continued he, & added that it became *una bella Bocca*—'

'And it had best be confined to such!' answered I.

After something further which I have forgotten, he asked me, in a tone of reproach—'Ma perche &c but *why* will you not answer me in Italian?' |

'Because I assure you I cannot.'

'*Ma*—but you have understood all I have said?'

'Some part—by accident, only.—'

'Well, Ma'am,' cried he in English, 'I hope that when I have the Honour to be further known to you, you will speak to me in no other Language! I think, Dr. Burney, that the *Spanish* is the Noblest Language in the World!—I would, if it was in my power, always speak Spanish to men, & Italian to Women. As to English—that is quite out of the Question, you know!—but for *French*,—I protest I am ashamed of speaking it! it is become so very vulgar & Common—⌐every body knows it!'¬

'See how it is,' cried my Father,—'the French Language, from Being spoken at every Court in Europe, & being reckoned the politest living Language—is now sunk to worse than nothing—to vulgarity!'

'I think I never knew a Foreigner,' said Mr Twiss, 'who spoke English so well as Baretti does,—but so very slow,

---

[39] Twiss notes in his *Travels through Portugal and Spain*, p. 156: 'The fury and ardour for dancing with which the Spaniards are possessed on hearing the fandango played, recall to my mind the impatience of the Italian race-horses standing behind the rope, which being fixed across the road breast-high restrains them; and the velocity and eagerness with which they set off, and run without riders the instant that that barrier is removed.'

(in a drawling Voice, turning to me) that—if—he—were
—to make—love—it—would—take—him—*tree*—Hours—
to—「make」—a—declaration—However, I am of opinion, Dr.
Burney, that the English bids fair to be the *standard* Language
at the European Courts, in another Century. Have you ever
seen, Ma'am, any of the great Dr. Johnson's curious
Handwriting?' |

He then put into my Hand a Letter from that *Colossos* of
Literature, as he is often called. I told him that I *had* seen his
Writing, (which is scarse legible,) 「some years since,」 in a
Letter to my Father. However, he shewed me one Word (it
was *Testimony*) that I could not possibly make out.[40] 'But,
Ma'am,' added he, 'you write so well yourself!—I have the
Spanish Queries that you did me the Honour to Write—&
upon my Word, it is very seldom a *lady* writes so 「well」—

'O,' cried I, 'I am particularly proud of the *spelling* of the
Spanish Words!—I hope you Admired that?' [He had already
pointed out a mistake I had made. He looked quite
shocked.][41]

Mrs Young then began to speak of Ireland, where her
Husband had some thoughts of going.[42]—She asked Mr Twiss
if he had been there? Not having well attended to what was
said, he took it into his Head that *she* was of that Country, &
answered very civilly—'I reserved the *best* for the *last*, Ma'am.
Pray do you speak *Erse*, Ma'am?'

'Who *I*, Sir?' Cried Mrs Young, staring—

'I did not know, Ma'am—I thought that being an *Irish*
lady, perhaps you might. Well, I declare solemnly, the more I
go out of my own Country, the more I admire it—as to

---

[40] Johnson's letter to Twiss is missing. Johnson gave qualified praise to Twiss's
Travels when the book came out the next year, and gave him letters of introduction for
his trip to Ireland (see *Life*, ii. 345–6; *Boswell: The Ominous Years, 1774–1776*, ed. C.
Ryskamp and F. A. Pottle (New York, 1963), p. 131; Johnson, *Letters*, ed. R. W.
Chapman (Oxford, 1952), ii. 27–8; below, p. 135). The letter from Johnson to CB
that FB mentions is also missing, unless she means one of the extant letters written
much earlier; the latest is the one dated 16 Oct. 1765 (MS draft, Hyde), printed in
Letters, i. 178.

[41] Added by FBA.

[42] Young made his first trip to Ireland in 1776.

Ireland and Scotland, I mean to include them,[43] but I have Travelled from the Age of 17, & return with double satisfaction to England.—And of all the Countries that I have seen, upon my Honour I would not take a *Wife* out of my own for the Universe, for though I may prefer a Foreign lady to Dance or sing with, & though they have a certain *agrement* that is charming in the vivacity with which they make acquaintance with strangers; yet in the English Women, there is a reserve, a modesty—& something so sensible—that [*sic*] are *too* sensible, indeed, to be intimate with strangers:—yet I admire them for it:—though I own the *Spanish* ladies charmed me much—& the Portugese—O, Ma'am (to me) if you are fond of *Clubs*,[44] you should see the Portugese ladies' Hair—they have them thus Broad—& they wear no Caps—only a few Jewels—or Flowers—or—

'What,' interrupted Mrs Allen with a sneer,—'& I suppose some of those pretty shining things? those *Glow-Worms* that you mentioned—'

⌐'They⌐ are caught in great plenty in Spain,' said he to *me*, (taking no Notice of Mrs Allen's palpable sneer) '& they have an exceeding pretty effect in the ladies' Hair:—but then, *you* must shut your Eyes—or they won't shine![45]—'

'There's for you, my dear!' cried Mrs Allen—⌐O Christ⌐—'

'Nay, Ma'am,' said Mama, 'it was not said to *you*'—'

The Conversation soon turned upon Dancing, Mr Twiss spoke of it in very warm terms, 'I love Dancing most exceedingly—I prefer it to any thing—'

'I blush for you,' Cried my Father, Laughing—'is this you who pretend to love music?'

'Ay,' said Dr. Shepherd, 'what becomes of music?'

'O—Dancing beats all music!—I should prefer a Country

---

[43] See below, p. 191. Twiss went to Ireland in 1775 and had also visited Scotland by the following year (see his *Tour in Ireland* (1776), p. 177 and *passim*).

[44] i.e., hair worn in a club-shaped knot or tail at the back; fashionable in the 2nd half of the 18th c. (*OED* s.v. Club, *sb.* 6).

[45] Meaning, of course, that their light would be eclipsed by FB's bright eyes (or her eyes would so shame them that they would not shine). Mrs Allen's reaction may be to the hyperbole, or, missing the compliment, she may have simply taken Twiss's remark as yet another 'traveller's lie'.

Dance,—with *you* [Ma'am][46]—to all the music in the World!
—but this is only for *your* Ear, Ma'am.—*You* must not hear
this, Doctor. Don't *you* love Dancing, Ma'am?'

'Me, Sir?' said I—'O, I seldom Dance—I don't know—'

'What Assemblies do you frequent, Ma'am?'

'Me, Sir?—⌐Lord¬—I never Dance—I go to none!—'

'To None?—⌐God¬ bless me!—but—pray Ma'am—will
you do me the Honour to accept any Tickets?'

'Sir, I am much obliged to you, but I never—'

'No, Sir,' said my Father, she does Nothing of that sort.'

He seemed extreamly surprised—but continued—'I Danced
last Thursday till past two o'Clock, but I was so unlucky as to
fix upon a very stupid Partner, from whom I hardly could get
a Word— | all the Evening—I chose her because she was a
pretty Girl,—Miss Ladbroke—[47]

'How could a pretty Girl be stupid?' cried Dr Shepherd.

'Ay,' said my Father, 'her Eyes should have sufficed to
make her Eloquent: but English Girls are often shy.—'

'Shall you go to the Lock Hospital Oratorio,[48] Ma'am?'

'No, Sir.' answered I.

'To that at the Foundling?[49]—O!—I hope it!—'

'No, Sir. I seldom go out.'

'Well, my dear, cried Mrs Allen, you have it all!—poor Susy
is Nothing to Night!—'

She said these kind of speeches, in a sort of whisper, so
often, that I was exceedingly frightened lest Mr Twiss should

---

[46] Inserted by FBA.

[47] Perhaps Ann Ladbroke (d. 1791), m. (18 Aug. 1774) Thomas Littler; younger
daughter of Sir Robert Ladbroke (?1713–73), MP, prominent London banker, and a
former lord mayor of London (Namier; *GM* xliv (1774), 390, xlvii (1777), 195, lxi¹
(1791), 286).

[48] Held annually in the Lock Hospital chapel. The Lock Hospital for women with
venereal disease was established in 1746. The oratorios were instituted by the
Hospital's chaplain, Martin Madan (*c*. 1725–90), writer and composer. In 1774 the
performance took place on Wed., 30 Mar.; the oratorio was *Ruth*, music by Giardini.
See *Morning Chronicle*, 30 Mar.; *New Grove*, s. v. London, I, 5, Martin Madan.

[49] The Foundling Hospital for abandoned children, established by Thomas Coram
(1668–1751) in 1739. An annual performance of Handel's *Messiah* in the chapel, for
the benefit of the Hospital, was begun by Handel himself in 1750. This year's
performance took place on Tuesday, 29 Mar. The performances were discontinued
after 1777 (*Daily Adv.*, 29 Mar.; R. K. McClure, *Coram's Children: The London Foundling
Hospital in the Eighteenth Century* (1981), pp. 69–71 and *passim*).

hear her: & Mrs Young fixed her Eyes with such curious Observation———my Father too began to grow very grave;—so that all together I was in a very embarrassing situation, which I believe was pretty obvious, for they all endeavoured to turn Mr Twiss away from me, & my Father made several attempts at changing the Conversation, though the ⌜young man⌝ was too flighty to regard them.

However, at length, he attacked Susy, & talked a little French with her:—but as I was more conveniently situated for him, he returned again soon to me.ꞁ

'Have you Read Miss Aiken's[50] Poems? Dr. Burney they have been much admired. There is one poem in them, Come here fond youth,—that describes the symptoms of Love, which all the ladies I meet with, have by Heart. Have *you*, Ma'am?'

⌜'God,⌝ no, Sir! ⌜I never—I know nothing of these things—'⌝

'But, Dr. Burney, of all the Books upon this subject, none was ever equal to Eloise![51] what feeling! what Language! what fire! have you Read it, ma'am.

'No, Sir.'

'O, it's a Book that is *alone*!—'

'And *ought* to be *alone*, said my Father very gravely.

Mr Twiss Perceived that he was angry, and with great eagerness, cried—'why I assure you I gave it to my sister![52]—who is but 17, & just going to be married.

'Well,' returned my Father, 'I hope she Read the Preface,—& then flung it away?'

'No, upon my Honour! she Read the Preface first, & then the Book. But pray, Doctor, ⌜have⌝ you ever met with a little

[50] Anna Laetitia Aikin (1743–1825), m. (1774) the Revd Rochemont Barbauld (d. 1808); poet and miscellaneous writer. Her 4to vol. of *Poems*, pub. in 1773, went through 3 edns. the first year and a 4th in 1774. 'Come here fond youth' is the first of her songs in this vol. (1773 edn., pp. 66–9). FB met Mrs Barbauld and her husband in 1783. Toward the very end of her days she confided to Samuel Rogers that she repeated to herself every evening some lines from Mrs Barbauld's poem *Life* (*DL* ii. 238–9; *HFB*, p. 490).

[51] *Julie ou la nouvelle Héloïse* (1761), by Jean Jacques Rousseau. Despite CB's disapproval below, he owned two copies of the 1761 printings, besides an English translation of 1764 (presumably William Kendrick's, first pub. in 1761). See *Lib.*, p. 49.

[52] Not further traced.

Book upon this subject, called the Dictionary of Love?[53] it is a most elegant Work.—I am surprised you have not seen it:—but *it* is difficult to procure, being out of Print. It is but a Duodecimo, but I gave half a Guinea for it.— | indeed, Davies[54] had a commission from me to get it for 5 Guineas, but it took him 3 years. I have it now, Binding in Gold, for a present to a young lady. But first I shall do myself the Honour to shew it to you, Ma'am—though *you* cannot want it—you have it all ready—it is only for such Bunglers as me.'

I made no Answer—he spoke this rather in a low Voice, & I hoped that Nobody heard him, for I was quite ashamed of receiving such an offer—& did not seem even to hear him myself.

His next attempt was for music. He began a most urgent & violent entreaty to me to play—

'I will kneel to you,—for a quarter of an Hour!—' I answered very seriously that I could not possibly but he would not *be* ⌐answered⌐—'To whom must I apply?—Dr. Burney?—pray—speak for me!—'

'Sir,' said my Father, half Jesting, half earnest, 'the young Women in this House, like those in Spain, do nothing before they are married!'

He was silent for a few moments. & then turning to Mama, with a supplicating Tone, said—'Will you use your influence, Ma'am—I will kneel to *you* to obtain it—' Sir, said she. ⌐I give up the⌐ Duenna!' [xxxxx *3–4 words*]

'Duenn*a* Ma'am, said he, is the pronunciation.' |

---

[53] *The Dictionary of Love. In which is contained, the Explanation of most of the Terms used in that Language*, pub. by Ralph Griffiths in 1753. This little book is an anonymous effort by John Cleland and was his second most popular work, after *Fanny Hill*. He presents humorous, lightly cynical definitions based on the *Dictionnaire d'amour* of Jean-François du Radier (Paris, 1741); he pretends to aim at the true meanings behind lovers' protestations. The definitions range from 'Absence' to 'Zone'; the latter is defined thus: 'The Virgin Zone. Whatever stuff this zone was made of, which the virgins of antient times wore about their waists, it is at present so lightly wove, that it is apt to give way at the least touch.' A new edn. appeared in 1776, pub. by John Bell and Christopher Etherington, with the notice: 'This Book was first printed in London, near thirty years ago, and as it has become exceeding scarce, it has been thought proper to re-print it'. Twiss recommended it again in a note to his *Tour in Ireland* (1776), p. 51. See P. Sabor, 'Introduction' to *Memoirs of a Woman of Pleasure*, by John Cleland (Oxford, 1985), p. xi.

[54] Presumably the bookseller Thomas Davies (above, p. 9 n. 18).

'What shall I say! *one* air, before I go—only *one* air—will make my sleep so delightful!—'

'If you would go to sleep *first*, perhaps—'

'Why ay, Fanny,' said my Father, *do* play him to sleep!'

'No, no, Dr. Burney—not to sleep!—but my Dreams *after* it will be so fine—'

'Well,' cried Mrs Young, 'here's a lady who *can* play, if she will—' turning to Susan.

He immediately arose, & went & flung himself on his knees to Susy. She refused his request, & changed her place—he followed her, & again prostrated himself—

'Well, however,' cried Mrs Allen, 'I am glad he is got to Susy, at last!'

This scene lasted but a short Time—finding he sued in vain—he was obliged to rise—& Dr. Shepherd, who had been quite out of his Element all the Evening, rose to depart, & proposed to take Mr Twiss with him. This was agreed to—& ⌜all our Company departed.⌝

I think this was the most extraordinary Evening I ever passed. Mr Twiss is such a [xxxxx *1 word*] man as I never [saw][55] before, or scarsely any one whose Character ⌐ even⌐ *resembled* his. He piques himself upon having Travelled ⌜so⌝ many years, & when ⌜so⌝ very young, without a Tutor;—but I am apt to attribute greatly to this very circumstance the extravagant strangeness of his manners. Always his own master, ⌜& allowed what money he pleased,⌝ he has scampered from place to place, met with new Customs & new men every month, without any sensible or experienced friend ⌜to Guide him, &⌝ to point out the good or Evil that he saw,—he is really a Creature of *his own* forming; for he seems to have seen every thing, & Copied Nothing.

Nothing could be more improper, more injudicious than the Conversation which he chose to enter into. Indeed I often wondered where he would stop. It is however, evident that he *meant* no offence or impertinance, by his prating at such a rate, before my Father & mother; yet what a Novice would we conclude any man who could imagine that any Father would approve of such a sort of Conversation! More especially, ⌜the

---

[55] Inserted by FBA.

[xxxxx *2–3 words*] *not* considered,⌐ that any man of Letters would be entertained by so much frivolous gallantry—⌐

But perhaps he is of that Number of men who conclude that all ⌐Women⌐ take Nonsense for politeness; & that it is necessary to banish sense & reason in order to be understood. ⌐It seems [xxxxx *1–2 words*] that these obliging conformists to the Capacity of *the fair*, are frequently found among men who Travel very young, & I suppose it may in some measure be attributed to the general levity of the Women on the Continent, I mean of the *general run*.⌐

He has really put our House into a Commotion, his behaviour was so extraordinary, that he has been the sole topic of Discourse since his curious ⌐visit. Mrs. Allen is quite amazed at him, & cannot speak of him with Decency, calling him at every Word, *impudent Fellow*! audacious puppy! &c. Mama, too, has taken a thorough aversion to him & always mentions him in a passion.⌐ Even my gentle & candid Father says that *he has quite mistaken the Thing*, & that he shall never see a *Table Cloth* in his House again, or be invited ever more into the ⌐Parlour.⌐

[April][56]

⌐Mrs. Allen is gone to Lynn. She made her visit here last near 6 months, however the old lady was never at all in our way, for notwithstanding her Caprice, she ever behaved to Susy & me with the utmost civility, & even kindness.

Miss Davis,[57] her mother & sister, spent an Afternoon here last week. I am amazed to hear that this young woman is engaged in perpetual Quarrels at the Opera, as she appears to be made up of Nothing that is not pleasing—& as, added to

---

[56] Inserted by FBA.

[57] Cecilia Davies (?1753–1836), called l'Inglesina, English soprano. Her mother was widow of the composer and flautist Richard Davies (d. Dec. 1773), whom she had married before 1744; she was still living in 1786, but her date of death (and maiden name) have not been found. Miss Davies's sister was Marianne Davies (*c.* 1743–?1816), a celebrated performer on the glass harmonica, for whom Mozart and other composers wrote original pieces.

CB praises Cecilia Davies's talents in *Hist. Mus.* (Mercer, ii. 879–80). FB also admired her as an artist and person and came to her aid *c.*1832 when she was living in poverty. See *New Grove*; Highfill; Rees, s.v. Armonica; *Tours*, ii. 95; *Mem.* ii. 19–20; *JL* xii. 811–12; CB to Mrs and Misses Davies, 17 Feb. [1786] (Osborn); below, *passim*.

manners infinitely engaging, she is very sensible. I am sure that she must have very bad Counsellors & I fancy that she owes all that is wrong in her Conduct to the Advice & interference of her Termagent sister, to whom she seems to pay implicit respect.[58]

My Father has at length settled with Sig^r Giardini, & has paid him 120 pounds for his Tickets.[59] Many letters passed between him & Mr. Twiss upon the subject. This Gentleman has twice Called here—the first Time he only gained a short entrance with Mama in the passage, who did not ask him to Walk in, & the second Time he was admitted to my Father in the study, but not before Susy & I were sent off. He went to join us afterwards in the parlour, but my mother told him we were all engaged, with great Coldness.⌐|

In one of his Letters to my Father concerning ⌐the plates of Giardini,⌐ he says 'Inclosed is the form of folding Italian Billet Doux, which I promised to the Young ladies.'

As to *promised*, which is a strange Word, & which only this strange man would use, all that passed concerning the Billets was That he asked if my Father had ever shewn me the Italian method of folding them? I answered No. 'Then pray ask the Doctor, said he,—*I* dare not!—' I begged to be excused, & niether said or thought more upon the subject. And this he calls a *promise*!

The Billet is folded in form of a Heart; & very prettily. It is sealed with a very fine impression of the Emperor.[60] The Direction was

Alla più bella.

⌐Sukey⌐ & I both refused to open it. Perhaps the Gentleman fancied we should pull Caps upon the occasion! However my Father himself saved us that trouble. Within were these Words written in an elegant Hand.

Di questa parte, i Cicisbei Italiani scrivono loro Lettere

---

[58] Cecilia Davies, with her mother and sister, had returned to England from the Continent in 1773 and sang at the Opera in the 1773–4 season. Her main dispute with the Opera's management seems to have been over the right to sing elsewhere, over which issue she sued the Opera. See below, pp. 79–80, 106–8, 150.

[59] See above, p. 12 and n. 28. The letters mentioned by FB are missing.

[60] Joseph II (1741–90), Holy Roman Emperor, 1765–90.

gallanti ed amorosi alle loro Dame, essendo la Figura di questa Carta, forma |ᵞ[xxxxx *1 word*] del Core, ch'essi danno a queste signorine.⌐

I shall now go from an odd *Young*, to an odd *old* man, both new Acquaintance to us.

Soon after the publication of the German Tour, my Father received a Letter from a stranger who called himself Mʳ Hutton[61] of Lindsey House Chelsea, & a friend of Dr. Hawkesworth. It contained some criticisms on the German Anecdotes, concerning the poverty & wretchedness of that Country; he said that he had frequently Travelled there, but had always met with *White Bread*;[62] & vindicated several other particulars which seemed to bear hard upon Germany; concluding with supposing that my Father's servant, or other people, must have misinformed him; & signed himself his real well wisher, & a great admirer of all *other parts of his Charming Book*.[63]

My Father wrote an immediate, & angry Answer to this Letter,[64] Acquainting Mʳ Hutton that his Veracity, which had never before been disputed, was what he should most carefully & invariably defend, & Adhere to, That the Accounts he had given of the miserable state of the Empire, was from his *Observations*, made with his *own* Eyes; & not the result of *any* information; that if Mʳ Hutton found that Country more reasonable,[65] fertile & flourishing, he was sure he must have Travelled before the last War,[66] when the most terrible

---

[61] James Hutton (1715–95), son of the Revd John Hutton, a non-juring divine, was principal founder of the Moravian Church in England. Lindsey House, his home, was a meeting place of the Moravians in London. Hutton's initial letter to CB, dated 2 July 1773, is in the Osborn Collection; he introduces himself as 'Mr Hutton of Lindsey House Chelsea (whom Dʳ Hawkesworth takes friendly notice of) ...'.

[62] Hutton had not read the *German Tour* itself, but Bewley's anonymous review of it, with excerpts, in the *Monthly Review* for June 1773 (xlviii. 457–69). 'Mr H. never found want of white Bread, & excellent too, in every even Market Town He went through ...' (James Hutton to CB, 2 July 1773).

[63] 'Dʳ B. therefore has been misinformed & when the Electress of Bavaria reads his charming Book, she will reckon the Dʳ to have been out of luck during that Voyage. ... all Health to the Dr.'

[64] Dated 17 July 1773 (letter signed copy, Osborn).

[65] Hutton thought that CB had exaggerated the expense of travelling in Germany.

[66] The Seven Years War, 1756–63.

ravages were Committed by the king of Prussia[67] & that
whatever reasons he might have for defending Germany, they
could not be more powerful than those which would ever
impel himself to defend his own Honour;—then after answering particularly to his several Remarks, he told him that if he
desired any further satisfaction, or had any remaining doubts,
he would at any Time receive him, & endeavour to convince
him, in Queen Square.

Soon after this, poor Dr. Hawkesworth brought a Letter
from Mr Hutton,[68] filled with apologies & concessions, &
allowing that he *had* Travelled before the last war: he protested that his Letter was extremely well meant, & expressed
the greatest concern & contrition that he had given offence.

With this Letter, Dr. Hawkesworth gave a character of M^r
Hutton, the most amiable that could be drawn; he said that he
was his old & intimate friend; that a more worthy Being did
not exist; but that he was singular, & wholly ignorant of the
World;—that he was a man who was a true lover of mankind,
& made quite miserable with the idea of hurting or dis-
pleasing any living Creature. In short he made his Portrait
so full of benevolence & simplicity, that my Father, whose
Heart is replete with all the 'milk of Human kindness,' Wrote
to him immediately a Letter of reconciliation, apologising in
his Turn for his own hasty Answer to his first Epistle, &
begging the continuance of his esteem & friendship.

The much regretted Death of Dr. Hawkesworth, which
happened soon after,[69] did not put an End to this strangely
begun Correspondance. Mr Hutton wrote Letters that were
truly *his own*, being unlike any, either Printed or manuscript,
which we ever before saw.[70] They contained a good deal of
humour, very oddly Worded, & the strongest expressions of
kindness. About 3 months Ago, he called here. I heard him
parleying in the Passage, & delivering his Name,—which
induced me, (having only Susy at Home) to ask him in. He

---

[67] Frederick II (1712–86), the Great, King of Prussia, 1740–86.
[68] This letter is missing, as is CB's reply to it (below).
[69] In Nov. 1773 (see *EJL* i. 324).
[70] Extant are letters from Hutton to CB of 24 Jan. and 2 Apr. 1774 (Osborn; see below).

looks about 60[71]—good humoured, clever & kind Hearted. He
came up to me, & said 'Is your Father at Home? for I am
Deaf.' He had not heard the man's answer. He stayed a little
while with us, & desired his respects & love to my Father.
'Tell him,' said he, 'that I know him very well, though I never
saw him!' |

Last Good Friday [1 April], he called again, & then had the
good fortune to meet with my Father. He was also introduced
to Mama & all the Family. He came with open Arms, & my
Father was very soon extremely intimate with him. He enquired concerning us all, & whether one Daughter [EBB]
was not married? Yes.—'And pray, said he, are you a *Grand
Father, Young Gentleman?*'[72]

My Father has, indeed, a remarkably young look. He said
many other humourous things ⌜before he went,⌝ & left us all in
high good humour with him.

The next Day, I received a Letter in an Hand that I was
unacquainted with—& to my great surprise saw the Name of
Hutton at the Bottom. The Letter is so extraordinary, considering the manner of his being known to us, that I will
Copy it.—though I hate the *Dear Miss* at the Beginning, the
rest of the Letter is worth preserving. There was in it one
Inclosed to my Father.[73]

Dear Miss,

I have written[74] here a longish kind of Letter to your dear
Papa, whom I saw with infinite pleasure you love so tenderly.
As you | love him therefore so much, I shall recommend to you
to give him this Letter when he is in some degree at leisure for
the babble of a friend of his, ⌜perhaps after Dinner on Monday
[4 April], or some such Time, or you may leave the Disposal
of it to your Mama:[75] he is at least[76] as well off in one of you as

---

[71] He would be 59 in Sept.

[72] EBB was, in fact, currently expecting her 3rd child, Charles Crisp Burney (born
6 Nov.; see below, p. 54).

[73] Hutton to CB, 2 Apr. 1774 (Osborn). The original of Hutton's ALS to FB, 4
pp. double sheet 4to, dated 2 April [1774] and addressed 'To Miss Burney | at Dr
Burney's | Queen's Square | Ormond Street', is in the Barrett Collection. Variants
from FB's copy are indicated in the footnotes.

[74] 'wrote'

[75] 'to your Mother if you should be going out:'

[76] 'almost'

in the other. How well does he deserve you both.⌐ I mentioned to him the use of the steam of Coffee for his Eyes, so well employed for himself, his family,[77] & for all who have Taste in the World.[78] You & your Mama together will know how to surprise[79] him into the use of it, ⌐as I express it in the Inclosed,⌐ for if you Consult much with him, he may perhaps, as most other studious men do, till it be too late, desire to be excused. ⌐But if he should be averse to it after the first surprise, do not teize him for the World: for you will teize him I know in Nothing else, & should[80] be sorry if I was the occasion of[81] his being teazed.⌐[82] I will tell you something else, Miss, if my skill in physiognomy has not totally deceived me, he is happy in his lady[83] & Children, & you in him. This gives me a high pleasure, as Domestic happiness is all Harmony & melody, capable of being expressed with a thousand Graces, the irregular & New, as well as the Grave Old[84] of 40 years ago: the thousand small attentions accompanying the solid fundamental melody, charm beyond expression.

May ye all, all of ye[85] be blessed together! Happy will that man be who shall be blessed with *your* Hand, or I am totally out!—how do I wish my young friend, as I call your Father, may have Nothing but blessings in his Children & Grand Children! ⌐Pray where does your Brother in Law live, that I may run & take a peep at Him & your Sister?⌐[86]

You will always be married *sat citê si sat bene*.[87] But how shall

---

[77] 'for his family'

[78] After recommending that CB sit a proper distance from the fire, Hutton notes that 'the great [Albrecht von] Haller whom you mention as a Poet, recommended to a Gentleman at Lausanne while I was there, that the steam of Coffee, the Eyes held over it, would strengthen the Eyes . . . do not hold your Eyes too near the Liquor . . . to scorch them'.

[79] 'continue to surprise'

[80] 'I should'

[81] 'if I should be a means of'

[82] FB's two spellings ('teize,' 'teazed') are so in the MS.

[83] 'Family'

[84] 'old grave'

[85] 'you'

[86] '& your Sister? & what is his Name?' EBB and Charles Rousseau Burney lived in Charles St., Covent Garden.

[87] Properly, *sat cito si sat bene*, 'fast enough if [only] well enough'; a proverbial expression attributed by St Jerome to Cato the Elder (H. T. Riley, *Dictionary of Latin Quotations* (1860), p. 408). Hutton cites the phrase correctly, both in his letter to FB and his letter to CB.

we find a man who will deserve a Daughter who loves her Parents as you do? Your Father is the properest[88] person to explain that Latin phrase to you.[89] If I Live till next Good Friday, I may perhaps meet with your Father again at Home; or on some Sunday, when his Book is finished: though then I shall Rob all of you of part of the pleasure his leisure gives you, which at present you can have but little of. An old man as I am is garrulous, & deaf people often are so. Now I am both old & Deaf—Discretion bids me finish. I hope you believe
that I am with the greatest esteem
your obed[t] hum[ble] ser[t] James Hutton |

P.S.[90] I was married 34 years ago, by recommendation of friends, as our Princes used to be;[91] & have had Nothing to make me repent.[92] If I had chosen for myself perhaps[93] I might not have been so well off, for I have had Domestic Happiness in the highest degree, & have still as much esteem & tender friendship & Love,—& it is reciprocal,—as in the first[94] month: am not I happy? I believe this little anecdote may give pleasure in Queen Square, & therefore I mention it; else I know it is not fashionable for a man to talk of his Domestic happiness.
　　Lindsey House
　　Chelsea.[95]

[88] 'proper'

[89] To explain, but never to teach the language. When Dr Johnson later offered to teach FB Latin, CB forbad it on the grounds that 'Latin was too Masculine for Misses' (*Thraliana*, i. 393, 502).

[90] The 'P.S.' is not in the original.

[91] Presumably an allusion to the maverick marriages of George III's brothers Prince William Henry (1743–1805), D. of Gloucester (to Maria, Countess-Dowager Waldegrave, in 1766) and Prince Henry Frederick (1745–90), D. of Cumberland (to Mrs Anne Horton, in 1771), which resulted in the Royal Marriage Act of 1772.

[92] Hutton married at Marienborn, Germany, 3 July 1740, a Swiss Moravian, Louise Brandt (b. 1709), granddaughter of an advocate of Neuchâtel. The match was recommended by Hutton's mentor Nicolaus Ludwig Zinzendorf (1700–60), C. of Zinzendorf and Pottendorf, founder of the Moravian Brethren in Germany, who performed the ceremony. Mrs Hutton died on 10 Nov. 1778 (Hutton to FB, 5 Apr. 1781, Berg). See D. Benham, *Memoirs of James Hutton* (1856), pp. 56, 518–22.

[93] 'myself I fancy'

[94] 'very first'

[95] FB has transposed 'Lindsey House | Chelsea' from just after Hutton's signature and has omitted his date of 'April 2. ⌜Saturday⌝ in the Evening'.

Perhaps Mr Hutton thought the intelligence of his marriage was necessary, after so civil a Letter, to prevent any *mistakes* on my part!

However, he is an exceeding good man—& I like him very much—nevertheless his Letter was so odd, that I could not attempt to answer it. ⌈Indeed I find that 2 Correspondants[96] are as much as I can comfortably write to, because those two expect so very much from me.⌉

Some Time after my mother met this Gentleman ∣ ⌈in the street⌉ & he sent me a reproach for not Writing—which I therefore was then obliged to do, excusing myself as well as I could.[97]

The very Day after, he called here again[98]—he came up to me & shook my Hand—'Thank you for your Letter—you thought I wanted a *performance*, but I only wanted the Heart—but I have got *that*, & a performance too!'

It seems he had been speaking very highly of my Father to the King—who he was accidentally admitted to the speach of, by being one morning in the Apartment of M. Salgas,[99] who is a preceptor of the Prince of Wales, when the King came in, & entered into the Conversation with great complacency & Condescendsion. He had given an account of this to my mother ⌈in his street *encounter*⌉—she told him now, that my Father was much pleased to have had so good a friend speak of him before the King.—

'Madam, cried he, I will speak of him before God, & that is doing much more!'

Since this, I have received another Letter from him[1]—much

---

[96] Presumably SC and MAR.

[97] This letter is missing.

[98] This visit took place on Saturday, 23 Apr. (Hutton to FB, 24 Apr. 1774, Barrett, printed *ED* i. 309–12).

[99] Charles Jean de Salgas (b. *c.*1729), subpreceptor to George Augustus Frederick (1762–1830), Prince of Wales (later George IV) and Frederick (1763–1827), D. of York, *c.*1772–6. Salgas left the King's service in 1776 and drew an allowance from Oct. 1776 to 1795, the presumed year of his death. Hutton, who was childless, called Salgas 'my son' and was present at his wedding in Holland in 1778. See RHI; Benham, *Memoirs of James Hutton* pp. 518, 525–6; also Horace Walpole, *Last Journals*, ed. A. F. Steuart (1910), i. 557–8; *The Later Correspondence of George III*, ed. A. Aspinall (1962–70), i. 572 and *passim*.

[1] Presumably Hutton to FB, 24 Apr. 1774 (above n. 98). Again, FB's reply is missing.

in the style of the former—very much desiring me to write to him—which I yesterday did. Though I think few young persons have Entered into a more singular Correspondance. ⌐

[*two or more leaves and top of page cut away*]

⌐to *depreciate*—the latter, indeed, was out of the Question. I therefore made no answer at all—though I could not help laughing, as I saw an amazing Broad Grin upon Bessy's Face—What he thought I know not, but he did not then pursue or afterwards raise the subject.

Since this, accidentally Drinking Tea at Mrs. Strange's, I met with the *Young* Clergyman [Mr. Mann][2]—who I there soon discovered to be a very Coxcomb—full of affectation & airs—Lord Berriedale[3] also was there—he is just the reverse —he is, indeed, not *meerly* unaffected—he is even without that *Polish* which his connections, Rank & Education *ought* to have given him. Nevertheless I was ashamed to see the Conceit, the half witted liveliness, of the *English* youth, when contrasted by the manly manners, solid ⟨sense,⟩ & entertaining *Humour* of the Youth of Scotland.⌐ |

[*top of page cut away*]

⌐&⌐ my Father has bought A House in St. Martin's Street Leicester Fields—an odious street.—but well situated, & nearly in the Centre of the Town; & the House is a large & good one. It was built by Sir Isaac Newton![4]

⌐We have made an exceeding pleasant Excursion for 3 Days to Chesington. Mama, Bessy & Charlotte went a Week before my Father, Dick & me, who brought them Home. My beloved Mr. Crisp looks very well, though he is never long free from the Gout. He tells me he has a Plan of an Invite to *me* for a longer Time this summer—but *our* History [CB's *Hist. Mus.*]

---

[2] Inserted by FBA. Perhaps the Revd Daniel Mann (d. 1788), dissenting minister at Burwash in Sussex (*GM* lviii[1] (1788), 273).

[3] John Sinclair (b. *c.*1756), styled Ld. Berriedale; 11th E. of Caithness (Scotland), 1779. Currently an ensign in the 17th Foot, he had been sent to Paris to complete his education, where he was committed to the good offices of Mrs Strange's brother Andrew Lumisden. He died by his own hand in 1789. See Dennistoun, ii. 130, 134–8.

[4] Sir Isaac did not build the house, but moved into it in 1711, and added a small observatory to it. The Burneys occupied their new residence in Oct. (below, p. 52; see also Wheatley, ii. 489; *Survey of London*, xx. 107–8; C. Hill, *The House in St. Martin's Street* (1907).

now requires its secretary & I am almost certain it will not be possible to separate them till the Work is finished.

However, I saw but little of Mr. Crisp, as he & my Father were *closeted* almost constantly between⌐ ⌐ [?our arrival there and our return.]

[*three leaves cut away*]

⌐I shall be heartily glad if my dear Mr. Crisp's plan *can* take place, & I may have another visit to Chesington.[5]

O but then this inglorious Youth[6] returned to the Garden— after his unexpected failure of success. He said as he mounted his Horse—'Lord—she's so monstrous *Coy*, there's no making any thing of her'—⌐

My good old new Friend, Mr Hutton, made me two Visits while my mother was at Chesington, ⌐before *my* Jaunt thither. I have also had another Letter from him,[7] & which, though much too ⟨cool,⟩ is still more in the *way of the World*, than the two former, & is really very clever—yet I have not answered it—as I think *3* Letters in this airing are sufficient.⌐

We had a good deal of Conversation upon Lord Chesterfield's Letters, ⌐which have lately been published.⌐[8] I had the satisfaction to ¦ find that our opinions exactly coincided—that they were extremely well written, contained some excellent *hints* for Education—but were written with a tendency to make his son a man wholly unprincipled; inculcating immorality; countenancing all *Gentlemanlike* vices; *advising* deceit; & *exhorting* to Inconstancy.

'It pleased me much,' said Mr Hutton, 'in speaking to the King about these Letters, to hear him say—'*For my part, I like more streight forward work.*'

---

[5] See below, pp. 45–52.

[6] Perhaps the young clergyman, Mr Mann, mentioned above (p. 32).

[7] Presumably Hutton's letter to FB of 16 May (Berg).

[8] On 7 Apr. They were advertised in the *Daily Adv.*, 8 Apr. as: 'Elegantly printed in two volumes, Royal Quarto ... Letters written by the late Right Honourable Philip Dormer Stanhope, Earl of Chesterfield, to his Son Phillip [*sic*] Stanhope, Esq. later Envoy Extraordinary at the Court of Dresden. Together with several other Pieces on various Subjects. Published by Mrs. Eugenia Stanhope; from the Originals now in her Possession. Printed for J. Dodsley, in Pall-Mall.' CB owned a copy of the 4-vol. edn. published later this year (*Lib.*, p. 10). The letters were addressed to Chesterfield's natural son Philip Stanhope (1732–68), diplomatist, and published by Stanhope's widow, Eugenia née Peters (d. 1783). See *YW* xxviii. 145 n. 14; 146 n. 25.

⌐I found that he had known Miss Kinnaird—& that he much loved her—which indeed is a natural consequence of knowing her—he told me that she is now gone to Scotland, to reside.[9] I cannot help being sorry.

Signor Corri, the Italian who Dined with us, with Martinelli, 2 summers ago,[10] has made us 2 or 3 visits lately. He has been, with his⌐ |

[*The top of the page has been cut away. The 'Foreigners' whom FB visited (or who visited her) may have been the Castells (below, p. 39).*]

⌐[?I have made the]m two visits since, in the course of which [I have] [spo]ken more bad French than in all the former part [of] my life together but there is a civility, & such an [exc]lusion of *apparent* ridicule, in Foreigners (I except Italians) that it gives a Courage which among [?my own countrymen I could never find.]⌐ |

[*top of page cut away*]

I have had the Honour, not long since, of b[eing] in Company with Mr Keate, Author of An accoun[t] of Geneva;[11] Ferney, & some other things, chiefly Po[et]ical. He is an Author *comme il faut*, for he | [is] in affluent circumstances, & Writes at his leisure & for his amusement. It was at the House of 6 old maids, all sisters, & all above 60, that I met him. These Votaries of Diana are exceeding worthy Women,

---

[9] With her grandmother in Edinburgh (James Hutton to FB, 16 May 1774, Berg).

[10] Actually the summer of 1771 (see *EJL* i. 168). Signor Corri had gone to Edinburgh that year with his wife, the singer née Baccheli, but returned to London this year for the production of his opera *Alessandro nell'Indie* at the King's Theatre, 3 Dec. 1774. It is also likely that Signora Corri sang the role of Sandrina in *La Buona figliuola* at the King's Theatre on 17 Mar. 1774. Both Corris performed in several of CB's musical evening parties during this stay in London; they returned to Edinburgh in 1775.

In the missing conclusion of this paragraph FB may have mentioned Corri's having been with his wife at Edinburgh. See *New Grove*; Highfill; Corri's 'Life', quoted in *The Scots Musical Museum*, ed. J. Johnson and W. Stenhouse (Edinburgh, 1853), i. pp. lxx–lxxii; below, p. 149–50.

[11] *A Short Account of the Ancient History, Present Government and Laws of the Republic of Geneva* (1761), by George Keate, miscellaneous writer. For his poem *Ferney* see *EJL* i. 77. A bibliography of Keate's writings is in K. G. Dapp, *George Keate* (Philadelphia, 1939), pp. 169–75.

of the name of Blake;[12] & I heartily [wish][13] that *I*, who devote myself to the same Goddess, should I be as ancient, may be as good.

Mr. Keate did not appear to me to be very brilliant; his powers of Conversation are not of a shining Cast,—& one disadvantage to his speeches, is his Delivery of them, for he speaks in a slow & sluggish Voice. But what principally banished him from *my* Good Graces, was the conceited manner in which he Introduced a Discourse upon his own Writings.

'Do you know, Mrs Blake, (addressing himself to the senior Virgin) I have at last ventured upon Building?—in spight of my resolution, & in spight of my Ode?'[14]

Mrs Blake fell into his ⌐Plan,¬ without being sensible that he had laid one—'O Mrs Burney, (cried she to Mama) that Ode was the prettiest thing! I wish you could see it!'

'Why I had determined, & indeed promised,' said he, | 'that when I went into my new House, I would either give a Ball, or write an ode—& so I found the Ode was the most easy to me—but I protested in the Poem, that I would never undertake to Build.'[15]

All the sisters then poured forth the Incense of Praise upon this Ode, to which he listened with the utmost *nonchalance*, reclining his person upon the back of his Chair, & kicking his Foot now over, & now under, a Gold Headed Cane.

---

[12] A Mrs Jane Blake (d. 1798) and her sisters Rachel (d. by 9 Dec. 1785), Diana, Elizabeth, Anne, and Sarah (all d. by 1 Oct. 1793). Jane Blake, the eldest, was the recipient of a set of verses from Keate with a present of a pair of hand-screens; in the poem he addresses her as 'Cousin'. At his death in 1797 Keate bequeathed her a sum for mourning, and Mrs Keate left an annuity to a former servant of hers in 1800. See Dapp, *George Keate*, pp. 78–9; *GM* lxviii[1] (1798), 447; *The Poetical Works of George Keate, Esq.* (1781), ii. 168–70; wills of Rachel Blake, PCC, prob. 9 Dec. 1785; Sarah Blake, prob. 1 Oct. 1793; Jane Blake, prob. 21 May 1798; Diana Blake and Elizabeth Blake, both prob. 8 Oct. 1798 (PRO).

[13] Inserted by FBA.

[14] 'A Burlesque Ode, on the Author's Clearing a New House of Some Workmen' (see Dapp, *George Keate*, p. 84; below).

[15] After his marriage Keate moved from the Temple into a brick corner house at No. 8 Charlotte St. The house needed considerable renovation, but Keate found his craftsmen lazy and inefficient and drove them off in a fury. After writing himself into a good humour by composing his 'Burlesque Ode', he engaged his friend Robert Adam to help finish the work (Dapp, *George Keate*, pp. 84–5).

When these effusions of civility were vented, the good old
ladies began another subject—but upon the first cessation of
speech, Mr Keate broke the silence he had kept, & said to
Mama—

'But the Worst thing to me, was that I was obliged to Hang
a Carpenter in the course of my Poem.'[16]

'O dear, aye,'—cried Mrs Blake— 'that part was vastly
pretty!—⌈lord,⌉ I wish I could remember it——dear M^rs
Burney, I wish you could see it—Mr Keate, it's a pity it
should not be seen.'—

'Why surely, (cried he affectedly) you would not have me
Publish it?'

'O, as to that—I don't know—' answered, with the ⌐utmost
simplicity, Mrs Blake! '*You* are the best Judge of that. But I *do*
wish you could see it, Mrs Burney—'

'No, faith,' added he, 'I think that if I *was* to collect my
other Brats, I should not, I believe, put this among them.'

'If we may judge,' said Mama, 'of the Family *unseen*, by
those in the World, we must certainly wish for the pleasure of
knowing them all.—'[17]

Having now set the Conversation upon this favourite topic
again, he resumed his posture & his silence, which he did not
again break, till he had again the trouble of renewing himself
the Theme to which his Ear delighted to listen.

⌈He⌉ sat attentive to his own Applause.—[18]

My Father,—who thank Heaven, is an author of a different
stamp, pursues his Work at all the leisure moments he can
snatch from Business or from sleep. ⌈But he afforded us one
Evening last Week, to accompany us to Vauxhall.[19] Mr. &
Mrs. Young, Mama, Bessy, & Charlotte made the rest of the
Party.

The Gardens were very much Crowded & we Could only

---

[16] He does this to frighten the other workmen back to their jobs.

[17] Keate did publish the 'Burlesque Ode', in his *Poetical Works*, ii. 174–85. It is
republished (in abridged form) in *The New Oxford Book of Eighteenth Century Verse*, ed.
R. Lonsdale (Oxford, 1984), pp. 574–7.

[18] Cf. Pope's *Epistle to Dr Arbuthnot*, l. 210.

[19] The evening entertainments in the Spring Gardens, Vauxhall, began this year
on 16 May (*Daily Adv.*, 16 May).

procure a Box to sup in within a Dark kind of recess—however my Father was in excellent [|] spirits, & we were all very Gay.

Among the Faces that I knew, were those of Captain Debbieg & his son Clement.[20] I was glad to see them again, though they did not, I believe, know us. Indeed, the height & the uniform of Captain Debbieg, may well account for *his* being remembered by those *he* has forgot. Even the *sight* of an old acquaintance, I mean such as we have had pleasure in sharing, causes an agreeable sensation in the mind—I experienced this, though not unmixed with regret, when last Week, in passing through Broad Street, I saw at a Dining Room Window my old friend Mrs, Pringle. I passed ⟨quick⟩ly by—I cannot tell whether she saw or recollected me—I have no reason to wish that she did—but I was really quite glad to see *her* & in apparent Health. [|]

I also saw Dr. Smith[21] at Vauxhall—and Mr. Barthelemon, who played a solo, which I was so unfortunate as to miss hearing. I had likewise the Honour of a Bow from Lord Berriedale—& a kiss of the Hand from Sir John Turner,[22] who met & joined us for some Time. His Daughter Fanny is returned to Norfolk. And these are all the Adventures I met with in this *Elyzium*.

Mr. & Mrs. Young have, since, left Town.[⌐]

Sunday Night——
June 26th

Mama—with Bessy & Dick, are gone for a few Days to Bradmore, on a Visit to Mrs Young.

A message came this Evening, While my Father & I were

[20] For the Debbiegs and Mrs Pringle (below), see *EJL* i and below, pp. 102–4, 150, 153.

[21] Probably James Carmichael Smyth, MD, the Stranges' family physician (see *EJL* i. 198).

[22] Sir John Turner (1712–80), 3rd Bt., of Warham, Norfolk. Sir John was MP for King's Lynn from 1739 to 1774. He was a cousin of CB's friend Charles Turner, and had procured for CB the post of organist at Lynn in 1751. Sir John evidently had a difficult personality; MAR later this year expressed her 'dread' of him (MAR to FB, 24 Aug. 1774, Berg). The daughter mentioned here was Frances Turner, who in 1775 married Sir Martin Browne Folkes, 1st Bt. See *EJL* i. 87; Namier.

Tête à Tête in the study, from Mr Coney[23] of Lynn, with Compliments, & that he was coming to pay a Visit here, with an intimate friend of my Father's. Not conjecturing who this might be, & knowing that Mr Coney did not merit the sacrifice of an Evening, Word was sent that my Father was in the Country; ⌐however⌐ they had left Home before the ˡ messenger returned—& were therefore told the same Tale at this Door—however, they came in to see me—Mr Coney first—& then Mr Bewley, my Father's very learned & philosophical friend,—who is come to Town only for this one Evening! I protest I was quite Confounded at the sight of him;—I well knew that my Father would as earnestly desire to see Mr Bewley, as he had *Not* to see Mr Coney;—I was upon the point of saying, *tout de bon*,—at sight of him—Mr Bewley, my Father *is* at Home—but the recollection of the 3^d of a second told me what a gross affront that would be to Mr Coney, whose name had already been sent, & without success. I therefore restrained myself—& to my great concern, after about a quarter of an Hour spent in Chatting, I was obliged to suffer Mr Bewley to march off in the same ignorance that his Companion did.

My Father has since sent half the Town over in search of ⌐him⌐ but in vain—⌐for the result of the enquiry was that he left Town very ⟨early⟩—⌐ for I could not procure any satisfactory account of his place [of]^24 abode, which indeed he did not seem to know himself. He was so extremely *distrait* during the visit, that I believe he was uncertain whether he was in Queen Square in reality or in a Vision.[25]

Mr Coney, who piques himself upon having the address of ˡ a man of the World, & who is very conceited, gave himself the air of being *diverted* at Mr Bewley, for his Absence, ignorance of the Town, &c. He protested he had done nothing but laugh

[23] Carlos Cony (*c.*1726–1806), attorney, had recently become solicitor to Ld. Orford in Norfolk (*YW* xxiii. 560, xlii. 338 n. 1; MI, St Nicholas, Lynn). He was a subscriber to *Hist. Mus.*

[24] Inserted by FBA.

[25] Bewley alludes to his ill-fated visit in a letter to CB, 5 Sept. 1774 (Osborn): 'My laborious midnight expedition from Billingsgate to Queen's square so *recent!*—performed—after a journey of 4 score miles, with the express intention—waving all other business—of spending with you three out of four, or perhaps all the four, *waking* hours, that the niggard fates would allow me to spend in London!—'

since they arrived. Ah! thought I, my merry Gentleman—
however you may presume upon your external acquirements
—that quiet, unassuming man who makes your diversion,
may also from *you*, receive his *own!*[26]

[*The bottom of the page has been cut away. The unnamed woman in the next passage is probably the singer Cecilia Davies, who had returned from the Continent in 1773 and who was involved in a dispute with the managers of the Opera (see above, pp. 24–5).*]

⌐managers, I did not venture to be inquisitive. Our Conversation therefore turned upon Italy & Germany, & foreign
Persons & customs. For she has been in both those Countries,
& speaks in a very sensible and intelligent manner concerning
them.

The Castells[27] have spent an afternoon here since my last
visit to them—my Father was out—Mama cannot speak a
Word of French—I was obliged therefore to do all the
Honours—& to blunder on⌐ |

[*bottom of page and top of following page cut away*]

I have been interrupted by a Visit from Dr. Armstrong. He
must be very old[28]—& looks very ⌐ill⌐ but he still retains his
Wit & his gallantry. When I regretted my Father's being out,
& thanked him for coming in to *me*—'To *you*? repeated he,
(shaking my Hands) do you think there is Any body I would
sooner come in to see than *you*?'

Speaking afterwards of physicians, I said that it appeared to
me to be the most melancholy of all professions, though the
most useful to the World. He shook his Head, & said that
indeed he had never been happy till he was able to live
Independant of his Business, for that the pain & the anxiety
attendant upon it were inconceivable. |

[*The top of the page has been cut away. The child referred to below was perhaps EBB and Charles Rousseau Burney's infant son Richard Allen, born the previous October.*]

[26] The Burneys' aversion to Cony was shared by Horace Walpole, who called him a 'rascal' and dismissed him upon succeeding as E. of Orford in 1791 (*YW* xxv. 131, xlii. 356).

[27] Presumably acquaintances from CB's visit to France in 1764 or 1770. Not further identified.

[28] He was about 65.

⌜[?I had the] satisfaction of seeing that the Child thrives & is taken very good care of. The last Time that I went with only our Dick with me, I met Mr. Garrick Walking with another Gentleman. I was passing by him very quick—not knowing whether to *wish* to be seen, as he had not spoken to any of our family since Mr. Burney's quitting Drury Lane ⟨without a⟩ Word[29]—but his penetrating Eye had already caught mine— & he stopt me. & after asking me how I did, 'I thought, said he, that I knew that Face!—Well but—your Father—why he never Calls—& *I* have been exceeding busy.'

'And *he* has been exceeding busy, too, Sir' answered I—

'But I have been exceeding *ill*, too, cried he—I was laid up at Hampton—I am but just come to Town.'—[30]

'But what did you do meantime with your *looks*', said⌝ |

[*a leaf or leaves missing*]

16 [Queen Square,
late July 1774]

To Susanna Elizabeth Burney

AL fragment (PML), late July 1774
Single sheet 4to, 2 pp.
The beginning and end of the letter are missing. It seems to have been addressed to SEB at Barborne Lodge, where she was apparently visiting the Worcester Burneys with her sister EBB (see below, p. 46).

The fragment begins with FB's description of her father's first meeting, at the Admiralty, with the famous Omai (*c.*1753–80), a native of Raiatea near Tahiti, who was brought back to England on board the *Adventure* in July 1774. For a very full account of Omai see E. H. McCormick, *Omai: Pacific Envoy* (Auckland, 1977).

[29] Charles Rousseau Burney had been a Drury lane musician at least for the season 1766–7 (Highfill). The present passage suggests that he may have continued playing there as late as 1773, when he was either dismissed by Garrick or quit in a huff over some slight; SC alludes to his pride in an obliterated passage in a letter to CB, 17 Dec. 1776 (Berg; Osborn). CB and Garrick had made up by Mar. 1775 (see *EJL* i. 322; below, p. 80).

[30] Garrick came to town on 1 or 2 July after having been ill through the month of June (Stone, p. 673; Garrick, *Letters*, iii. 941, 944).

of that Country.—Capt. Furneaux[31] has brought him to Town with him—& he was at the admiralty where my Father had the satisfaction of seeing him. I find myself very curious to have the same sight. He was dressed according to the fashion of his Country, & is a very good looking man—my father says he has quite an *interesting* Countenance. He appeared to have uncommon spirits, & laughed very heartily many Times. He speaks a few English words—& Capt. Furneaux a few Otaheite words.—They had got M[r] Banks there, on purpose to speak with him—but M[r] Banks has almost forgot what he knew of that language. But you must know we are very proud to hear that our *Jem* speaks more Otaheite than any of the ship's *Crew.*—This Capt. F. told my father, who was Introduced to this stranger, as Jem's Father—he laughed, & shook Hands very cordially, & repeated with great pleasure the name thus *Bunny*! O! *Bunny*! immediately knowing who was meant, & the Capt. says that he is very fond of *Bunny*, who spent great part of his Time in studying the Language with him.[32]

Jem will be quite a *Lyon* on his return—Mr. Maxey Allen has invited him to Lynn, & M[rs] Henley[33] to Docking—&

---

[31] Tobias Furneaux (1735–81) was commander of the *Adventure*, which accompanied Capt. Cook's ship the *Resolution* on Cook's second voyage of discovery. JB had been transferred from the *Resolution* to the *Adventure* in Nov. 1772 (see *EJL* i. 220 n. 98). The two ships were separated in bad weather, and the *Adventure* returned alone to England, reaching Portsmouth on 14 July. Furneaux immediately went to London with Omai and called with him on Lord Sandwich at the Admiralty the morning of 15 July. CB had probably gone to the Admiralty to inquire after JB (McCormick, *Omai*, pp. 93–4).

[32] JB had befriended Omai when the latter came on board the *Adventure* the previous September. He describes him in his private journal of the voyage as 'a fellow of quick parts—very intelligent, has a good memory & takes great notice of every thing he sees. he is possessed of many good qualities—is Strong, active, healthy & as likely to weather the hardships of a long Voyage as any of us ...' (*With Captain James Cook in the Antarctic and Pacific: The Private Journal of James Burney ... 1772–1773*, ed. B. Hooper (Canberra, 1975), p. 70).

[33] Catherine née Hare (d. 1778), only child and heir of the Revd Hugh Charles Hare of Docking, Norfolk; widow of Henry Holt Henley (d. 1748), MP, whom she married in 1739. Mrs Henley was a friend of Dorothy ('Dolly') Young and step-mother of MAR's friend Mrs Styleman of Snettisham, Norfolk. In an undated letter to FB written earlier this year (Berg), MAR mentions a gift from Mrs Henley of '3 fine White hens and a Cock' from one of Mrs Henley's *fermes ornées* at Summerfield and Sunderland (see also MAR to FB, *c.*15 June 1774 (Berg); *EJL* i. 138; Sedgwick; Mrs Henley's will, PCC, dated 5 Aug., prob. 4 Dec. 1778).

every body in Town who knows our Family, inquire after, & desire to see him.

It seems Capt. Cooke is to stay another year—but this ship of Capt. Furneaux' has been so maul'd in a storm, & by sickness of the men, added to the loss of 10 Hands, that it was obliged to return to England, not being able to pursue the original design. I am heartily glad that they *are* returned—& I hope that a Country so savage as New Zealand will never more be visited by my Brother.[34]

I have seen my little Nephew[35] *2ce* this Week—for once he came *here*, at mama's request. He is vastly well—& Crawls upon the Carpet with amazing Dexterity—he Can lift himself *half* way up already—Indeed he thrives extremely. Pray tell my sister [EBB] she may *depend* upon my accounts.

Send me off the inclosed Frank, if possible, immediately. You was very kind in sending two so speedily.[36]

And now, my dear Susy—whether to bid you adieu— |

[The remainder of the letter is missing. The Journal for 1774 continues.]

But now let me come to a matter of more importance, & at the same Time more pleasure. My Brother is returned;—in Health, spirits & Credit. He has made what he calls a very fine Voyage;—but it must have been very dangerous: indeed he has had several *personal* Dangers[37]—& in these Voyages of

---

[34] See below, p. 43. Capt. Cook returned to England in July 1775 after making two further trips to the Antarctic and another winter cruise to the Pacific islands. The *Resolution* and the *Adventure* were parted during a gale off the coast of New Zealand on 30 Oct. 1773. After the separation Furneaux set sail again for the Antarctic but was forced by high seas and intense cold to change his course for Cape Horn. By the time the *Adventure* approached the Cape Furneaux was short of supplies, his men were falling ill, and his ship was no longer in condition for further Antarctic exploration. The *Adventure* arrived at the Cape of Good Hope to refit on 19 Mar. 1774, and a month later left for England (*With Captain James Cook* ..., p. 93 n. 1; J. C. Beaglehole, ed., *The Voyage of the* Resolution *and* Adventure *1772-1775* (Cambridge, 1961), p. 283).

[35] Richard Allen Burney (b. 22 Oct. 1773), EBB's infant son. He grew up to become a divine and Master of St Mary Magdalen Hospital, Winchester (1804). He died in 1836.

[36] The franks were presumably supplied by Sir John Turner, MP for Lynn. MAR mentions using 'a Frank of Sir John Turners' in her letter to FB, 6 June 1773 (Berg). SEB's two franked letters to FB are missing.

[37] In his private journal, s.v. 'Sunday, 12th Decr in Shag Cove' (in New Zealand), JB noted 'Kemp, Rowe, Omy & myself in the Great Cutter—Narrow Escape there—' but did not elaborate (*With Captain James Cook* ..., p. 90).

hazard & Enterprise so I imagine, must every Individual of the ship.

Captain Cooke was parted from in bad weather accidentally—in the passage from the Society Isles to New Zealand, in the second & so fatal Visit which they made to that Barbarous Country, where they lost 10 men in the most inhuman manner.

My Brother, unfortunately for himself, was the witness & Informer of that horrid massacre.

Mr Rowe,[38] the acting Lieutenant, a midshipman, & 8 men, were sent from the ship, in a Boat to shore, to get some Greens. The whole ship's Company had Lived so long upon good terms with the New Zealanders, that there was no suspicion of treachery or ill usage. They were ordered to return at ¹ 3 o'clock; but upon their failure, Capt. Furneaux sent a Launch, with Jem to Command it, in search of them. They Landed at 2 places without seeing any thing of them— they went among the people & bought Fish—& Jem says he imagined they were gone further up the Country, but never supposed how *very* long a way they were gone. At the 3^d place —it is almost too terrible to mention—they found—

[*At this point half a page has been left blank. FB evidently intended to supply the details of what JB and his party found, but never got up the courage. Upon landing in Grass Cove JB and his men came upon the partial remains of Rowe and his crew, who had been massacred and eaten by the Maoris (on 17 Dec. 1773). They brought on board their launch '2 Hands—one belonging to Mr Rowe, known by a hurt he had received in it the other to Thomas Hill known by a tattoo . . . & the head of the Capt^{ns} Servant [James Swilley]—these with more of the remains were tied in a Hammock & thrown overboard . . .' (JB's report to Capt. Furneaux, printed in* With Captain James Cook . . ., *pp. 95–9). The details of the massacre were ascertained by Capt. Cook when he returned to Queen Charlotte Sound in 1777. Despite JB's disclaimer of tension between the ship's company and the natives, it was the culmination of increasing hostility. The immediate spark was probably a quarrel over the Maoris' theft of some food. The Europeans fired two muskets and killed two natives, whereupon*

---

[38] John Rowe (*c*.1745–73), master's mate, was related to Capt. Furneaux by marriage. The midshipman was Thomas Woodhouse. The other 8 men were Francis Murphy (b. *c*.1740), quartermaster; William Facey (b. *c*.1747); Thomas Hill (b. *c*.1745); Edward Johns, boatswain; Michael Bell (b. *c*.1751); John Cavanagh (b. *c*.1742); William Milton (b. *c*.1753); and James Tobias Swilley, Furneaux's servant, 'a negroe' (*With Captain James Cook*, p. 98; Beaglehole, pp. 889–91).

the others attacked and killed all the white men. The bodies were immediately cooked and eaten. Capt. Cook, like JB, believed that the massacre was not premeditated and that the Europeans were probably partly to blame because of their impulsive behaviour (ibid., p. 92 n. 1).

Perhaps a month of journal is missing here. 'Miss Phipps' in the next passage was Henrietta Maria Phipps (d. 1782), daughter of Constantine John Phipps, 1st B. Mulgrave, who m. (1776) Charles Dillon Lee (1745–1813), 12th Visc. Dillon (1787). Her brothers included Constantine John Phipps (1744–92), later 2nd B. Mulgrave (Ireland) and B. Mulgrave (Great Britain), a noted naval captain, who in 1773 led an expedition to find the north-west passage and who on his return became a political connection of Lord Sandwich; and Henry Phipps, later E. of Mulgrave, whom FB had met in 1770 (see EJL i. 118).]

┌purpose of seeking Entertainments of a rational & Instructive Nature. This seems to be the case with Miss Phipps in a great degree. She appears to have a curiosity after every thing worthy exciting it & I was not the less pleased with her, for observing that she is excessively fond of my dear Father.┐

The present *Lyon* of the Times, according to the Author of the Placid man's[39] term,—is Omy, the Native of Otaheite;— & next to him, the present Object is M[r] Bruce,[40] a Gentleman who has been Abroad 12 years, & spent 4 of them in Abyssinia, & places in Africa, where no English man before has gained admission. His adventures are very marvellous. He is expected to publish them, and I hope he will. He is very intimate with the Stranges, & one Evening Called here with Miss Strange.

His Figure is almost Gigantic! He is the Tallest man I ever

[39] *The Placid Man: or Memoirs of Sir Charles Beville* (1770), a novel by Charles Jenner (1736–74). The use of 'lion' in the sense of 'a person of note or celebrity who is much sought after' did not originate with Jenner but is traced by *OED* (s.v. Lion 4b) to Lady Mary Wortley Montagu's *Town Eclogues* (1716).

[40] James Bruce (1730–94), African explorer, called 'Abyssinian' Bruce. He had gone to Africa in 1763 with the ultimate goal of finding the source of the Nile. He entered Abyssinia in 1769, and late the following year reached the source of the Blue Nile (not the main river, or White Nile). He left Abyssinia in Mar. 1772 and arrived back in London in June 1774. Irritated by the widespread disbelief of his 'traveller's tales' (which were substantially true), he did not publish his *Travels* until 1790.

Bruce was a relation of Mrs Strange (her mother was a Bruce), and Robert Strange had engraved plates of Bruce's drawings of Paestum in Italy for a work never published. See Dennistoun, i. 269, ii. 44–50, 52; J. M. Reid, *Traveller Extraordinary: The Life of James Bruce of Kinnaird* (1968), *passim*; below, *passim*.

saw,⁴¹ ⌐& exceeding⌐ well made, niether too fat or lean in proportion to his amazing height [*sic*]. I cannot say I was charmed with him, for he seems rather arrogant, & to have so large a share of good opinion of himself, as to have nothing left for the rest of the World, but Contempt. ¦ Yet His self approbation is not that of a *Fop*; on the contrary, he is a very manly Character, & looks as [*sic*] dauntless & intrepid, that I believe he could never in his life know what fear meant.

September 1ˢᵗ

My Father received last Week a Note from Lord Sandwich,⁴² to invite him to meet Lord Orford & the Otaheitan at Hinchinbrook, & to pass a week with him there;—& also to bring with him *his son the Lieutenant.*

⌐They are both gone. I hope this prognosticates something good for Jem, for I think the first Lord of the Admiralty would never *desire* to see a young sea Officer for whom he had no good intentions.

I am sorry this Nobleman bears so bad a Character, for he has, ever since he knew him, endeavoured most assiduously & kindly to seek oppertunities [*sic*] of serving my Father.⌐ ¦

17   Chessington [?17–29] September [1774]
To Susanna Elizabeth Burney

AJLS fragment (Berg), ?17–29 Sept. 1774
Single sheet 4to, 10 pp.
The journal letter has been inserted into the Journal for 1774, where it is paginated 467–[74] and foliated 28–32.

Chesington,
Saturday, Septʳ [?17]

Willingly, my dearest Susy, do I comply with your request of *Journalising*⁴³ to you during my stay at this place—⌐I will

---

⁴¹ He was six-foot four.
⁴² Lord Sandwich to CB, 21 Aug. 1774 (PML).
⁴³ Underlined by FB, perhaps as a new coinage; quoted in *OED* (s.v. Journalize 3) as the earliest use of the word in the sense of 'to write letters in journal form'.

even send you all I had written before I received your Letter[44]
—you have a *claim* upon me for any thing of this kind that is in
my power. Though niether your *heart*, or my *Inclination*, can
enable me to *pay* you the debt I contracted while you was at
Barborne.[45]

I have no *adventures* to communicate. However, I will write
all that I possibly can, & much more than I should, were I to
scrawl only for my self.

My Father is infinitely better. He has had a very good
night; & as his complaint is *local*, being confined to one
shoulder, & unattended by any Fever but what the *pain* at
Times brings on, we hope he will very soon be quite well.[46]

I was truly sorry that *you* could not be sent for. But there is
not Room in the House for a Cat more than it now holds. &
there has never, thank Heaven, been any [xxxxx *1 word*]⌐

Mᵉˡˡᵉ Courvoisyois[47] ⌐has made her appearance amongst us.
I have not yet seen much of her, but if it is fair to judge so
soon, she⌐ seems to be good natured & agreeable ᶦ enough, but
to have what may be called a merry Heart, & a shallow Head!
She laughs eternally. Niether her own illness, or other people's
can make her grave.

⌐I like her very well, & had not my Father been taken ill,
was growing very intimate with her. She⌐ speaks very good
English, for a French woman, for so she is as to Language,
though Born in Switzerland.

⌐I have not Time now to write to my sister [EBB]. But I will
by my mother,[48]—I would also to Jem if I thought it would be
agreeable to him to *answer* me, but I don't love Writing Letters
well enough to do it *unprofitably*. My best Love to him, however, & to all your Fire side, if, like us, you have begun that
first of indulgences, on Cold Evenings. Don't I talk like a good
old Nurse?⌐ ᶦ

[44] Missing.

[45] See above, p. 40.

[46] CB had suffered a severe attack of his chronic rheumatism.

[47] A Swiss lady who was paying 'a visit to Mlle. Rosat' (FBA's addition). She was
apparently a tutoress (see below). Not further traced.

[48] EAB returned to London on 20 Sept. (see below). If FB sent a letter by her to
EBB, it is missing.

[*The bottom of this page is blank, and the top of the next page has been cut away.*]

⌐Wednesday Sept^r [28]

My dear Susy will be very happy to hear that last Night my Father was so well as to insist upon my leaving his Room, & sleeping with Kitty Cooke again, for ever since my mother went to Town, which was yesterday a week [20 Sept.], I have only *reposed* upon a Truckle Bed, without undressing; & to ⟨say⟩ the Truth, I began to look so Wretchedly haggard, that all the good folks here grew uneasy for me.

They have all noticed my *Change of Countenance* (for all Countenances are capable of change) in different⌐ |

[*top of page cut away*]

One thing which diverts me a good deal, & which is equally at least a diversion to Mlle Rosat, is that not a soul in the House can pronounce Mlle Courvoisyois' Name, except Mr Crisp, & *he* never will, as he always calls her *petite mechante*. Mrs Hamilton calls her Miss *Creussy*, Mrs Simmons,⁴⁹ Miss— *what's your Name*; Mrs Moon⁵⁰ calls her Miss *Creusevoye*; & Kitty, to cut the matter short as possible, & to save trouble, only says Miss *Crewe*, which ⌐you will [xxxxx *1 word*] Judge is amazingly like the real name.⌐

Mrs Simmons, who, because she can smoak the | folly of her sister Moone, thinks *herself* a prodigy of Wisdom &, I dare say would think herself an immediate descendant from Minerva, if she had ever happened to hear of such a person; for her conceit raises her to the utmost height of her *conceptions* ⌐in her own mind;⌐—well, this wise lady holds poor Courvoisyois more cheap than any other person in the House;—& I really believe she took a dislike to her from finding she could not pronounce her Name. When she spoke of her, it was generally in this manner 'that Miss *what's her name*, there, Miss *Fid Fad*, as I call her,—there she has been laughing, till she has made

---

⁴⁹ Mrs Elizabeth Symons (d. 1794), wife of Capt. (later Adm.) John Symons (*c*.1733–99), under whom JB served on the *Cerberus* the following year. She was Kitty Cooke's cousin (see Manwaring, p. 57; *GM* lxix² (1799), 1093; FB's MS Journal for 1778, p. 673, Berg; MI, St Mary's Church, Bury St Edmunds; below, p. 48).

⁵⁰ Or 'Moone' (below and FBA's 'List' for 1774), Mrs Symons's sister. Not further traced.

my Head ache ready to split;—yet I gave her a good *set to* just now; I suppose she won't like me—who cares?—not I, I promise her! I think she's the greatest fool that ever *I see*.—She should not be a Tutoress to my Cat.'

I have almost, though very undesignedly, occasioned a *grand fracas* in the House, by a ridiculous ⌐joke¬ which I *sported* for the amusement of Miss Simmons[51] & Kitty. We had been laughing at some of poor Moone's queer phrases, & then I mentioned some of Kitty's own,—her Cousin joined in laughing violently, & as I proceeded from one absurd thing to another, I took Miss Simmons herself to task upon some speeches she had made; & in conclusion, I told them that I intended to write *a Treatise upon politeness* for their Edification. All this was taken as it was said, *in* ⌐*Joke*,¬ & we had much laughing in consequence of my scheme, which I accompanied by a thousand flighty speaches.

After this, upon all indecorums, real or fanciful, I referred to my Book for Instruction—& it became a sort ˡ of standard joke among us, to which we made every thing that passed applicable, & Miss Simmons, who enjoyed hearing me *run on*, as she called it, introduced the subject perpetually. Indeed the chief amusement I have made myself when with the two Cousins, has been in indulging ⌐myself¬ in that kind of Rhodomantide Discourse, that it will be easy to you to recollect some Instances of, ⌐my dear Susy, with all their *ludicrousness*.¬

All this did very well among ourselves;—but the Day after the Simmons left us, while we were at Dinner, Kitty blundered out 'Good people I tell you what;—*she's* going to write something about politeness, *& that*, & it's to be for all of you, here at *chiss* [Chessington].

'I'm sure, cried Mlle Courvoisyois, we shall be very much *obligè* to the lady.'

'I'll subscribe to the Book with all my Heart, cried Mlle Rosat. I beg leave to bespeak the first Copy. I am sure it will be a very useful Work.'

---

[51] Presumably Mrs Symons's daughter. A Miss 'Simmons' is listed as CB's student in his pocket memoranda book for 1768 (Berg). She is last mentioned by FB in 1777 and has not been further traced.

'She's to tell you all what you're to do, resumed Kitty, & how you're to do this—& all that.'

'Exceedingly well defined, Kate.' said Mr Crisp, 'but pray, Fannikin, what shall you *particularly* treat of?'

'O Sir,' cried I, all parts of life! it will be a very comprehensive work.—& I hope you'll all have a *Book*.

'Pray what will it cost?' demanded Mrs Moone.

'A Guinea a Volume,' answered I, '& I hope to comprize it in 9 Volumes.'

'O lord!' exclaimed she, 'I shan't give *no such money* for it.'

'*I* will have 2 Copies,' said Mlle Rosat, 'let it Cost what it will. I am sure it will be exceeding well Executed.'

'I don't doubt *in least*,' cried Mlle Courvoisyois, 'of politeness of Miss Burney—but I should like to see the Book, to see if I should *sought* the same.'

'Will it be like Swift's Polite Conversation?'[52] said Mr Crisp.

'I intend to Dedicate it to Miss Notable,' answered I. It will contain all *the newest fashioned* regulations. In the first place, you are never again to Cough.'[53]

'Not to *Cough*?' exclaimed every one at once, 'but how are you to help it?'

'As to *that*, answered I, 'I am not very clear about it myself, as I own I am guilty sometimes of doing it. But it [is][54] as much a mark of ill breeding as it is to *Laugh*, which is a thing that Lord Chesterfield has stigmatized.'

'Lord, well, for my part, said Mrs Moone, 'I think there's no fun without it.'

'Not for to *Laugh*!' exclaimed Courvoisyois, with Hands uplifted—'well, I declare I *did* not *sought* of such a *sing*!'

'And pray,' said Mr Crisp, making a fine affected Face, 'may you *simper*?'

'You may *smile*, Sir,' answered I. 'But to *laugh* is quite abominable. Though not quite so bad as *sneezing*, or *blowing the Nose*.'

---

[52] *A Complete Collection of Genteel and Ingenious Conversation, according to the Most Polite Mode and Method now used at Court, and in the Best Companies of England. In Three Dialogues* (1738). Miss Notable is one of the ladies in the dialogues.

[53] Cf. FB's satirical 'Directions for Coughing, Sneezing, or moving, before the King and Queen', in her letter to EBB 17 Dec. 1785 (printed *DL* ii. 352–3).

[54] Inserted by FBA.

'Why, if you don't blow it,' cried Kitty, 'what *are* you to do with it? ⌜Don't you think it nastier to let it *run* out perhaps?'⌝

I pretended to be too much shocked to answer her.

'But pray, is it permitted,' said Mr Crisp, very drily, 'to *Breathe?*'

'*That* is not yet, I believe, quite exploded.' answered I, 'but I shall be more exact about it in my Book, of which I shall send *you six* Copies. I shall only tell you in general, that whatever is Natural, plain or easy, *is* entirely banished from polite Circles.'

'And all is sentiment & *Delicacy*, hay Fannikin?' |

'No, Sir, not so,' replied I, with due gravity, '*sentiments* & *sensations* were the *last* fashion; they are now done with—they were *laughed* out of use, just before laughing was abolished.[55] The *present Ton* is *refinement*;—nothing *is to be*, that *has been*; all things are to be *new polished*, & *highly finished*. I shall explain this fully in my Book.'

'Well, for my part,' cried Mrs Moone, who ⌜I believe⌝ took every word I said seriously, 'I don't desire to read *no* such *tiddling* Books. I'm very well as I am.'

It's well you think so. thought I.

'Pray ma'am,' said Mlle Rosat, 'is it within the Rules of politeness to *pick the Teeth?*'

'Provided you have a little *Glass* to look in before you.' answered I, & rose to go up stairs to my Father.—

'& pray, Ma'am,' cried she again, 'is it polite, when a person talks, if you don't understand them, to look at another as if you said 'what Nonsense she says!'

'I should imagine not.' answered I, moving ⌜to the Door,⌝ as I found these Questions were *pointed*.

'Pray is it polite, Ma'am,' cried Mlle Rosat again, to make *signs* & to *whisper?*'

'I suppose not.' cried I, opening the Door.

'And *pray*,' cried Kitty colouring, 'is it *pelite* to be *touchy*? & *has* people any business to suspect, *&* to be suspicious?'

---

[55] FB was no doubt thinking of Goldsmith's campaign against sentimental comedy in *She Stoops to Conquer* (1773), heralded by his 'Essay on the Theatre; or, a Comparison between Laughing and Sentimental Comedy' (first published in the *Westminster Magazine*, Jan. 1773). Goldsmith had just died the previous Apr. See *EJL* i. 254.

'O,' cried I, these are things that don't come into my Cognisance—' & away I ran.

My Father, however, sent me down again to ask | Mr Crisp up stairs to play at Back Gammon. I found them all silent. Mr Crisp went up immediately, & presently every body went out but Kitty, Courvoisyois, & me.

I told Kitty, who I saw was swelling with anger, that I began to be sorry she had mentioned the Book—'O,—it does not signify,'—cried she, bursting into a violent fit of Tears—'I don't mind—if people will be cross—it's nothing to *me*—I'm sure I'm as obliging as I can—& if people don't like me, they must let it alone.'—

We tried to pacify her. Courvoisyois gave her a Glass of wine, & insisted on her Drinking it—'I did not *sought*,' said she, 'that Miss Rosat did mean you—I am sure she always says you are very good—'

'You're very obliging, Miss *Crewe*,' cried Kitty, sobbing, 'but I can *see*, as well as other people—& I know what Miss *Rossiter* meant—(N.B. She calls her *Rossiter*, no one knows why, not even herself) 'because the thing was, that one Day my Cousin & I were together, & so *Rossiter* came in—& I'm sure I did not more than I do at this moment—my Cousin can witness for me—but she went out of the Room in a huff, Nobody knows for what,—& then afterwards, she goes & tells my aunt ⌐Hamilton⌐ that when she came into the Room, I said *Humph*!—now I *purtest* I never said *no* such a thing ⌐as *Humph*,⌐—& so my Cousin would say, if she was here—for I should scorn it—& though I a'n't so *pelite* as Miss *Rossiter*, I'm sure I always try to be as obliging as I can, & if ever she wants any thing, at any Time, I'm always ready to | go for her.'

'I'm sure I always *hear* her say so, Miss Cooke,' cried Courvoisyois, 'I *sink* you are certainly *of* a mistake.'

I was very glad *she* spoke, for *I* could not, ⌐for her⌐ account of the cause of the disagreement was told so very ridiculously, that it required a painful effort to forbear laughing ⌐violently⌐ —it was all I could do ⌐to be decent:⌐ however, after some Time, we consoled her, & made her dry up her Tears, which she did, all the while protesting *that she 'would not say such a thing as Humph for the World,'*—& that 'Nobody was *further from it.*'

They are now upon very good terms again. Poor Kitty has

as honest & worthy a Heart as any human Being, & cannot bear to be thought ill of. Yet I can never cease to be astonished that she can have Lived so many years under the same Roof with such a man as Mr Crisp, & yet be so *very* unformed, ⌐so really vulgar.¬

I often wish it was possible to set down, as they occur, the strange speeches which she makes, as I am sure they would highly divert you.

Thursday, Goose Day [Michaelmas Day, 29 Sept.]

⌐Your Letter,[56] which arrived here last Night very late, has extremely raised spirits [xxxxx *1½ lines*] but I have no Time to say more at present. I will write for the post to morrow. God bless you, my Susy, & believe me, with the greatest Truth & Constancy *Yours*, F. Burney¬ |

[*The Journal for 1774 resumes. The top and bottom of the page have been cut away.*]

St. Martin's Street
Leicester Fields
Octr 18th

My Father, very much recovered, & myself, left Chesington 10 Days Ago. ⌐Mr. Crisp & Mr. Featherstone rode with us to Kingston. We left the whole Party well, & endeavouring to the last minute to prolong our stay. But my Father had given every moment that he could possibly afford, to the persuasions of Mr. Crisp.¬

We came immediately to this House, which We propose calling *Newton House*, or *The Observatory* or some thing that sounds *grand*. ⌐By the way,¬ Sir Isaac's identical observatory is still subsisting, & we shew it to all our Visitors, as our principal Lyon.

I am very much pleased with ⌐the House & still more with this part of the Town.[57]

---

[56] Missing, as is FB's promised reply. It may have contained news of EBB's improved health in her pregnancy (see below, p. 54).

[57] See above, p. 32 n. 4, and the illustration. The Burneys moved from their house in Queen Square because of difficulties respecting its title (*Mem.* i. 288). CB and his wife remained in St Martin's St. until 1789, when they moved permanently to Chelsea

2. The Orange Street Chapel, St Martin's Street, formerly the Burney family residence. From an engraving executed by Charles John Smith and published by William Pickering, Chancery Lane, London, in 1837. Newton's observatory shows on the top of the building.

We found my mother, Susy, Charlotte & Dick all well.
James is on a visit in Norfolk, at Mr. Rishton's, & is to visit
Mr. Coke[58] at Holkham before his return. [xxxxx *1 line*]⌐ ⌐

[*top and bottom of page cut away*]

⌐I had the most sanguine hopes for my Father's Health
when we left Chesington; but we had not been 2 Days in Town
before he had a Relapse, attended with more Fever & Illness
than ever!—He had, however, immediate advice, & I thank
God, he is recovering,—nevertheless I am at this moment
Writing in his Chamber, though just 2 o'clock, as I have sit up
all night with him.

Upon these occasions of Nocturnal Nursing, when I opine
that my *Patients* sleep, & when I have reason to hope they are
in a very fair way, I am obliged to do any thing in the World
by way of occupation, to keep off drowsiness on one Hand, &
the gloom of sick reflections on the other.

My dear Hetty, too, is not well, though a short Time, I
hope, will make her so, as she Daily expects to increase her
Little Family.[59] Upon this account, Susy & I sleep at her
House[60] alternately every other night, for though we cannot
boast of being very *useful*, her affection & our Anxiety, make
our being with her a mutual comfort.⌐ ⌐

[*at least 4 leaves missing*]

[xxxxx *8 lines*]

The first Opera was performed last Tuesday.[61] The
morning before, Mrs Brooke, ⌐who lives in Market Lane,⌐

College. The observatory was dismantled about 1850, and the rest of the house was
pulled down in 1913. The site is now (1990) covered by the Westminster Reference
Library. The panelled pine walls, carved mantel, and other woodwork of the fore-
parlour were acquired by Mrs Grace K. Babson and are incorporated in the Babson
Institute Library, Wellesley, Massachusetts. See G. K. Babson, *A Descriptive Catalogue
of the Grace K. Babson Collection* ... (New York, 1950), illustration facing p. 32 and
passim.

[58] Thomas William Coke (1754–1842), cr. E. of Leicester (1837). He later became
famous for the agricultural reforms he introduced on his estate at Holkham. He was a
friend of Martin Rishton. See A. M. W. Stirling, *Coke of Norfolk and his Friends* (2nd
edn., 1912).

[59] She gave birth to a second son, Charles Crisp Burney, on 6 Nov. Charles Crisp
died in 1791 ('Worcester Mem.').

[60] In Charles St.

[61] The opera season opened on Tues., 8 Nov., with a performance of *Armida*, a new
pasticcio with music by Sacchini and others, the libretto by Giovanni Gualberto

Called here, & very civilly invited my mother, Susy & me to ⌜go with her⌝ to the Opera the next Day. ⌜The managers of public places are the only people to whom I care to be obliged, as all *pecuniary* obligations are odious & insupportable.⌝ We were very desirous to hear the new singer, Rauzzini, of whom my Father has said so much in his German Tour,[62] & we agreed to wait upon Mrs Brooke about seven.

Accordingly we went. Her House in Market Lane, by means of divers turnings & windings, has a passage to the Opera House. We intended to have sat in her Box, & have seen only her, but when we went, we found she was up stairs with Mrs Yates,[63] ⌜& when she came down,⌝ she immediately asked us to go up stairs with her. This we declined, but she would not be refused, & we were obliged to follow her.

⌜It is very disagreeable that the Yates are half managers with the Brookes, nor can I understand how a woman of Character & reputation, such as Mrs. Brooke, can have reconcil'd herself to becoming intimate with one whose fame will bear no scrutiny.⌝[64]

We were led up a noble stair case, that brought us to a most magnificent Apartment, which is the same that belonged to the famous Heideger,[65] & since his Time, has always been the property of the Head manager of the Opera. Here we saw M^rs

Bottarelli. It was performed 13 times (*LS 4* iii. 1847 and *passim*; F. C. Petty, *Italian Opera in London 1760–1800* (Ann Arbor, 1980), pp. 140–2).

[62] 'Signor Rauzzini, a young Roman performer, of singular merit ... he is not only a charming singer, a pleasing figure, and a good actor; but a more excellent contrapuntist, and performer on the harpsichord, than a singer is usually allowed to be ...' (*The Present State of Music in Germany, the Netherlands, and United Provinces* (1773), i. 126; see also i. 148–9). CB first heard Rauzzini at Munich. Rauzzini contributed several of his own songs to *Armida* (Petty, *Italian Opera*, p. 143 n. 6).

[63] Mary Ann Graham (1728–87), who m. (*c.*1756) Richard Yates (*c.*1706–96), actor. She and her husband had become joint managers of the Opera with the Brookes in 1773.

[64] FB presumably alludes to reports of Mrs Yates's early life. John Taylor recorded, in his *Records of My Life*, that she had once lived 'together about two years' with his friend, a Mr Donaldson (cited in L. McMullen, *An Odd Attempt in a Woman: The Literary Life of Frances Brooke* (Vancouver, 1983), p. 156); gossip also linked her with the E. of Huntingdon (see *Theatrical Biography; or, Memoirs of the Principal Performers of the Three Theatres Royal* (1772), ii. 5). Despite the occasional innuendo, she seems to have given up gallantry in her later years, and she came to be Mrs Brooke's closest friend (McMullen, p. 154).

[65] John James (Johann Jakob) Heidegger (1666–1749), Swiss impresario active in London. He was manager of the Opera from 1713 until at least 1745 (*New Grove*; Highfill).

Yates, seated like a stage Queen surrounded with gay Courtiers, & dressed with the utmost elegance & brilliancy. What most provoked me was that ⌐a Brother[66] of the Miss Garricks was among the Gentlemen in the Room, it will therefore, in all probability, *travel* to that family, that we visited Mrs. Yates for⌐ as we entered the Room, our Names were announced in an *audible* Voice. All I can comfort myself with, is, that it was at the *Opera House* we met, & that of *late years* Mrs Yates has had no harm said of her ⌐but it was mortifying [xxxxx *2–3 words*] that *her* acquaintance [xxxxx *½ line*] should be inseparably annexed to that of Mrs. Brooke, which we ⟨would much rather choose⟩ to cultivate.⌐

Mrs. Yates to a very fine Figure, joins a very handsome Face, though not now in her *premiere Jeunnesse* [*sic*]; but the expression of her Face is infinitely haughty & hard.[67]

With an *over done* civility, as soon as our Names were spoken, she rose from her seat hastily, & rather *rushed* towards us, than meerly advanced to meet us. But I doubt not it was meant as the very *pink of politeness*.

As to poor *M^r* Yates, he presumed not to take the liberty, in his own House, to act any other part than that of Waiter, in which capacity he arranged the Chairs.

We were not absolutely seated, when the Door was opened by an Officer. Mrs Yates again started from her seat, & flew to receive him, Crying, 'General Cholmondeley[68] I am happy to see you!' Then turning to her *Jerry*,[69] 'Mr Yates, pray get the General a Chair.' Mr Yates obeyed, & then we rose, to go to the Opera:—We were to sit in a Box by [ourselves.][70]

---

[66] This would have been Carrington (1751–87), David (?1754–95), or Nathan (1755–88) Garrick, nephews of David Garrick (Stone, p. 654).

[67] Mrs Yates was very much the prima donna and quarrelled with Garrick, among others. The antiquary Richard Gough wrote in 1772 that 'Mrs Yates is beloved by none of her associates' (letter to Michael Tyson, 30 Jan. 1772, printed in Nichols, *Lit. Anec.* viii. 579).

[68] Hon. James Cholmondeley (1708–75), army officer; Gen., 1770. Cholmondeley's brother George, 3rd E. of Cholmondeley, had been a patron of CB's father, James Macburney (Lonsdale, p. 4). His niece Mary (Mrs Robert) Cholmondeley (née Woffington), called 'Polly', society hostess, was a long-time friend of Mrs Brooke (McMullen, *An Odd Attempt in a Woman*, p. 12).

[69] i.e., jerry-sneak, or henpecked husband, from a character of that name in Samuel Foote's *The Mayor of Garratt* (1763). See *OED* s.v. Jerry *sb.* 6.

[70] Inserted by FBA, probably from the next missing leaf.

[*A leaf or leaves are missing. The following passage seems to regard another excursion to Chessington (see below, p. 63).*]

⌜of the Party, but as I had so lately made an *Excursion* there, I found it not easy to obtain permission, & therefore stopt short with as good a Grace as I could assume. [xxxxx *1½ lines*]⌝

[*At this point FB gives an account of Omai's first visit to St Martin's Street. As it overlaps with a much fuller account in the following letter to SC, the journal narrative is here omitted except for additional or corroborating details cited in the footnotes to that letter.*

Some additional details are also cited from FBA's record of the visit in Mem. *In 1775 FB continued to write parallel accounts of memorable evenings in her journal and in her letters to SC. Fifty years later, in preparing* Mem.*, she would patch together composite letters from her journals and her letters to SC, with additional material from memory (or, in some cases, fancy). The editor's practice here is to give in full the longer account or, when the accounts are roughly the same length, the earlier one. Purely verbal or stylistic differences tend to be insignificant and are ignored.*]

18   St Martin's Street,
                       1 December [1774]

To Samuel Crisp

ALS (Barrett), 1 Dec. 1774
2 double sheets 4to, 8 pp., *pmk* 1 DE wafer
Addressed: Saml Crisp Esqr, | at Mrs Hamilton's, | Chesington near | Kingston | Surrey.
Annotated (by FBA): *Omai*: I N° 6 1774 ✳

St. Martin's Street
Thu[r]sday Night.
1st Dec^r

My dear Daddy,

What you have thought of me & of my promises, I know not—but Evil Communication!—Ever since I found myself *defrauded* of my own proper Goods & *Chattels*, by a certain Gentleman whom I had held in the highest veneration for Honesty;—I have insensibly found myself reconciled to a certain *easiness of Promise*, & a *cavalier carelessness* of *performance*, which formerly I was Goth enough to be greatly averse to.

The Truth is—for at last I find I have still some *gothiness*[71] left,—that while you thus inflexibly continue to hoard my *old* papers, it is with some *effort* that I send you *new* ones.[72]

Hang her papers! you Cry—if there is this fuss about them, I wish they were all at old Nick!—prithee let her have them—

Well—if I get them at any rate, I don't care. So you may abuse as much as you please, if you will but convey them to me. To *you* they *can* only furnish entertainment, if any, from the first perusal;—but to *me*, who know all the people & things mentioned, they may possibly give some pleasure, by rubbing up my memory, when I am a very Tabby, before when I shall not think of looking into them. But the *return was* the *Condition*, so give me my *Bond*.[73]

I told you that as to Writing, a Lyon stood in the way—Now you will not easily conjecture that a Lyon could wear so gentle a face, & kind an aspect, as the one who has stood between my pen & me—it is, moreover, of the female kind, & *hight* Eliz. Simmon[s.] For I had made a resolution that I would *certainly* go to visit her before my next Letter—& indeed I could not have prevailed with ⌐ myself now to have broke the resolution, if I had not this morning seen her, & fully convinced her that it has been my *misfortune* not my fault, that I have not hitherto waited upon her. I will not trouble you, therefore, with a long story; I will only tell you that I am now recovering from a very severe Indisposition,[74] which began by a violent cold; & that I am still a forlorn body, & *denied admitance* into the [xxxxx *1 word*] Air.

And now, my dearest sir, to make you some amends for all the scolding & impertinence with which I have begun this Letter, I will tell you that I have seen Omai. And if I am, as I intend to be, very minute in my account, will you shake Hands & be friends?

Yes, you little Devil you!—so *to business*, & no more words. Very well, I obey. You must know, then, in the first place,

---

[71] *OED* does not give this facetious nonce word.

[72] FB is referring to SC's retention of her Teignmouth Journal and of MAR's Geneva Journal (see *EJL* i. 320). SC had written to her in July, 'as to Fanny's papers, unless I have her positive, *angry* Commands; my answer is; *I don't care to part with them*—they are a Fund of Entertainment to me oftner than you think' (SC to FB, 18 July 1774, Barrett).

[73] See below, p. 64.

[74] Of '⌐about a fortnight⌐' (Journal for 1774, fo. 36).

that glad as I was to see this great personage, I extremely regretted not having *you* of the party, as you had half promised you would be,—& as I am sure you would have been extremely well pleased, & that the Journey would have more than answered to you: but the notice was so extremely short it was impossible. Now to facts.

⌜Susy &⌝ my Brother went last Monday to the play of Isabella at Drury Lane,[75] ⌜they⌝ sat in one of the Upper Boxes, from whence ⌜they⌝ spied Omai & Mr Banks—Upon which, ⌜as Susy was next neighbour to some very civil & genteel kind of women, she gave Jem leave to quit her while he went⌝ to speak to his friend. Omai received him with a hearty shake of the Hand, & made room for him by his side. Jem asked Mr Banks when he could see him to Dinner? Mr B. ⎮ said that he believed he was engaged every Day till the holy days, which he was to spend at Hinchinbrooke. ⌜Jem then returned to Susy.⌝ However, on Tuesday night, very late, there came a note which I will write down.[76] It was directed to my Brother.—Omai presents his Comp^{ts} to Mr Burney. & if it is agreeable & convenient to him, he will do himself the Honour of Dining with Mr Burney to morrow. But if it is not so, Omai will wait upon Mr Burney some other Time that shall suit him better. Omai begs to have an answer, & that if he is to come, begs Mr Burney will fetch him.

Early on Wednesday morning, Jem called at Mr Banks, with my Father's Comp^{ts} to him & to Dr. Solander, & begging their company [also]. But they were Engaged at the Royal Society.

Mr Strange & Mr Hayes, at their own motion, came to Dinner to meet our Guest. We did not Dine till 4, but Omai came at 2, & Mr Banks & Dr. Solander brought him, in order to make a short visit to my Father. They were all just come from the House of Lords, where they had taken Omai to hear the King make his speech from the Throne.[77]

For my part, I had been confined Up stairs for 3 Days

---

[75] Garrick's *Isabella; or, The Fatal Marriage*, adapted from Southerne's play (1680), was first staged in 1758, and was performed again at Drury Lane on Friday, 25 and Monday, 28 Nov., with Mrs Yates in the title role (*LS 4* iii. 1851).

[76] The original is missing.

[77] The King opened the current session of Parliament on Wednesday, 30 Nov. (see *GM* xliv (1774), 591–2).

—however, I was much better, & obtained leave to come
down, though very much wrapt up, & *quite a figure*. But I did
not chuse to appear till Mr Banks & Dr. Solander were gone.
I found Omai seated on the Great Chair, & my Brother next
to him, & talking Otaheite as fast as possible. You cannot
suppose how fluently & easily Jem speaks it. Mama & Susy
were opposite. As soon as there was a *cessation* of talk, Jem
Introduced me, & told him I was another sister. He rose, &
made a very fine Bow. & then seated himself again. But when
Jem went on, & told him that I was not well, he again directly
rose, & muttering something of the *Fire*, in a very polite *manner*, without *speech* insisted upon my taking his seat,—& he
would not be refused. He then drew his chair next to mine, &
looking at me with an expression of pity, said 'very well to
morrow-morrow?'—I imagine he meant *I hope* you will be very
well in *two or 3 morrows*.—& when I shook my Head, he said
'*No? O very bad!*'—

When Mr Strange & Mr Hayes were Introduced to him, he
paid his Compliments with great politeness to them, which he
has found a method of doing without *words*.[78]

As he had been to Court, he was very fine.[79] He had on a
suit of Manchester velvet, Lined with white satten, a *Bag*, lace
Ruffles, & a very handsome sword which the King had given
to him. He is tall & very well made. Much Darker than I expected to see him, but had a pleasing Countenance.

He makes *remarkably* good Bows—not for *him*, but for *any
body*, however long under a Dancing Master's care. Indeed he
seems to shame Education, for his manners are so extremely
graceful, & he is so polite, attentive, & easy, that you would
have thought he came from some foreign Court. You will
think that I speak in a *high* style; but I assure you there was
but one opinion about him.

At Dinner I had the pleasure of sitting next to him, as my
Cold kept me near the Fire. The moment he was helped, he

[78] 'He seemed particularly pleased with Mr Hayes, whose white Hairs & chearful
Countenance could not fail of engaging the Native of a Country where Age is held in
the greatest veneration, which Jem says is the case at all the Islands of the South Seas
where he has been' (Journal, fo. 37).
[79] 'He had ... been admitted to a private audience of his Majesty, whom he had
much entertained' (*Mem.* i. 284). Omai had first been presented to the King and
Queen at Kew on 17 July (E. H. McCormick, *Omai: Pacific Envoy* (Auckland, 1977),
p. 95).

presented his plate to me, which, when I declined, he had not the *over shot* politeness to offer *all around*, as I have seen some people do, but took it quietly Again. He Eat heartily, & committed not the slightest blunder at Table, [|] niether did he do any thing *awkwardly* or *ungainly*. He found by the turn of the Conversation, & some wry faces, that a Joint of Beef was not roasted enough, & therefore when he was helped, he took great pains to assure mama that he liked it, & said two or three Times '*very dood*—very *dood*.' It is very odd, but true, that he can pronounce the *th*, as in *Thank you*, & the *W*, as in *well*, & yet cannot say *G*, which he uses a *d* for. But I now recollect, that in the beginning of a word, as *George*, he *can* pronounce it.[80]

He took a good deal of Notice of Dick, yet was not quite so well pleased with him as I had expected him to be.

During Dinner, he called for some Drink. The man, not understanding what he would have, brought the Porter. We saw that he was wrong. However, Omai was too well bred to send it back. He took it in his Hand, & the man then brought him the small Beer;—he laughed, & said 'Two!'—however, he sent off the *small* Beer, as the *worse* of the *two*. Another Time he called for *port wine*. & when the Bread was Handed, he took two Bits ⌈up⌉ & laughed & said '*one—two*.'—

He even observed *my abstinence*, which I think you would have laughed at, for he turned to me with some surprise, when Dinner was almost over, & said '*No wine?*'

Mʳ Hayes asked him, through Jem, how he liked the King & his speech. He had the politeness to try to answer in English, & *to* Mr. Hayes—& said '*very well, King George!*'

After Dinner, mama gave the King for a Toast. He made a Bow, & said '*Thank you, Madᵃᵐ,*' & then *tost off King George!*

He told Jem that he had an Engagement at 6 o'clock, to go with Dr. Solander to see no less than 12 Ladies.—Jem [|] translated this to us—he understands enough of English to find out when he is talked of, in general, & so he did now, & he laughed heartily, & began to Count, with his Fingers, in order to be understood—'1. 2. 3. 4. 5. 6. 7. 8. 9. 10.—*twelve*— *Woman!*' said he.

---

[80] Both *g*s in *George* are soft, of course, unlike the hard *g* in *good*. FB fails to think phonetically.

When Mr Banks & Dr. Solander went away, he said to them *good bye—good bye.*

He never looked at his Dress, though it was on for the first Time. Indeed he appears to be a perfectly rational & intelligent man, with an understanding far superiour to the common race of *us cultivated gentry*: he could not else have borne so well the way of Life into which he is thrown.

When the man brought him the *two* Beers, I forgot to mention that in returning them, one hit against the other, & occasioned a little sprinkling. He was *shocked* extremely— indeed I was afraid for his fine Cloaths, & would have pin'd up the wet Table Cloth, to prevent its hurting them—but he would not permit me; &, by his *manner* seemed to *intreat* me not to trouble myself!—however, he had thought enough to spread his Napkin ⌐out⌐over his knee.

Before 6, the Coach came. Our man ⌐came in, &⌐ said 'Mr Omai's servant.' He heard it at once, & answered *'very well.'* He kept his seat about 5 minutes after, & then rose & got his Hat & sword. My Father happening to be talking to Mr Strange, Omai stood still, niether chusing to interrupt him, nor to make his Compliments to any body else first. When he was disengaged, Omai went up to him, & made an exceeding fine Bow,—the same to mama—then seperately to every one in the company, & then went out with Jem to his Coach.

He must certainly possess an uncommon share of ¦ observation & attention. I assure you every body was delighted with him. I only wished I could have spoken his Language. Lord Sandwich has actually studied it so as to make himself understood in it. His *Hands* are very much *tattooed*, but his Face is not at all. He is *by no means* handsome, though I like his *Countenance.*

The Conversation of our House has turned ever since upon Mr *Stanhope* & *Omai*—the 1st with all the advantage of Lord Chesterfield's Instructions, brought up at a great school, Introduced at 15 to a court,[81] taught all possible accomplishments from an Infant, & having all the care, expence, labour & benefit of the best Education that any man can receive,—

---

[81] Chesterfield's natural son Philip Stanhope attended the Westminster School from 1743 to 1746. His first presentation to a court was at Dresden in 1748, while on the Grand Tour (see *The Letters of the Earl of Chesterfield to his Son*, ed. C. Strachey (1924), i. 228).

proved after it all a meer *pedantic Booby*:[82]—the 2[d] with no
Tutor but Nature, changes after he is grown up, his Dress, his
way of Life, his Diet, his Country & his friends;—& appears
in a *new world* like a man [who] had all his life studied *the
Graces*, & attended with [unre]mitting application & diligence
to form his manners, [to] render his appearance & behaviour
politely easy, & *thoroughly well bred*: I think this shews how much
more *Nature* can do without *art*, than *art* with all her refinement, unassisted by *Nature*.

If I have been too *prolix*, you must excuse me because it is
wholly owing to the great curiosity I have heard you express
for whatever concerns Omai. My Father desires his love to
you, & says that if you will but come to Town, as soon as
Omai returns from Hinchinbrooke, he will promise you that
you shall have a meeting with him. |

⌐As to our Chesington Jaunt, I fear Jem's letter[83] quite
frightened you. My sister [EBB] continues very weak, but
hopes to be able to go. Mr. Burney can only stay one night.
For *my* part, I have not yet mentioned my *thinking* of such a
scheme [xxxxx *3½ lines*]

My kind love to Kitty, ⌐her Gown ⟨came home⟩ to Day.
Pray will it do to send it when Jem goes to Chesington?¬ Adieu
my dear sir,

I beg you to believe me
your ever affectionate
& obliged
F. Burney

[The Journal for 1774 concludes:]

Not having opportunity of proceeding in my *ingenious*
Narration, it has laid by so long, that I have now forgot all I
intended to have added, & I cannot give myself the trouble of
Recollection, not being in a prosing humour—I shall therefore
take an abrupt & rather Cavalier leave of this adventure; & as
I am already much in arrears with some *New* ⌐ones,¬ I shall
reserve all my forces for those, by way of *amende honorable*—

[82] This judgement is excessive. Though Stanhope never achieved the polished
manner that Chesterfield wished, James Boswell, who met him at Dresden (where
Stanhope was the British envoy) in 1764, observed that 'he was, in truth, a sensible,
civil, well-behaved man' (*Life*, i. 266 n. 2; *Boswell on the Grand Tour: Germany and
Switzerland, 1764*, ed. F. A. Pottle (1953), pp. 128–34).
[83] Missing. EBB's weakness presumably related to her recent pregnancy.

[St Martin's Street,
2 February 1775]

To Samuel Crisp

ALS (Barrett), 2 February 1775
Double sheet 4to, 4 pp., *pmk* 2 FE wafer
Addressed: Mr Crisp, | at Mrs Hamilton's | Chesington near | Kingston
upon | Thames | Surrey
Annotated (by FBA): Declining to suffer these Journal Letters to be sent to
Mr. Crisp's sisters. ✠ N° 2 1775 Feb. 74 *or* 75 N° 28.

My dear Sir,

I have been so long & so much distressed how to Answer
your last Letter,[1] that I at length have taken up my Pen with
all my irresolution upon my Head, from the fear that if I
thought much longer, I should not be able to Answer it at all.

You will believe I was a little startled to find my Letter had
Travelled so far;—but when I came to the request for the
Journals, I was quite confounded!—your sister's[2] Letter is,
indeed, highly flattering, & I think myself extremely indebted
to her *Good Nature*; I would trust to her Candour & her
Honour, & frankly comply with her Desire—or rather let me
say *yours*, which are sacred with me—*if* I was at liberty—*if*
I had not—as I have—insuperable objections to the contrary.

I have felt, & do feel, so much unwillingness & reluctance
to refuse one whom I am happy to receive any request from,
that I have delayed Day after Day sending an Answer. I will
give you my reasons simply as they stand, but must entreat
you not to undertake to confute them, because I know that I

[1] SC to FB, 25 Jan. 1775 (Barrett).

[2] Sophia Crisp (*c.*1706–91), who m. (1724) Philip Gast (d. by 1748) of Rotterdam,
a Dutch merchant. A learned and amiable lady, she lived at Burford, Oxfordshire,
with her sister (for whom see below). Letters from SC to Mrs Gast, 1779–82, are
printed in W. H. Hutton, *Burford Papers* (1905), pp. 24–84. FB met her in 1776.

SC had shown Mrs Gast FB's letter to him of 1 Dec. 1774, describing the visit of
Omai. In his letter to FB, he copied part of one from his sister, in which she praises
FB's 'cleverity' and asks 'to see the [Teignmouth] Journal, she is so eager to get into
her own hands again'. SC also asks FB's permission to lend to Mrs Gast MAR's
Geneva Journal of 1771–2.

cannot withstand your arguments, even when I am inwardly convinced that an *equal* Disputant certainly *would*. |

Mrs Rishton, ever since her marriage, has regretted that her Journal was ever out of her own Hands, & she has a thousand, nay a million of Times, conjured me both by Letters & by word of mouth, to endeavour to get them all, & to *Burn every scrap*:[3] Now I will not pretend to say that I *have* Burnt them, but I have saved them from the flames with no other view than giving her the greater satisfaction by Burning them before her Face.

As to the concealment of who she is, &c, I have been looking over the papers, & I see it would be *utterly impossible*, there are so many allusions to her situation, to us all & to her *proper* self.

They are of a nature that [ought to be held sacred][4]—in short—perhaps I am scrupulous—but I must say, that I should think it a real Breach of Trust reposed in me, if without her leave, which would never be obtained, I were to make one more Confident than she has allowed of.

I am sensible that you could answer all this, & though I could urge many more strengthening reasons, yet I well know you could if you would over set them all: but still I am sure you could not reconcile to myself the risking her being known to her [xxxxx *1 word*] own risk when | she has, I know, the firmest reliance upon my discretion, & observance of the old Golden Rule.

I am very uneasy at the thought of disobliging you, & very sorry to withhold any Entertainment from your sisters,[5] who have given me the most flattering motives to love & reverence them: but indeed I cannot answer this affair to myself, as I am satisfied that no pretences would make me pardon it in another.

In regard to my own [Tingmouth][6] Nonsence, there is

---

[3] Most recently in her letter to FB, 1 Jan. 1775 (Berg).

[4] Substituted by FBA for an obliterated passage, not recovered.

[5] SC's other sister at Burford was Ann Crisp (c.1696–1776). She was an old friend of Mrs Delany, who, writing in 1751, alludes (not unkindly) to her middling understanding and notes that she 'has vowed to live and die a virgin' (*Delany Corr.*, iii. 52–3; see Hutton, pp. 10–12; *Oxford Journal*, 24 Sept. 1776; *DL* ii. 195–6).

[6] Inserted by FBA.

neither *subject* or any thing else to make it worth a stranger's Reading; however, if there should be any conveyance for it, I would without fuss tr[ust] it to them, though meerly as a proof how re[adil]y I would comply with any request they should honour me with, & that you should desire, *except* what concerns *other People*—though, in fact, no *Journal* can be Confined to the writer, but *must* contain anecdotes, &c of others.

Now pray don't be angry, but represent something as ⌐comical & as¬ excusable as you possibly can to your sisters—I should be very much concerned to have their *partial* opinion of me changed to a *prejudiced* one. ⌐

⌐My Father continues much the same as he has been for this month, that is to say, his General Health, spirits & appetite are pretty good, but his Rheumatic shoulder & Gouty Hand still torment & distract him. My mother is very well again.

I beg my love to dear Hetty, & respects to Mrs. Ham. I am ever, my dear Daddy, y^rs most faithfully F. Burney.¬

AJ (Early Diary, viii, paginated 489–[570], foliated 1–56, Berg), Journal for 1775.

Originally a cahier of large double sheets. Now 43 single sheets and 8 double sheets 4to, 118 pp. (including 8 by SC inserted by FB), with 3 paste-overs and a cover *dated* 1775 *and numbered* 8.

The beginning of the Journal is missing.

Feby 28th

Yesterday morning, my mother, Susan & self, accompanied by Mr Twining,[7] went ⌐to the opera House, in expectation of hearing a new Comic Opera[8] Performed, but the indisposition of Signora Sestini occasioned it being pos[t]poned. The morning being then broken into, we went to console ourselves⌐ to Sir Joshua Reynolds' to see his Pictures. Here we were very much delighted; the ease & elegance of this Painter, as Mr Twining observed, seem unrivalled among English Artists. ⌐Among other Portraits, we saw Signor Sacchini, which is taken for the Duke of Dorset;[9] it is finely done & makes a most charming Picture. Sir Joshua himself, speaking of it to my

---

[7] Thomas Twining (1734–1804), divine, linguist, classicist; curate of Fordham, Essex, 1764; rector of St Mary's, Colchester, 1788. One of the eminent scholars of his day, he initiated a learned and amusing correspondence with CB in 1773 and soon became his close friend. He was a signal help to CB in the preparation of his *Hist. Mus.* See esp. Lonsdale, p. 134 and *passim*; R. S. Walker, 'Thomas Twining's Letters' (unpub. typescript on deposit in Cambridge University Library).

[8] *La Marchese giardiniera*, music by Pasquale Anfossi (1727–97), opened at the Opera on 7 Mar. (*New Grove*; Highfill; *LS 4* iii. 1874). The production was marked by the London début of Signora Giovanna Sestini (*fl.* 1774–91), prima buffa, who had come from Lisbon. FB and the others were of course hoping to attend a pre-opening rehearsal of the opera. See below, p. 79.

[9] John Frederick Sackville (1745–99), 3rd D. of Dorset, 1769. Dorset was a patron of Sacchini, whose new opera *Motezuma* was dedicated to him (see below, p. 78). CB had been introduced to Dorset at Rome in 1770 (*Tours*, i. 201; *YW* xxiv. 90 n. 2). The Duke paid £36. 15*s.* for the picture. It was sold at Sotheby's on 17 Mar. 1982 to Colnaghi's for £17,600, and subsequently resold to an anonymous client. See the illustration (information courtesy of Ms Valerie Vaughan, Librarian, the National Portrait Gallery, Ms Lucy Hodson, Sotheby's, and Ms Jennifer A. Lunan, Colnaghi's; see also A. Graves and W. V. Cronin, *A History of the Works of Sir Joshua Reynolds* (1899–1901), iii. 857, iv. 1403).

Father, said that Sacchini was the high style of manly Beauty.⌐

But what most delighted me, was the beautiful Mrs Sheridan, who is taken seated at a Harp⌐sichord,⌐ a whole Figure, in Character of Saint Cecelia, a denomination she greatly merits. My Father is to supply Sir Joshua with some Greek music to place before her.[10]

⌐When we had made a long visit here, my mother, not being very well, went Home, & we then proceeded with Mr. Twining to Mr Merlin, the famous mechanic, to hear his new Invented Harpsichord,[11] ∣ the tone of which is the sweetest I ever heard. We found there a young man, Mr. Clementi,[12] who plays the second Harpsichord at the Opera, & he, very good naturedly, sat down & showed the Instrument off to great advantage. He has studied & understands it, & is a very good player. Indeed, Mr. Burney excepted, I do not recollect ever hearing a better. Mr. Burney is such a *Giant* in playing, that he makes Figures[13] of all other performers upon his Instrument.

We found very good Entertainment here for above an Hour, &⌐ then we went to Miss Reid, to see her paintings, which, in Crayons, seem really to nearly reach perfection; their not standing[14] appears to me the only inferiority they have to Oil Colours: while they are new, nothing can be so soft, so delicate, so blooming.

---

[10] On Wednesday, 1 Mar., Sir Joshua, who lived in Leicester Fields 'scarcely twenty yards' from CB's own street (*Mem.* i. 330), sent CB a note thanking him 'for the Musick' and inviting him to join Mrs Sheridan, 'who is going to sit for her Picture today', as his guest for dinner (Fitzwilliam Museum, Cambridge). His portrait of Mrs Sheridan as St Cecilia, seated at an organ (not harpsichord), was exhibited this year at the Royal Academy. Horace Walpole described it as 'most simple and beautiful'. It is now in the collection of Waddesdon Manor, Buckinghamshire. See E. Waterhouse, *The James A. De Rotschild Collection at Waddesdon Manor: Paintings* (1967), pp. 86–9.

[11] Presumably the 'compound harpsichord' patented by Merlin in 1774 (see *EJL* i. 267 n. 37; A. French, M. Wright, and F. Palmer, *John Joseph Merlin: The Ingenious Mechanick* (1985), pp. 97–9).

[12] Muzio Clementi (1752–1832), the well-known composer and virtuoso keyboard performer. He had been brought to England from his native Italy by Peter Beckford in 1766 and spent the next 7 years studying and practising the harpsichord at Beckford's Dorset estate. In 1773 he went to London and enjoyed immediate success in the King's Theatre orchestra. See Highfill; *New Grove*.

[13] i.e., objects of ridicule.

[14] i.e., keeping their colours.

3. Antonio Sacchini. From a portrait by Sir Joshua Reynolds, 1775.

We went afterwards into the Room where Miss Reid, & her lively Neice were sitting. As she is very Deaf, I believe she did not hear me speak Mr Twining's Name, & she was so intent upon what she was about, that I am sure she never saw him: she is a very clever woman, & in her Profession has certainly *very* great merit; but her turn of mind is naturally melancholy, she is Absent, full of Care, & has a Countenance the most haggard & wretched I ever saw, added to which, she Dresses in a style ¦ the most strange & Queer that can be conceived, &, which is worst of all, is always very Dirty.

The unhappiness of her mind, I have heard attributed to so great & extraordinary an unsteadiness, not only of Conduct, but of principle, that in regard to her Worldly affairs, she is Governed by all who will Direct her, & therefore acts with inconsistency, & the most uncomfortable want of method; & in her Religious opinions, she is guided & led alternately by Freethinkers & by Enthusiasts. Her mind is thus in a state of perpetual agitation, & uneasiness. If she was a Woman of weak intellects, I should not wonder at her being so unfixed & wavering; but that is by no means the Case, she has a very good Understanding, & when the *foul fiend* is not tormenting her, she is even droll & entertaining.[15]

We found her Trying on a Coat[16] she was altering, in a fit of Housewifery, herself, upon Nelly Beatson, who seemed to think the *favour* was all of *her* granting, in permitting her Aunt to meddle with her. It was curious to see the ill managed contrivance of poor Miss Reid, who was so ignorant how to make the alteration she found necessary, that she was peicing a blue & white Tissue with a large Patch of black silk! I believe there are few *men* in the World who would not figure more creditably as mantua makers.

She had on a large dirty wing Cap, made of muslin, ¦ & an half Handkerchief tyed over it, as a Hood; a German Dress made of old lutestring excessively faded & colorless, & a *shawl*, that *had* been a very fine spotted one, but which was more

---

[15] Mrs Ellis reports a tradition in the Strange family that Mrs Read's unhappiness was due in part to an old and unrequited love for Mrs Strange's brother Andrew Lumisden (*ED* i. 283 n. 1).

[16] Changed to 'petticoat' by FBA.

soiled than if she had been Embraced by a chimney sweeper, was flung over her shoulders.

She did not stop her Employment, or even lift up her Head, though she very civilly enquired after our Healths, was very glad to *see* us, &c for her inattention is the effect of Absence, not of wilful ill breeding. I asked Nelly to shew us some of *her* Drawings. 'There they are, yonder,—' said she, in her usual easy manner. 'Well but, won't you Come Yourself, & shew them to this Gentleman?' 'No, I can't,' said she gravely, 'pray how does Charlotte do?' 'You little Cross Patch, cried I, you *must* come with us—I won't have you so idle—'

'No, I can't ⌐indeed,¬ answered she very Composedly, but come another Time, & I will'.[17]

Her Aunt bid her stand a little way off, that she might see how her Coat set: she immediately marched to the Door. 'Nay now, Nelly,' cried Miss Reid; 'I can't see at all,' 'O Lord, what signifies?' returned she, 'I shan't try it any more—' & Jumped out of it, leaving it on the Ground.

As we were going, Miss Reid called me to her, & said that she wanted to speak to me, 'I have a favour to ask of you,' said she, 'which is that ˡ you will sit to me in an Attitude,—' I burst out in Laughter, & told her I was then in haste, but would Call soon & talk about it.

I cannot imagine what she means; however, if it is to finish any *Burlesque* Picture, I am much at her service.[18]

Mr Twining confessed that he was not *more*, though *differently* Entertained by Miss Reid's Paintings than by Miss Reid herself: for her knowledge of her Profession is not more remarkable than her Ignorance of the World. However, it is a great pity that a Girl of the Parts & understanding of Nelly Beatson should be so miserably Educated.

Mr Twining was excessively agreeable—He assumed no manner of superiority, nor yet, as is often the Case with People of Learning, as well as with ⌐men of Distinction,¬[19] affected a

---

[17] This year the precocious Miss Beatson exhibited 6 paintings at the Society of Artists, of 'A card party', 'A Fortune-teller', 'Blindman's Buff', etc. (A. Graves, *The Society of Artists of Great Britain 1760–1791* . . . (1907), p. 27).

[18] There is no evidence that FB ever sat for Miss Read.

[19] Changed by FBA to 'Persons of Rank'.

certain *put on* equality;—a Condescendsion which mortifies a thousand times more than ⌜Insolence⌝[20] itself.

Not being much in Town, the new *Vis-à-vis*[21] were not familiar to him, 'That is to me a most disagreeable looking Carriage,' said he,—'from want of Custom, perhaps; for it is true that a Chariot or Chaise will only hold *two* people, any more than a *vis-à-vis*, but the Thing is, that one only *thinks* of two people at sight of a Chariot; but there is something in a *Vis-à-vis* which looks as if it meant to *Exclude* a Third Person: it seems ⌜as if it were⌝ *spiteful*.' |

⌜He affects a droll kind of ignorance of the ways of the world & demands advice & admonition with great seriousness & a humourous, pretended simplicity. He had Engaged himself to Dine at his mother's[22] & appeared to be ⟨late⟩ but he would not ⟨hasten,⟩ therefore when we left Miss Reid, I begged him to speed away, & leave us to proceed at leisure; he would not listen to this, insisting upon seeing us Home, I therefore grew *peremtory*, knowing that he was in anxiety all the Time, & told him that he *must* go, that we *desired* & *insisted* upon it. 'But how queer you will think me, said he, if I should be so rude as to leave you by yourselves.'

'The Rudeness, said I, is all mine, for you find I desire no more of your Company; I am *trying* to get rid of you.—So pray go.'

'Well but now, said he, don't let me do wrong. Don't say when I am gone, lord! what an ill bred, black fellow that Mr. Twining is!'

We persisted in ⟨harass⟩ing him—at length he went. This morning he Called, & told me he found himself unfortunately in very good Time, 'which made me very uncomfortable,' explained he, 'for *if* I had made Dinner wait, or had found it half over, I would have forgiven myself for leaving you, but

---

[20] Changed to 'Arrogance' by FBA.

[21] 'New' to Twining. The vis-à-vis, a light carriage for 2 persons sitting face-to-face, had been introduced at least 25 years before. Cf. Sterne on the vis-à-vis in *A Sentimental Journey*, ed. I. Jack (1968), p. 13 (see *YW* xxiv. 260 n. 4; *EJL* i. 65).

[22] Twining's stepmother Mary née Little (1726–1804), who m. (before 1748) Daniel Twining (1713–62). She lived in Devereux Court, the Strand, where her son Richard Twining (1749–1824), Thomas Twining's half-brother, managed the prosperous family tea business (R. S. Walker, 'Thomas Twining's Letters', Preface, p. 6, Introduction, p. 11).

when I found myself in good Time I was quite provoked & shocked.'⌐ |

21 [St Martin's Street,
2 March 1775]

To Samuel Crisp

ALS (Barrett), 2 March 1775
2 double sheets 4to, 8 pp., *pmk* 2 MR wafer
Addressed: Saml Crisp Esqr | at Mrs Hamilton's | Chesington near | Kingston upon Thames | Surry.
Annotated (by FBA): Agujari March 75. N° 3 of this Year. ✳ 1775. N° 29.
This letter parallels a 6-page account of Agujari's visit in the Journal for 1775, pp. 488–93. The journal account is omitted except for extracts in the notes to this letter, and the final paragraph given afterwards. FBA embellishes the episode in *Mem.* ii. 21–6.

My dear Daddy

I hope, by your Letter[23] to my mother, that you are now restored, tolerably at least, to Health; & therefore I immediately take pen in Hand to send you a long Detail of affairs, taking it for Granted that you are now well enough to have renewed the ⌐old⌐ exquisite Taste which you have formerly Expressed for my marvellous, miscellanious Hodge Podge of Intelligence. Now Don't call me Jewess, & Jessica, & so forth, for not writing till you are in Capacity to answer; because I really would not have waited for that ⌐but⌐ only your short Letter gave me no encouragement; but much concern to find you so ill: & I don't know how it is, but I cannot persuade myself to write nonsense to a person who I believe to be all the Time in pain.

As to my stupid Tingmouth stuff—I am quite surprised that you should think it worth sending so far: however, I feel a thousand Times more repugnance to suffering your sisters to see such folly, since its return to me because I have Read it myself: *They* have not *your* long acquaintance & partiality to our *system*, which makes Apology for blunders & stupidity:

[23] Missing, as is his letter to FB mentioned below.

And if I *had not* been so dissatisfied myself, I could not have borne to have sent the Journal without a line or two from you, to tell them that it was at *your* Desire it went, not in consequence of any *vanity* of mine. ˈ

But now to new matters.

I really don't know what to begin with—I am quite over stocked with materials:—So I think, to prevent waste of Time in considering, I will take people *Alphabettically*; & go through as many Letters as three sheets, which I propose filling, will hold. ˈMr. Stephen Allen & his wife have been lately in Town. Stephen is grown a man of prodigious consequence, he talks perpetually of *his possessions, property* & so forth [xxxxx *3 lines*]—And in this manner, he takes every possible opportunity of making mention of his own Importance [xxxxx *½ line*]

As to his Wife, she is much improved—she has Cast off the Hoyden, & is well behaved & [xxxxx *1 word*]ˈ

Signora Agujari,[24] detta Bastardini, sent very particular Compliments to my Father by Dr. Matty, of the [British] Museum, regretting that she had not seen him when he was Abroad, & very much desiring to be Introduced to his Acquaintance. It was somewhat remarkable, that this is the second Capital Female singer who has sent ˈ to *solicit* my Father's Acquaintance, & both of them by men of learning; for Miss Davies commissioned Dr. Johnson to deliver *her* message of Compliments.[25]

An Evening was accordingly appointed, & Mr Burney & Hetty came here to meet this *silver side* lady,[26] who is reckoned, next to Gabriella,[27] the greatest singer in the world.

Dr. Matty, who is a little, formal man, very civil, & very affected, Handed the Bastardini into the Room, she is of

---

[24] Lucrezia Aguiari *or* Agujari (1743–83), Italian soprano; called 'La Bastardina' or 'La Bastardella' because of her alleged illegitimate birth. She came to London this year and sang in the Pantheon concerts until the fall of 1777. She was one of the most sought-after singers in Europe. Mozart praised the range and beauty of her voice, and she was also remarkable as an actress. See *New Grove*; Highfill; below, *passim*.

[25] The message is missing.

[26] Agujari reputedly had a silver plate in her side, due to her having been mauled by a hog or dog when an infant.

[27] Caterina Gabrielli (1730–96), Italian soprano. Known as one of the most eminent and perfect singers of the time, she made her London début later this year. See *New Grove*; Highfill; below, p. 77 and *passim*.

middle stature, & a little Lame; she has a very good Complection, & was *well*, not *absurdly*, Painted; she has fine, expressive, languishing Eyes, & all together is a handsome Woman,
& appears about 4 or 5 & Twenty.[28]

She was Accompanied by Signor Colla,[29] who is maître de
[musique à][30] la Cour at Parma, & who attends her in her
Travels, & is, like her, pensioned by the Duke. He is a Tall,
thin, spirited Italian, full of fire, & not wanting in Grimace.

Dr. Maty also Introduced two more Gentlemen, both
clergymen, to be of the Party; the name of one of them, I have
forgot, he was a *yea & nay* man, not worth remembering: the
other was the famous Mr Penneck,[31] that worthy & gentle, &
pious Parson, who knocked down Mr Colman upon suspecting
his having a *Penchant* for a Miss Miller, an Actress. This man
is half a mad man, he looks dark & designing, & all together
ill favoured.

This was our Party, & if I could write & spell | French &
Italian, I would give you a sketch of the Conversation, which
was lively & Entertaining; but as that is out of my power, I
can only mention two or three circumstances.

We were all of us excessively eager to hear her sing, but as it
was not convenient to offer her her Pantheon-price of 50
Guineas a song, we were rather fearful of asking that favour:
however, my Father ventured to hint at it to Signor Colla; who
told us that she certainly *would* sing—*but* that she had a bad
cold, & slight sore Throat!

As to Signor Colla, he was *so* Civil to my Father! talked so
much of his *Fame* Abroad, & of the *ardent* Desire which he had
of the *Honour* of knowing so *celebrated* a person! It seems he

---

[28] She was about 32.

[29] Giuseppe Colla (1731–1806), Italian composer. From 1766 he was *maestro di
capella* at the court of Ferdinand (1751–1802), D. of Parma. Agujari was appointed
virtuosa di camera by the court in 1768. She and Colla had long had a liaison but did not
marry until 1780 (*New Grove*; Highfill).

[30] Inserted by FBA.

[31] The Revd Richard Penneck (*c.*1728–1803); chaplain to Ld. Orford; keeper of
the reading room of the British Museum. The Miss Miller in question was an actress
at Covent Garden from 1769 to 1774 and was probably one of Colman's mistresses
after the death of his wife in 1771. Penneck, described by FB as 'twice the height at
least' of Colman (Journal for 1775, p. 489), had accosted him in the street and
knocked him down twice in Feb. 1773. It was Penneck who had married Colman and
Sarah Ford in 1768! See Highfill; *YW* xxxii. 97–8 and nn. 19–20; *EJL* i. 40 n. 15.

Composes for Agujari, who he suffers not to sing any music but his own.[32] He talked of *her* as of the greatest Wonder of the World,—'*c'est une prodige!*' He said that Nature had been so very lavish of it's gifts to her, that he had had hardly any trouble in teaching her—every thing was ready done!

One very ridiculous circumstance I cannot forebear mentioning: Susette had, I know not how, understood by Dr. Maty, that Signora Agujari was married to Signor Colla: This she told to Hetty & me, & we therefore concluded that it was only a *foreign* custom, that she still kept her name; as it is the case with many other singers. Well, when my sister was asked to play, she pleaded want of Practice, & said to Agujari that she had other Things to mind than Harpsichords.—

'Et qu'avez vous donc, Mademoiselle?' demanded the Bastardini. 'Des Enfans!' answered Hetty. 'Ah Diable!' exclaimed she, (for that is her favourite Exclammation) et vous etes si juine [*sic*] encore! & combien [en][33] avez vous?'

'J'en ai trois.' answered Hetty—

'Ah Diable! C'est bien extraordinaire!'

'Avez *vous* une Enfant?' asked Hetty,—

She stared—& after some Gestures of surprise, said 'Moi!—je ne suis pas mariée, moi!'

Hetty was quite confounded,—she begged her pardon, & said 'mais en verité j'ai toujours cru que ce monsieur étoit votre epoux!'

'Non, Mlle' answered the Bastardini, 'c'est mon maître.'

This was a very ridiculous mistake, however, she took it ⌜very⌝ good naturedly, & without being offended, as it was evident that it was not designed.

Dr. Maty has assured us that she bears an unexceptionable character, & that she is therefore visited by his Wife & Daughters.[34] She has been strongly recommended to him from abroad.

---

[32] CB noted in *Hist. Mus.*: 'She sung hardly any other music while she was here than her husband's, Signor Colla, which, though often good, was not of that original and varied cast which could supply the place of every other master, ancient and modern' (Mercer, ii. 883). A leaf from a programme to a Pantheon concert (Berg) gives as the final piece a song by Colla, *Per salvare il mio Bene*, sung by Agujari.

[33] Inserted by FBA.

[34] His 2nd wife, Mary née Deners (*c.*1716–1802), and his daughters Louisa (1746–

Her Behaviour was very *proper*, and she displayed none of her airs, though it was not difficult to see that she *could* behave otherwise; for she betrayed, perhaps involuntarily, a consciousness of her greatness, superiority & consequence by a thousand little speeches & looks. I believe that she allows *Gabriella* to be a *Rival*; all the rest of the world she holds in Contempt. She has not even the curiosity to *hear* any singing but her own. She said she had not been once to the opera; & when we asked her if she had ever heard Rausini [Rauzzini], she answered 'No! mais on dit qu'il Chante joliment.'! My Father asked her how she liked *Galluci*,[35] a new woman who sings at the Pantheon, as well as Agujari. She answered that she had never heard her! that she went into her own Room the moment she had done singing herself. How conceitedly incurious!

'Mais vous, monsieur,' said she, 'vous avez entendu la Gabriella? n'est-ce pas?'

My Father told her that Gabriella was in Sicily when he was in Italy, & therefore he could not hear her.[36] 'No?' said she, 'mais vraiment c'est dommage!

My Father then asked if *she* had heard her? |

'O no,' she said, & Signor Colla added that they two could never be in the same place together.

'Two suns,' said Dr. Maty, 'never appear at once.'

'O, ce n'est pas possible!' cried Agujari.

After Tea, we went into the Library, & Hetty was prevailed upon to play a Lesson of Bach of Berlin's, upon our Merlin Harpsichord.[37] It was very sweet, & ⌜*she*⌝ [Agujari][38] appeared

---

1809), m. (1776) Rogers Jortin (*c*.1732–95), attorney; Ann (b. 1748), m. John Obadiah Justamond (1737–86), FRS, surgeon and translator; and Martha (b. 1758, living 1812) (Nichols, *Lit. Anec.* iii. 259; *GM* xlvi (1776), 191; lvi¹ (1786), 270; lxxii¹ (1812), 286; IGI; wills of Matthew Maty, PCC, prob. 17 Aug. 1776; Louisa Jortin, prob. 8 Apr. 1809).

[35] FB calls her 'the second to herself [Agujari] at the Pantheon' in the Journal for 1775, p. 491. 'Signora Gallucci' is named after Agujari in an advertisement for a subscription concert at the Pantheon, 6 Feb. 1775 (*Morning Chronicle*, 6 Feb.). She was never engaged at the Opera and is not further traced.

[36] Gabrielli was at the end of a 3-year engagement at Palermo during CB's trip (1770).

[37] The chronology implied by this letter suggests that this was *not* the 'compound harpsichord' seen by FB on 27 Feb., but an earlier model purchased previously.

[38] Inserted by FBA.

to be *really* much pleased with it, & spoke highly of the *Taste* & *feeling* with which ⌜she⌝ [Hetty][39] played. Mr Burney sat down next. They all stared, as usual, at his performance. And the Bastardini, after thanking him, expressed herself to be *extremely* concerned that it was not then in her power to sing, saying it w[ould] give her particular pleasure: but she added, th[at] she would come some other Time, & bring some of her best songs, & sing *comme il faut*.

When she went away, she again said 'O! je viendrai absolument!'

And so Ended this visit. Signor Colla has been here since, & had a long discourse with my Father concerning *poetry* & *music*. He is a mighty *Reasoner*. But what was most provoking, was that He came again yesterday, & the Bastardini with him,—& we were all unfortunately at the Stranges.ˈHowever, I hope we shall see her by appointment soon, as my Father has promised Mr Twining to let him know when she comes, that he may be of the Party.

I have been interrupted, & am on the brink of missing the post—Must therefore conclude in the greatest haste yours ever & ever F.B.

[*FB's journal account of Agujari's visit concludes:*]

This singer is really a *slave* to her Voice; she fears the least Breath of air—she is equally apprehensive of Any heat—she seems to have a perpetual anxiety lest she should take Cold; & I do believe she niether Eats, Drinks, sleeps or Talks, without considering in what manner she may perform those vulgar duties of Life so as to be most beneficial to her Voice. However, there are so few who are gifted with eminent Talents, that it is better to cultivate them even labouriously, than to let them suffer Injury from Carelessness or Neglect.ˈ

[*The Journal for 1775 continues. The top of the page has been cut away.*]

Motezuma[40] is a delightful opera. Rauzini sings *only* second to Millico. We met that youth at Mrs Brooke's, last week, & were much pleased with his vivacity & drollery. He afterwards

[39] Inserted by FBA.
[40] Sacchini's new opera opened at the King's Theatre on 7 Feb. with Rauzzini singing the title role (*LS 4* iii. 1868 and *seq.*)

went, as well as ourselves, to a Rehersal of a new comic opera, in which the excellent Lovattini,[41] & Signora Sestini, sing. *The Sestini* is excessively pretty, & is a charming singer.[42]

[*Next follows the journal account of Agujari's visit, the conclusion of which has been given above. After this section, FB continues:*]

And now I have said so much of this great *Italian* singer, I will condescend to mention our great *English* singer, Miss Davies.

We had a Visit from her, her mother & sister last Week: & we had here to meet her, Mr Twining, a clergyman, who is come to Town for a few Weeks from his *parsonage* near Colchester.[43] He is a man of Learning, is very fond of music, & a good performer both on the Harpsichord & Violin. He commenced a Correspondance with my Father upon the publication of his German Tour,[44] which they have kept up with great spirit ever since, for Mr Twining, besides being very deep in musical knowledge, is a man of great humour & drollery.

Cecelia was ⌜as⌝ engaging ⌜as ever,⌝ but would not be prevailed upon to sing, to the great disappointment of Mr Twining; but she said that she *dared* not, for that ⌜her⌝ Law suit was not yet decided, & her articles with the Opera managers tied her down to never singing to any Company: she invited our Family, however, to visit *her*, & said that *at Home*

---

[41] Giovanni Lovattini (*fl.* 1760–82), Italian singer. The opera was *La Marchese giardiniera*, by Anfossi. Lovattini was primo buffo at the Opera from 1766 to 1775. CB praised his 'sweet and well-toned tenor' as well as 'his taste, humour, and expression'. He left England this summer and subsequently retired to his native Bologna (Highfill; Mercer, ii. 872).

[42] CB, commenting on the opening performance (7 Mar.), observed: 'Her face was beautiful, her figure elegant, and her action graceful. Her voice, though by nature not perfectly clear and sweet toned, had been well directed in her studies, and she sung with considerable agility, as well as taste and expression' (Mercer, ii. 881).

[43] Twining was curate of Fordham, 5 m. NW of Colchester. He also maintained a town house in Colchester, where he and his wife wintered.

This 'introductory' passage on Twining seems an afterthought by FB. It properly belongs earlier in the journal (and FBA shifted it there for publication), but the chronology is correct because of the sequence of FB's attendance at rehearsals of Anfossi's opera (above, p. 67).

[44] Actually several weeks prior to the publication. Twining had met CB briefly a decade earlier and was aware of his work on *Hist. Mus.* (Lonsdale, pp. 120, 135; Twining to CB, 28 May 1773, BL).

she supposed she might be allowed to *practice*, & therefore if it would be any Amusement to us, she would be happy to do whatever was in her power.

Modesty, & an unassuming Carriage, in people of Talent & Fame, are irresistable. How much do I prefer for an acquaintance, the well bred & obliging Miss Davies, to the self sufficient & imperious Bastardini though I doubt not the superiority of her powers as a singer. |

ᵀThe Law suit is a very singular one. If the managers lose it, they will [have] the Costs to pay, & a whole season's salary to Miss Davies, though she has never sung a Note for them, & though the singer[45] who has succeeded her, & who must also be paid, has never been a favourite with the Public, which is always a most cruel circumstance to the managers. And if Miss Davies fails, she will have lost a whole year's singing & have the Damages to pay. Where the *Right* lays I know not, but it is not possible to be in Company with Miss Davies & not wish her success.[46]

And now that I am upon the subject of Public Characters, I must not omit to mention that my Father and Mr. Garrick have met, & are reconciled, if I may use that Word, to speak of the cessation of a displeasure which never amounted to a Quarrel.ᵀ[47]

My Brother James has left us some time; he has an appointment for the Cerberus, & is ordered to America, which I am not at all pleased at, though I thank Heaven there is no prospect of any Naval Engagement, their Business being only to Convoy the General Officers.[48] I am sure I shall earnestly pray for peaceable measures. Jem & I Correspond,[49] & I am glad to find he is not himself displeased at his designation.

---

[45] The German singer Signora Schindlerin, a pupil of Rauzzini whom he had brought from Venice. She sang in the Opera from Nov. 1774 to May 1776. CB sneered at her 'moderate abilities, and more feeble voice' (Mercer, ii. 881; see also *LS 4* iii. 1831 and *passim*).

[46] Miss Davies eventually won the suit. See below, p. 150.

[47] See above, p. 40.

[48] JB was appointed 2nd Lt. of the *Cerberus*, a 28-gun frigate, on 9 Dec. 1774. The ship set sail for Boston on 21 Apr. with Maj.–Gens. Howe, Clinton, and Burgoyne on board. See Manwaring, pp. 52–5; below, *passim*.

[49] See below, p. 91 n. 71. JB was presumably at Portsmouth, where the *Cerberus* was fitting out.

Mr Bruce, that *great Lyon*, has lately become very intimate with my Father, & has favoured him [|] with two delightful Original Drawings, done by himself, of Instruments which he found at the Egyptian Thebes, in his long & difficult & Enterprising Travels; & also with a long Letter concerning them, which is to be Printed in the History.[50] These will be great ornaments to the Book; & I am happy to think that Mr Bruce, in having so highly obliged my Father, will find, by the Estimation he is in as a Writer, that his own Name ⌜& Assistance⌝ will not be disgraced, though it is the first Time he has signed it for any publication with which he has hitherto favoured the World.

⌜Susy & I frequently see Barsanti at present, for we now Live very near to her,[51] & can *make opportunities* of calling upon her whenever we go out. & really she ⟨continues⟩ so good a Girl, living wholly with her mother & being almost always at Home, except when obliged to be at the Theatre, that I think she deserves calls, the attention & kindness which can be paid to her, & upon this consideration, I have at length given up my former *delicacy* of not visiting her privately, partly tempted by the great pleasure I have in her Conversation & partly by a kind of Hope that the continued & manifold regard shown her by those friends whom she retains, & wishes to be thought well of by, will have some influence in encourageing & re-paying her perseverence in meriting their Regard.⌝ [|]

March 4th

I had Yesterday the Honour of Drinking Tea in Company with his *Abyssinian majesty*, Mr Bruce, for so Mrs Strange Calls Mr Bruce.[52]

My mother & I went to Mr Stranges, by Appointment to

---

[50] The letter (now Osborn), dated 'Kinnaird Octr 20 1774', is printed in *Hist. Mus.* i. 214–24 (Mercer, i. 177–83). The drawings, of a Theban harp and Abyssinian lyre, are reproduced in Plates 5 and 8.

[51] Jenny Barsanti lived in Queen St., Golden Square (Westminster Rate Books for St James's, Westminster Reference Library). On 17 Jan. 1775 she created the role of Lydia Languish in Sheridan's *The Rivals* (Highfill).

[52] FB repeats this account of Bruce (and the account of his visit later to St Martin's St.) in her joint letter with CB to SC, written in late Mar. (below). See also *Mem.* i. 298–318.

meet M^r & Mrs Turner of Lynn, who are lately become acquainted in that Family, & who are in Town for the Winter. & this majestic Personage Chanced to be there.

He has been Acquainted intimately with Mrs Strange all his Life, & is very much attached to her & her Family. He seldom passes a Day without Visiting her; but Miss Strange, who has told me of many of his singularities, says that he is generally put into a *pet* when they have any Company, as his excessive haughtiness prevents his being sociable with them, & makes him think them impertinant if they take the liberty to speak to him.

Indeed, she also told me, he has been really very ill used from the curiosity, which, previous to his provocation, he *did* satisfy: for many people gathered anecdotes & observations from him, & then printed them.[53] This ⌜was shameful, &⌝ as he intends ⌜some Time or other⌝ to publish his Travels himself, ⌜it⌝was most abominably provoking.

It is not enough to say that this has put him *upon his Gaurd*, it has really made [him] shy of being asked how he does? or what's o'clock?—Haughty by Nature, his extraordinary Travels, & perhaps his long Residence among savages, have contributed to render him one of the most imperious of men. He is, indeed, far the most so of any that *I* every saw.

He is more than six foot high, is extremely well proportioned in shape, & has a handsome & expressive Face. If his *vanity* ⌜is⌝ half as great as his *pride*, he would certainly ⌜become⌝ more courteous if he knew how much smiles become him, for when he *is* pleased to soften the severity of his Countenance, & to suffer his Features to relax into smiling, he is quite another Creature, ⌜& looks indeed very handsome.⌝

⌜As we went in, we met Miss Strange's younger sister, Bell,[54] who was coming to invite my Father to be of the Party,

---

[53] For instance, Boswell had interviewed Bruce the preceding Aug. and 'dug from him' information for an essay in the *London Magazine* (Aug. and Sept. 1774). FB wrote to SC that 'there is *now* ⌜printing⌝ in Germany, a History of his Travels, in 2 vol^s Octavo!' But no evidence of such a work has been found. See *Boswell for the Defence, 1769–1774*, ed. W. K. Wimsatt and F. A. Pottle (New York, 1959), pp. 271–5, 283–4; *Boswell: The Ominous Years 1774–1776*, ed. C. Ryskamp and F. A. Pottle (New York, 1963), pp. 45–6.

[54] Isabella Katherina Strange (1759–1849). See Dennistoun, i. 257, 284, 312, ii. 273; Nora K. Strange, *Jacobean Tapestry* (1947), pp. 133–5.

at Mr. Bruce's request. As we knew he was out, we made her return up stairs with us. Mrs Strange Introduced my mother to Mr. Bruce, & seated her next to him. He enquired after my Father several Times, for he has frequently been visited by him of late on account of his Egyptian Communication.⌐

Mr Bruce, as my Father did not accompany us, I doubt not wished himself alone with the Stranges, for he looked so important, that he awed almost into total silence M^r & Mrs Turner, who secretly wished the same. Mr Turner, who is a very *Jocular* man, could not bear to be deprived of his Laugh, & yet had not courage sufficient to venture at Joking before so terrible a ⌐man,⌐ who looks as if Born to command the World! Besides, he had heard so much of his Character before they met, that he was *prepared* | to fear him. & Mrs Turner is too little used to the Company of strangers, to be at her Ease when in it.

As to my ⌐self,⌐ I sat next to Miss Strange, & was comfortable enough in Conversing with her: till my mother, finding herself little Noticed by ⌐his Majesty,⌐ quitted her seat, & went & placed herself next to Mrs Turner, saying 'Well, I shall come & sit by you, & leave Mr Bruce to the young ⌐Ladies.⌐

I do heartily hate these sort of speeches, which *oblige* one to be ⌐Noticed;⌐ nothing can be more provoking. Mr Bruce, accordingly, turning towards me, said 'Well, Miss Burney, I think you can do no less than take the seat your Mama has left.'

I did not half like it, but thought he would suppose me *afraid* of him, if I refused, ⌐& therefore I⌐ changed Chairs; but ⌐making⌐ Miss Strange move next to me, I immediately renewed our Conversation, lest he should think himself obliged to take further Notice of me.

A ⌐very strange⌐ Advertisement had been put in the Papers the Evening before, which said that Mr Bruce was *Dying* or *Dead*;[55] my Father, who knew he was well, wafered the paragraph upon a sheet of paper, & sent to his Lodgings. My mother asked him if he had seen it? 'I thought, answered he, 'it had come from *Brucey*' (for Miss Strange, who was

---

[55] 'James Bruce, Esq; the celebrated Traveller, lies dangerously ill without Hopes of Recovery, at his House in Leicester-fields' (*Public Advertiser*, 1 Mar.)

Christianed [*sic*] *Bruce*, he always calls *Brucey*). 'Yes, I ⌐saw it, & Read my Death with great Composure.' Then turning himself to me, he added 'Was not you sorry, Miss Burney, to Read of my Death?'

These immense sized men speak to ⌐little⌐ Women as if they were Children; I answered that as my Father had seen him the Day before, I was not much *alarmed*. Mʳ Turner, then, gathering Courage, said 'Well, Sir, I think as Times go, it is very well that when they killed you, they said no ill of you.'

'I know of no reason they had to do otherwise,' answered Mʳ Bruce, so haughtily, that Mʳ Turner, failing in his first attempt, never afterwards spoke to him.—or indeed, ⌐hardly⌐ opened his mouth.

Soon after, a servant came in with General Melville's⁵⁶ Compliments, & a desire to know if it was true that Mʳ Bruce was ⌐so⌐ Dangerously ill? Mʳ Bruce answered drily, 'Yes,—tell him I am Dead.'

'Ah poor soul!' cried Mʳˢ Strange, 'I dare say he has been vexed enough! Honest man! I don't think that man ever wronged or deceived a human Being!⁵⁷

'Don't you, faith?' cried Mʳ Bruce: 'that's saying more than I would! Can you really suppose he has risen to the Rank of General with so little trouble?'

'O, you know, it's only the *Women* that are ever deceived; & for my part, I never allowed that the best among you could deceive *me*, for whenever you say pretty Things, I make it a Rule to *believe* them true!' ⌐

Bell Strange then carried him his Tea; ⌐she is a very good sort of Girl, & very sensible [xxxxx *1 word*] & well made, though very plain.⌐ Mʳ Bruce turning to me, said 'Do you know, Miss Burney, that I intend to run away with Bell? We are to go to Scotland together. She won't let me rest till I take her.'

'How can you say so, Sir?' cried Bell, 'pray, Ma'am, don't believe it.'

---

⁵⁶ Robert Melville (1723–1809), soldier and antiquary; Maj.-Gen., 1766; Gen., 1793 (*AL* (1807), p. 2).
⁵⁷ Melville was noted for his humanity as Governor of Grenada and the other ceded islands in the West Indies, 1763–70 (*DNB*).

'Why, how now, Bell,' returned he, 'what! won't you go?'
'No, Sir.'

'This is the first lady,' said Mr Bruce, rising, 'who ever refused me!' Then addressing Mrs Strange, he asked her if she had heard of Lord Rosemary[58] lately? They then joined in drawing a most odious character of him, especially for avarice; after which, Mr Bruce walking up to me, said 'And yet *this man* is *my Rival!*' 'Really?' cried I, 'I am sure I wonder that he should—(I *meant* upon account of his prodigious Figure) 'O, answered he, 'it's really true! Mrs Strange, is it not that he is my Rival?' 'O yes, they say so.' said she.

'I am surprised that he *dares*, said my mother, [be][59] Rival to Mr Bruce, for I wonder he does not apprehend that his long residence in Egypt made him so acquainted with magic, that—'

'O!' cried Mr Bruce, I shall not poison him!—but I believe that I shall Bribe his servant to fasten a string across his stair Case, by which, as I dare say ⌐he¬ never uses a Candle to Light him, he may fall down & Break his Neck.'[60]

⌐He went out of the Room soon after, I asked ¦ Miss Strange what all this meant? She told me that it was reported that Mr. Bruce was going to marry Lady Anne Lindsay,[61] sister of the handsome Lady Margaret Fordyce, of whose beauty I have spoken. She said that she did not know whether it was true, but that certainly Lord Roseberry paid his Addresses to her Ladyship.[62]

I should rather suppose it to be mere *Badinage*, by her

---

58 Bruce's derisive name for Ld. Rosebery, i.e., Neil Primrose (1729–1814), 3rd E. of Rosebery.

59 Inserted by FBA.

60 Ironically, Bruce met his death falling down a staircase in 1794 (J. M. Reid, *Traveller Extraordinary: The Life of James Bruce of Kinnaird* (1968), p. 308).

61 Lady Anne Lindsay (1750–1825), eldest daughter of the 5th E. of Balcarres; authoress of 'Auld Robin Gray' (see *The New Oxford Book of Eighteenth Century Verse*, ed. R. Lonsdale (Oxford, 1984), pp. 573–4). For FB's mention of her sister see *EJL* i. 200.

62 Lady Anne rejected both Rosebery and Bruce. She m. (1793) Andrew Barnard (d. 1807), Secretary to the Colony of the Cape of Good Hope. Rosebery, like Bruce a widower in search of a 2nd wife, rebounded instantly to wed (17 July 1775) Mary Vincent (*c.*1752–1823), only daughter of Sir Francis Vincent, 7th Bt. Bruce, the following year, wed Mary Dundas (d. 1785), daughter of one of his neighbours, Thomas Dundas of Fingask and Carron Hall (Reid, pp. 296, 301).

talking with so little Ceremony upon the subject. When he returned into the Room, he asked⌐ Miss Strange how she could let her Harpsichord be so much out of order? 'I went down, said he, to try it, but upon my Word it is too bad to be touched: However, while I was at it, in comes Bell, & seats herself quietly behind me; but no sooner did I rise, then away she flew down a flight of stairs, quite to the Cellar, I suppose; expecting, no doubt, that I should follow! but, added he drily, 'I did not. Well, Bell, what do you *Glowr* at? (I don't know if I spell the word right) do you understand Scotch, Miss Burney?'[63]

'I Believe I can go so far as that word, Sir.'

'But, *Brucey*, why are you so negligent of your music?—you play, Miss Burney?'

'Very little, Sir.'

'O I hope I shall hear you; I am to come to your House some Day, with Mrs Strange, & then—'

'When we have the Honour of seeing you, Sir, cried I, I hope you will hear a much better player than me.'

'O as to that,' answered he, 'I would not give a *fig* to hear a *man* play, comparatively.' |

'Well,' said Mrs Strange, 'I knew a young lady who was at a Concert for the first Time, & she sat & sighed, & groaned, & at last she said Well, I can't help it! & burst into Tears!'

'There's a Woman,' cried Mr Bruce with some emotion, 'who could never make a man unhappy! Her soul must be all Harmony!'

We then joined in recommending it to Miss Strange to Practice; & Mr Bruce took it into his Head to affect to speak to me in a Whisper, bending his Head, not without difficulty, to a level with mine; what he said I have forgot, though I know it was something of no manner of consequence; but really I saw every body's Eyes struck with his attitude ⌐yet⌐ fixed upon him in total silence, so that I hardly heard him from the embarrassment I was in.

Except what I have Written, ⌐almost⌐ every Word that he said, was addressed *en badinage* to plague Bell, or in diverting

[63] FB's spelling is one of the accepted 18th-c. variants. The word was in general dialectical use in Scotland, Ireland, and England (*OED*; *EDD*; *SND*).

himself with Miss Strange's Parrot. He seemed determined not to Enter into Conversation with the Company in general, nor to speak upon any but trifling Topics.

It is pity that a man who seems to have some generous feelings, that break out by starts, & who certainly is a man of Learning & of Humour, should be thus run away with by Pride.

March 10th

We had a large Party here last ⌈Sunday⌉ [5 March], the first of the kind we have had in this House.

Mr Bruce, who is very fond of music, had appointed that Day to accompany Mrs Strange hither│to hear Mr Burney play upon our Merlin Harpsichord. Mr Twining also brought his Wife[64] & another lady with the same view. These, with Miss Strange, my sister [EBB] & ourselves, formed the Party.

Mr Bruce, however, did not appear till very late. Mr Twining & *his ladies* came before six; he apologised for his unfashionable Hour; 'But,' added he, honestly, 'I not only wished for a long Evening here, but also to avoid having to Enter the Room after your Company were assembled.'

M^{rs} & Miss Strange came soon after. We enquired after his Abyssinian majesty; they said he Dined at General Melville's, & was to join them here. We Waited Tea about an Hour, during which Time the Conversation was too general & mixed to be remembered; the *Tea* Equipage was then ordered, & we had all done, & Mr Burney, followed by Mr Twining, had gone into the library, where our music was to be, & which joins the ⌈dining Room, where we all were,—when a Thundering Rap called up our attention.⌉ Mr Bruce was announced, & he Entered the Room like a monarch.

We soon found that he was disconcerted; he complained to Mrs Strange, who Enquired after the General, that he had Invited a set of stupid people to meet him; & he seemed to have left the Party in disgust. He took one Dish of Tea, & then desired to speak to my Father, concerning his Letter that is to

---

[64] Elizabeth Smythies (1739–96), m. (1764) Thomas Twining. She was the daughter of Palmer Smythies (1692–1776), Master of the Colchester Free Grammar School, where Twining had prepared for Cambridge. The other lady is not identified.

be Printed in the History. My Father asked him into his study, which is a very comfortable *snug* Room within the Library; ⌐As they went out,⌐ Mʳ Twining was returning to the Dining Room, & my Father Introduced him to Mʳ Bruce; they Exchanged Bows, & went on. Mʳ Twining lifted up his Hands & Eyes in a droll kind of astonishment, when Mʳ Bruce was out of sight, & coming up to us, said, 'This is the most awful man I ever saw!' & added, 'I never felt myself so little before!'

'Troth, never mind,' cried Mʳˢ Strange; 'if you was 6 foot high, he would *look over you*; & he can do no more now!'

Mʳ Twining then sat down, but said he felt in fear of his life; 'For if he should come in, hastily, & Overlook me, taking his Chair to be empty, it will be all over with me! I shall be Crushed!'

After some Time, finding they did not return, Mʳ Twining, impatient to hear Mʳ Burney, begged him to go to the Harpsichord; accordingly, we all went into the Library, & Mʳ Burney fired away in a Voluntary.[65]

Mʳ Twining, at once astonished & delighted at his performance, Exclaimed: 'Is not this better than being Tall?'

⌐When Mr. Bruce & my Father joined the Party, Mrs. Strange Introduced Mr. Burney & my sister to the former saying, in allusion to Mr. Strange's having given away Hetty at her marriage,

'These, Sir, are both Children of Mr. Strange's, though you have never seen them before.' Bows & Curtsies over, Mr. Bruce answered 'Have a care that he has no children that *you* have never seen, in his perigrinations to the Continent!'

Mr. Strange is at present abroad.[66]

Music was then announced, & lasted almost without intermission till Ten o'Clock. Nobody played but Mr. Burney, except that Hetty accompanied him in 2 Harpsichord Duets, one very pretty, by Mr. Burney himself, & another of most exquisite Composition, by Müthel.⌐[67]

---

[65] 'A piece played by a musician extempore, according to his fancy. This is often used before he begins to set himself to play any particular composition, to try the instrument, and to lead him into the key of the piece he intends to perform' (Rees, s.v. Voluntary).

[66] See below, p. 111.

[67] Johann Gottfried Müthel (1728–88), German composer. The piece performed

Mr Twining was enraptured: Mrs Strange listened with silent wonder & pleasure; & Mr Bruce was Composed into perfect good humour! He forgot the General, discarded his sternness, & wore upon his Face smiles, attention & satisfaction.

As to *M^{rs}* Twining—she seems a very stupid Woman—I marvel that Mr Twining could chuse her! She may, however, have Virtues unknown to me;——perhaps, too, she was *rich.*[68]

The whole Party were asked to a Family supper, when, to a general surprise, Mr Bruce consented to stay! an Honour we by no means expected: however, he was implicitly followed by the rest of the set.

Mr Bruce sat between Mrs Twining & me. That lady & he did not fatigue themselves with Exchanging one Word the whole Evening; however, Mr Bruce was exceeding courteous, & in great Good humour. He made me seem so very short as I sat next to him, that had not Mr Burney, who [is][69] still less than myself, been on my other side, I should have felt quite ⌜mean &⌝ pitiful. But what very much diverted me, was that whenever I turned to Mr Burney, I ⌜saw⌝ his Head leaning behind my Chair, to *peer* at Mr Bruce. ⌜Indeed, no Eye⌝ was off him, though I believe he did not perceive it, as he hardly ever himself looks ǀ at any body.

The Conversation during supper turned upon madness, a subject which the Stranges are very full of, as a lady[70] of their acquaintance left their House but on Friday in that terrible disorder. We asked how she happened to *be* with them? They ⌜said⌝ that she had seemed recovered. Mr Bruce, who ⌜was

---

was undoubtedly Müthel's duetto for 2 clavichords, 2 harpsichords, or 2 pianofortes, published at Riga in 1771. Writing some 30 years later, CB observed that 'the duet is still a curious composition, manifesting a powerful hand, great fertility of invention, and a taste and refinement unknown, at the time, to all Europe, except to the Bach school' (Rees; see also *Tours*, ii. 240–1; *New Grove*).

[68] FB, in her letter to SC, describes Mrs Twining as 'a very silent, dull Woman'. She mistakes silence for stupidity. Mrs Twining had wits enough to study Latin and Greek as a girl and to handle Twining's household accounts; she was *not* rich, and Twining truly loved her. This is one of FB's happily rare lapses into sheer cattiness. See R. S. Walker, 'Thomas Twining's Letters', Introduction, pp. 19–20 (typescript on deposit in Cambridge University Library); also, *ED* ii. 22 n. 2.

[69] Inserted by FBA.

[70] Not identified.

there & saw⌐ her, was very inquisitive about her. Mrs Strange said that the beginning of her *Wandering* that Evening, was, by ⌐going⌐ up to her, & asking her if she could *make Faces?*

'I wish,' said Mr Bruce, 'she had asked *me*!—I believe I could have satisfied her that way!'

'O,' said Miss Strange, 'she had a great desire to speak to you, Sir; she said that she had much to say to you, ⌐but I made her promise me not to speak.⌐

'If,' said Mr Bruce, 'without any preface, she had Entered the Room, & come up to me making Faces; I confess I should have been rather surprised!'

'I am sure,' cried I, '*I* should have made a Face without much difficulty! I am amazed at Miss Strange's Courage in staying with her!'

'I have been a great deal with her,' answered Miss Strange, '& she particularly minds whatever I say.'

'But how are you to answer for your life a moment,' cried Mr Bruce, 'in Company with a mad Woman? When she seems most quiet, may she not snatch up a pair of scissars, or whatever is near her, & destroy you,? or at least run them into your Eyes, & blind or maim you for life?'

'While I tried to hold her from going into the street,' said Mrs Strange, 'she scratched my arm, as you see,—' |

'Did she fetch Blood?' cried Mr Bruce; 'if she did you will surely go mad too. Nay, I would Advise you to go directly to the sea, & be dipt! I assure you I would not be in your situation!'

He said this so drily, that I stared at him, & could not forbear beginning to Expostulate, when turning round to me, I saw he was Laughing.

'If you are bit by a mad *Cat*,' continued he, 'will you not go mad? & how much more by a mad *Woman?*'

'But I was *not* bit,' answered Mrs Strange, 'I only felt her Nail, & where there Enters no *Slaver*, there is no Danger.

'I hope,' said my mother, 'that her friends will not place her in a private mad House; there is so much iniquity practiced at those places, that in order to keep them they will not let their friends know when they are really recovered.'

'Ay, indeed?' cried Mr Bruce, 'why this is very bad Encouragement to go mad!'

And now I must have done with this Evening, unless I were to Write horrid Tales of madness; for that shocking subject being started, every body had something terrible to say upon it.

March 13th

Inclosed in a Letter to myself, I received on Tuesday [March 7] one for Miss Strange, from my Brother,[71] to thank her for a Letter she had honoured him with to a Relation at Boston.[72] I went in the Afternoon with it to Mrs Strange & found her & her two daughters at Tea, with Mr Bruce. |

I told Miss Strange that I had just received Dispatches from Portsmouth; but as her Letter was from a Gentleman, I delivered it before her mother—for fear of consequences!—

'From Portsmouth? said Mr Bruce, 'What, from Collins,[73] *Brucey?*'

'It is from a very honest Tar.' Answered I.

'Then pray, *Brucey*, let me look at the seal, to see whether he has sent you 2 pigeons billing? or a bleeding Heart? or a Dove Cooing?'

When he found my Brother was the Person in Question, & that he was going to America, he said he was sorry for it, as there was going to be another South Sea Expedition, which would have been much more desirable for him. 'And,' said I, much more *agreeable* to him, for he wishes it of all things; he says he should now make a much better Figure at Otaheite, than when there before, as he learnt the Language of Omai in his Passage Home.

'Ah weel, honest lad,' said Mrs Strange, 'I suppose he would get a Wife, or something pretty, there.'

'Perhaps Oberea?[74] added Mr Bruce.

---

[71] None of the letters mentioned here survive. In an earlier letter (Berg), JB asked FB to clarify whether his correspondent was Mrs or Miss Strange and suggested that she might draft a reply which he would 'make no scruple to father as my own production'. This is the only extant letter from this period between JB and FB.

[72] According to JB, 'a Lady in Boston', not further identified.

[73] Not traced.

[74] Purea, the ambitious wife of the high chief Amo of Papara, in Tahiti. The explorer Wallis met her in 1767, when she was 40 or 45 and at the height of her power. Banks met her 2 years later, on the first of Cook's voyages; by then she and her husband had been defeated in a factional war, though she retained some influence. In his journal Banks implies that he evaded an invitation to her bed. The 2 were coupled

'Poor Oberea,' said I, 'he says is dethroned.'

'But,' said he archly, 'if Mr *Banks* goes, he will reinstate her!—But this poor fellow, Omai, has lost all his Time; they have taught him Nothing; He will only pass for a consummate Lyar when he returns; for how can he make them believe half the Things he will tell them? He can give them no idea of our Houses, Carriages, or any thing that will appear probable.'

'Troth, then,' cried Mrs Strange, 'they should give him a set of Doll's Things, & a Baby's House, to shew them; he ¦ should have every Thing in miniature, by way of model: Dressed Babies, Cradles, Lying In Women, & a' sort of pratty Things!'

There is a humourous Ingenuity in this thought, that I really believe would be well worth being tried.

Masquerades being mentioned, the *comely* Mrs Tolfray,[75] ⌐who accompanied Miss Allen & me to one,¬ was spoken of. She Exhibited herself as ⌐a shepherdess at the King of Denmark's masquerade,[76] at which Miss Strange was with her, & she was remarked about her *fat* & her size the whole Evening. Since then, said Mrs. Strange, she is become more *grand*, she has been¬ a *Queen* ⌐ever since.¬ She was once Queen of the Amazons; after that Queen of Scots; & last of all Andromache—'

'I should think she must have appeared *in Character*,' cried I, as Queen of the Amazons.'

'I own I should like to have seen her,' said Mr Bruce, but how was she Dressed?'

'O,' answered Miss Strange, 'in *Buskins*—& her Hair about her shoulders—'

'But there was a peculiar Custom,' said Mr Bruce, among the Amazons, which ought to have been attended to;—which

---

in a series of anonymous indecent lampoons, starting with *An Epistle from Oberea, Queen of Otaheite, to Joseph Banks, Esq.*, published in 1773. Purea or Oberea died in 1775 or 1776. See E. H. McCormick, *Omai: Pacific Envoy* (Auckland, 1977), pp. 3, 11–12, and *passim*.

[75] Perhaps the Margaret, wife of Samuel Tolfrey, who had 2 sons at Eton at this time. Not further identified.

[76] Christian VII (1749–1808), King of Denmark, gave a masquerade ball at the Opera House in Oct. 1768, while on a visit to England. His wife, Queen Caroline Matilda, was sister of George III (*YW* xxxv. 407 n. 12; see also ibid, xxiv. 104).

was, that they Cut off the left Breast. Now Mrs Tolfray has both right & left Breast so very entire, that there is scarce any part of them suffered to be lost, even or lessened, even to public View. What Dress had she for Andromache?'

'Black Velvet & Hoop.' answered Miss Strange. |

'And who the Devil was to know that was Andromache?' cried he, 'does Nobody else wear Black?'[77]

'She had better have been in a Gown of her own spinning.' quoth I.[78]

Mrs Strange enquired of Mr Bruce, if he was acquainted with M^r & Mrs Bodville? the former of whom she gave great encomiums to, saying he was the most ingenious man, & never idle Night or Day; or scarce spending a moment of his life but in his peculiar branch of studies.[79]

'Then what ⌈the deuce⌉ did he *marry* for?' demanded Mr Bruce. 'I think his Wife is but little obliged to him;—Now a man is certainly right to give his Day to his studies,—but the *Evening* should be devoted to society;—he should give it to his Wife; or his friends; or to Conversation,—or making Love.—'

'Now do you know I adore you for that!' Exclaimed Mrs Strange.[80]

We have been to return the Visit of Signora Agujari: she was all civility ⌈to us,⌉ & has renewed her promise of another & a musical Evening: she speaks of it with an undisguised Consciousness of the great pleasure she is to give us. If Mr Bruce is the *proudest* man I ever saw, so is the Bastardella the *vainest Woman!*

She says she Lives quite alone, & that it is *Charity* to visit her: she proposed cultivating very much with our Family; for she said that she hardly ever saw any body, as she was always *refused* to Gentlemen: she certainly has great merit in this

---

[77] Andromache was the widow of Hector.

[78] FB alludes to Hector's admonition to Andromache: 'No more—but hasten to thy Tasks at home,/There guide the Spindle, and direct the Loom' (Pope's translation of *The Iliad*, Bk. vi ll. 632–3, ed. M. Mack, Twickenham Edition, vii (1967), p. 358).

[79] Mr Bodville seems to have published nothing 'in his peculiar branch of studies'. He and his wife have not been further traced.

[80] Mrs Strange alludes to her desertions by Robert Strange in pursuit of his career.

Conduct, as, besides her Talents, she is a fine Woman, & must be ⌐ ⌐very much courted.[81]

I am more & more pleased with our House; it is so centered, that we are surrounded with acquaintance; the Stranges in Castle Street, Barsanti in Queen Street, Miss Davies in Pall Mall, Mrs. Brooke in Market Lane; Dr. Hunter in Windmill Street, & in Leicester Fields the *Great* Mr. Bruce.

I have just Called again upon Miss Reid, & find she wants me to sit *in an Attitude* to finish a Picture of a Miss March,[82] a Young lady who is just going to Madrass, & just of my size and make, but who cannot, Heaven knows why, sit herself.

March 23^d

Yesterday morning, as Susette & I were returning from Mr. Burney, we met the celebrated Actress, Mrs. Abington, walking & alone, in Tavistock Street. Susy proposed our turning back, & following her; the weather was beautiful, & [we] accordingly Traced her Foot steps, which were made very leisurely, as she looked at all the Caps as she passed. When we came to the End of the street, at the Corner of Charles Street who should we see but Mr. Garrick? He touched his Hat, & made a motion towards meeting. Mrs. Abington, who was just before us, returned a Courtesie, & crossed over to him, While we Walked gravely on, taking no sort of notice of his Bow, which we did not know who was meant for. They went down Charles Street together, & when we were out of their sight, we again turned,⌐

[*At least one leaf has been cut away, and the top of the next page. In the interim Garrick seems to have left Mrs Abington and joined FB and her sister.*]

from her.

⌐When he came to the bottom of Southampton Street, he offered us each a Hand to Cross the Strand, but we declined, & told him we were not going that way.

'Arn't you? Cried he—well then, *I'll* go *your* way.'

So saying, he put himself between us, entertaining both

---

[81] Signor Colla was her lover (above, p. 75 n. 29).

[82] The reading is uncertain. Miss 'March' may have been one of the 2 ladies whose portraits by Miss Read were exhibited at the Royal Academy in 1776 (A. Graves, *Royal Academy of Arts ... 1769 to 1904* (1905–6), vi. 243).

himself & us with a humourous, sportive kind of gallantry, which, *from him*, was infinitely agreeable.

He again proposed calling a Coach, & making away with us. 'It will make an excellent Paragraph in the Papers' added he—He then noticed that Sukey was Grown—& turning to me, & tapping my Cheek, asked which of us was Eldest? 'I am, Sir, answered I, & ought to be Tallest, only she has been so wicked as to out grow me'⁷ |

[*top of page cut away*]

March 26ᵗʰ

Two Days after the above mentioned *rencontre*, early in the morning, this most entertaining of mortals came.

He marched up stairs immediately into the study where my Father was having his Hair Dressed, surrounded by Books & Papers innumerable; Charlotte was Reading the News paper, & I was making Breakfast. The rest of the Family had not quitted their Downy Pillows.

My Father was beginning a laughing sort of Apology for his letters & so forth,—but Mʳ Garrick interrupted him with—'Ay, now, do be in a little Confusion,—it will make things comfortable!'[83]

He then began to look very gravely at the Hair Dresser; He was himself in a most odious scratch Wig, which | Nobody but himself could dare be seen in: He put on a look, in the Abel Drugger style, of *envy* & sadness as he examined the Hair Dresser's progress;—& when he had done, he turned to him with a dejected Face, & said '—pray Sir,—could you touch up *This* a little?' taking hold of his frightful scratch.

The man only Grinned, & left the Room.

He shook Hands with me, & told my Father that he had *almost* run away with me a Day or two before.

He then Enquired after some Books which he had lent my Father, & how many he had?

'I have 10 of the Memoirs of the French academy.'[84] said my Father.

---

[83] Apparently Garrick had written several letters to CB which CB had not got around to answering. There are no extant letters between Garrick and CB in 1775.

[84] There is no series under that title. Perhaps CB meant the *Mémoires pour servir à*

'And what others?' Cried Mr Garrick.

'I don't know. Do you, Fanny?'

'O—what—' cried Mr Garrick, archly, 'I suppose you don't chuse to know of any others?—O very well!—pray Sir make free with me!—pray keep them, if you chuse it.'

'Charles will know, Sir,' said I.

'What, *Cherry Nose*? cried he (for so he has Named poor Charles, ⌐on account of his Nose being rather of the brightest).

'O, cried I 'Cherry Nose will be quite unhappy when he hears you have been here without his seeing you.'

'Why' said he, I am very good friends with Cherry Nose. I enquired he should like to go to the Play? & Cherry Nose smirks, & simpers—⌐ But pray, Doctor, when shall we have the History out? Do let me know in Time, that I may prepare to Blow the Trumpet of Fame'—

He then put his stick to him mouth, & in a *raree* show man's Voice, cried—Here is the only true History— ⌐ Gentlemen, please to Buy—please to Buy—⌐Gad,⌐ Sir, I shall Blow it in the very Ear of yon scurvy magistrate (meaning Sir John Hawkins, who is writing the same History).

He then ran on with great humour upon twenty subjects, but so much of his drollery belongs to his Voice, looks & manner, that *Writing* loses it almost all.

My Father asked him to Breakfast; but he said he was Engaged at Home with Mr Boswell[85] & Mr Twiss. He then took the latter off, as he did also Dr. Arne,[86] very comically; & afterwards Dr. Johnson, in a little Conversation concerning his borrowing a Book of him;—'David—will you lend me Petraca [*sic*]?' 'Yes, Sir.' 'David,—you sigh?—'Sir, you shall have it!' Accordingly, the Book—finely bound!—was sent; but scarse had he received it, when uttering a Latin

l'histoire des hommes illustres dans la république des lettres, by J. P. Niceron *et al.* (43 vols., Paris, 1727–45), sold at the auction of Garrick's library in 1823. Garrick had a collection of over 2,700 titles. See Stone, p. 173; R. Saunders, *A Catalogue of the Library ... of David Garrick* (1823), p. 51.

[85] James Boswell (1740–95), the biographer of Johnson. Boswell records in his journal, s.v. Friday 24 March: 'Breakfasted with Mr. Garrick. He was hurried and I saw little of him'. He does not mention Twiss (*Boswell: The Ominous Years, 1774–1776*, ed. C. Ryskamp and F. A. Pottle (New York, 1963), p. 93).

[86] Thomas Augustine Arne (1710–78), Mus.D. (Oxon.), 1759; composer and CB's former music master.

Ejaculation, (which Mr G. repeated) in a fit of Enthusiasm—over his Head goes poor Petraca,—Russian Leather and all!'

He soon after started up, & said he must run—'Not yet!' cried I.—He turned to me, & in mock Heroics cried—'ah! I will make *your* Heart ache!—*you* shall sigh—'

He then went out of the study, followed by my Father, & he took a survey of the Books in the Library.—Charlotte & I soon joined them—he called Charlotte his little Dimpling Queen—'See, how she follows me with her blushes!—& here comes another with her smiles—(to me) ay—I see how it is! all the House in Love with me!—here is one (to Charlotte) whose love is in the *Bud*—& here (to me) here it is in *blow*:—& now, (to my Father) ^| I must go to one whose is full *blown*—*full blown*, egad!'

He would not be prevailed with to lengthen his visit—we all followed him down stairs—though he *assured* us he would not ⌐steal⌐ any thing! 'Here is a certain maid here, said he, whom I love to speak to, because she is *Cross*;[87]—Egad, Sir, she does not know the great Roscius!—but I frightened her this morning a little:—Child, said I,—you don't know who you have the happiness to speak to!—do you know I am one of the first Genius's of the Age?—Why, Child, you would *faint away* if you knew who I am!'

In this sportive manner he continued till the Door was shut. He is sensible that we all doat on him—but I believe it is the same thing where ever he goes, except where he has had a personal Quarrel, which I am sorry to hear is frequently the case with those who have been his best friends.

He promised he would often Call in the same sort of way, *to plague us*; we assured him we would freely forgive him if he did. In truth, I desire no better Entertainment than his Company affords.

[87] Presumably little Sarah Harriet Burney, 2½ years old.

With Charles Burney to Samuel Crisp

AL and ALS (Barrett), late March 1775
3 double sheets 4to, 12 pp.
Annotated (by FBA): ✳ N° I of Mr. Bruce. 2ce with Mr. Twining, M^{rs}
Strange, &c & Mr. Bruce, Nesbit, &c March 1775 N^0 30
The letter begins with a half-page 'Prologue' by CB, followed by a 10½-
page letter from FB. CB concludes with most of another page, to which FB
appends a short postscript.
The parts by CB are omitted, as are FB's accounts of Bruce already given
in the Journal for 1775.
SC replied to this letter on 27 March (Barrett).

My dear Daddy,

I need not, I am sure, tell you how much I was concerned at
Kitty's account of your illness:[88] I have been, indeed, much
disappointed, to find the Winter pass away, without your even
peeping at London——But as to my thinking you do not
sufficiently value my Favours—vous vous moquez de moi!—But I was
a little shocked to find, soon after I sent you my Last Letter,[89]
that Hetty had written to you upon the same subject, the
Bastardini, just before. I am afraid between us, you must be
quite tired of this poor *silver side*, you have doubtless heard the
story of the Pig's Eating half her side, & of its being repaired
by a silver kind of machine. You may be sure that she has not
Escaped the witticisms of our *Wags* upon this score: it is too
fair a subject for Ridicule $^|$ to have been suffered to pass
untouched. Mr. Bromfield has given her the Nick name of
Argentine: Mr Foote has advised her, (or *threatened* to advise
her) to go to the stamp office, to have her *side entered*, lest she
should be prosecuted for secreting silver contrary to Law: &
my Lord Sandwich has made a Catch, in Italian, & in Dialogue between her & the Pig: beginning *Caro Mio Porco*—

[88] Kitty Cooke's letter is missing, as is EBB's letter to SC mentioned below.
[89] FB to SC, 2 Mar. 1775 (above).

the Pig answers by a Grunt;—& it Ends by his exclaiming *ah che bel mangiare*! Lord S. has shewn it to my Father, but he says he will not have it set, till she is gone to Italy.[90]

I think, by what I recollect, that I can take no subject which will be so *agreeable* to you as M[r] Bruce—& therefore I will devote to him this Letter. But first, let me tell you that my Father's most excellent Correspondent, M[r] Twining, has been in Town for a month: he is just gone, which we are all sorry for:[91] he has not only as much *humour* as *Learning*, but also as much *Good Nature* as either. We saw him almost every Day, & as he *could* not be much with my Father, whose Engagements are now at their *height*, why he even took the House as he found it, & came to the Little, when he could not get the Great. You are sure he was not less our favourite for that: indeed it reminded us of *him* who is (out of this House) our Greatest Favourite, & who took the same kind of pot luck Company, in those Days when he was not so shy of London as at present.

[*Here follow FB's accounts of Bruce, omitted.*]

M[rs] Strange called here a few Days after [FB's last meeting with Bruce], & said 'Do you know I am now come with a message from the King of Abyssinia—& he sends his Compliments to you all—& he was ravished last ⌈Sunday!⌉ & he has said so much of his Entertainment from the Duet, that there is a M[r] Nesbit,[92] a very musical friend of his, who ⌈he wants⌉ to hear it.'

Next ⌈Sunday⌉ therefore, is appointed for this Lion to make his second appearance in S[t] Martin's Street. ⌈Let me know how you do by Hetty—I beg my Love to her, & as I have not time to write to her, if *you please*, let *her* Read this Letter and take it for an answer.⌉

---

[90] CB had the good taste not to set it.

[91] Twining wrote to CB from Fordham on 26 Mar. (BL).

[92] Described by FB to SC, 14 Apr., as a young Scot, heir to a 'monstrous' fortune, he was probably William Nisbet (1747–1822), eldest son of William Nisbet (d. 1783) of Dirleton and heir of entail of James, 5th Ld. Belhaven (d. 1777). A musician and composer of some repute, he had once been cornet player in the Prince of Wales's Regiment of Dragoon Guards. He m. (1777) Mary, daughter of Ld. Robert Manners. 'By marriage and inheritance Nisbet became one of the wealthiest lairds in Scotland' (Namier; see also R. C. Nesbitt, *Nisbet of that Ilk* (1941), pp. 46–8).

Adieu, my dear sir, I hope to hear of your being soon better, & pray believe me

in all sincerity
your affect^e
F. Burney.^I

[CB's concluding paragraph is omitted.]

Now if you don't thank me some how or other, for getting you this, I'll say you are a very bad man, as haughty as Mr Bruce—as vain as the Bastardini—& as much an Actor as Garrick!

[The Journal for 1775 resumes.]

April 3^d

A few Days since,[93] Mrs Strange Called, with a very civil message from the *King of Abyssinia*, importing, that he had had so much pleasure from the Harpsichord Duet he had heard here, that he could not forbear speaking of it in high terms to a friend of his, Mr Nesbit, a very musical man, whose curiosity he had so much raised | to hear it, that Mr Bruce promised him to endeavour to fix a Day with my Father for his coming hither.

Accordingly, last ⌐Sunday¬[94] we had another music meeting. Our Party consisted of Mr Bruce; M^{rs} & Miss Strange; Mr Nesbit, who is a Young man infinitely *fade*; M^r & Miss Bagnall; Dr. Russel,[95] a phisician who is but lately returned from Aleppo, where he met with Mr Bruce, & Mr Solly,[96] another great Traveller, who was Acquainted with Mr Bruce at Grand Cairo & Alexandria: he had likewise met with my

---

[93] Actually a few weeks earlier (see above, p. 99).

[94] The evening before, 2 April.

[95] Patrick Russell (1727–1805), physician and naturalist; MD. He became physician to the English factory at Aleppo in 1753. A specialist in Eastern diseases, he treated Bruce for malaria there in 1767. Russell returned to Edinburgh in 1772 and settled that year in London. See J. M. Reid, *Traveller Extraordinary: The Life of James Bruce of Kinnaird* (1968), pp. 53, 115.

[96] Probably Samuel Solly (*c.*1724–1807), a merchant in the Italian and Levant trade. FB elaborates in her letter to SC, 14 Apr. (below), that he met CB 'all accidentally' at Bologna, Florence, Rome, and Naples, and that he was '⌐Brother of a merchant in the City¬', viz. Isaac Solly (*c.*1725–1802). Samuel Solly was elected FRS in 1792. See *GM* lxxii^I (1802), 189, lxxvii^I (1807), 92; subscription list to *Hist. Mus.*

Father at almost every great Town in Italy. He is a lively man, full of Chat, & foreign *shrugs* & ⌜Actions.⌝

Dr. Russel is, I believe, very clever: but he is so near sighted, that he *peers* in every body's Face a minute or two before he knows them; & indeed *after* too, for he never casts his Eyes upon the Fire, Ground, or any thing inanimate; for he is so fond of the *Human Face divine*,[97] that he looks at Nothing else. ⌜Sukey⌝ & I could hardly keep our Countenances from observing his perpetual stare from Face to Face.

Mr Bruce was quite *the Thing*; he addressed himself with great gallantry to us all alternately—First going up to my mother, who was talking with Mrs Strange—'Madam, I was looking for *you*, to pay my Respects to you.' Soon after he came to my sister—'Mrs Burney, I hope your Finger is better? Miss Strange told me you had hurt it?'[98] '*Mrs Burney's* Fingers,' Cried Dr. Russel, 'ought to be exempt from Pain.'

'O,' returned Mr Bruce, 'I prayed to Apollo for her.'

'I don't doubt, Sir,' said Hetty, 'your influence with | Apollo!' 'Madam,' answered he, 'I *ought* to have some, for I have made myself a slave to him all my life!' Then turning to me, 'Miss Burney, I hope *you* intend to *begin* the Concert to Night? Yes, you must indeed, for perhaps you may not like so well to play after *these Folks*.' pointing to Mr Burney & my sister.

When he found he could make Nothing of me, he addressed himself to Sukey, & told her that she must not refuse to play for that he had *Dreamt* some very great misfortune would happen to him if she did ⌜not.⌝ After this, he and Mr Nesbit got together & sat Whispering for some Time; & I have since heard, from Miss Strange, that the delicate Mr Nesbit, was Acquainting Mr Bruce with an apointment [*sic*] which a *certain lady of Quality* had made with him for the Evening, at the opera the Night before![99]

---

[97] Cf. Milton, *Paradise Lost*, iii. 44.

[98] '⌜He had heard that she had had a bad Whitlow⌝', i.e., a sore or swelling in a finger (FB to SC, 14 Apr.).

[99] 'He was telling Mr Bruce of a certain lady of quality he had seen at the opera the night before, who was so well pleased with him, that she appointed him to wait on her the next Evening, at 9 o'clock, & therefore, he said he must shorten his visit at your

What a thorough Coxcomb! even his friend M[r] Bruce held his Communication in so ridiculous a light that he told M[rs] Strange of it laughingly.

M[r] Bagnall was far the most elegant man in the Room. Indeed he must be so almost every where. His Daughter is rather improved, & somewhat less reserved & shy than formerly.[1]

M[r] Bruce told us that Dr. Russel was a Performer on the Violin. 'A very fine [one][2] too, added he;—'though we used rather to disgrace his Talents at Aleppo, by making him play English Country Dances.'

The Doctor then mentioned a Concert at which | he had been in Aleppo, I think, which lasted 3 Days, & which was frequent upon occasion of marriages.

'Three Days!' exclaimed M[r] Bruce. 'Why matrimony is more formidable *there* than *here*!'

The Duet—M[r] Burney's & my sister's playing, were much Admired, & the Evening passed very agreeably.[3]

┌April

As I was Walking out lately, just before me who should I see but our old friend Mrs. Pringle.┐ I felt as much ashamed, from having so long dropt her Acquaintance, as if I had done her an injury; I put my Handkerchief up to my mouth, & Walked quietly on: she saw me—looked earnestly, & presently recollected me—'Miss Burney?—God bless me! I hardly knew you! What an Age since I have seen you!' I asked after her Health & her Family. She said, in her hearty manner, shaking Hands with me, 'well, I am vastly glad to see you! & how does your sister [EBB] do? Has she any Family?—well, she was as fine a Girl as ever I saw—& I was like a fond

House' (FB to SC, 14 Apr.). The opera performed on Saturday evening, 1 Apr., was Sacchini's *Motezuma* (*LS 4* iii. 1881).

   [1] 'She is Tall & well made, with a fair complection; but otherwise is rather plain ┌than not,┐ having very bad Features. She is sensible, & reserved; yet by no means seems worthy of such a Father as she has to boast of, for her manners are unformed, & rather uncoothe' (FB to SC, 14 Apr.).

   [2] Inserted by FBA.

   [3] FBA gives an account of this evening in *Mem.* (i. 319–29), and at this point adds a few humorous anecdotes told by Bruce at supper.

Parent, for I thought she could not do well in the World. And how is little Charlotte?'

'O, she is *great* Charlotte now, cried I.

'Well do pray come & see me & bring Charlotte—I shall be vastly *glad* to see you, I assure you. ⌐I Live in Broad Street, just by.' She gave me a ¦ card, & then we took leave.¬ I was ⌐really very¬ glad to see her, & quite [h]appy that she made me no reproaches. I should like [ex]tremely to renew my Acquaintance with her, as Mr. Seton is now out of the question, except from Mr Crisp's dislike; but I fear it will be impossible, as my mother has [q]uite an Aversion to her.[4]

⌐The Day after this *rencontre*, I was going to Golden Square [xxxxx *3 lines*] & saw Mrs Pringle at her own Door—[xxxxx *3 words*] she saw me, & called to me—[xxxxx *2 lines*] I knew I could not repeat my visit, however, I accepted her invitation, & accompanied her into her Drawing Room.¬ She was very friendly & cordial, & sensibly avoided all such Conversation as led to Family affairs. She never once mentioned Mr Seton; her son the Captain she said was at Newfoundland, & Andrew still at the East Indies.

Captain Debbieg she told me was promoted to be major.[5]

She told me a Circumstance concerning Mr Crawford, who she said was still *single* & in London, that rather surprised me: I knew that he *admired* Hetty; but she says that he made *her* the Confidante of his passion, entreating her leave to see Hetty at her House, till he could arrange his affairs so as to offer himself to her. But, continued she, I would not hear of it—I always ¦ hated the Character of a *match maker* beyond all others, & besides, I told him it would never do, for that your Family was too large for the Daughters to have much Fortune, & that he was not in a style to marry without. & so I assured him he should never, with *my* knowledge or Contrivance, see your sister more at my House. So when he found he failed with me, he made his sister Visit You, but her Visit was never returned,—& then he offered Tickets for a Concert—but they were not accepted; now how glad was I to find your sister

---

[4] Both SC and EAB seem to have suspected Mrs Pringle of trying to engineer the ill-fated match between EBB and Alexander Seton. See *EJL* i.

[5] This occurred in 1772 (see *EJL* i. 199 n. 43).

behaved with so much prudence, & that *I* had put off the affair in the same manner! for I was sure she could have no Objection to Visiting Miss Crawford upon *her own* Account, only to avoid her Brother.[6]

She enquired very particularly after all our Family,—spoke warmly of the great regard she had had for us;—traced our Acquaintance to its beginning—but stopt short of proceeding to its Conclusion.

'*You*,' said she, 'was a particular favourite with me before ever I saw you; for I had heard of you from Mrs Sheele whose House you were at, when a Child when you lost your mother;—& she told me that of the Hundred Children she had had the Care of, she never saw such affliction in one before—that you would take no Comfort—& was almost killed with Crying.

She repeatedly invited me to Visit her, & to bring Charlotte. ¦

23   [St Martin's Street, 14 April 1775]

To Samuel Crisp

ALS (Barrett), 14 April 1775
2 double sheets 4to, 8 pp., *pmk* 14 AP wafer
Addressed: Samuel Crisp Esqr, | at Mrs Hamilton's | Chesington, near | Kingston upon Thames | Surrey
Annotated (by FBA): ✳ 2^d Mr Bruce Mr Nesbit—Admiral Burney!—Miss Davis. Mr. Bruce &c N° 7 N° 31 N° 5. 24 [*sic*] ap. 75
FBA has retraced five pages of the letter, due to fading of the ink. Omitted here is the account of Bruce's latest visit, already given in the Journal.

My dear Daddy
I have complied with your commands, without *prudery* I do assure you, though by no means without real reluctance—I

[6] But neither EBB nor FB had any great desire to visit Miss Crawford (or Craufurd). See *EJL* i. 72.

am very sorry your sister[7] is to have the perusal of so very trifling & insignificant a Pacquet, but as it is now past, I will not trouble you with *speechyfying* [*sic*].

My last Letter was so *enormous*, that I am pretty sure I need not apologise for not being more speedy in sending another. Indeed it is utterly impossible for me to send such overgrown Epistles *very* frequently;—but I hope you Read it at your leisure.

You enquire so much after Jem that I am tempted to send you one of his Letters to me, in which he gives a good & satisfactory account of his Captain[8] & fellow Lieutenant. He Corresponds with me with tolerable regularity; where he at present is I am not certain, but I fancy still at Portsmouth. It is true that there have been Removals among the officers of his ship, in so much that only the 1st Lieutenant remains the same as when Jem went on Board. The Cerberus is ordered to carry the three General officers, viz General Burgoigne,[9] Genl Cleveland[10] & another, to America,—but we have no certain information at present when they will sail. Jem in his Last Letter tells me that he is quite in the Dark about it himself. There is much talk of [an in]tended South Sea Expedition; Now You must [know] there is nothing that Jem so earnestly desires | as to be of the Party, & my Father has made great Interest at the Admiralty to procure him that pleasure: & as it is not to be undertaken till Capt. Cooke's return, it is just possible that Jem may be returned in Time from America.

---

[7] Mrs Gast. SC had written to FB, 27 Mar. (Barrett): 'My Sister has again wrote about the [Teignmouth] Journal & does not care to be refus'd; so do, prythee send it her.'

[8] James Chads (d. 1781), Capt., RN, 1766. The original captain had been Hugh Dalrymple (d. 1784), Capt., RN, 1763. The 1st Lt. was William Bristow (d. 1803). See Manwaring, pp. 52–4; *GM* li (1781), 95; ship's logs of the *Cerberus*, PRO (Kew); D. B. Smith, *The Commissioned Sea Officers of the Royal Navy* (1954), i. 108, 156, 227.

[9] John Burgoyne (1723–92); Maj.-Gen., 1772; Lt.-Gen., 1777; 'Gentleman Johnny', mainly remembered for his defeat at Saratoga in 1777.

[10] FB presumably means Samuel Cleaveland (*c.*1716–94), at this time Lt.-Col. in the Royal Artillery but with the temporary rank of Brig.-Gen. Cleaveland did not go on the *Cerberus*, however. The other officers were William Howe (1729–1814), Maj.-Gen., 1772; Gen., 1793; afterwards 5th Visc. Howe; and Henry Clinton (1730–95), Maj.-Gen., 1772; Gen., 1793; KB, 1777. The *Cerberus* sailed on 21 Apr. See Namier; *GM* lxiv[2] (1794), 864; *The Private Papers of John, Earl of Sandwich*, ed. G. R. Barnes and J. H. Owen (1932–8), i. 168.

This intended Expedition is to be *the Last*: they are to carry Omai back. & to give him a *month for liking*, at the End of which, if he does not again relish his Old Home, or finds himself not well treated, he is to have it in his power to Return hither again.

We made a visit yesterday morning to Miss Davies. She told us her Law Suit was not yet decided; for the managers did every thing in their power to delay & procrastinate. Her mother, Miss Dumpty her sister, (for so Lady Edgecumbe[11] calls her, because she is short, crooked & *squat*) & herself Drank Tea with us while Mr Twining was in Town, & we invited him to meet them. As he never heard her sing, we were in hopes of being able to procure him that gratification ⌐which he very much wished for.⌐ My Father made an attack, by saying he wished she would try the power of music upon his Rheumatism, which had withstood every thing hitherto: but the *medicinal* power of a song from her he dared believe would prove very ˡ efficacious. Miss Davies looked down, & was silent for a minute—upon which my Father repeated his request.—She then, in a hesitating voice, said—'I should be very ready to—but you know, Sir, how I am situated.' Nobody spoke: every body looked disappointed: & she proceeded to explain herself by saying that her *articles* were so strict that she dared not infringe them, but that if my Father & *us females* would give her our *companies* at her House, she would try to tire us; for she supposed that she might at least be allowed to *practice* a little at Home.

Poor Mr Twining looked very blank. I was sorry she did not include him in the Invitation ⌐though I really believe that had he been away, she would not have scrupled to have sang meerly to our own Family.⌐ Mr Twining was, however, much pleased with her, & agreed that she was a sensible, well bred, & engaging Girl. She ⌐has a very good House in Pall Mall, opposite to Carlton House[12] where she lives⌐ with great

---

[11] Emma Gilbert (1729–1807), daughter of John Gilbert, Archbishop of York; m. (1761) George Edgcumbe (1721–95), 3rd B. Edgcumbe of Mount Edgcumbe, later E. of Mount Edgcumbe. She was an accomplished amateur musician and hostess of musical evening parties. See below, p. 171 and *seq.*

[12] Cecilia Davies's house was at No. 1 St Alban's St., Pall Mall (Highfill). Carlton House had been the residence of the Princess Dowager of Wales (d. 1772) and

reputation of Honour. ⸢She complained of being very ill used & much abused in the news papers. She has, unfortunately, some *Scribbling Enemies*[13] who perpetually harass her with despite.⸣ |

[*The account of Bruce's visit, 3¾ MS pages, is here omitted.*]

⸢Since the writing of this, we have been to Drink Tea with the Simmons—where I was extremely sorry to hear of the Illness of your sister—I am doubtful whether to send this scrawl but think at any rate I will not add to it further than by my best wishes, & [beg] you to believe me to all

> Your most affectionate & obliged
> Frances Burney |

If—my dear Daddy—you should be prevented by ill health or ill spirits from writing to me & if it should happen that you should nevertheless desire to hear from me let Kitty acquaint me how things are.

I beg my love to her & to Mrs. Hamilton.⸣

[*The Journal for 1775 continues with the first leaf of a letter from SC, inserted by FB, with her annotations:* From Mʳ Crisp to Miss Frances Burney. 1775 Nº 6.
The rest of the letter is missing.]

Chesington Ap. 18.

Dear Fannikin.

Tho' Fingers are Crippley & left Arm lame I shall not spare them, to tell You, You are at last (after a hard fight with You) a tolerable (not *very tolerable* Observe) good Girl—you make such a Rout about my sisters seeing what You are pleas'd to call, *your trifling stuff, &c, &c, &c* that I could beat You—I thought You had more Taste—but no—'tis not want of Taste; 'tis a Way Young Girls have got by Habit, & as it were mechanically, of making *mille façons* without a shadow of Reason—you cannot but know, *that trifling, that negligence, even*

---

became the residence of George, Prince of Wales (afterwards George IV) in 1783 (Wheatley).
[13] Not identified. Presumably they were hack writers employed by the Opera's managers or by a cabal of rival singers.

incorrectness now & then, in familiar Epistolary writing, is the very soul of Genius & Ease & that if your letters were to be fine labour'd Compositions, that smelt of the *Lamp*; I had as lieve they ⌐smelt of Air⌐—So, no more of that, Fany [*sic*], & thou lov'st me—Dash Away, whatever comes uppermost; & believe me, You'll succeed better, than by leaning on your Elbows, & studying what to say—One thing more, & I have done—rest assur'd that the unconnected rattle You tax Yourself with, is exactly the same sort of thing, as that *Nonsense*, which we are told, *is Eloquence in Love*—Now for Jem's letter, which I am much pleas'd with—what I am so much pleas'd with above the rest, is to Observe that Caution & ⏐ Guardedness in his ⌐actions⌐ & Accounts, that indicate a maturity of Judgment, that is more frequently to be Wish'd than found in a Warm, Wild, Buck of his time of Life & Profession—this uncommon & Valuable Quality at so early a Period promises, & seems almost to insure future success—

I am so far from being tir'd with your long letters as You call them, that I only wish them a quire apiece; & all that stuff about reading them at my leisure, & the impossibility of getting thro' them at once, &c &c &c, is of a piece with the ringing of the Bellman,—being come to the bottom of your Page, & the rest of those usual sprightly Conclusions which if You'll take my Opinion, are rather too much hackneyd for my Fanny's Use—You Young Devil You, You know in your Conscience I devour greedily your Journalizing letters, & You once promis'd they would be *Weekly* Journals; tho' now you fight off, both in your Declarations & your Practice—I desire You would reform both—take my word for't, Miss Davis will lose her Law suit—I am glad to find the Abyssinian King mends upon your hands—pray are not the Stranges going to live abroad?—⌐I think I saw an advertisement of Mr Strange to that purpose⌐[14]—Write me more about y^r Daddy—will he come here at Whitsuntide?—⌐[xxxxx *3 lines*]

You must know, I suspect, I am some how out of favour with your mama, that she is *up* at something—tho' I cannot guess what—not the least hint of this, for your life.⌐[15]

---

[14] See below, p. 111.
[15] See below, p. 109.

[St Martin's Street]
24 April [1775]

To Samuel Crisp

ALS (Barrett), 24 April 1775
2 double sheets 4to, 8 pp., *pmk* 24 AP seal
Addressed: Sam¹ Crisp Esqr, | at Mrs Hamilton's, | Chesington near | Kingston upon Thames | Surrey.
Annotated (by FBA): ✻ *3^d Mr. Bruce. Mr. Hutton. Dr. King. Stranges* N° 8 Monday 24 Ap. 1775 N° 32. N° 6.

April. 24

Dear Daddy
⌐I do faithfully assure you that as to your suspicions of my mother's being displeased, I believe them to be totally Groundless. At least as far as appearance goes, there is no reason for thinking she is. She has never dropt a Word hinting that way that I have either heard, or heard *of*. As to my Correspondence with you, I pretend not to suppose it is *agreeable* to her, but it is now of too Long a Date to occasion any offence —though to this Day, I never receive a Letter from *Mrs. Rishton* which does not cause displeasure, frowning & a thousand Questions—as many as if the *last* Letter was always the *First*, & a *new thing*.

If any thing should arise that way, you are never to think differently, I will honestly tell you.⌐[16]

So you prohibit speechifying?—very well, sir, I have done!—to say the truth, I am exactly of the same mind, as to all Letters which I *receive*—but as to those I *write*—& to *you*—I was only afraid of your thinking me *too free* & *easy*, & therefore made a few apologies, in order to save my credit. Nevertheless, I must frankly own I am far from being satisfied

---

[16] This censored passage shows EAB's deep insecurity about her stepdaughters and continuing resentment of her daughter MAR. By this time she had largely alienated the Burney children because of her domineering and abusive behaviour, born in the main of jealousy over CB. They in turn had united in a kind of cabal against her, to which SC was increasingly a party. MAR had deeply offended her mother by her elopement with Martin Rishton. See *EJL* i.

in regard to showing my *Tingmothiad* to y^r sisters. However, I won't now renew that exhausted Theme.

I thought you would like Jem's Letter—but pray, sir, does it follow that you must *keep* it? If you return it in your next, I will reward you with the sight of a short, but characteristic Letter I have had from Mr Hutton lately.[17] That worthy, good, ⌜half mad⌝ man calls here pretty often. There is something in his flightiness which speaks so much Goodness of Heart, & so much ignorance,—or *contempt*, (I know not which) of the World, that his Conversation is quite singular.

Jem left England last Tuesday.[18] Added to the ship's Company were 3 Generals, 3 aid de Camps, 2 Gentlemen passengers, & 6 or 7 servants. The Government allows Capt. Chad £400 to maintain them. Their stay is quite uncertain. Jem prays for his return in Time to go to the South Seas. He says that if they have fine Weather, they shall have a Jovial Voyage —but if *bad*—God help them, & all these useless Hands! I expect they will fling the Land officers over Board if there should be a storm.

As to his Majesty of Abyssinia, I have only had the Honour of seeing him for 2 or 3 minutes since my last Letter, which was on occasion of ⌜Carrying⌝ Miss Bell Strange ⌜Home⌝ after she had been with my mother & me to the School[19] Ball in Queen Square. He was extremely *out of sorts*, because there was some Company in the Room (Dr. Smith & a lady)[20] who

[17] The letter is missing.

[18] Actually, the *Cerberus* left Portsmouth on Friday, 21 Apr. Gen. Burgoyne's aide was Capt. Henry Gardner (d. 1792), later Lt.-Col., an officer in Burgoyne's 16th (or Queen's) Regiment of (Light) Dragoons. One of the passengers was Robert Woolf, an agent on business with the Royal Marines, and among the servants was Gen. Clinton's French valet. The other aides, passengers, and servants have not been identified. The Lords of the Admiralty approved the £400 to Chads at their meeting of 11 Mar. See *A Journal Kept in Canada ... by Lieut. James M. Hadden*, ed. H. Rogers (Albany, 1884), p. 242 and n.; W. B. Willcox, *Portrait of a General: Sir Henry Clinton in the War of Independence* (New York, 1964), p. 36; *GM* lxii^2 (1792), 866; Admiralty Orders and Instructions, ADM 2/99 p. 327, PRO (Kew); Admiralty Minutes, ADM 3/81, s.v. 11 Mar., 7 Apr. 1775, PRO (Kew).

[19] Presumably Mrs Sheeles's school (see *EJL* i. 147 n. 17) or the more prestigious school of Mrs Stevenson, which came to be known as 'The Ladies' Eton' (see G. H. Hamilton, *Queen Square: Its Neighbourhood and Its Institutions* (1926), pp. 34–5).

[20] Perhaps Mary Holyland, only child and heiress of Thomas Holyland of Bromley, Kent, whom Dr Smyth married this year. Mrs Smyth died in 1806 (*GM* lxxvi^1 (1806), 586).

did not please him—how Dr. Smith offended him I know not, but as to *the lady*, Miss Strange told me, she had *too much Tongue*, & had fatigued his Majesty.

Last Night Andrew Strange[21] Drank Tea here. He is the 2ᵈ son, & now at Oxford—he is a very pretty young man:—he told us that he had been in the morning with a Party who had the Honour of seeing Mʳ Bruce's Collection of curiosities. He spoke of them very highly, particularly of the Drawings, which he ⸢says⸣ are delightful. He said it was to be the last morning of Exhibiting them, as he only wishes them to be sufficiently seen to make their Fame induce the Government to be at the Expense of publication. He sends them all to Day privately to ᐟDr. Hunter's[22] Museum: 'but, said Andrew, he intends the World should think they are gone to Scotland, that he may not be solicited to shew them any more.'

He added, that the morning had proved very agreeable not only because ⸢his⸣ Collection was extremely curious, but also, he said, 'Because his Majesty was less Relentless than usual.'

I am very sorry to tell you that the Advertisement you have seen about the Stranges is true; the whole Family are going Abroad—they say for 2 years, but I fear for Life. ⸢We shall miss them most grievously, who are the most comfortable & agreeable neighbours we ever had.⸣ I shall extremely regret *all* of them, though most particularly *Mʳˢ Strange*, who has more *goodness* & *wit* than I ever besides saw *united* in one Woman. ⸢Her Daughter [Mary Bruce Strange] is a worthy, good Girl, &⸣ all the Family merit regard & esteem.

⸢Mr. Strange [xxxxx *1½ lines*] his Furniture, &c will be sold. He then goes on a visit to Scotland, to Mr. Bruce, & after that, they all go to Paris.⸣ The reason of his quitting England is a *disgust* he has taken at being excluded from being a

---

[21] Thomas Andrew Lumisden Strange (1756–1841). He had matriculated at Christ Church, Oxford, in 1774. He later became a distinguished jurist, serving as Chief Justice of Nova Scotia (1789–97) and Chief Justice of Madras (1800–17). Knighted in 1798, he devoted his later years to an authoritative treatise on Hindu law, published in 1825.

[22] John Hunter (1728–93), anatomist and surgeon; brother of the Stranges' close friend Dr William Hunter. He kept a museum of anatomy and pathology in his house in Jermyn St., to which travellers often sent rarities. Bruce failed in his scheme to induce the government to publish his drawings. He eventually took his collection of relics, manuscripts, and drawings back with him to Scotland.

member of the Royal academy. You know his principles, & therefore will not wonder either at the Ex[c]lusion or the Disgust.[23]

My Father's History goes on very slowly indeed at present. The Town is very full. He teaches from 9 to 9 almost every Day, & has scarce Time to write a page a week. Nobody besides himself could write a word so circumstanced. His Health & Hand are, I hope, *rather* better—however, very little, for never, surely, was an attack more obstinate. He [*sic*]

I have been just interrupted by a visit from Dr. King—which as it proved short, & very ridiculous, I cannot forbear relating.

I think you know him—if you do, you must remember how prosing, affected, & *very fine* he is. But this morning he took it in his humour to be quite flighty. Mama was out—Sue & I at home. After the first Common Speeches, He Enquired of me for *his snuff*. (You must know he a long Time since gave me some snuff in charge for him, as he likes a *pinch* now & then, though he does not regularly take it. This snuff I have always unfortunately mislaid or lost, & been frequently upbraided, I had therefore promised to put it in a box for him—but after he went, I had thought no more of it—)

Shamming a little confusion, I confessed I knew not where it was. He reproached me with great gravity, said he had depended upon *me*, but found he had *mistaken his man*—but desired me to take no more trouble about it. 'You come so seldom, cried I, that it is too much for me to remember from Time to Time.'

'What!' cried he, 'you forget me then?'

---

[23] Strange had fought for Bonnie Prince Charles in the Rising of 1745, but his Jacobite principles were largely borrowed from the future Mrs Strange, who had made his support of Charles a condition of their courtship. After the Rebellion Mrs Strange's ardent Jacobitism apparently continued to be a hindrance to his career, and he felt that the Royal Academy's exclusion of all engravers was aimed at himself. (Matters were not helped by his brother-in-law, Andrew Lumisden, having been secretary to the Old Pretender at Rome.) Before moving his family to Paris he aired his grievances by publishing (on 1 June) *An Inquiry into the Rise and Establishment of the Royal Academy of Arts*. Later this year the Stranges moved to the rue d'Enfer in Paris, where they were to remain for 5 years. See below; Dennistoun, ii. 175–80; *Daily Adv.*, 1 June.

God forbid I should *not*, thought I! but only *said* 'I forget your *snuff*, sir.'

'Very well.' answered he, solemnly. I find I was mistaken! I had pitched upon *you*! There is my good friend Mrs Burney would most chearfully have undertaken the charge—There is ⌜Sukey⌝ *wished* to have had it—& Bessy almost Quarrelled with me about it—but I picked *you* out of the Herd, ˡ as the one whom I expected most from—'

'O! I have just recollected, exclaimed I, the reason why I did not Buy ⌜the⌝ Box—you must know I put it off in order to chuse it at the Fiera in Mascherata²⁴ to Night—I was determined it should be elegant—& I thought you would like it the better for the place it came from.'

'No, No,' said he, 'don't take any more trouble about it.'

Then starting up, he ⌜said⌝ he could stay no longer, but that he would not take any further notice of *me*! He then went up to ⌜Sukey⌝, & casting a look of reproach at me, said—'Come— I'll shake Hands with ⌜Sukey⌝—'

I bore this *great stroke* with all imaginable patience, though I believe he expected I should have wept at least—& I suffered him very quietly to go to the Door—which he had no sooner reached, than—unable, I suppose, to act with so much cruelty—he turned hastily back, & hurrying up to me, took my Hand, patted my Cheek, & genteely called me a *little Hussey*,—

I again wished him Good Morning. He then renewed his reproaches—& said if *any other person* had ⌜said⌝ him so ill, he should not have minded it—but—cried he, in a raised voice, & suddenly flinging himself into a Theatrical attitude—

But *There*—where I had Treasured up my Heart! *There*— where—O fye! fye! fye!—

He then opened the Door—& half shutting it again, repeated in an *Emphatic Manner*

Excellent wretch!—perdition catch my soul—²⁵ ˡ

---

²⁴ 'At the King's Theatre in the Hay-market, This Day will be a grand FIERA In MASCHERATA. (Being the Last Masquerade at the King's Theatre this Season.) ... The Doors to be opened at Ten ... Tickets, at One Guinea and a Half each' (*Public Advertiser*, 24 Apr.).

²⁵ Cf. *Othello*, III. iii. 90.

He did not wait to finish his Rhapsody—but ⌐left¬ the House suddenly, on seeing John, the man, coming into the Parlour.

⌐Let me, however, beg you never to Laugh or speak about this man to my mother, because he is a very great favourite with her.

As to Barsanti she is very ill, Susy & I have called upon her several Times. She Lives very near us, & she is a very good Girl, & worth our regard & attention which we can pay her no other way, & she is always most ardently rejoiced to see us. She is to do Clarinda in the Suspicious Husband[26] for the first Time at her Benefit, if she is well enough. Her old complaint in her Head is returned with great fury.[27] Sir John Pringle[28] & Mr. Hunter both visit her, out of regard to her mother, their Country woman. I earnestly hope she will be soon better. She is frightened to Death lest she should not be able to act on the 5th of May, which is her Night.[29] She frequently enquires after you, & is most pleased when I tell her how often we write about her. We have the pleasure of finding her almost always quite alone. Her poor Father is confin'd now to one Room, being superannuated, though I really believe he has still more Brains left than ever his fair Wife had in her Life. Barsanti's engagements that my Father made for her with Mr. Colman will finish with this season. They were for 3 years, 3 gns. the first season a week—4 the next, & 5 the present. She hopes to have then her salary raised.¬[30]

I think I never told you that Mr Hutton—curious after every thing & body,—had a most anxious desire to be Introduced to Mr Bruce—whose *Enterprise* he regards with a kind of veneration, & *reveres* the man who has made Travels so extraordinary & dangerous.—Accordingly he begged my

[26] By Benjamin Hoadly (1706–57), first performed in 1747.

[27] Laetitia Hawkins remarked that some years after her début Barsanti fell into 'a sad continuity of ill health' and that 'ill advised sea-bathing subjected her to excruciating pains in the head' (cited in Highfill).

[28] Sir John Pringle (1707–82), 3rd Bt.; prominent physician and President of the Royal Society.

[29] She was not well enough to appear, and, in addition, her father died. But the benefit was performed, with Mrs Mary Bulkley playing in her stead (*LS 4* iii. 1890; below, p. 135).

[30] See below, p. 162.

Father to speak of him to Mr Bruce, ⌜& to gain his permission for him to visit him.⌝ My Father, who loves the Character of this original man, complied with his request, & spoke of him in Terms so advantageous to the Abyssinian King, that he graciously condescended to admit him. He was very civil also to him, which I think is somewhat to his Honour, considering that Mr Hutton's appearance is by no means in his favour, as he wears an old Wig, & shabby Cloaths. But he is a good Being, & I think you would all together, oddities & all, like him.

⌜As to the [xxxxx *1 word*] affair, I have promised my sister to leave that subject to her.

We have seen—but not *heard* the Bastardini twice since I told you of her last. She is extremely *charmée* [xxxxx *2 words*] & all that, whenever ⟨we meet,⟩ but says nothing now of singing till after the Pantheon is ⟨closed,⟩ & *then* she will ⟨honour⟩ Her *promise.*⌝

Adieu—my dearest sir—I will write again next Monday, according to your desire—provided I hear of—or from you—between this & then. I do assure you I could not wade through so much writing were it not for the Reward of seeing your Hand in return. ⌐

⌜All sorts of love & Compliments attend you, pray don't you intend to write to my Father?⌝

My love & comp^ts & so forth. & I am ever

     My dear Daddy

       Your obliged & affectionate

          F. Burney.

[*The Journal for 1775 continues.*]

              May 8th

This month is Called a *tender* one—It has proved so *to* me— —but not *in* me—I have not breathed one sigh,—felt one sensation,—or uttered one folly the more for the softness of the season.—However—I have met with a youth whose Heart, if he is to be Credited, has been less guarded—indeed it has yielded itself so suddenly, that had it been in any other month—I should not have known how to have accounted for so easy a Conquest.

The First Day of this month I Drank Tea & spent the Evening at Mr Burney's, at the request of my sister, to meet a very stupid Family, which she told me it would be Charity to herself to give my Time to.

This Family consisted of M^rs O'Connor, & her Daughter, by a first marriage, Miss Dickenson, who, poor Creature, has the misfortune to be both Deaf & Dumb. They are very old acquaintances of my Grandmother Burney, to oblige whom my sister Invited them. My Grandmother & 2 aunts therefore were of the Party:—as was, also, Mr Barlow, a young man who has Boarded with M^rs O'Connor for about 2 years.[31]

Mr Barlow is rather short but handsome, he is a very well ˹behaved, civil,˺ good tempered & sensible young man. ˹He bears an excellent˺ ˡ character, both for Disposition & morals. He has Read more than he has Conversed, & seems to know but little of the World; his Language is stiff & uncommon, he has a great desire to please, but no elegance of manners; niether, though he may be very worthy, is he at all agreeable.

Unfortunately, however, he happened to be prodigiously Civil to me, & though I have met with much more gallantry occasionally, yet I could not but observe a *seriousness* of attention much more expressive than Complimenting.

As my sister knew not well how to *wile away the Time*, I proposed, after supper, a round of Cross Questions. This was agreed to. Mr Barlow, who sat next to me, took near half an Hour to settle upon what he should ask me,—& at last his question was—'what I thought most necessary in Love?' I answered. *Constancy*. I hope, for his own sake, he will not remember this answer long, though he readily subscribed to it at the Time.

The Coach came for me about Eleven. I rose to go. He earnestly entreated me to stay only 2 minutes. I did not, however, think such compliance at all requisite, & therefore ˡ only offered to set my Grandmother down in my way. The

---

[31] Thomas Barlow was 24 years of age, in 'Easy' circumstances, and living with Mrs O'Connor in Hoxton (see below). Probably of a merchant family, he may have been the Thomas Barlow who later had 3 children christened in St Leonard Shoreditch (in 1785, 1787, and 1790; see IGI), but he has otherwise not been further traced. Mrs O'Connor and Miss Dickenson have also eluded further identification.

Party then broke up. M^{rs} O'Connor began an urgent Invitation to all present to return the visit the next Week. Mr Barlow, who followed me, repeated it very pressingly, to *me*, hoping I would make one. I promised that I would.

When we had all taken leave of our Host & Hostess,—my Grandmother, according to custom, gave me a kiss & her blessing. I would fain have eluded my aunts, as Nothing can be so disagreeable as kissing before young men; however, they chose it should go round; & after them, M^{rs} O'Connor also saluted me, as did her Daughter, desiring to be better Acquainted with me. This disagreeable Ceremony over, Mr Barlow, came up to me, & making an apology which, not suspecting his intention, I did not understand,—he gave me a most ardent salute! I have seldom been more surprised. I had no idea of his taking such a freedom. However, I have told my friends that for the future I will not chuse to lead, or have led, so contagious an Example.

He came down stairs with us, & waited at the Door, I believe, till the Coach was out of sight.

Four Days after this meeting [5 May], my mother & ⎮ Mrs Young happened to be in the Parlour, when I received a Letter which from the strong resemblance of the Hand writing to that of Mr Crisp, I immediately opened & thought came from Chesington. But what was my surprise, to see Madam, at the beginning, & at the Conclusion

your sincere Admirer &

very humble serv^t Thos Barlow

I Read it 3 or 4 Times before I could credit my Eyes. An Acquaintance so short, & a procedure so hasty astonished me. It is a most tender Epistle & contains a passionate Declaration of Attachment, hinting at hopes of a *return*, & so forth.

[*The original ALS, single sheet 4to, 2 pp., is in the Barrett Collection. FB omitted it from her journal as too* 'high flown' *(below, p. 139). The present editor includes it here for its obvious interest.*]

Mad^m

Uninterrupted happiness we are told is of a short duration, & is quickly succeeded by Anxiety, which moral Axiom I really experienc'd on the Conclusion of May day at Mr Charles Burney's, as the singular Pleasure of your Company

was so soon Eclips'd by the rapidity of ever-flying Time; but the felicity, tho' short, was too great to keep within the limits of one Breast, I must therefore intreat your Pardon for the Liberty I take, in attempting to reiterate the satisfaction I then felt, & paying a Tythe of Justice to the amiable Lady from whom it proceeded, permit me then Mad^m, with the greatest sincerity, to assure you, that the feelings of that Evening were the most refined I ever enjoy'd, & discovered such a latent Spring of Happiness from the Company of the Fair, which I had positively before then been a Stranger to; I had 'til then thought, all Ladys might be flattered, but I now experience the contrary, & am assur'd, Language cannot possibly depict the soft Emotions of a mind captivated by so much merit; & have now a Contest between^l my ardorous Pen, stimulated by so pleasing & so just a subject on the one side, & a dread of being accused of Adulation on the other; however, endeavouring at Justice, & taking Truth (in her plainest Attire) for my Guide, I will venture to declare, that the Affability, Sweetness, & Sensibility, which shone in your every Action, lead me irresistably to Love & Admire the mistress of them & I shoud account it the road to the highest Felicity, if my *sincerity* might in any degree meet your Appro-bation; as I am persu[a]ded *that is the first Principle* which can be offer'd as a foundation for the least hope of a Ladys regard; & I must beg leave to observe, I greatly admire that Quality which yourself so justly declar'd, was most necessary in Love, I mean CONSTANCY, from which I woud presume to infer, that we are naturally led from Admiration, to Imitation & Practice: All which in being permitted to declare to you— woud constitute my particular happiness, as far as Expression coud be prevail'd on to figure the Ideas of the mind; mean while I woud particularly Request, you woud condescend to favour me with a Line, in which I hope to hear you are well, & that you will honour us with your Company with good Mrs Burney & Family some day next week, which that Lady is to fix; in which request I trust we shall not be deny'd, as 'twill not be possible to admit separating so particularly desirable a part of the Company and as I am persuaded we are honoured with your Assent to the Engagement: I am Dr Miss Fanny's
most sincere Admirer & very hble Servt
Thos Barlow.

I took not a moment to deliberate.—I felt that my Heart was totally insensible—& felt that I could never Consent to unite myself to a man who I did not *very* highly value.

However, as I do not consider myself as an independant member of society, & as I knew I could depend upon my Father's kindness, I thought it incumbent upon me to act with his Concurrence. I therefore, at Night, before I sent an answer, shewed him the Letter. He asked me a great many Questions—I assured him that forming a Connection without attachment—(& that I was totally indifferent to the Youth in Question) was what I could never think of. My Father was all indulgence & goodness; he at first proposed that I should write him [|] Word that our acquaintance had been too short to authorise so high an opinion as he expressed for me; but I objected to that, as seeming to infer that a *longer* acquaintance might be Acceptable. He therefore concluded upon the whole, that I should send no answer at all.

I was not very easy at this determination, as it seemed to treat Mr Barlow with a degree of Contempt, which his partiality to me by no means merited from myself; & ⌐as¬ I apprehended it to be possible for him to put, perhaps, *another* & more favourable interpretation upon my silence. I shewed Hetty the Letter next Day. She most vehemently took the young man's part: urged me to think differently, & above all advised me to certainly Write an answer, & to be of their party, according to my promise, when they went to M^{rs} O Connor's.

I told her I would speak to my Father again in regard to writing an Answer, which I wished much to do, but could not now without his consent: but as to the Party, I could not make one, as it would be a kind of tacit approbation & assent of his further attentions.

I went afterwards to call on my Grandmother; my sister followed me, & directly told her & my aunts of the affair. They all of them became most zealous Advocates for Mr Barlow; they [|] spoke most highly of the Character they had heard of him, & my aunt Anne humourously bid me beware of her & Beckey's fate!

I assured them I was not intimidated, & that I had rather a thousand Times Die an old maid than be married, except from affection.

When I came Home, I wrote the following Answer which I proposed sending, with my Father's leave.

Miss Burney presents her Compliments to Mr Barlow; she is much obliged for, though greatly surprised at the good opinion with which on so short an Acquaintance he is pleased to Honour her; she wishes Mr Barlow all happiness, but must beg leave to recommend to him to Transfer to some person better known to him a partiality which she so little merits.

My Father, however, did not approve of my Writing. I could not imagine why, but have since heard from my sister that he was unwilling I should give a No without some further knowledge of the young man.

Further knowledge will little avail. In Connections of this sort, the *Heart* ought to be heard. |

My sister was not contented with giving her own advice; she Wrote about the affair to Mr Crisp, representing in the strongest light the utility of my listening to Mr Barlow. He has written me such a Letter! God knows how I shall have Courage to answer it. Every body is against me but my beloved Father. ⌈My mother, indeed, knows nothing of the matter ⟨& yet⟩ has had a downright Quarrel with me upon the subject & though Hetty was at first very kind, she has at last also Quarrelled with me. My 2 aunts will hardly speak to me—Mr. Crisp is in a *rage*.⌉

They all of them are kindly interested in my welfare; but they know not so well as myself what may make me happy or miserable. To unite myself for Life to a man who is not *infinitely* dear to me, is what I can never, never Consent to. Unless, indeed, I was strongly urged by my Father. I thank God most gratefully he has not interfered.

They tell me they do not desire me to *marry*, but not to give up the *power* of it, without seeing more of the proposer: but this reasoning I cannot give into.—it is foreign to all my Notions: how can I see more of Mr Barlow without encourageing him to believe I am willing to think of him? |

[*FB inserts SC's ALS, double sheet 4to, 4 pp., dated 8 May. EBB's letter, which he quotes in part, is otherwise missing.*]

Chesington May 8.

So much of the future Good or Ill of your Life seems now depending, Fanny, that I cannot dispense with myself from giving You (without being call'd upon) my whole sentiments on a subject which I dare say you already guess at—Hetty, (as she told You she would) has disclos'd the affair to me—the Character she gives of the Young man is in these Words.

'—a Young man, whose Circumstances, I have heard are Easy, but am not throughly inform'd of them—but he bears an extraordinary Character for a Young man now a Days— I have it from some who have known him long, that he is remarkably even-temper'd, sedate & sensible he is 24 Years of Age, is greatly esteem'd for Qualities rarely found at his Age—Temperance & Industry—well Educated, under-stands Books & Words, better than the World. Which gives him something of a stiffness & formality, which discovers him unus'd to Company, but which might wear off'—

Is all this true, Fanny?—if it is, is such a man so very deter-minately to be rejected, because from the overflowings of an innocent, honest mind (I wont call it *ignorant* but) *untainted with* the World, (instead of a thousand pitiful Airs & disguises, mixt perhaps with treachery & design) he with trembling & diffidence ventures to write, what he is unable to declare in person, & forsooth, to raise your indignation to the highest pitch, is so indelicate as to hint, that his intentions aim at *matrimony*—⌜god damn my blood but You make me mad!—⌝ if you dont put me in mind of Moliere's[32] Precieuses Ridicules! —Read it; [xxxxx *2–3 words*] You Young Devil, & blush!—tis scene the 4ᵗʰ & ⌐instead of Gorgibus & Madelon, read Crispin & Fanchon & the Dialogues will run thus.

Fanchon.

La belle galanterie que la sienne! Quoi, débuter d'abord par la mariàge!

---

[32] Molière (Jean-Baptiste Poquelin) (1622–73). *Les Précieuses ridicules* was first performed in 1659. SC's quotation is almost exact.

Crispin.

Et par où veux-tu donc qu'il débute? par la concubinage? n'est-ce pas un procedé, dont vous avez sujet de vous loüer, aussi-bien que moi? est il rien de plus obligeant que cela? et ce lien sacré, où il aspire, n'est-il pas un témoignage de l'honnêteté de ses intentiòns?

Fanchon.

Ah mon Pere! ce que vous dites là est du dernier Bourgeois. Cela me fait honte de vous oüir parler de la sorte, & vous devriez un peu vous faire apprendre le bel air des choses.

How does this happen? Were there Fanchons in Moliere's days, or are there Madelons now?—But seriously, Fanny, all the ill-founded Objections You make, to me appear strong & invincible marks of a violent & sincere Passion—what You take it into your head to be displeas'd with, as too great a Liberty, I mean, his presuming to write to You, & in so tender & respectful & submissive a strain, if You knew the World, & that villanous Yahoo, call'd man, as well as I do, You would see in a very different Light—in its true light—fearfulness, a high opinion of You, a consciousness (an unjust one I will call it) of his own inferiority; & at last, as he thinks the happiness of his Life is at stake, summoning up a trembling resolution of disclosing in writing the situation of his mind, which he has not the courage to do to Your Face—& do You call, or think this—can You judge so ill, as to look on this as an undue, or impertinent Liberty?—Ah Fany [*sic*], such a disposition promises a thousand fold more happiness, more solid, ˡ lasting, home-felt happiness, than all the seducing, exterior Airs, Graces, Accomplishments, & Address of an Artful ⸢⟨rake⟩⸣— such a man, as this Young Barlow, if ever You are so lucky, & so well-advis'd, as to be united to him, will improve upon You every hour; You will discover in him Graces, & Charms, which kindness will bring to light, that at present You have no Idea, of—I mean if his Character is truly given by Hetty— that is the grand Object of Inquiry—as likewise his Circumstances. This last, as the great sheet Anchor, on which we are to depend in our Voyage thro' life, ought most minutely to be scrutiniz'd. Is he of any profession, or only of an independent

Fortune?—if either, or both, sufficient to promise a ⌜⟨really⟩⌝ comfortable [Income,][33] You may live to the Age of your Grandmother, & not meet with so Valuable an offer—Shakespear says,

> There is a Tide in the affairs of men,
> Which taken at the heighth, leads on to Fortune;
> But being neglected, &c[34]

I forget how it goes on, but the sense is, (what You may guess,) that the Opportunity is never to be recover'd—the Tide is lost, & You are left in shallows, fast aground, & struggling in Vain for the remainder of your life to get on—doom'd to pass it in Obscurity & regret—look around You Fany—look at y[r] Aunts—*Fanny Burney* wont always be what she is now!—M[rs] Hamilton once had an Offer of £3000 a Year or near it—a parcel of young giggling Girls laugh'd her out of it—the man forsooth was not quite smart enough, tho' otherwise estimable—Oh Fany this is not a marrying Age, without a handsome Fortune!—⌜how happy does Hetty feel herself to have married [xxxxx *5 words*]⌝[35]—Suppose You to lose y[r] Father—take in all Chances. |Consider the situation of an unprotected, unprovided Woman—

Excuse my being so Earnest with You—Assure Yourself it proceeds from my regard, & from (let me say it, tho' it savours of Vanity) a deep knowledge of the World—Observe, how far I go—I dont urge You, hand over head, to have this man at all Events; but for Gods sake, & your own sake, give him & yourself fair Play—dont decide so positively against it—if You do, You are ridiculous to a high degree—if You dont answer his letter, dont avoid seeing him—at all Events, I charge You on my blessing to attend Hetty in her Visit to the O'Connors, according to y[r] Promise, & which You cant get off without positive rudeness—this binds You to Nothing; it leaves an opening for future Consideration & Inquiry, & is barely decent—I have wrote so much on this subject, (which is now next my heart) that I cannot frame myself to any thing

---

[33] Supplied by FBA for a word not recovered.
[34] Cf. *Julius Caesar* IV. iii. 217 ff.
[35] Not recovered, but presumably a swipe at Charles Rousseau Burney's poverty.

else for this bout—so Adieu, You have the best wishes of y^r Affectionate Daddy   SC ˈ

The Visit to M^{rs} O Connor was made yesterday. I Commissioned my Aunts——though they would hardly hear me—to say that I was prevented from Waiting on her by a bad Cold. How the message was taken, & what passed, I know not; but this morning, while we were all at Breakfast, except my Father, who was in the study; John came into the Parlour, & said that a Gentleman ⌈wanted⌉ me.

I guessed who it was—& was inexpressibly Confused. Mama stared, but desired he might walk in—the Door opened—& he appeared.—He had Dressed himself elegantly —but could hardly speak.—He Bowed two or three Times—I coloured like scarlet, & I believe he was the only person in the Room who did not see it.

'M^{rs} O Connor—he called—my Cold—he understood—he was very sorry—'

He could not get on.—My voice too, failed me terribly—for his silence at his first Entrance made me fear he was going to reproach me for not answering his Letter.—I told him my Cold had been too bad to allow me to go out—but I was so terribly frightened lest my mother should say *what Cold—I did not know you had one*!—that I ˈ had great difficulty to get out the Words: & he himself ⌈after wards⌉ took Notice that my *Voice* spoke how bad my Cold was!—though in fact I have no Cold at all: my mother then asked him to sit down—& Sukey, very good naturedly, entered into Conversation with him, to our mutual relief,—particularly to his, as he seemed so confounded he scarse knew where he was. I sat upon Thorns from the fear he would desire to speak to me alone—I looked another way, & hardly opened my mouth, ⌈& when,⌉ in about ½ an Hour, he rose to go, ⌈I kept my Eyes from him—& Sukey went to the Parlour Door with him.

I don't know what my mother thought, but she has not said a Word.⌉ Whether he was induced to make this visit from

---

^{36} Correctly, May 14th.

expecting he might speak to me, or whether in order to see if I had any Cold or not, I cannot tell: but it proved cruelly distressing to him, & confusing to me.

Had I sent an answer, this would not have happened: but it is now too late. I am very sorry to find this young man seems so serious;—however, an attachment so precipitately formed, so totally discouraged, & *so* placed—cannot be difficult to Cure.

25   [St Martin's Street, 15 May 1775]

To Samuel Crisp

ALS (Berg), 15 May 1775
Double sheet 4to, 4 pp.
Annotated (by FBA): ✿ *From Miss Frances Burney to Mr Crisp.* on Mr Barlow and marriage 10th [*sic*] May 1775 N° 35–34 N° 9
The letter has been inserted into the Journal for 1775, where it is paginated 529–[32].

And so it is all over with me!

& I am to be given up—to forfeit your blessing—to lose your good opinion—to be doomed to regret & the Horrors—*because*—I have not a mind to be married.

Forgive me—my dearest Mr Crisp—forgive me—but indeed I cannot act from *Worldly motives*—you know, & have long known & laughed at my Notions & Character. Continue still to *Laugh* ⌐at me¬—but pray don't make *me* Cry—for your last Letter really made me unhappy—I am grieved that you can so earnestly espouse the Cause of a person you never saw—I heartily wish him well—he is, I believe, a worthy young man—but I have ⌐long¬ accustomed myself to the idea of being an old maid—& the Title has lost all its terrors in my Ears. I feel no repugnance to the expectation of being ranked among the Number.

As to the Visit to Hoxton—my dear Daddy, *how* could I make it, without leaving Mr Barlow to infer—the Lord knows what?—by what he says in his Letter, it is evident he would have taken it to himself:—he is hasty—& I dreaded being some how or other entangled—I have no dislike to him—the whole party were strongly his friends—& upon the whole, I though it necessary to keep away. I would not for the World be thought to *trifle* with any man. ⌐ [I could not][37] now have made that Visit without giving him reason to draw conclusions very disagreeable to me.

Don't imagine by what I say that I have made a *Vow* for a single Life—no. But on the other Hand I have no *Objection* to it, & have all my life determined never to marry without having the highest value & esteem for the man who should be my Lord.

Were I ever so well disposed to follow your advice & see more of this Youth—I am convinced he would not let me;—he is so extremely precipitate—I *must* either determine for or against him—or at least enter into such conditions as I should think myself in honour bound to abide by.

If you ask my Objections—I must frankly own they are such as perhaps will only satisfy myself—for I have none to make to his Character—Disposition or person—they are all good; *but*—he is not used to Company or the World—his Language is stiff, studied, & even affected—in short—he does not *hit my fancy*—

> I do not like you, Dr. Fell—
> The Reason why I cannot tell—
> But I don't *like* you, Dr. Fell![38]

Hetty, & the Party, went on Saturday [13 May] to Hoxton. I desired them to say I was not well—how the Day passed I know not—they have all Quarrelled with me about this affair, & I don't care to go either to ⌐Queen Street or York Street.⌐[39] But while we were at Breakfast yesterday ⌐ morning—John came in & said a Gentleman desired to speak to me.—M^r

---

[37] Supplied by FBA for a tear in the page.

[38] FB's condensation of a well-known quatrain by Thomas Brown (1663–1704), addressed to Dr John Fell (1625–86), Dean of Christ Church, Oxford, where Brown was a student.

[39] FB's grandmother and aunts Nanny and Becky lived in York St. Apparently her sister EBB and Charles Rousseau Burney had just recently moved from Charles St. to Queen St.

Barlow came in—to enquire after my Health—*You* would
have Laughed had you been present—for I was so much
frightened ⌜lest my mother should blab my being well, &⌝ lest
he should desire to speak to me—that I quite lost my
Voice—in so much, that he himself afterwards took notice
how bad my Cold was—though in fact I have none at
all!—while on the other Hand, he was so terribly confused
that he made 3 several Bows before he could get out a word.
My mother, Bessy & Charlotte all stared with amazement,
wondering who he was, & what his visit meant—as to Sukey,
she could not keep her Countenance at first—though soon
after, she very good naturedly entered into Conversation with
Mr Barlow, to our mutual relief.

I am very uneasy at not having answered his Letter—I
should be equally grieved to have him take my silence either
for *Contempt* or for *Compliance*; but my Father to whom I
shewed it, desired me not to answer it.—*why* I cannot imagine. If *he* sided against me—I could not resist the stream—
for Sukey is firmly his friend—but I thank Heaven he does not
interfere—he is all indulgence—& to quit *his* Roof requires
inducements which I am sure I shall never have. I never—
never can love any human being as I love him!

Once more I entreat your forgiveness—& that ⎮ you will
write me word you forgive me—

Don't be uneasy about my welfare, my dear Daddy, I dare
say I shall do very well.—I cannot persuade myself to *snap* at
a settlement—& I do assure you this young man would not
suffer me to deliberate long.—

Had marriage from prudence & Convenience been my
desire—I believe I had it quite as much in my power ⌜if I
designed it⌝ as now—there was a certain youth, not *quite* so
hasty to be sure, as Mr Barlow, but not far otherwise, who
took much pains for ⌜⟨increasing⟩⌝ our Acquaintance—I
happened to Dance with him at a private ⌜masquerade at Mr.
Lalauze's—⌝[40] & he called two or 3 Times afterward, & wrote
2 notes, with most pressing ⌜requests that Hetty & I would
accept Tickets for Balls & that⌝ *he might exist again*—however,

---

[40] See *EJL* i. 97–107, 114–15, 118–19 for Mr Lalauze's masquerade (in 1770) and
FB's young would-be suitor who came as a Dutchman.

after the answer he received to the 2ᵈ Note, I heard of him no more. In short, I long since settled to either attach myself with my whole Heart—or to have the Courage to lead Apes.⁴¹

I have now—& I shall ever have the most grateful sense of your kindness, & of the interest you take in my concerns.—I heartily wish I *could* act by your advice, & that I could return an attachment, which, strange as it seems to me, I so little deserve.

After all—so long as I live to be of some comfort (as I flatter myself I am) to my Father,—I can have no motive to wish to sign myself other than his & your

> ever obliged & ever affectionate & devoted
> Frances Burney to
> the End of the Chapter.
> Amen!

As to his ⌐circumstances,¬ I have made no Enquiries—for I honestly [c]onfess they wᵈ have but little Influence with me one way or other. ⏐

26   [St Martin's Street,
                                       *c.*22–5 May 1775]

To Samuel Crisp

ALS (Barrett), May 1775
2 double sheets 4to, 8 pp., seal
Addressed: Samˡ Crisp Esqʳ | at Mʳˢ Hamilton's | Chesington near | Kingston | Surrey
Annotated (by FBA): ⚌ Concert Mr. Burney, Esther, Baronness Deiden, Miss Phips, Mr. & Miss Louisa Harris, [17]75 Nᵒ 35 May 12ᵗʰ
FB repeats her accounts of the concert and of her visit to Aunt Becky in the Journal for 1775, fos. 25–29. See also *Mem.* ii. 11–18.

My dear Daddy,

I was extremely happy at the Receipt of your last Letter,⁴² because you assure me you are not angry with me, though,

---

⁴¹ 'To lead apes in hell' was the proverbial fate of old maids.
⁴² Missing.

believe me, I cannot with unconcern Read your cautions & prognostics. I am *not triumphant*—but I am not *desponding*: & I must again repeat what I have so often had the hardiesse to say, that I have no idea why a single Life may not be happy. Liberty is not without its value—with women as well as with men, though it has not *equal* recommendations for both,—& I hope never without a prospect brighter to myself to lose mine: & I have no such prospect in view.

Had I ever *Hesitated* about Mr Barlow, your advice, my dear sir, would have turned the Balance on his side; but I never did or could. So now to other matters.

Our Concert[43] proved to be very much *the Thing*: The Company consisted of

The Baron Deiden,[44] the Danish Ambassadour.

The Baronness, his Lady. She is young, pretty, well made, polite & amiable. We were all charmed with her.

Miss Phipps, sister of the famous Capt. Phipps. & Daughter of Lord Mulgrave. She is a very sweet Girl. Her Face is not handsome, but full of *Expression* & *intelligence*. She is arch, clever, & Engaging.

Sir James & Lady Lake.[45] You have already had my opinion of this Couple, which is not at all altered.

Miss Lake,[46] sister of Sir James. A very agreeable *old maid*. I *respect* & *admire*—& wish to *imitate* her.

Sir Thomas Clarges. He is just returned from Italy, whither he was sent by his Relations, upon account of a violent passion

---

[43] Presumably on Sunday, 21 May.

[44] Wilhelm Christopher von Diede (1732–1807), Danish envoy extraordinary to England, 1767–76; m. (1772) Ursula Margrethe Constantia Louisa von Callenberg of Huset Muskau (1752–1803) (*YW* xxiii. 402 nn. 10, 13). The Baroness subscribed to *Hist. Mus.* FB added in the Journal, fo. 25: 'She is reckoned one of the best lady Harpsichord players in Europe'.

[45] Sir James Winter Lake (*c.*1742–1807), 3rd Bt; antiquary and collector; m. (1764) Joyce Crowther (*c.*1747–1834), daughter of John Crowther, Esq., of Bow, Middlesex (*GM* xxxiv (1764), 302; civ² (1834), 447). FB wrote in the Journal, fo. 25: 'Sir James Lake, who, as heretofore, was sensible, cold & reserved. Lady Lake, who, as heretofore, was. all ⌈Condescendsion⌉ politeness & sweetness'.

[46] Mary Lake, m. (1782) Maj. William Webb, of Mansfield Woodhouse, Notts. (*GM* lii (1782), 94). FBA named the 'Misses Lake' in her 'List' for 1773. The other Miss Lake was perhaps Mary Lake's younger sister Anne, who died unmarried in 1834.

which he had for Miss Linley, now Mrs Sheridan;[47] he is a
very Tall youth, & has not by his Travels lost his native |
bashfulness & shyness.[48]

· Mr Harris of Salisbury, author of 3 Treatises, on Happiness,
music, &c & of some other Books, particularly one just
published, called Philosophical arrangements.[49] He is a
charming old man,—well bred even to humility, gentle in his
manners, & communicative & agreeable in his Conversation.

Mrs Harris,[50] his wife. A so, so, sort of woman.

Miss Harris,[51] his Daughter. She has a bad figure, & is not
handsome. She is reserved, modest & sensible. She has
Acquired a *name* as a lady singer, & is a scholar of Sacchini's.

Mr Earl.[52] A very musical man.

Mrs Ord,[53] a very musical woman.

Miss Ord,[54] a fine Girl, but totally inanimate & insipid.

Mr Merlin, the very ingenious mechanic, who is also a very
[entertaining][55] character. There is a *simplicity* so unaffected &

[47] Sir Thomas had proposed to Miss Linley but been refused. He went abroad in
Dec. 1772, after denying that he had proposed. See R. B. Sheridan, *Letters*, ed. C.
Price (Oxford, 1966), i. 68; W. F. Rae, *Sheridan: A Biography* (New York, 1896), i. 243,
256.

[48] 'He ... scarce speaks, but to make an answer, & is as shy as if his last residence
had been at Eton, instead of Paris' (Journal, fo. 25). Clarges eventually mastered his
shyness enough to stand for Parliament and give at least two speeches in the Commons
(as MP for Lincoln, 1780–2; see Namier).

[49] *Philosophical Arrangements; Containing a Variety of Speculations, Logical, Physical,
Ethical, and Metaphysical, derived from the Principles of the Greek Philosophers, and Illustrated
Examples from the Greatest Writers, Both Ancient and Modern.* Harris's book was listed in
this month's *GM* (xlv (1775), 244). CB's copy is listed *Lib.*, p. 23.   ·

[50] Elizabeth Clarke (d. 1781), daughter of John Clarke of Sandford, Bridgwater;
m. (1745) James Harris (*GM* li (1781), 492). For a different appraisal of her talents,
see *ED* ii. 57 n. 3.

[51] Louisa Margaret Harris (1753–1826) (*JL* i. 163 n. 52).

[52] William Benson Earle (1740–96), philanthropist. Earle was a friend of James
Harris and, like Harris, was very actively involved in the musical life of Salisbury. An
excellent musician himself, he composed several glees and a 'Sanctus' and 'Kyrie'
which were still occasionally performed in Salisbury Cathedral a century after his
death (see *DNB*; Nichols, *Lit. Ill.* v. 346–8).

[53] Anna Dillingham (*c.*1726–1808), m. (1746) William Ord (d. 1768) of Newcastle;
a noted bluestocking. This was her first recorded meeting with the Burneys. She
became a close friend of the family but ostracized FB after her marriage (1793) to M.
d'Arblay. See *DL* and *JL passim*.

[54] Charlotte Ord (1753–95) (*JL* i. 75 n. 9).

[55] Substituted by FBA for an obliterated word not recovered.

so uncommon, in his manners & Conversation that his Company always gives me ⌜pleasure.⌝ He ⌜⟨gives⟩⌝ his opinion upon all subjects, & about all persons without the least disguise; he is humbly grateful for all civility that ⌜is shewn to him,⌝ but at the same Time, he shews an honest & warm resentment if he meets with any slight. He pronounces English very comically, for though he is never at a loss for a word, he almost always puts the *emphasis* on the wrong syllable.

Mr Jones,[56] a Welch Harper. A silly young man.

[Mrs. Anguish, a *keen, sharp, clever* woman.][57]

Miss Harrison. Daughter of the late Commodore Harrison.[58] She is rather pretty, very young, proud, I believe, & uninteresting.

Mr Burney, Hetty, & our Noble Selves bring up the Rear.

The Company in general came early, & there was a great deal of Conversation before any music; but as the party was too large for a *general Chatterment*,[59] we were obliged to make parties with our next Neighbours. I had the satisfaction of having Mr Harris for mine till the Concert began.

As we had no violins, we were obliged to be contented without any overture; & the Concert was opened by Mr Burney at the desire of the Baroness Deiden. He Fired away, with his usual successful velocity, to the amazement & delight of all present, particularly of the Baroness, who is a very celebrated lady performer;—it was to her that Boccherini[60] & Eichner, whose Lessons you have so very much admired, Dedicated their music, as have many other Composers of less merit.

---

[56] Edward Jones (1752–1824), Welsh harper, historian, and composer. He had recently left Merionethshire to start a career in London. He evidently struck FB as immature at this time, but later distinguished himself as a historian and recorder of Welsh music. See *New Grove*.

[57] Inserted by the editor from FB's Journal, fo. 26. This was probably Sarah, née Henley (d. 1807), daughter of Henry Holt Henley of Docking, Norfolk and Leigh, Somerset, whose husband, Thomas Anguish (c.1724–85), FRS, a Master in Chancery, subscribed to *Hist. Mus.* See *GM* lxxvii[1] (1807), 92; above, p. 41 n. 33.

[58] Presumably Capt. Thomas Harrison (d. 1768), formerly commodore of the British squadron in the Mediterranean (*GM* xxxviii (1768), 94; D. B. Smith, *The Commissioned Sea Officers of the Royal Navy 1660–1815* (1954), ii. 412). His daughter was perhaps the Miss Harrison of Highgate who married 'John Hatton, Esq; in Queen-square' in 1778 (*GM* xlviii (1778), 439). She has not been further traced.

[59] FB's humorous construction is noted in *OED*.

[60] Luigi Boccherini (1743–1805), Italian composer (*New Grove*).

Mr Burney played a Concerto of Schobert,[61] & one of my Father's, & a great deal of Extemporary Preluding.

When he rose, my Father petitioned the Baroness to take his seat—o no! she would not hear of it[62]—she said it would be like a Figurante's Dancing after Mlle Heinel![63]—Miss Phipps joined violently in intreating her, & the Baron seemed to wish her to comply—& she was at length prevailed with. She played a Lesson of Schobert. I think her the best lady player I ever heard. She is a good musician,—does not blunder or make false steps,—has a remarkable strong left Hand—& plays with much *meaning*, as well as Execution. She is, at the same Time, so modest & unassuming, & so pretty, that she was the general object of admiration. When my Father went to Thank her, she said she had never been so frightened before in her life.

My Father begged her to favour us with some thing else. She was going to play again[64]—but the Baron, looking at my sister Hetty, said—'après, ma chere.' 'Eh bien, cried Miss Phipps, who is her intimate friend, après Madame Burney.'

She immediately, & very gracefully rose, & gave her place to Hetty, who, to avoid the appearance of *emulation*, with great propriety chose to begin with a *slow* movement, as the Baroness had been Exerting all her Execution.

She played *your bit* of Echard.[65] & I may safely say that I never heard her play it better, if so well; Merlin's Harpsichord made it divine—& the Expression, feeling & Taste with which she performed it raised a general murmur of applause

---

[61] Johann Schobert (*c.*1735–67), composer (ibid.)

[62] FB notes in the Journal, fo. 26, that she spoke in French, 'which she almost always speaks'.

[63] Anne Frédérique Heinel (1753–1808), French dancer; m. (1773) M. Fierville; m. (1792) Gaëtan Apolline Balthazar Vestris. She had first come to London in 1771 and was considered the finest dancer in Europe. CB observed that her 'grace and execution were so perfect as to eclipse all other excellence' (Mercer, ii. 878; Highfill).

[64] 'Another German Composition which he had heard her play at Lord Mulgrave's' (Journal, fo. 26).

[65] Johann Gottfried Eckard (1735–1809), German composer. EBB played a 'Lesson' or sonata movement by Eckard (Journal, fo. 26), presumably from one of the 8 sonatas published in 1763 and 1764 (op. 1 and op. 2). Of his sonatas, CB commented: 'There is an elegance of style built upon such sound principles of harmony and modulation as few have surpassed' (Rees; see also *New Grove*; *Mus. Lib.*, p. 29).

& satisfaction from all. Mr Harris enquired eagerly whose it was? Every body seemed to feel & to be enchanted with it. If a Pin had dropt, it would have made a Universal start! Every one was silent, attentive, & pleased.

After this, she played a very difficult Lesson of my Father's; but she was flurried, & niether did that or herself Justice.

At my Father's request, Miss Harris then consented to sing.

Her Father accompanied her on the Piano Forte. She sung a most beautiful slow song of Sacchini's,[66] which has never been printed, but which we remembered having formerly heard him sing. She has very little voice, scarce any, indeed,—having niether power, compass, or sweetness, *and yet*—which is wonderful—her singing gave us all pleasure! She is extremely well taught, & makes up for the deficiencies of Nature by the acquirements of Art; for she sings with great Taste & feeling, & in an excellent style.

She protested she was more frightened at singing to *such an audience*, than she should have been in a Theatre. She consented, however, to sing another Air, when somewhat recovered: & she gave us a new & favourite Rondeau of Rauzzini's, which he sings in the New opera of Piramo & Tisbè.[67]

After this, followed the *great Gun* of the Concert, namely a Harpsichord Duet between Mr Burney & my sister.[68]

It is the Noblest Composition that was ever made.

They came off with flying Colours—Nothing could exceed the general applause. Mr Harris was in *extacy*; Sr James Lake ⌐who is silent & ⌐shy,⌐ broke forth into the warmest expressions of delight—Lady Lake, more prone to be pleased, was quite in raptures—the charming Baroness repeatedly declared she had never been at so agreeable a Concert before; & many said They had never *heard music* till then.

What would I give that you could hear it? It is not possible for Instrumental music to be more *finished*.

---

[66] 'Some Recitative & an Air of Sacchini's' (Journal, fo. 27).

[67] Rauzzini's best-loved opera. It had opened on 16 Mar., but was first staged at Munich in 1769. The rondo was 'Fuggiam dove sicura' (Journal, fo. 27; see also F. C. Petty, *Italian Opera in London: 1760–1800* (Ann Arbor, 1980), pp. 141–3; *LS 4* iii. 1876; *New Grove*; *A Selection from Pyramus and Thysbe* (1775), pp. 18–22).

[68] By Müthel (Journal, fo. 27).

The Baroness was then again Called upon—but she excused herself from playing any more—&, with the Baron & Miss Phipps, soon after took her leave.

I quite forgot to speak of Mr Jones, who played upon a Harp with new pedals constructed by Mr Merlin: it is a sweet Instrument.[69] He plays very well, he is precisely neat, & has a good deal of Execution: but the poor young man has no *soul* to spare for his playing.

The Concert concluded by another song from Miss Harris, it was a Bravura, a MS. of Sacchini's. A fine song, & very well sung.

The Company [xxxxx *2–3 words*] went away to all appearances extremely well pleased; & we who remained at Home were in all reality the same. ⌐We kept Mr Merlin to supper, & we had much amusement in hearing his Comments.⌐

So much for our Concert.

⌐I was truly sorry to hear of your Illness. My father does not remember how the *fixed* ⟨*air*⟩[70] was managed & confined, but he has written to Mr Bewley, since I asked the Question, & has enquired the particulars of him; whenever an answer arrives, I will immediately acquaint you with it. Whether it is to be *bought*; & all that, my Father cannot, of *his own Head*, tell. I hope it will not be long ere we hear from Mr Bewley.⌐

My Father desires his kind Love to you—but fears it will be impossible as he must go to sea Bathing & as he cannot leave Town at all till his Book is published. However, he *very much* wishes to see you, & says that if he *possibly* can get to you for one Day or so, he will spare no Pains to procure himself that satisfaction.

As to my mother—she talks of certainly going to Chesington for a few Days during the summer.

The Rishtons were in Town only a week. They are very well

[69] Jones opened the concert (Journal, fo. 26). See A. French, M. Wright, and F. Palmer, *John Joseph Merlin: The Ingenious Mechanick* (1985), pp. 110, 140–1; Scholes, ii. 204.

[70] A conjectural reading. Later this year William Bewley wrote to CB about his experiments with 'fixed air', or carbonic acid gas (carbon dixoide). SC may have been interested in conducting some experiments of his own. The letters between Bewley and CB referred to here are missing. See Bewley to CB, 1 Dec. 1775 (Osborn).

& very comfortable. They are gone to make a Tour to Wales & will return through Town in about a month.

Poor Barsanti is still a bit indifferent, though much better than she has been. Her Benefit[71] proved a very good one, though inferior to her 2 former ones which I attribute to her not acting. She goes next week to Bristol, where she is engaged in Reddish's[72] Company of comedians.

Mr. Twiss has never Entered the House, in spite of repeated endeavours. His Travels[73] proved to be very dull & dry, he was so fearful of his natural flightiness being perceived, that he has cut out every thing that could have been entertaining, & left nothing but tame description.

Dr. Johnson, with much less materials, has built a Book worth a million of Mr. Twiss's.[74]

Thursday May [25]

And now, my dear Mr Crisp, I am going to ask you advice, for I am in some perplexity.—all concerning this Mr Barlow.

My Grandmother, 2 aunts & sister [EBB] spent the Day with us last Wednesday [17 May]. They told me that my *Cold* was very well swallowed at ⸢Hoxton⸣ & that Mr Barlow was *immensely shocked*, & all that.[75]—My Aunt Beckey teized me to Drink Tea with her the next Day [18 May]—⸍ I was engaged,

---

[71] On 5 May. She received £148. 8s. 6d. from her benefit of 10 May 1773, and £174. 7s. from the benefit of 23 Apr. 1774 (*LS 4* iii. 1721, 1805, 1890).

[72] Samuel Reddish (1735–85), an actor at Drury Lane Theatre, was principal manager of the Theatre Royal, Bristol, 1774–7. Barsanti performed for him the summers of 1774 and 1775 (Highfill; K. Barker, *The Theatre Royal, Bristol, 1766–1966* (1974), pp. 26–7, 32–7, 42).

[73] Richard Twiss's *Travels through Portugal and Spain* was published earlier in the year. It is listed in the *GM* for May (xlv. 244). CB's copy is listed in *Lib.*, p. 60.

[74] Johnson's *A Journey to the Western Islands of Scotland* was published on 18 Jan. (*Daily Adv.*, 18 Jan.). CB's copy is listed in *Lib.*, p. 28.

[75] Charles Rousseau Burney was also of the party in St Martin's St. FB adds in the Journal, fo. 27, that she asked the 'remarkably good Tempered' Aunt Becky about Hoxton: ⸢I dared not ask Hetty or my aunt Anne, because they were so mad with me for not joining the Party, & though *Beckey* was at first equally provoked, it is by no means difficult to *mollify* her. She does not think deeply enough to harbour resentment of any sort.⸣ FB asked 'whether they had forbore, as I had earnestly entreated that they would, to betray their knowledge of Mr Barlow's secret; for it is certainly incumbent upon every Female who refuses a man to keep from the World his unsuccessful choice'. Aunt Becky observed that when Barlow 'saw you was not there, he looked ready to drop!'

& could not, but said I would on Saturday [20 May].[76]
Accordingly I went. I ran up stairs, as usual—but when I
opened the Door, the first object I saw was M[r] Barlow.[77] I was
much surprised, & rather provoked,[78] fearing that my aunt
Beckey, whose Temper is much superior to her Understanding,
had purposely led me to this meeting.[79] You will believe I was
tolerably shy & forbidding, at first, but afterwards I tried to
behave as if I had never received his Letter, & it was not
difficult to me to appear quite unconcerned, & as usual.

⌐I made my visit [xxxxx *2–3 words*] very short, & was
hurrying away as soon as Tea was over when I found that I
should not be allowed to go [xxxxx *1½ lines*] had I slipt out, he
would have followed me. I therefore sat down again,
determined to wait till he went, or till I was sent for by the
Mama.⌐

I have since wished that I had let him have his way—speak
to me—⌐&⌐ answered him,—to End the affair for ever. But at
the Time, I really had not sufficient presence of mind:—he
appeared so humbly at my service, that I dreaded lest, in the
fear of being impertinent, I should be involved in some scrape
from being *civil*;—in short, I much wished to avoid a private
Conversation in which I could hear nothing that would be
agreeable to me, & could say nothing that would not be
highly *dis*agreeable to him.—I am heartily sorry his Letter
was not answered at once. It is now too late to take any Notice
of it. He was excessively urgent with my Grandmother to fix a
Day for another visit to ⌐Hoxton⌐ *with me*; & he *entreated* me not
to have a Cold then! I laughed the Cold off as well as I could,
but would by no means promise to be of the Party—niether,
indeed, would I do any single thing that he requested, lest he

---

[76] 'She asked me to ⌐Dine with her⌐ the next Day—⌐I told her that perhaps I
might call in the Afternoon: but cried she, generously, "you will be more likely to
meet Mr. Barlow in the *morning*".
    I thanked her kindly, & told here that for that very reason I should not go. . . .
    I told her, however, that I would wait on her some time on Saturday⌐' (Journal,
fos. 27–28).
[77] 'Seated with my Grandmother, Aunts, & M[rs] Powel, a niece of M[rs] O Connor'
(ibid., fo. 28). Mrs Powel has not been further traced.
[78] ⌐'monstrous mad⌐' (ibid.).
[79] 'the more so, as, though he seemed much pleased, he did not appear at all
surprised at my Entrance' (ibid.).

should construe | even common complaisance into a wish of obliging him.

I should be quite sorry for the apparent *seriousness* of this young man's attachment, but that I am p[r]etty persuaded what so easily came, will without difficulty depart.

I hope—as I endeavoured—that my *general manner* has convinced him of his having chosen ill. Nevertheless,—I beg you to advise me what to do whether to go to ⌜Hoxton⌝ & force myself to say (as Lord Ogleby expresses it) *shocking* things to Him[80]—I don't care to say any thing more to my Father about it.—I could not resist *him*.

I certainly ought not to keep ⌜him⌝ [Barlow] in *suspence*, if it is *possible* he can think himself so. Pray Instruct me—only remember that *I* am *fixed*.

Adieu my dear sir, I am now and ever

most faithfully & truly yours,
Frances

27   [St Martin's Street,
                            2 June 1775]

To Samuel Crisp

ALS (Barrett), 2 June 1775
Double sheet 4to, 4 pp., *pmk* 2 IU wafer
Addressed: Saml Crisp Esqr, | At Mrs Hamilton's, | Chesington near Kingston | Surrey.
Annotated (by FBA): ※ Mr. Barlow & rejection N° 11 N° 36 2 May 1775

Friday Night

My dear Sir,

My Father can not see you before Sunday, when he proposes to be with you as s[oo]n as he can. Whether *alone*—or with any body else—or whether your anecdote-monger will accompany him, as yet none but the *great gods can tell*!

---

[80] Cf. Garrick and Colman, *The Clandestine Marriage*, Act IV, sc. iii.

If I do *not* see you—I must take this opportunity of en-treating & convincing you not to use your Influence with my Father for Mr B. in case he should mention that personage to you. I have not Time at present to tell you *all about it*—but a great deal has passed since I wrote last, & I have suffered the most cruel & terrifying uneasiness—I am *now* again at peace & hope to continue so. Should my Father happen to speak to you of what *I* have said,—(as it is ^| well known that I write very openly to you) I entreat you to assure him that I have expressed the greatest aversion to forming a connection with Mr B. I have not dared to speak so much to the purpose myself,—for I have been—& I am, determined at all Events not to oppose *his* will & advice—but I know he wishes only for my happiness, & I am sensible that I should be wretched for ever if induced to marry where I have no manner of affection or regard.—O Mr Crisp—it is dreadful to me to think of Uniting my Destiny—Spending my Time—Devoting my Life —to one whose Face I never desire to see Again!

Had I with equal bluntness expressed myself to my Father, I am certain he would not ever think of Mr B. more—but—his interference was so unexpected—it silenced, confounded, & frightened me.

I see you did not care to send me your advice—which, however would be too late—as Mr B. is no *Dreaming Lover.*—I hope all is over. ^|

I don't think my mother will be able to be with you, as Miss Lidderdale of Lynn is expected here—but all this is unsettled.

Adieu, my dear Daddy,

I am ever most truly yours
F. Burney

[*The Journal for 1775 resumes. FB's account of her visit to Aunt Becky, which begins the June 6 entry, is omitted.*]

June 6th

A Week passed after this, without my hearing or seeing any more of Mr Barlow & I hoped that he had resigned his pre-tensions. But on Saturday morning [27 May], while we were at Breakfast, I had a Letter brought me in a Hand which I immediately knew to be Barlow's.

As it by no means is so *high flown* as his first, I will Copy it.[81]

Madam,

I have somewhere seen that powerful Deity Cupid, & the invincible Mars habited in a similar manner, & each have in their Train several of the same dispositioned [|] Attendants: the propriety of which Thought I own pleased me, for when drawn from the Allegory, it is acknowledged both Love & War are comparative in several particulars; they each require Constancy, & the hope of success stimulate each to perseverance, & as the one is warmed & encouraged by the Desire of Glory, so the óther is much more powerfully fired & transported by the Charms of the Fair sex: I have been told that Artifice & Deception are connected to both; but those Qualities I should determine to discard, & substitute in their place an open Frankness, & undisguised Truth & Honour, & for Diligence, Attention, Assiduity & Care,[82] which are essential to both, & which some place in the Catalogue of the Labours of Love, I should have them happily converted to pleasures, in the honour of devoting them to Miss Fanny Burney, if the Destinys auspiciously avert a disagreeable sequel, for as the bravest General may miscarry, so the most sincere Lover may lose the wished for Prize; to prevent which, I should continue to invoke my Guardian Genius, that she may ever inspire me with such Principles & Actions as may enable me to reach the summit of my Ambition, in Approveing [*sic*] myself not unworthy the Esteem of your amiable self, & not unworthy— but stop, Oh *ardurous*[83] *Pen, & presume not*—'till in the front you can place Permission to hope—ascending such sublime heights.

⌐It has given me great uneasiness that the excessive⌐ [|] hurry of Business has so long prevented me the honour of Waiting on You, & enquiring after your Welfare, which I earnestly wish to hear; but I determine, with your leave, ere long to do

---

[81] The original undated ALS, single sheet 4to, 2 pp., is in the Barrett Collection. Some minor variants are recorded in the notes.

[82] 'Assiduity, Care, & Attention'.

[83] The editors of *OED* found only one instance of this form, dated 1814. There, as here, it is probably a slip for 'ardorous'. Barlow is echoing his earlier letter (above, p. 118).

myself that pleasure, as methinks Time moves very slowly in granting me an opportunity to declare, in some small degree, (for I could never[84] reach what I should call otherwise) how much I am, with the greatest Respect immaginable, ⌜dear Miss Fanny,⌝

Your most Devoted & most Obedient servant

Tho[s] Barlow.

[Hoxton][85]

Notwithstanding I was at once sorry & provoked at perceiving how sanguine this youth chose to be, I was not absolutely concerned at receiving this 2[d] Letter, because I regarded it as a fortunate opportunity of putting an unalterable Conclusion to the whole Affair. However, ⌜as I had begun by asking my Father's advice,⌝ I thought it my duty to speak to Father before I sent an Answer, never doubting his immediate concurrence.

My mother, Sukey & I went to the opera that Evening;[86] it was therefore too late when I returned to send a Letter to Hoxton—but I went up stairs into the study, & told my Father I had received another Epistle from M[r] Barlow which I could only attribute to my not answering, as I had wished, his first; I added that I proposed, with his leave, to Write to M[r] Barlow the next morning.

My Father looked grave, asked me for the Letter, put it in his Pocket unread, & wished me good Night.

I was siezed with a kind of pannic—I trembled at the idea of his Espousing, however mildly, the Cause of this young man:—I passed a restless Night, & in the morning dared not Write without his permission, which I was now half afraid to ask.

About 2 O'clock, while I was dawdling in the study, & Waiting for an opportunity to speak, ⌜we heard a Rap at the Door—& soon after, John came up,⌝ & said 'A Gentleman is below, who asks for Miss Burney,—M[r] Barlow.'

I think I was never more ⌜mad⌝ in my life—to have taken

---

[84] 'not'.

[85] In the original.

[86] The works performed were *Piramo e Tisbe* and *La Difesa d'Amore* (a pasticcio) (*LS* 4 iii. 1899).

pains to avoid a private Conversation so highly disagreeable to me, & at last to be forced into it at so unfavourable a Juncture,—for I had now 2 Letters from him, both Unanswered & consequently open to his Conjectures. I exclaimed ⌜"Lord!"⌝— how provoking! what shall I do?'

My Father looked uneasy & perplexed:—he said something about not being hasty, which I did not desire him to explain, ⌜but only said as I left the Room—

'Well, I must soon tell him I *have* answered his letter, & so send one tomorrow, & let him think it kept at the Post office.' In this determination, I⌝ went down stairs.—I saw my mother pass into the Back Parlour; which did not add to the *Graciousness* of my Reception of poor Mr Barlow, who I found alone in the Parlour. I was not sorry that none of the Family were there, as I now began to seriously dread any protraction of this affair.

He came up to me, & with an Air of *tenderness* & satisfaction, began some anxious Enquiries about my Health, but I interrupted him with saying 'I fancy, Sir, You have not received a Letter I ⌜⟨have written to you⟩⌝—I—'

'A Letter?—no, Ma'am!'

'You will have it, then, to-morrow, Sir.'

We were both silent for a minute or two, when he said 'In consequence, I presume, Ma'am, of the one I—'

'Yes, Sir!' Cried I.

'And pray—Ma'am—Miss Burney!—may I—beg to ask the contents? that is—the—the—' he could not go on.

'Sir—I—it was only—it was merely—in short, you will see it to-morrow.'

'But if you would favour me with the Contents now, I could perhaps Answer it at once?'

'Sir, it requires no Answer!'

A second silence ensued. I was really distressed myself to see *his* distress, which was very apparent. After some time, he stammered out something of *hoping*—& *beseeching*,—which, gathering more firmness, I announced—'I am much obliged to You, Sir, for the great opinion You are pleased to have of me—but I should be sorry you should lose any more Time upon my account—as I have no thoughts at all of changing my situation.'

He seemed to be quite overset: having, therefore so freely explained myself, I then asked him to sit down, & began to talk of the Weather. When he had a little recovered himself, he drew a Chair close to me, & began making most ardent professions of respect & regard, & so forth. I interrupted him, as soon as I could, & begged him to rest satisfied with my Answer.

'*Satisfied?*' repeated he—'my dear Ma'am—is that possible?'

'Perhaps, Sir,' said I, 'I ought to make some apologies for not answering your first Letter—but really, I was so much surprised—upon so short an Acquaintance.'

He then began making Excuses for having written but as to *short acquaintance*, he owned it was a reason for *me*—but for *him*—fifty Years could not have more convinced him of my &c &c.

'You have taken a sudden, & far too partial idea of my character, answered I. 'If you look round among your older Acquaintance, I doubt not but you will very soon be able to make a better choice.'

He shook his Head: 'I have seen, Madam, a great many Ladies, it is true—but never—'

'You do me much honour;' cried I, 'but I must desire you would take no further trouble about me—for I have not, at present, the slightest thoughts of ever leaving this House.'

'*At present?*' repeated he, eagerly,—'no, I would not expect it—I would not *wish* to precipitate—but in future—'

'Niether now or ever, Sir,' returned I, 'have I any view of changing my situation.'

'But surely—surely this can never be! so severe a resolution—you cannot mean it—it would be wronging all the world!'

'I am extremely sorry, Sir, that you did not receive my ⌈Letter⌉—because it might have saved you this trouble.'

He looked very much mortified, & said, in [a][87] dejected voice—'If there is any thing in me—in my connections—or in my situation in Life—which you wholly think unworthy of You—& beneath you——or if my Character or Disposition meet with your disapprobation—I will immediately forgo all—I will not—I would not—'

---

[87] Inserted by FBA.

'No, indeed, Sir,' cried I, 'I have niether seen or heard any thing of ⌐your character⌐ that was to your disadvantage—& I have no doubts of your worthiness—'

He thanked me, & seemed reassured; ⌐but⌐ renewed his solicitations in the most urgent manner. He repeatedly begged my permission to acquaint my Family of the state of his affairs, & to abide by their decision—but I would not let him say two words following upon that subject. I told him that ⌐the⌐ Answer ⌐I had written⌐ was a final one, & begged him to take it as such.

He remonstrated very earnestly. 'This is the severest decision!—⌐I am persuaded, Madam, you cannot be so cruel?⌐— Surely you must allow that the *social state* is what we were all meant for?—that we were created for one another?—that to form such a resolution is contrary to the design of our Being?—'

'All this may be true,—' said I;—'I have nothing to | say in contradiction to it—but you know there are many odd Characters in the World—& I am one of them.'

'O no, no, no,—that can never be!—but is it possible you can have so bad an opinion of the married state? It seems to me the *only* state for happiness!—'

'Well, Sir, *You* are attached to the married Life—*I* am to the single—therefore, *every man in his humour*—[88] do *you* follow *your* opinion,—& let *me* follow *mine*.'

'But surely—is not this—*singular*?—

'I give you leave, Sir,' cried I, laughing, 'to think me singular —odd—Queer—nay, even whimsical, if you please.'

'But, my *dear* Miss Burney, only—'

'I entreat you, Sir, to take my Answer—You really pain me by being so urgent.—'

'That would not I do for the World!—I only beg You to suffer me—perhaps in future—

'No, indeed; I shall never change—I do assure you you will find me very obstinate!'

He began to lament his own Destiny. I grew extremely tired of saying so often the same thing;—but I could not absolutely turn him out of the House, & indeed he seemed so dejected &

[88] FB's forced levity is an echo, of course, of Ben Jonson's play.

unhappy, that I made it my study to soften my refusal as much as I could without leaving room for future expectation.

About this Time, my mother came in. We both rose.—I was horridly provoked at my situation—

'I am only come in for a Letter,' cried she,—'pray ⎸don't let me disturb you.—' & away she went.

⌐Very obliging indeed!⌐

She was no sooner gone, than Mr. Barlow began again the same story, & seemed determined not to give up his Cause. He hoped, at least, that I would allow him to enquire after my Health?—

'I must beg you, Sir, to send me no more Letters.'

He seemed much hurt.

'You had better, Sir, think of me no more—if you study your own happiness—'

'I *do* study my own happiness—more than I have ever had Any probability of doing before—!'

'You have made an unfortunate Choice, Sir; but you will find it easier to forget it than you imagine. You have only to suppose I was not at Mr Burney's on May Day—& it was a mere chance my being there—& then you will be—

'But if I *could*—could I also forget seeing you at [old]⁸⁹ Mrs Burney's?—and if I did—can I forget that I see you now?—'

'O yes!—in 3 months Time you may forget you ever knew me. You will not find it so difficult ⌐a Task⌐ as you suppose.'

'You have heard, Ma'am, of an Old man being Growed young?—perhaps you believe *that*?—But you will not deny me leave to sometimes see you?—'

'My Father, Sir, is seldom,—hardly ever, indeed, at Home—'

'I have never seen the Doctor—but I hope he would ⎸not refuse me permission to enquire after your Health? I have no wish without his Consent.'

'Though I acknowledge myself to be *singular* I would not have you think me either *affected* or *trifling*,—& therefore I must assure you that I am *fixed* in the Answer I have given You; *Unalterably* fixed.'

---

⁸⁹ Inserted by FBA.

His entreaties grew extremely ⌈urgent & very⌉ distressing to me:—he besought me to take more Time, said it should be the study of his life to make me happy. 'Allow me—my *dear* Miss Burney—only to hope that my future Conduct—'

'I shall always think myself obliged, nay honoured by your good opinion—& you are entitled to my best wishes for your Health & Happiness—but indeed, the less we meet the better.'

'What—what can I do?' cried he, very sorrowfully.

'Why—go & ponder upon this affair for about half an Hour—then say, what an odd, queer, strange Creature she is! & then—think of something else.'

'O no; no!—you cannot suppose all that?—I shall think of nothing else; *your* refusal is more pleasing than any other Lady's acceptance—'

He said this very simply, but too seriously for me to Laugh at it. Just then, Sukey came in—but did not stay two minutes. It would have been shocking to be thus left purposely as if with a declared Lover, ⌈& yet⌉ I was not sorry to have an opportunity of preventing future doubts or expectations.

I rose & Walked to the Window, thinking it high Time to End a Conversation already much too long; & when he again began to entreat me not to be so *very severe*, I told him that I was *sure* I should never alter the Answer I made at first; that I was very happy at Home, & not at all inclined to try my fate elsewhere; I then desired my Compliments to M^rs O'Connor, & Miss Dickenson, & made a *reverence* by way of leave taking.

'I am extremely sorry to detain you so long, Ma'am,—' said he, in a melancholy Voice. I made no answer. He Walked about the Room; & then again besought my leave to ask me how I did some other Time—I absolutely, though Civilly, refused it; & told him frankly that, fixed as I was, it was better ⌈⟨for himself⟩⌉ that we should not meet.

He then took his leave:—returned back—took leave—returned again:—⌈he had then a new Petition, for then I took a more formal leave of him,⌉ expressing my good wishes for his Welfare, in a sort of way that implied I expected never to see him again—he would fain have taken a more *tender* leave of me,—but I repulsed him with great surprise & displeasure. I did not, however, as he was so terribly sorrowful, refuse him my Hand, which he had made sundry vain attempts to take in the course of our Conversation; when I withdrew it, as I did presently, I rang the Bell, to prevent him again returning from the Door.

Though I was really sorry for the unfortunate & misplaced attachment which this Young man professes for ⌐ me, yet I could almost have *Jumped* for Joy when he was gone, to think that the affair was thus finally over.

Indeed I think it hardly possible for a Woman to be in a more irksome situation, than when rejecting ⌐an honest⌐ man who is all humility, Respect & submission, & who throws himself & his Fortune at her Feet.

I had no opportunity of speaking to my Father all that Day. In the Evening Mr Burney & Hetty came. Hetty told me, that the Day before, M^rs O Connor had Called on her, & ⌐told her of Mr. Barlow's having owned to her⌐ his Attachment to me, & requested ⌐of her to let him⌐ know, first, whether I had any pre-engagement, & secondly, whether I had ever expressed any *Antipathy* to him. She answered both these in the Negative, & then M^rs O'Connor, in Mr Barlow's Name, entreated her to be his Advocate; which she readily promised.

After his Conversation with me, he Called on her himself. She says he was all dejection & sadness. He expressed the greatest *Respect* for me, feared I thought him wanting in it;—apologised for his early Declaration, which, he said, resulted from his sincerity, & his having no Experience either in the arts, or the ways of men.

My Father sent for Hetty up stairs, & made a thousand Enquiries concerning Mr Barlow.

The next Day [29 May]—a Day the remembrance of which will be never erased from my memory—my Father first spoke to me *in favour* of Mr Barlow! & desired me not to be *peremtory* in the Answer I ⌐was going⌐ to Write. |

I scarce made any answer—I was terrified to Death—I felt the utter impossibility of resisting not merely my Father's *persuasion*, but even his *Advice.*—I felt, too, that I had no *argumentative* objections to make to Mr Barlow, his Character—Disposition—situation—I knew nothing against—but O!—I felt he was no Companion for my Heart!—I wept like an

Infant—Eat nothing—seemed as if already married—&
passed the whole Day in more misery than, merely on my
own account, I ever did before in my life,—except upon the
loss of my own beloved mother—& ever revered & most dear
Grandmother![90]

After supper, I went into the study, while my dear Father
was alone, to wish him Good Night, which I did as chearfully
as I could, though pretty evidently in dreadful uneasiness.
When I had got to the Door, he called me back, & asked
me concerning a new mourning ⌜Gown I had bought for the
mourning of ⟨Queen Caroline—⟩[91] he desired to know what
it would come to, & as our ⟨allowance⟩ for Cloaths is not
sumptuous, said he would assist⌝ Sukey & me which he accordingly did, & affectionately embraced me, saying 'I wish I
could do more for Thee, Fanny!' 'O Sir!—' cried I—'*I* wish
for Nothing!—only let me Live with you!—' —'My life!' cried
he, kissing me kindly, 'Thee shalt live with me for ever, if Thee
wilt! Thou canst not think I meant to get rid of thee?'

'I could not, Sir! I could not!' cried I, [I could not out-
live][92] such a thought—' | I saw his dear Eyes full of Tears! a
mark of his tenderness which I shall never forget!

'God knows'—continued he—'I wish not to part with my
Girls!—they are my greatest Comfort!—only—do not be too
hasty!—'

Thus relieved, restored to future hopes, I went to Bed as
light, happy & thankful as if Escaped from Destruction.

I had, however, written my Letter before my Father spoke,
& as I had expressly told Mr Barlow it contained a Refusal, I
thought it would be even ridiculous to alter it, ⌜& I rather⌝
determined, if my Father had persisted in desiring it, to *unsay* a
rejection, than not to write it after having declared I already
had. This is the Copy:

[90] FB's Grandmother Sleepe.
[91] George III's sister, Caroline Matilda (1751–75), who m. (1766) Christian VII,
K. of Denmark. She had died 10 May, and a general mourning was ordered, which
lasted from 24 May to 5 July (*YW* xxxii. 238 n. 6).
[92] Substituted by FBA for an obliterated phrase, not recovered.

St Martin's Street
29 May [1775]

To Thomas Barlow

ALS copy (Berg), 29 May 1775
The original is missing. FB's copy is in the Journal for 1775, fo. 35^v.

St Martin's Street
Leicester Fields.

Sir,

I am much concerned to find that my silence to the first Letter with which you honoured me, has not had the Effect it was meant to produce, of preventing your giving yourself any further trouble upon my Account.

The good opinion you are pleased to express of me, however extraordinary upon so short an Acquaintance, certainly claims my Acknowledgements; but as I have no intention of changing my present situation, I can only assure You of my good wishes for Your Health & Happiness, & request & desire that you will bestow no further Thoughts, Time, or Trouble upon,

Sir,

Your most humble servant,

F. Burney.

[*The Journal for 1775 resumes.*]

From that Day to this, my Father, I thank [H]eaven, has never again mentioned Mr Barlow. |

June [8]^{93}

I called at my sister's lately, & was very sorry to hear that Mr Barlow, who has been again to visit her, expressed himself to be as strongly as ever Attached to me, & requested of her to suffer him to meet me some Day at her House, by letting him know when I was with her. She told him I should be very angry with her—he promised to appear so much sur-

---

^{93} Corrected from '9th'.

prised, that I should never know the meeting was not accidental,—& she was at length prevailed with to promise him her assistance.

However, reflecting upon it afterwards, she repented, & therefore told me of what had passed. I Assured her I was extremely glad she had saved me so disagreeable [a][94] Task as a second refusal should have been—for as *his* motives are obvious, so *my* resolution is unalterable.—but by my Father, who, I am sure is too indulgent to require me to give my Hand without my Heart.

I Commissioned her, when she saw him, to tell him that she found by my Conversation I was so *determined*, that she thought it was only exposing both of us to uneasiness to promote a meeting.

I wish this young man Well—I believe him to be worthy—but am sorry he will not be Answered. |

⌐Signor Celestini has had a Benefit at Carli[s]le House—to which we all went. The affair concerning him & Madame Giordani[95] has been *Compromized*. He gave a good Concert, but had little Company. He begged my Father to use his Interest for him, which he did, & I believe got off some Tickets for him.

We met Mr. & Miss Louisa Harris there & while we were talking with them, most of the Performers in the Concert came up to them. They addressed us, & entered into Conversation with the Harris's, who seem never so pleased as when Engaged with the most eminent singers & players.

Mr. Merlin, Clementi, & Jones also joined us, & we had much amusement with the Observations of Mr. Merlin, which are natural & ingenious.

Celestini was extremely pleased to see us, & promised to visit us again.

The Coris also have had a Benefit, to which some of us went.[96] They are now gone for Another year to Scotland. They

---

94 Inserted by FBA.

95 Probably Nicolina Giordani, called 'La Spiletta'; singer. The 'affair' was perhaps a financial dispute. No advertisement has been found for Celestini's benefit. See Highfill; *LS 4* iii. 1874, 1881, 1896.

96 The benefit was held on 28 Apr. at the Hanover Square Rooms under the

spent one afternoon here, in which Signora Bichelli sung to us very sweetly. She has had three Children since she was first in London & has lost some of her beauty, though she still retains a very pleasing share of it. |

In returning from Barsanti's, with my sister, not long since, we met Mrs. Pringle. She *recognized* us immediately, & joined us—Hetty Coloured, & was as much embarrassed as she had been at our first meeting; but it soon wore off, upon Mrs. Pringle's cordiality. She stopt & chatted a few minutes. She desired a renewal of acquaintance, asked Hetty's Direction, & promised to make the first Visit.

Miss Barsanti has lost her Father, who was a very worthy man, though superannuated before his death. Her Health Continues to be very indifferent, she was so ill on the Night of her Benefit, that she Could not Act,—she is now gone to Bristol, where she is Engaged for the summer.[97] Sukey & I are equally sorry we can see her so seldom; we were always sure of passing our Time very agreeably ⟨with her,⟩ whenever we could have her, & independent of her Talents, I love her for her Character & Disposition. Indeed she is a very charming Girl, & her good Conduct gives me the greatest pleasure. I hope to *preserve* my friendship for her to the End of my Life, & to *encrease* my power of shewing it.

Mr. & Mrs. Rishton have been in Town lately, though for a very short Time. Just as they were, they continue to be all happiness & love! |

Miss Davis, to the great Consternation of the managers, has gained her cause. They will lose near £2200.[98]

direction of Bach and Abel (*Morning Chronicle*, 28 Apr.). The Corris returned to Edinburgh, where they remained until about 1790, when they came back to London. The children mentioned here have not been traced and may have died young. A daughter, Sophia Giustina, was born to Signora Corri (née Baccheli) just after her return to Edinburgh. Sophia m. (1792) the composer Jan Ladislav Dussek and died in 1847. See *New Grove*.

[97] See above, p. 114 and nn. 27, 29; p. 135 and nn. 71–2.

[98] See above, p. 25. Miss Davies won her case in the Court of Common Pleas on 31 May. The Opera managers were obliged to pay her £1,500 plus costs and £500 for her lost benefit (Highfill).

Friday, June [9][99]

We this Evening expect the long promised *musical* visit from
Signora Agujari.

Miss Lidderdale of Lynn has been at our House to spend a
[few][1] Days, in her way to Wales, where she is going to pass
the summer.⌐ On Wednesday morning, while my mother & ⌐I
were with her, [xxxxx *½ line*] the maid came up stairs, & said
a *Gentleman* was in⌐ the Parlour, waiting for me—'Did not he
send up his Name?' cried Mama. 'No, Ma'am,' answered she.
'Do you know who he is?' 'No, Ma'am.'

I supposed it was Mr Barlow, & heartily wished I had been
out. I went down stairs, ⌐⟨nevertheless,⟩ perforce,⌐ & found
him Alone. He Bowed. I curtsied. He seemed at a loss what to
say—& as I determined not to ask him to sit down, or to say
any thing that might encourage him either to stay, or to repeat
his Visit, I was silent also. At length, he stammered out 'I
hope—Ma'am—you—are well?—'

'Very well, I thank You, Sir,' was my laconic reply.

Another silence; & then—'Your Cold?—I hope, Ma'am, I
hope you have quite—'

'O it is quite gone,' cried I; 'I am perfectly well.'

'I am very happy to hear it—I could not,—Ma'am—I
could not deny myself—the satisfaction of enquiring after
your Health.—'

'I am sorry, Sir,' answered I very gravely, that You should
have taken the trouble to Call.'

'Does it give you—I hope, Ma'am—it does not give you—
any *uneasiness?*—'

I made no answer, but went towards the Window, where I
saw Dick & Miss Fydell,[2] a lady who was coming to see Miss

[99] Corrected from '10th'.

[1] Inserted by FBA.

[2] Probably either Elizabeth Fydell, m. (1776) John Betts of Boston, Lincolnshire;
or her younger sister Fanny, m. (1777) Thomas Rogers, daughters of Richard Fydell
(?1709–80) of Boston. Miss Lidderdale later bequeathed a miniature of herself to
their brother Thomas (1740–1812). See Sedgwick, s.v. Richard Fydell; G. P. Judd
IV, *Members of Parliament, 1734–1832* (New Haven, 1955), p. 202; IGI; wills of Dorothy
Young, PCC, prob. 18 Feb. 1805; Richard Fydell, prob. 3 May 1780; Elizabeth
Fydell, prob. 6 Feb. 1783 (PRO).

Lidderdale, ⌐in the street;⌐ I was rejoiced at so speedy an opportunity of Ending our Tete à Tete, & flew myself to the Door to ⌐let them in.⌐ I then began to talk with Miss Fydell, all the Time standing myself, that I might not be obliged to ask Mr Barlow to sit.

He seemed a good deal agitated. I was truly quite sorry to be so rude to him—but what can ⌐a Woman do⌐ when a man will not take an answer? I would with all my Heart, have been civil & sociable with him in a friendly manner, from gratitude for the real regard he seems to have for me—but I have ⌐heard⌐ too much of mankind to believe he would not draw *Inferences*, & entertain *Expectations* from such *friendliness*, that might greatly distress & embarrass me: besides, ever since the Day that my *Father* spoke for him, I have quite dreaded the continuation of his addresses.

His situation was too uneasy to be long supported, &, after enquiring about the Family, he took his leave, with a look so mortified & unhappy, that I felt shocked at myself for what, in fact, I could not help.—⌐how ever, when I heard the street Door opened, I just shewed my self in the Passage,⌐ & called out that I wished him a good Walk. He started back & seemed going to return—but I immediately came into the Parlour, yet not before I could see by his change of Countenance that he was pleased at this little mark of Civility.

I hope, however, that this Visit will be his last. I think he will never have the courage to make Another. I have not mentioned it to my Father. Indeed I dare not renew a subject which has caused me so much uneasiness & fright. Sorry as I am for Mr Barlow, who is a worthy young man, I cannot involve myself in a Life of discomfort for his satisfaction.

I have had the great pleasure of a Letter[3] from my dear Mr Crisp, in answer to my pleas against marrying *Heart-whole*, in which he most kindly gives up the Cause, & allows of my reasoning & Opinion.

What my mother thinks of the Affair I know not, but the other Day, when Hetty & Mr Burney were here, she suddenly, in a *laughing way*, turned to me, & said 'O but—Fanny!—was

---

[3] Missing.

you cruel?—or kind, the other morning?—upon my Word—it is Time to enquire!—a Gentleman *whose Visits are admitted*!'

I only laughed, not caring to be serious so publicly, but really it was a very provoking *turn* to give to Mr Barlow's Calls;—& will make me doubly desirous that they should not be renewed.

I forgot to mention that one Evening, about a fortnight since, as we Were all Walking in the Park, we met Mrs Pringle again. I introduced to her her *young old* friend, Charlotte, & they were mutually glad to see each other. She was extremely cordial in her Invitation to all of us, & I much wish it was in my power to accept them.

We also saw poor Miss Laluze,[4] whose Face immediately shewed that she recollected my Eldest sister & me; however, we Walked on, wishing to avoid speaking to her: but when we were at Spring Garden Gate, she just touched my shoulder, as she came suddenly behind us, & said 'Miss Burney!—how do you do, ⌐Ma'am?¬'—

I answered her rather coldly—& Hetty turned from her abruptly. I was afterwards very sorry that I did not speak with more kindness to her, for Sukey says that she looked greatly disappointed. It is, however, impossible & improper to keep up acquaintance with a Female who has lost her character, however sincerely they may be objects of Pity. What way this unfortunate Girl is in, at present, I know not; but Miss Strange believes her to be as culpable as ever. She was with [a][5] very decent looking Party, & was very genteely Dressed, without shew or frippery, & looked very handsome.

Much is to be said in Excuse of a poor credulous young Creature, whose Person is Attractive, while her mind is unformed. Should she quit her way of life before she grows more abandonned, I shall have great pleasure in shewing her any Civility in my circumscribed power, from the remembrance of her Innocence when I first knew her. Miss Strange has heard the story of her *marriage* all contradicted.

[4] See *EJL* i. 98.
[5] Inserted by FBA.

To Samuel Crisp

AL (Barrett), 10 June 1775
2 double sheets 4to, 8 pp., wafer
Addressed: Saml Crisp Esqr, | at Mrs Hamilton's, | Chesington near
Kingston | upon Thames | Surrey.
Annotated (*by FBA*): ⊞ ✳ 1775 N° 13 N° 38 on Mr. Barlow,—marriage,
and Agujari.
The first half of the letter repeats FB's latest journal account of Mr Barlow
and is here omitted.

At length—we have heard Agujari!—We wished for you!—
I cannot tell you how *much* we wished for you! the great singers
of former years, whom I have heard you so emphatically ⌜speak
of⌝ seem to have all their Talents revived in this wonderful
singer. I could compare her to nothing *I* ever *heard* but only
to what ⌜I have heard of⌝—Your Carestino—Farinelli—
Senesino[6]—alone are worthy to be ranked with the Bastardini.
Such a powerful voice!—so astonishing a Compass—reaching
from C in the middle of the Harpsichord, to *2* notes *above* the
Harpsichord! Every tone so clear, so full—so charming! Then
her *shake*—so *plump*—so true, so open!—it is [as][7] strong &
distinct as Mr Burney's upon the Harpsichord.—

Besides it's great power, her voice is all sweetness,—&,
when she pleases, all softness & delicacy. She sings in the
highest style of Taste, & with an *Expression* so pathetic, it is
impossible to hear it unmoved. She ⌜does⌝ the greatest difficulties that are possible to be given to her, with all the ˡ ease
& facility that I could say ⌜what's o'Clock?⌝

She came before 7—& stayed till 12, & was singing almost
all the Time![8] She permitted us to encore almost every song.

[6] Giovanni Carestini (*c*.1705–*c*.1760), Farinelli [Carlo Broschi] (1705–82), and
Senesino [Francesco Bernardi] (d. by 27 Jan. 1759) were famous Italian castrato
singers (*New Grove*).
[7] Inserted by FBA.
[8] FB adds in her journal account (fo. 39^v) that she came with Signor Colla, who

She sung in 20 different styles. The greatest was son Regina &
son[o] amante from Didone.[9] Good ⌈God⌉! what a song! &
how sung! Then she gave us 2 or 3 *Cantabiles*, sung divinely,
then she ⌈chanted⌉ some *Church Music*, in a style so nobly
simple & unadorned, that it stole into one's very soul! Then
she gave us a Bravura, with difficulties which seemed only
possible for a Instrument in the Hands of a great master—
Then she spoke some Recitative—so nobly.—

In short—whether she most astonished, or most delighted
us, I cannot say—but she is really a *sublime* singer.

We had not a soul here but our own Family, which was her
particular desire.[10] She gave us some hopes of coming once
more before she quits England—if she does—& if we know it
in Time—could you resist coming to Town for one Night?
Papa could introduce *You* to her as one who desired to be
admitted, because your Health would not permit you to hear
her in the Pantheon. Indeed, it would | *greatly* answer to you.

Besides her musical Talents she has really a great deal of
⌈Wit⌉ & would entertain you by her conversation.

She also has great ideas of action—& grew so animated in
singing an *Arria* Parlante from Didone,[11] that she acted it
through out, with great spirit & feeling.

I could not help regretting to her that she should sing at the
Pantheon, when she was so much formed for the *Theatre*. She
made Faces & shrugs, in the Italian way, & said 'oui—*comme
une* statue!—*comme une petite Ecoliere!*'—& then she took up a
Book, to take herself off when singing at the Pantheon.

We all hoped that, After the Gabriella was gone, she would
return to England, & to the Opera House. She said that if ever
she did—it should be through the means of Dr. *Burney*—into

accompanied her on the harpsichord, and that she began with a minuet of his composition. Cf. also *Mem.* ii. 26–31.

[9] *Didone* by Metastasio, set by Colla (1773).

[10] FB notes in the journal (fo. 39ᵛ) that the evening's recital was actually opened
by Charles Rousseau Burney. She also qualifies somewhat her praise of Agujari by
extolling the superior *'feeling'* or *'sensibility'* of Millico (fo. 40ʳ).

[11] *'Non hai ragione, Ingrato'* (Journal, fo. 39ᵛ). FB records (ibid.) that 'she was
desirous that we should all understand the words, before we heard the music, & in a
Voice softly melodious, she repeated the song through before she sang it, & then
Translated its *sense* into French.'

whose Hands she would put her Engagements—& to *no one else!*[12]

She professes great contempt for the managers.

By the way, Miss Davis has gained her Cause, & the managers will lose near £2000.

Among other things, Agujari sung a *Rondeau,* [*3 words cut away*] for she says she detests [*ces miséres là! ils me font guignon!*']^[13] is not, for her Talents are so very superior that she cannot chuse but hold all other performers cheap. The Gabriella, her only Rival, she never heard, & consequently she has never met with any singer equal to herself.

She is a wonderful Creature!—

Adieu, my dear Daddy—my Father cannot yet fix his Day for dear Chesington. I wish I could fix *mine*! My love to Kitty, & respects to Mrs. H. [*bottom 3 lines cut away*]

[*The Journal for 1775 resumes. FB's journal account of Agujari has been omitted, except for the citations in the notes to the preceding letter. The top of the first page following has been cut away.*]

″exquisitely charming.

Captain Bloomfield's[14] contemptible Rival, Sir Martin, called here 2 or 3 Times upon Mr. Rishton, & *consulted* with him concerning Miss Turner, for though he at present *thinks* of marrying her, yet he says he is *afraid she will dispute the point with him*,—& when Mr. Rishton desired him to explain himself, he could only discover a general fear, of being made a Jerry! But I fancy the real objection is that he has not the spirit or generosity to offer himself without *hesitation*, to a Woman of small fortune, though as he has actually been Jilted by *2* Women of *large* Fortune, he declares he will never offer himself to a third.″[15]

---

[12] She never performed at the Opera, but, after a trip back to Italy, returned and sang at the Pantheon until 1777 (see her letter to CB, 'Parma', 18 Dec. 1775, Osborn).

[13] Supplied from the journal, fo. 40ᵛ. The bottom 3 lines of the page are cut away.

[14] See *EJL* i. 109.

[15] In letters to FB earlier this year (1 Jan., 17 Feb., Berg), MAR calls Sir Martin Folkes 'that silly Proud wretch' and an 'insignificant little Reptile'. In a letter of 10 Sept. (Berg), she probably alludes to him and to Frances Turner: 'As for the Affair you ask about a Certain gentleman and a friend of mine it is either at a dead stand or quite of [*sic*]—you know my opinion of him it is not mended—as for her she is superior to all her sex and theirs too he is a dirty little Fellow.' The two women who

[*top of page cut away*]

I called lately upon my Grandmother, & found her at Cards with my Aunts & M^rs O Connor, who I saw looked rather gravely upon me. I enquired after Miss Dickenson, & sat & chatted about a Quarter of an Hour, & then I said I must be gone, for Miss Cooke from Chesington, & M^rs & Miss Simmons were to Drink Tea with us. Just as I rose, & was taking leave, M^rs O Connor called out 'No! stop a moment!—' I stood, suspended,—& in a solemn kind of manner, she addressed herself to my Grandmother & said 'Would you think this lady to be one of the greatest Cheats that ever was Born?'

They all stared, & she went on.

'Who—to look in her Face, & see so much good Nature would believe her to have *none*?—to be actually *cruel*?—here has she sat this half Hour—& never once had the common Civility to ask how my poor Mr Barlow does, whose Heart she has been breaking!—Fie!—Fie!'

I was much surprised at this Attack,—& made no immediate answer, hardly knowing whether she meant it seriously, or ⌐as badinage⌐—my aunts looked rather displeased, & my Grandmother said—'I'll assure you, I began to wonder what you *meant*, by Calling *my* Grand Daughter a Cheat!'

'O yes! cried M^rs O Connor, I expected to make you all angry!—I thought as much! but I could not contain—poor Mr Barlow! how will he wish *he* had happened to have been here, when I tell him—but you need not, I shall say, for she never once asked how you did!'

'If Mr Barlow would have been *the better* for any Enquiry, said I, I should certainly—

'O—if you meant *nothing else*,' cried she, 'it may be as well as it is! but you *will*—you *will* say *yes* yet?—'

'Let us hope, said my Aunt Anne, very judiciously, that they may *both* do better.'

'Ay—well—I don't know—I can't say—all I know is that

had jilted Sir Martin were apparently a Miss Williams and a Miss Harrison (MAR to FB, 17 Feb., 5 Nov. 1775, Berg). He married Miss Turner at the end of this year (on 28 Dec.).

poor Mr Barlow is almost dying with grief—you—you—
naughty thing! you have broke his Heart!'

'O, cried I (endeavouring to laugh it off) I dare say he will
survive—'

'O!—very well, Ma'am—very well—pray *exult*—it is
always the way with you young ladies—'

I determined to make no more answer, as I was quite affronted at this speech;—*Exult*—! I would not for the World!—
but how affected would it sound in *me* to *pity* a man for my own
cruelty, as she Calls it! |

'He is a good & most Worthy Young man,' continued she;
'& I have the greatest regard for him—however—perhaps—
before twice 7 years Time—you may *repent*—'

How excessively impertinent! I was quite silent, & so were
my Grand mother & Aunt Anne;—but my poor Aunt Becky
simply added to M^rs O'Connor's prediction, by saying—'Ay—
when you are *like us*!'

Perhaps ⌐she⌐ [M^rs O'Connor][16] thought she had gone
too far, for she afterwards seemed to endeavour to *soften* her
Attack by saying a great deal of the good *nature* of my *looks*;
—& wishing—though with an air of doubt—that I might be
happier.

As to my enquiring after Mr Barlow, ⌐I own⌐ I felt too
conscious to mention his Name, & had I *looked* so, & spoke of
him at the same Time, I am certain she would have put a
wrong construction upon it;—besides, Mr Barlow, I believe,
would *catch at a shadow*, & if he heard I meerly asked after his
Health, he would be anxious, I doubt not, to answer me himself, & I should be extremely uneasy to have, or to give, any
further trouble about this affair. |

30   [St Martin's Street,
                                        30 October 1775]

To Samuel Crisp

AL (Barrett), incomplete, 30 Oct. 1775, 1½ double sheets 4to, 6 pp.
Annotated (by FBA): ⚹ ‾30 Octr 75 S. Harriet—C.B. S. Payne FB.
F d'A

[16] Substituted for 'she' by FBA.

The last sheet has been cut away. It presumably contained a reference to Sarah Payne, for whom see below, p. 193.

My dear Daddy.

It is so long since I wrote to you that I suppose you conclude we are all gone a fortune Hunting in some other planet;—however though I cannot totally exculpate myself from the charge of Negligence, yet a great part of the Time during which I have been silent, has been employed in a manner that would have given you no pleasure to have heard of,—for my poor grandmother Burney, after a long painful, lingering Illness, in the course of which we all contributed our mites towards assisting as Nurses,—has Breathed her last.[17] I shall not dwell upon this melancholy subject, as I know your peculiar aversion to the *Horrors*,—but shall proceed to write upon those topics which you have yourself made choice of.

Now first as to that R[ogue] my F[ather]. He was at Buxton near three weeks, & Bathed 15 Times.—He went afterwards to sea Bathing, at Clay in Norfolk.[18] He has been returned Home about a fortnight, & I thank God is in good Health at present, though his Hand is still *obstinately bent*. The History has been this very Day, for the first Time since it's long Cessation, put into the Press. It is now *rough* written to the End of the 1st Volume, Preface & Dedication inclusive. When it is actually published, we intend to keep the Carnival.[19]

As to the Gabriellé—she has taken a House in Golden Square, & has had a Brass plate put on the Door, with *M^rs* Gabrielle on it. She & Rauzzini seem admirably suited for each other, for let her Live ever so much *en | princesse*, he will always keep her in Countenance by living *en prince*. He has had his Drawing room painted after the manner of the Card

[17] Mrs Ann (Cooper) Burney was buried in St Paul's Churchyard, Covent Garden, on Sunday, 1 Oct. (*The Registers of St. Paul's Church, Covent Garden*, ed. W. H. Hunt (1906–9), v. 102). FB's journal for the summer of 1775 was presumably taken up largely with her long final illness, and perhaps destroyed on that account.

[18] Cley next the Sea in North Norfolk. Buxton, a market town in North Derbyshire, is noted for its bracing climate and was formerly a popular watering place. CB presumably bathed in the thermal springs to ease his rheumatic arm and hand. See Lonsdale, pp. 155–66.

[19] See ibid., pp. 166–9. CB's Dedication to the Queen of *Hist. Mus.* was actually composed by Samuel Johnson.

Rooms at the Pantheon, with Pink & Green, & finely ornamented. The first opera is to be next Saturday,[20] when if you
do not come to Town I shall think & Conclude that you are
lost to all the St Cecelian powers of attraction. Indeed if niether
Agujari or Gabrielli have charms to allure you to the Opera or
Pantheon, one may imagine that you are become as indifferent
to music, as to Dancing or Horse-Racing. The opera is to be
Metastasio's *Didone*, which is the very opera that Agujari sung
to us 12 songs from, composed by her maestro Sig^r Colla. It is
to be a *half* pasticcio, but all the Recitatives by Sacchini, as
well as a Cantabile for Rauzzini, & *All the part* of la Gabrielli.
This I very much rejoice at, as I had rather hear her first
in music of his [Sacchini's] Composition, than of any other
maestro whose Works I am acquainted with.

I am extremely glad, also, that the squalling Galli is dismissed,[21] & Savoi once more taken as second man.[22] A sister
of Gabrielli[23] is to be 2^d Woman, & I hear she is very pretty
but no further has yet transpired.

The Rehearsals are begun, & the managers are very busy.
My Father, at the earnest invitation of M^r & Mrs Yates & M^{rs}
Brooke, Dined at their House last week, with the following
delicious party;—Rauzzini, Sacchini, the sister, & the Gabrielli
herself! He tells us that $^|$ she is still very pretty, & extremely
elegant, very well bred, & has the air & manner of a woman of
Rank. She did not sing, niether did any presume to ask her:
but she has invited my Father to her House, & desired to
cultivate his acquaintance. There's for you! He intends, not-

[20] 4 Nov. Actually, the season opened on Tuesday, 31 Oct., with a pasticcio,
La Sposa Fedele, repeated on 4 Nov. The first performance of *Didone*, slated for
7 Nov., was postponed to 11 Nov. (*LS 4* iii. 1925–7, 1929; below, p. 165).

[21] Caterina Galli, now in her fifties, had been a respected singer in her prime, but
by the 1770s had lost her voice. Nevertheless, after a long absence from England, she
sang at the Opera again from 1773 to 1776. If indeed she had been dismissed at this
time, she was subsequently reinstated, but rarely performed. See Highfill; *New Grove*;
LS 4 iii. 1910, 1950, 1952.

[22] Savoi first appeared this season in the roles of Count Lelio in *La Sposa Fedele* and
Araspe in *Didone* (*LS 4* iii. 1925, 1927).

[23] Francesca Gabrielli (b. *c.*1735) followed her sister everywhere and sometimes
deputized for her when she was ill. She sang 8 different roles this season. The reviewer
for the *Westminster Magazine* (iii. 568) called her 'a very capital Actress, and a good
singer', but Ld. Mount Edgcumbe dismissed her as 'a miserable performer' (Highfill;
New Grove).

withstanding the value of his Time, to shortly avail himself of this graciousness.

Nothing could ever exceed the expectatiorrs of people of all Ranks & all ways of thinking, concerning this so Celebrated singer. For my part, should any thing unfortunately prevent my hearing her first performance, I shall regard it ever after as a very great misfortune. ⌐

⌐Now to Barsanti. She has acted only in Charlotte Rusport since the House opened except that she performed in a foolish Prelude, which was but twice represented, at the beginning of the season.[24] It was a medley of the company—& [xxxxx *1 word*] she had a Tragedy ⟨speech they had⟩ given her to speak. The managers[25] desired her to take off Mrs. Yates & Miss Younge. The *first* she told them she could not if she would, & as to the last [xxxxx *4 words*] they pressed & made a point of it, but Barsanti, with a propriety & good manners which I hope you will approve of, told them that she had suffered so much abuse & ill will from her Imitations, that she was resolved not to do any more [xxxxx ½ *line*] what was provoking, was, that the Tragic speech notwithstanding all her desire to avoid it, was reported to be marked to *Miss Younge*.[26] ⌐ There was a good deal said about it in the Papers, & in particular one Letter written in the Morning Chronicle

---

[24] Jane Barsanti played the role of Charlotte Rusport in Cumberland's *The West Indian* on 22 Sept. On opening night (20 Sept.) she participated in a *New Prelude* consisting of 'the different Performers of the Theatre comparing notes together on their various successes, cast of parts, droll accidents, &c. &c. which they experienced during their different summer excursions' (*Westminster Magazine*, iii. 459; *LS 4* iii. 1911). The piece was presented again on 22 Sept. as *A Peep into the Green Room* (*LS 4* iii. 1912). The *Westminster* reviewer dismissed it as 'an unaccountable jumble, without the least seasoning of wit or humor'.

[25] The managers of Covent Garden at this time were Thomas Harris (d. 1820), Henry Dagge (d. 1795), James Leake (1724–*c*.90), Mrs Elizabeth Fisher (d. 1780), and Thomas Hull (1728–1808) (Highfill; *LS 4* iii. 1909; H. R. Plomer, G. H. Bushnell, and E. R. McC. Dix, *A Dictionary of Printers and Booksellers . . . in England, Scotland and Ireland from 1726 to 1775* (1932), p. 152; Garrick, *Letters*, ii. 595 n. 2). Elizabeth Young (*c*.1744–97), like Mrs Yates, was a popular actress at the rival Drury Lane until her defection to Covent Garden in 1779.

[26] 'After a variety of these curious stories, Miss *Barsanti* informs them, that the Managers have totally mistaken her talents, as she is calculated for deep Tragedy; and immediately gives a fine specimen of mimicry, both in voice and action, in which the tragical conceits of Miss Y—— are admirably hit off' (*Westminster Magazine*, iii. 459).

which attacked her for *Ill Nature*. She called here, alone, [xxxxx *1 word*] very full of it, & begg'd assistance to answer it, as she was very desirous of letting Miss Younge know *Publicly* that she had no design to *Burlesque* her. The Answer was accordingly written, sent, & printed [xxxxx *4 words*] If you have not seen it, you may, in a Morning Chronicle of about the 28th day of September.[27]

She met with great success at Bristol, & had kind encouragement from many very genteel Families in the Town. She has had very great offers sent her from the manager at Dublin,[28] & she thinks herself so much neglected here that she is determined to accept them for next season. I shall be very sorry to lose her, though I see her very seldom, for she is a most Charming girl, & I have a very great affection for her. She is now studying the part of Lady Dainty, in the Refusal."[29]

Now for Family. All Well. Bessy is to go to Paris as soon as Mrs Strange returns from Scotland.[30] Dick is at school at

---

[27] 'To the Printer of the Morning Chronicle. . . . I was present at Covent Garden Theatre the second night of performance. Respecting the Prelude, or what you please to call it, it is too low to say anything about; but I should be glad of information (if it does not proceed from ill-nature) why Miss B——i, in this, as well as at her first appearance on the stage, took so much pains in attempting to ridicule, or, as it is called, *take off*, Miss Y——e? If she would *take off* a piece of her tongue, it would be of much more utility, and possibly learn her to *speak* plain, and be as becoming as a pitiful subterfuge to depreciate the merit of an actress at least as valuable and improving as herself. [*signed*] INDIGNATION' (*Morning Chronicle*, 27 Sept.)

Barsanti's response 'To . . . Indignation' ran in part: 'In the few words I had to speak in the Prelude . . . there was nothing I so earnestly wished to avoid as attempting to *take off* ANY actress, as I have had but too much reason to regret that ever I did . . . I think myself extremely unfortunate in the present accusation, as I had taken particular pains to avoid any pointed imitation; and was even purposely extravagant in my action, from the desire I had of escaping censure. . . .' Even when she had purposely taken off actresses, 'it was never my intention to *burlesque*, but only to *imitate* . . .' (ibid. 28 Sept.).

[28] Presumably Thomas Ryder (1735–90), manager of the Smock Alley Theatre. Barsanti went over to act for him at the Crow Street Theatre for the winter season of 1776–7 (Highfill; L. Stockwell, *Dublin Theatres and Theatre Customs, 1637–1820* (1938), pp. 143–6).

[29] FB presumably means *The Refusal, or, The Ladies' Philosophy*, by Colley Cibber, first staged in 1721. The play had already been performed this season, on 24 Oct. (*LS* 4 iii. 1922). There is, however, no part of Lady Dainty, either in the original play or as it was acted on that date. It may have been a new role written into the piece as a showcase for Barsanti's talents, but *The Refusal* was not staged again, and Barsanti was used only sparingly throughout the year.

[30] See below, p. 192.

Harrow. Little Sally[31] is come Home, & is one of the most innocent, artless, *queer* little things you ever saw, & all together, she is a very sweet, & very engaging Child. Jem we hear nothing of yet,—but when he comes, it will be no fault of mine if I do not obey your kind Commands, & accompany him to Chesington. Niether will it be any fault of his, for I know he will both go himself, & make ¹ me, if it is in his power.

I have had the honour lately of a sort of Correspondance with Mrs Brooke, opera manager, & authoress of Lady Julia Mandeville &c &c—& she has been not a little civil upon the occasion, though she only wrote queries concerning my Father's absence, return, & so forth, when he was at Buxton.[32] Pray, if you are at any Time, when not well, or not busy, disposed for some *light summer Reading*, send for *The Correspondents:*[33] which you will find to be a *queer* series of Letters between a young widow, & an old *half* philosopher: Mrs Brooke, who is very Honourably mentioned by both of them, assures us that they are *genuine Letters* of the late Lord, & present *young* Lady Lyttelton, his son's Wife.[34] How they got to the Press seems so unaccountable, that it makes one doubt their authenticity whether one will or no.

My good friend & Correspondent, Mr. Hutton, called last week, in good Health & spirits, & was as droll, & affectionate, & odd as ever. My Father read to him his Dedication to the Queen, which mightily pleased him; for he almost adores her majesty.

In regard to Mr Barlow—I have not seen him for many months—but I *hear* of him very often, from a certain M^{rs} O'Connor, who was an old friend & favourite of my poor Grandmother, & continues to be so of my Aunts. It was by her

---

[31] FB's half-sister Sarah Harriet was 3 years old.

[32] This correspondence is missing.

[33] *The Correspondents, on Original Novel, in a Series of Letters*, published in Mar. 1775 (*YW* xxxii. 240 n. 10).

[34] The novel was meant to be taken as a series of authentic letters written *c.*1769 between George Lyttelton (1709–73), cr. (1756) B. Lyttelton of Frankley, poet, and his future daughter-in-law Apphia née Witts (1743–1840), widow of Joseph Peach, governor of Calcutta, who m. (1772) Thomas Lyttelton (1744–79), 2nd B. Lyttelton (1773). In 1782 FB met the young Lady Lyttelton herself, who confirmed her suspicion that the book was 'a very impertinent forgery'. A MS note on the title-page of a copy

means that he became acquainted with our Family, ⌐as he said he was [xxxxx ½ *line*]¬ This Gentle woman & I never meet, without her most officiously telling me ¹ Tales of his goodness, worth & so forth,—& expatiating upon my *cruelty*, & my *own loss*, & his *broken Heart*, & such sort of stuff. I have, however, sent her a message[35] by my Aunt Anne, desiring her to forbear these attacks, & letting her know, in as civil words as possible, that I was too much determined for them to answer any possible purpose. She has thought fit to make an Apology, & I hope she will desist in future. My Father, thank Heaven, has not once mentioned his Name, since the *Tragical tragedy*[36] which I gave you a hint of.

As to any *other* person—my dear Mᵣ Crisp your wishes for me are very kind,—but I am a queer sort of character, & without *particular inducements*, cannot bear ever the thought of uniting myself for life with one who must have full power to make me miserable, & perhaps none to make me happy—for it is such a Chance!—& as the constable[37] says, there are Gifts which God gives—& do not fall to the lot of every one.

But though I am difficult & saucy, as you call me, in regard to giving *another* the sole power of settling my fate, yet I am by no means difficult to be pleased & happy *as I am*,—on the contrary, I niether want spirits nor *pliability* of Temper, to enjoy all the *Good* that I can meet with: & as to the *Bad*,— though I am sometimes tempted to think I can never have *more*, yet, *upon the whole*, perhaps I shall never have *less*! & the more sensible I am of the Comforts I actually possess, the more careful it makes me of foregoing them. ¹

[*The rest of the letter is missing.*]

---

in the University of North Carolina Library claims that the author was 'Dr. Dodd', presumably William Dodd, the writer and divine whom Dr Johnson vainly tried to save from hanging (for forgery) in 1777. See *DL* ii. 74; *YW* xxxii. 240 n. 10; *ED* ii. 87 n. 2; L. McMullen, *An Odd Attempt in a Woman: The Literary Life of Frances Brooke* (1983), pp. 114–15.

[35] Missing.

[36] FB presumably alludes to Fielding's *The Tragedy of Tragedies; or the Life and Death of Tom Thumb the Great* (1731).

[37] Shakespeare's Dogberry. Cf. *Much Ado about Nothing*, III. v. 43. FB may have been anticipating seeing the play at Drury Lane the following week, with Francis Godolphin Waldron as Dogberry and Garrick as Benedick (see *LS 4* iii. 1927–8).

St Martin's Street
[13 November 1775]

To Samuel Crisp

ALS (Barrett), 13 Nov. 1775
3 double sheets 4to, 12 pp.
Addressed: Saml Crisp Esqr, | at Mrs. Hamilton's, | Chesington, near | Kingston, | Surrey
Annotated (by FBA): ✴ Gabriella's first appearance at the Opera House— and a concert in St. Martin's Street—Prince Orloff—Novr 1775 Novr 9 [*sic*] 15 N°
FB repeats the contents of this letter in the Journal for 1775, fos. 44–47. See also *Mem*. ii. 36–51.

The best apology I can make for the indolence you accuse me of, is by shewing more alacrity in future.[38] Don't you allow of that reparation?—as to my Correspondence with the Huttons—the Brooks—or so forth, it was only occasional, & niether did or could or can interfere with one which gives me a thousand times more real satisfaction & pleasure: besides, compared to what I write to *you*, all my other Letters are mere *Notes*.

So *you* are angry with Gabrielli for making Signor Onofrio Ill?[39]—what would you have been had you gone last Tuesday [7 Nov.] to the opera House, [xxxxx *1 word*] after seeing Didone advertised in all the papers, & then been told there was no Opera? Every one of the Family, but my mother, went. The Crowd was prodigious. They gave us Hand Bills on which were written *There can be no Opera this Evening on account of the Indisposition of the 2 Capital Serious Singers*.[40] People were in horrid passions. Some said it was scandalous;—others that it was a shame;—others called for the managers;—one gentleman blustered furiously, Vowing he had come 20 miles since Dinner on purpose to hear her.

[38] SC's letter to which this seems to be a reply is missing.
[39] Signor Onofrio or Onofreo, Italian tenor, sang the role of Jarba in *Didone* from 7 Nov. to 20 Jan. It is unlikely that Gabrielli's behaviour was the cause of his illness; the Opera's managers announced his death on 27 Jan. (*LS 4* iii. 1910–48 *passim*).
[40] These would have been Rauzzini and Gabrielli, but according to the *Public Advertiser* (8 Nov.), one of the ill singers was Signora Sestini (ibid. iii. 1927).

Poor Yates the manager, was obliged to stand at the Door from 5 till past 7 o'Clock, to appease the rage of the disappointed Public: though every person he sent away caused him a pang, as he could not but say—'There goes 3 shillings! there 5!— there half a Guinea!' Yet if he had not been there, the House would have been probably pulled down.

We all came Home horribly out of humour, & as to Hetty she determined from that moment not to like her; & prayed most devoutly that she might be Hissed whenever she should honour England with the sound of her Voice.

After this, we heard that she refused to let herself be heard even by the subscribers to the Opera, & would not sing at any Rehearsals, except at her own House. The next News was, that all the *Band* Complained, that when they assembled to accompany her, she would only give them Recitative.

My Father called on the managers to know the reason why the Opera was deferred on such short Notice. They *doubted* much whether Gabrielli was really ill, but told him that she had declared she could not sing. When they represented the fury of an English Audience upon such sort of disappointment, she told them, very easily, that, if that was the Case, she would Dress herself & make her Appearance,—that the Opera might be performed,—but that for herself, she would make a Curtsie, & *point to her Throat*, to excuse her singing.

You may be sure they knew too well the genius of our Nation to trust the safety of their Theatre to such a Trial of the forbearance of an Audience so big with expectation. Therefore the opera was put off till Saturday. The managers added, that she addressed them in the *mildest terms*, & with the most *obliging softness*, prefacing her refusal with '*mais, Madame, ecoutez! je donnerai très volontaire [sic] deux Operas la semaine prochaine*'—but the Deuce a bit has she kept her Word.

Mr. Bromfield the surgeon called here last Week, & said *he* had heard her, in a Trio,—& that though she did not exert herself, he *never heard such singing* before! He was so proud of it, that he could talk of nothing else, & he owned that he had not thought of any thing but her ever since he heard her. He had had a Note from her, & he shewed me her Hand writing, which was indeed a miserable scrawl, & her own Name signed by her own Hand.

As to my Father, he met with no opportunity of hearing her,

till Saturday Night at the Theatre. She requires more attendance & Courting than he has Time to give her.

Now for Saturday. My mother, partly from fear of the
Crowd, & partly from indifference to music, would not go. My
Father went in the Pit. Mr Burney, Hetty, Sukey, Charles,
Charlotte, Bessy Allen & me all sat in the Front Row of the 2^d
Gallery. ⌐We went before 5 o'clock, & were the first at the
Door, else we should have been crushed to Death, for the *mob*
reached through the Hall, stairs, & all the pavement of the
Haymarket before the Doors opened.¬ There was a prodigious
House, such a one as *November* can scarse ever have seen before;
unless, indeed, it was formerly more the fashion to come to
Town before Christmas than it is at present.

Well, Sir, expectations being raised so very high—can you
wonder they were not answered?

In the first scene, Rauzzini & Sistine [Sestini] entered, with
the *sister* Francesca Gabrielli. They prepared us for the Approach of the *blazing star*, who appeared in the second.

Nothing could be more Noble than her Entrance. She took a
sweep from the full length of the stage, amidst peels of Applause,
which seemed as if they would shake the foundation of the
Theatre. She Walked with great majesty, her person is rather
short, but charmingly proportioned, her Face is rather plump,
but very pretty, & her air is all dignity.

Though the Applause was so violent, she never deigned to
make the slightest acknowledgment, till she had finished her
Career, & marched from the furthest extremity of the stage,
which was open to the End, quite up to the Orchestra, when,
finding the Applause drowned the music, not a Note of which
could be heard, she made an *Italian Curtsie*; alias a *Bow*. They
continued to Clap, however, & made her make *2 more* Bows
whether she would or not before they were silent enough to
listen to her Voice.

Expectation was kept on the Rack long after her Appearance,
because she did not sing till after every other performer had
had an Air. & then came

Son Regina, & sono Amante

And now, I know not what to write. Opinions vary so much,
that I would to Heaven you would come & hear & Judge for
your self. In the Case of Agujari, I spoke boldly of her talents,

because there was but one mind among us; at present, I think I must speak separately of every one's sentiments, & leave you to suppose what you Can.

This *first* song was the *only* one of any consequence that she sang, all the rest being mere *bits*. The Trio, & the Duet were really charming. The difficulties in the Son Regina were all in the *Davis* style, in so much, that one would think Miss Davis had been Gabrielli's pupil.

To tell you I was not disappointed, is impossible.—you must already have perceived *your Tribunal* has pronounced well, for Agujari is still Alone & unrivalled!

Mr. Burney said he was prodigiously *let down* that she was not within 10 degrees of Agujari. |

Hetty, because she was not an Agujari, would allow her *Nothing*; declared that she would not quit her *Room* to hear her, that she did not care whether she went to another Opera the whole season, ⌜& that every shilling of the money ought to be returned—But Hetty is abominably provoked if she does not meet with every thing she expects. & will not allow *any* thing where there is the least deficiency.⌝[41]

⌜Sukey⌝ was rather more pleased with her. For my part, I was overborne by the torrent; but though I by no means could compare her with Agujari, I thought the *tone* of her Voice extremely sweet, that she sung in a *masterly* manner, Acted judiciously & gracefully,[42] & was only second to Agujari.

My Father, who has at once more *indulgence* & more *Judgement* than any of us, came Home in much better humour with her than his saucy Children. He pronounces her, *upon the whole, taking perfections & Imperfections* together, a very *Capital* singer.[43]

Disappointed as we were, there is no possibility, as yet, of knowing whether she *would* not, or *could* not do more, for she was most *impertinantly* easy, visibly took no pains, & never in the least exerted herself. All that can excuse her, is that she had really a bad Cold, Coughed often & was even *hoarse* at Times.

---

[41] This censored passage casts some additional light on the personality of FB's elder sister, whom she usually paints in all-flattering colours.

[42] 'As an actress, her motions are elegant & judicious; but she seems to want spirit & animation' (Journal, fo. 44).

[43] See CB's considered judgement in Mercer, ii. 881–2.

She has very *little* voice, though *sweetly* toned, & *polished*. She never gave us one shake, nor a [xxxxx *1 word*] *idea* of one, though I have heard she has a very fine one.

What could possibly put her out of humour, if in reality, she did not want the *power* but the *will* to do greater things? Nothing could be more flattering than her reception, & she had the most striking applause the whole Night.[44]

She is the universal subject of Conversation, & no 2 people think alike of her. In the Gallery, every one seemed to think that she gave herself Airs, & *would* not sing: in the Pit, near my Father, every body was *delighted* with her. So you see you must come & hear her yourself.

Others aver that she was in a terrible fright, & lost her steadiness and powers from fear. Indeed she actually told M[r] Bromfield that she *was* sure she should be terrified to Death. Upon the whole, there is no knowing what to say. So I will say no more, but change the subject, & *come* to *Yesterday*, to give you an Account of a *little Concert* we had, at which *Assisted* a most superb party of company. It was occasioned by the desire of Dr. King to have Prince Orloff[45] of Russia hear M[r] Burney & my sister in a Duet before he left England.

Prince Orloff is the identical man who was the Reigning favourite with the Empress of Russia at the Time the Czar was murdered. He is *said* to have seized the Emperor, but he is *known* to have immediately succeeded to the *good will* of the Czarina. This Prince was sent to negotiate peace at Constantinople, some little Time since, but in his absence, he was unfortunately supplanted in the favour of the Empress, by some other *Adonis*, &, though loaded with Honours, preferments & all sort of orders, he chose to *Travel* a little while, when, upon his return to Russia, he found the Empress had received another friend into her good graces.

He is now, therefore in England, where He Lives in great splendour, is perpetually at Court, & has had Entertainments made for him by all the ministers of state. &c

[44] 'Some say ... that her sister (a vilainous singer) being Hissed, put her so much out of humour, that she *would* not sing' (Journal, fo. 44).
[45] Alekseï Grigor'evich Orlov ('Orloff', 'Orlow') (1737–1808), Count. According to the *Daily Adv.* 10 Oct. he was 'a prince of the Roman Empire'. See next note.

Dr. King had him, when in Russia, for his *Patron*, & now proposed his coming here yesterday.[46] We had no performers but Mr Burney & Hetty, but a good deal of Company. I will Introduce them to you as they Entered, & hope to make my peace with You in relation to Indolence, by being as minute as I can.

Rat Tat Tat. Enter the Dean of Winchester.[47]

The Dean is a man of drollery, good humour, & *sociality*: but he is very *severe*, at Times, in his characters of men, though perfectly free from any Narrowness or contraction. He disdains *submitting* to the Great, or *Lording it* over the little, & was
                                                    Hetty
equally at his Ease with Prince Orloff—or Miss Sukey Burney.
                                                    Fanny
Dr. Burney. Was you at the Opera last night, Mr Dean? Dean of W. No, Sir. I made an *Attempt*, but *I* hate a Crowd— as much as the *Ladies* love it. I beg pardon! Bowing to us.

Mama then Entered into a defensive argument, which lasted till another Tat, Tat, at the Door.[48] Enter Dr. King.

---

[46] Orlov was the 3rd of the 5 Orlov brothers who helped Catherine II (1729–96) usurp the Russian throne in 1762. He was the leader of the group of officers who assassinated Czar Peter III (1728–62), but he was never Catherine's lover; FB confuses him with his brother Count Grigorii Grigor'evich (1734–83). Named Admiral of the Fleet during the 1st Russo-Turkish War (1768–74), Aleksei acquired considerable glory from the destruction of the Turkish fleet at the Battle of Tchesme Bay (July 1770).

It was his brother Grigorii who had been Catherine's emissary at a peace conference with the Turks at Fokshani in Moldavia in summer 1772. Hearing that he had been replaced by a new favourite, Alexander Semenovich Vasil'chikov (b. c.1745), Grigorii furiously rode 1,200 miles, only to be stopped at St Petersburg and ordered to retire to his estate at Gatchina.

In an unpublished fragment of his memoirs (Berg), CB records that Aleksei Orlov 'arrived in London from Paris ... when he came to England merely as an illustrious traveller without being accredited in a public character, he was unnoticed. Dr King ... was alarmed at this neglect, supposing it might be resented by the Empress & greatly injure our interest at her Court.' CB 'mentioned Dr King's fear to Lord Sandwich, who said it did not belong to his department but to the Prime Minister & Secretaries of State'. Orlov's visit to England lasted from 29 Sept. to 12 Dec. He was presented at Court on 25 Oct.

See *NBG*; H. Troyat, *Catherine the Great*, trans. J. Pinkham (New York, 1980); *passim*; I. Grey, *Catherine the Great: Autocrat and Empress of All Russia* (New York, 1961), pp. 153–69; *YW* xxiii. 441 n. 5, xxiv. 143–4 and nn. 13–15.

[47] Newton Ogle (1726–1804), DD (Oxon.), 1761; Dean of Winchester, 1769; Deputy Clerk of the Closet to George III. A 'very musical' and '*poetical*' man, he was a great favourite with the Burneys. See *ED* ii. 103 n. 1, 299.

[48] In lieu of this sentence FB inserts the following dialogue in her Journal account

He was as *fade* & as *imposing*, & as consequential, & as insipid as usual. He told us that the Prince was to Dine with Lord Buckingham,[49] & a multitude of others, & begged the Concert might not wait for him, as he was obliged to go in for a few minutes to Lady Harrington[50] before he came, it being her *Rout Day*.

Tat, Tat, Tat, Tat, Tat Two!—Enter Lady Edgecumbe.

We were all Introduced to her, & were honoured with a most gracious reception. She began a very animated Conversation, with my Father, & was all condescendsion, *repartee* (& *yet*) good humour.[51]

Dr. Burney. Your Ladyship was doubtless at the Opera last Night?

L.ᵞ Edge. O yes! But I have not *heard* the Gabrielli!—that is all I can say, I have not *heard* her! I won't allow that I have!

Dr. B. Your La'ship expected a greater & more powerful Voice?

L.ᵞ Edge. Why no, not much. But the *shadow* tells me what the *substance* must be.—however, I have not yet *heard* her. She had really a terrible Cold.

Dr. B. It is most fair not to Judge of her yet.

L.ᵞ Edge. She cannot have acquired the Fame of the first singer in the World for Nothing. But for me—I have heard Monticelli—I have heard Mingotti—& I have heard Manzoli![52] & I shall never hear them again!

Dr. King pushing himself forward. But I humbly submit to your Ladyship, whether Gabrielli has yet done herself Justice?

N.B. he knows nor cares a fig for music.

L.ᵞ Edge. Certainly not. But, Dr. Burney, I *have* also heard Agujari—& I shall never hear *Her* again!

(fo. 45): 'Dr. Burney. The Gabrielli is a very fine singer, but she has not Voice enough for the people of this Country;—she will never please *John* [*i.e., John Bull*]. Hetty. (pulling his sleeve.) Nay, Sir—now don't call *me* John!'

[49] John Hobart (1723–93), 2nd E. of Buckinghamshire (1756).

[50] Caroline Fitzroy (1722–84), daughter of Charles Fitzroy (1683–1757), 2nd D. of Grafton, m. (1746) William Stanhope (1719–79), 2nd E. of Harrington (1756).

[51] 'She seems to me a very clever, lively, quick, discerning Woman, & was totally free from airs & superiority' (Journal, fo. 45).

[52] Angelo Maria Monticelli (*c.*1710–64), Italian castrato soprano; Regina Mingotti, née Valentin (1722–1808), Austrian opera singer; and Giovanni Manzuoli (*c.*1720–82), called 'Succianoccioli', Italian castrato soprano. See *New Grove*; Highfill; Mercer, ii. 839, 854, 868.

Hetty Fanny, Sukey. O, Agujari!

Dr. B. Your Ladyship wins all their Hearts by naming Agujari. But I hope you *will* hear her again.

L^y Edge. Do pray, Dr. Burney, speak about her to Mrs Yates. Let her know that Agujari *wishes* to sing at the Theatre.

Dr. B. Their present Engagements with the Gabrielli must be first over; & then, I hope we shall bring Agujari back again.

L^y Edge. O! then I shall be quite crazy!^53

Dean of W. But, Lady Edgcumbe, may not Gabrielli [*sic*] have great powers, & yet not voice sufficient to fill a Theatre?

L^y Edge. O, Mr Dean, our Theatre is nothing to what she has been used to abroad. Agujari would *greatly* fill the Theatre— Indeed *she* could fill the Pantheon. By *Gabrielli*, Rauzzini seemed to have a great Voice;—by *Agujari* he appeared a Child.

   Tat, Tat, Tat,—Enter Mr. Charles Boone^54
   Salutations over,—

Dr. B. You were at the Opera last Night?

Mr. Boone.—No, my Cold was too bad. But I am told, by Mr Cooper,^55 an excellent Judge, that he heard enough to pronounce her the greatest singer in the World! |

   Tat, Tat, Tat Tat. Enter Mr. & Mrs. Brudenal.^56 Mr. Brudenal is second Brother to the Duke of Montague.^57 His

---

^53 '*Hetty. Fanny. Sukey.* O, I hope she will! *Dean of Winchester.* But why may we not have Agujari here *now*, & so hear them together? *Dr. Burney.* O that would be impossible; the Rivalry would be too strong,—they would be Cesar & Pompey. *Lady Edgcumbe. Pompey the little*, then, I am sure, would Gabrielli be!' (Journal, fo. 45).

   Pompey was known as 'the Great'. Lady Edgcumbe perhaps also meant a witty allusion to Francis Coventry's popular satire, *The History of Pompey the Little, or the Life and Adventures of a Lap-Dog* (1751).

^54 Charles Boone (*c*.1729–1819), of Barking Hall, Suffolk and Lee Place, Kent; MP (Namier).

^55 Perhaps Boone's fellow MP Grey Cooper (*c*.1726–1801), of Worlington, Suffolk; Secretary to the Treasury. One of his daughters was CB's scholar (ibid.; CB to FB, 2 Oct. 1786, Osborn).

^56 The Hon. James Brudenell (1725–1811), MP, cr. (1780) B. Brudenell of Deene, 5th E. of Cardigan (1790); m. (1760) Anne, née Legge (d. 1786), sister of William Legge (1731–1801), 2nd E. of Dartmouth (1750). 'Mr. Brudenal has a Tall & *imposant* figure; he is a good deal in the present *Ton*, which is not *macaronism*, but consists of a certain freedom of manners, & a dry, short, abrupt method of speech, by no means *to me* agreeable' (Journal, fo. 45).

^57 George Brudenell (1712–90), afterwards Montagu (1749), 4th E. of Cardigan (1732), cr. (1766) M. of Monthermer and D. of Montagu. James was actually the Duke's oldest brother.

Lady was the Hon. Miss Legge, a great Lady singer, & scholar of Mingotti.[58] She is a soft, obliging, pretty sort of Woman.

The Introduction over, the *Question of the Night* was repeated. How do you like Gabrielli?

Mrs. Brudenal. O, Lady Edgecumbe & I are exactly of one mind; we both agree that she has not sung yet.

Tat, Tat, Tat, Tat. Enter Mr. Chamier.[59]

Mr. Chamier, who is the most gallant of men, immediately seated himself by ⌈Sukey⌉ & me, & began a most lively & agreeable Conversation. & from this Time, the Company being large, divided into parties,—but I am resolved you shall hear *every body's* opinion of Gabrielli.

Mr. Chamier. Well, Ladies, I hope you were Entertained at the opera? I had the happiness of sitting next Dr. Burney.

Susy—I believe I saw you.

Mr. Chamier. I was very sorry I could not see *you*. I looked for you.

Fanny. O, we were at a humble distance!—in the Gallery.

Susy. I rather think we were at an *exalted* distance.

Mr. Chamier. I heard *where* you were, for though I had not the pleasure of seeing you, I enquired of the Doctor where you were. Was not the Gabrielli charming?

Susy. O, y—e—s.

Fanny. I never *expected* so much in my life—I was really in an *agitation*—I could not listen to the Overture—I could hardly *Breathe* till I had heard her.

Mr. Chamier. Well, & I am sure she did not disappoint you!—

Fanny—I must confess my Expectations were too high raised to be answered.

[58] 'a Female *Diletante* of great fame & reputation in the Beau monde as a singer' (Journal, fo. 45). The *Morning Chronicle*, 20 June 1775, carried an advertisement announcing the publication of 'Six Songs for the Violin, German Flute, or Harpsichord, composed by an African, dedicated to the Honourable Mrs. James Brudenell'.

[59] Anthony Chamier (1725–80), of Epsom, Surrey, was a wealthy financier who had gone into government service *c.*1763. Appointed this year an Under-Secretary of State, he also had wide cultural interests and was an original member of Dr Johnson's literary club. FB adds in the Journal (fo. 46) that he 'was the whole Evening constantly engaged with one or other of us [FB and SEB]. He is a *married* man, & an intimate Friend of my Father's, therefore we were by no means *shy* of him.' Chamier m. (1753) Dorothy Wilson (d. 1799), daughter and co-heiress of Robert Wilson, merchant, of Woodford, Essex. See Namier; *GM* lxix[1] (1799), 259.

M[r] Chamier. O, she was not in Voice;—you must regard this as a mere *echantillon*.[60]

Hetty. A very feeble & bad one! N.B. between her Teeth.

Mr. Chamier. I was kept at the Theatre a full Hour after the last Dance[61] before I could get to a Chair, for the Crowd. However, we got into a party in the Coffee Room, & settled the *affairs of the opera.* |

Fanny. Then I am sure there could be no dearth of Conversation, for the opinions of every one concerning Gabrielli are so various—

Mr. Cham.—O, I beg your pardon! I find it is the *ton* to be dissatisfied—'*C'est peu de chose*,' was echoed & reechoed *partout!*[62]

Tat, Tat, Tat. Enter M. le Baron de Demidoff.[63]

He is a Russian Nobleman, who Travels with the Prince. He is very musical, & subscribed to my Father's History of music before he left Russia. He brought News that the Prince was detained at Lady Harrington's Rout, but would be with us as soon as possible.

Lady Edgecumbe was engaged at the same place, but said she would defer her visit to the last moment. My Father, ⌐followed⌐ by her La'ship, Then went into the Library, & M[r] Burney seated himself at the Harpsichord. We all followed.

He was very much admired, but I can tell you nothing new upon that subject.

Tat, Tat, Tat. Enter M[r] Harris of Salisbury.

He is a most charming Old man, & I like him amazingly. Lady Edgecumbe arose, & went to meet him, saying he was an Old & particular friend of hers, & she rejoiced to meet him. When he ⌐was *done with* by the great folks⌐ he very civilly renewed acquaintance with us. I told him we were all afraid he would be tired of so much of *one thing*, for that there was

---

[60] A sample.

[61] The dance at the end of the opera was the 'New Grand Pantomine Ballet, *Pigmalion Amoureuse de la Statue*' (*LS 4* iii. 1925, 1926, 1929).

[62] '(with a macarony shrug)' (Journal, fo. 46).

[63] Pavel Grigor'evich Demidov (1738–1821). As a young man he travelled widely, indulging his interest in natural history and attending Linnaeus's lectures at Uppsala. He was a member of the principal learned societies of Europe. He is listed with his kinsmen 'M. Alex. de Demidoff' and 'M. Peter de Demidoff' as a subscriber to *Hist. Mus.* See *NBG*.

nothing for him again but the Duet.[64] 'That is the very reason I come, answered he, because I was never so much entertained as when I heard it before, & wish to renew the same pleasure.'

Mr Burney & Hetty then played a Duet on the Harpsichord & Piano Forte of Mr Burney's Composition, for they kept Muthel till his Highness arrived.

Lady Edgecumbe expressed herself in terms of the most lively pleasure, & was so animated & interested during the performance, that added to her adoring Agujari, I quite Adored *her*.[65] Indeed she was the life of the Company, for she was so *chatty*, spirited & easy, that she dispelled all sort of Ceremony, distance, or *fussation*.[66]

Tat, Tat, Tat—Enter Lord Bruce.[67]

He is *Younger* Brother to Mr. Brudenal, but an Uncle who took very much to him, settled his estate & *Barony* upon him. He *looks* a Tall, raw-boned Scotchman; but he *is* a most polite & agreeable man.[68]

He said he had been very unfortunate in losing a full Hour, from a mistake of his servants, who drove him to St Martin's *Lane*, where he had been Danced up & down from Top to Bottom, & at last, was in such a passion at their stupidity in not finding the House, that he jumped out of his Carriage, swore an oath or two, & began Enquiring himself, till he was directed right.[69]

Mrs. Brudenal was now so obliging as to sing. She gave

[64] 'as my Father had failed in his wishes & endeavours of varying the Entertainment by some *singers*, because every performer he applied to happened to be either Ill or Engaged' (Journal, fo. 46).

[65] 'Being herself a performer of reputation in the *lady world*, she was able to feel & to judge the merit of the performers & performance at once' (ibid.).

[66] Probably FB's humorous formation; cited by *OED* s.v. Fuss, *v.*

[67] Thomas Bruce Brudenell, afterwards Brudenell Bruce (1729–1814). He succeeded to the Barony of Bruce of Tottenham upon the death of his maternal uncle, Charles Bruce (1682–1747), 3rd E. of Ailesbury, who had obtained the barony in consequence of the failure of male issue, with remainder to his nephew. Together with the barony Thomas inherited vast estates in Wiltshire and Yorkshire. The earldom of Ailesbury became extinct upon his uncle's death, but he was made E. of Ailesbury (new creation) in 1776.

[68] 'Lord Bruce is a very polite & agreeable man, though of no *prévenant* Face; he is Tall, Thin, & plain' (Journal, fo. 46).

[69] St Martin's Lane is several streets east of, and parallel to, St Martin's St.

us a little *pastoral Cantabile*, of very elegant, sweet music, from Rauzzini's Piramo & Thisbe, with which you were much pleased at Chesington. She has a fine Voice, & sings, my Father says, in the style of the *good old school*: she has a very pretty shake, & sings very chastly [*sic*], not with vile graces & trills: but she was dreadfully frightened, which caused her to sing out of tune, at Times, though ⌐thank God¬ not *always*.

When she had done, I turned about, & said to Mr Chamier 'what pretty music!' He made no answer, but gave me *such* a look, expressive of *satire* & *drollery*, that, unable to keep my Countenance, I was forced precipitately to retreat into the drawing Room.

He soon after came there himself. I expostulated with him upon his cruelty in driving me out of the Room; he was pleased to say, that he was sure *I thought* what *he looked*. I told him, which is truth, that he was very *difficult* & *severe*. 'A singer who sings out of Tune cried he, is not to be borne!' 'She was extremely frightened, answered I, & that ought to be allowed for.' 'But, cried he, those who won't *open* their mouths (N.B. Mrs. Brudenal sings with her's almost *shut*) ought to be *Dumb*; & those who cannot sing in *Tune*, I could excuse from singing *at all*.' 'O! cried I, how many Voices would you silence at this rate! & how few lady singers would you leave!' 'No matter, returned he, a Candle that does not give a *good* light, ought to have an Extinguisher put on it.'

More music now called us back into the Library. Mr. Chamier was very curious to know if *that* was not the Room which *Sir Isaac* used to study in? & which my Father used for that purpose? ⌐God,¬ no, said I, '*this* is quite *superb* to the *study*; you never saw such a scene of Confusion as *that* is!

'It's quite a *Dungeon*, is it? Well, that's all as it¦ should be— But you have Sir Isaac's *Observatory*, have you not?'

⌐He is a horrid *smoaker*, for¬ I remember he once before asked me, very seriously, if I did not think that my Father's *real motive* for coming into this House, was that it had been Sir Isaac's.

Mrs. Brudenal now began another song. I told Mr Chamier that I should take care not to look at *him* when it was over, he promised he would not say a Word; but I mixed in with the *Crowd*, & would not trust myself near him.

I forgot to tell you, that Mr Harris is among those who admire the Gabrielli above all singers: ⌜& that, when Mr. Boone came in, his sword was broke—My Father inquir'd about it, & he said he had stumbled upon the stair, & that it was well he had not broke his neck.

'I am afraid, said my father, that the fault is in the *stairs*—but they were not of my constructing—they were Sir Isaac Newton's.[70]

'Sir Isaac Newton's! said he, why, was this Sir *Isaac's* House?' 'Yes, sir.' But I hope *he* did not have this fine Ceiling?' For the Dining Room ceiling is amazingly ornamented. 'Pray, answered my father, I hope you don't think that I did it? for I swear I did not!'⌝

I have filled my 3 sheets before my Time—but if you wish for the remnant of this evening, you have but to say so. ⌜I have not been able to finish this scrawl till to Day, & will not keep it longer. When you *write*, ⟨do as⟩ you would *speak* & you would never complain of want of materials. My love to Kitty. *Mrs. Bramble*[71] desires her Comp^ts. I told her of your complaining of her not writing, & she seemed well pleased. My Father's kind love—is monstrous busy.⌝ Write soon if you desire to have the Prince Introduced to you. I can't possibly without you send his Highness a Card first or, as I am your Sir Clement Cotterel,[72] why if you send one to *me*, I will endeavour to manage an Interview. Pray tell me your Health is better.

Yours [ever] & ever & ever
FB |

Gabrielli so fills up this Letter, that I must beg you to excuse any answer to your Letter till I write again, when I will tell you about the [xxxxx *1 word*], &c

---

[70] See above, p. 32 n. 4.

[71] FB's satiric name for her stepmother. In an undated ALS fragment to FB (Barrett), probably belonging to the end of this year, SC calls EAB 'that ____ honest Woman, your mother, my Friend, Goody Bramble'. The reference is probably to the unpleasant and domineering character of Tabitha Bramble in Smollett's *Humphry Clinker* (1771).

[72] i.e., his Master of the Ceremonies. This office, whose duties included formal introductions to the Sovereign, had been hereditary in the Cottrell Dormer family since 1640. FB names Sir Clement Cottrell Dormer (1686–1758), but the post was filled at the time of this letter by Sir Charles Cottrell Dormer (d. 1779). See *YW* xxxi. 10 n. 6; xlv. 756.

[*FB has inserted into her Journal for 1775 the following ALS, 2 pp., from SC, with the annotations: From Mr Crisp*—to Miss F. Burney ✳ Novr 19. *1775. The letter is between fos. 44 and 45, and paginated 547–[8]*].

Dear Fanny,

That I wish for the remnant of your Evening Concert, is saying nothing—you have learn'd from that R[ogue] your Father (by so long serving as Amanuensis, I suppose) to make your Descriptions alive[73]—send the remainder therefore without a moments delay, while breathing & Warm—I am now convinc'd, I had entertain'd a true & clear Idea of Mrs Gabriel; & form'd a just Estimate of the Comparative merits of her & Bastardini; for which I claim nothing to myself, but readily give it all to your faithful Portraits of both; the Pen, as well as the Pencil, sometimes exhibits Pictures with such strong marks of Nature that one instantly pronounces them like, without ever having seen the Originals—I can, not only excuse, but applaud Hetty, for her outrageous Preference of Agujari, & I love Charles for being *prodigiously let down*—as for that Rogue your Father, I could lick him for his affected Coolness & moderation ⌈(⟨Confound⟩ him he knows better)⌉ if it were not for one Consideration, which it must be own'd, has & ought to have some weight with him—I mean, the Rank he holds in the musical World; which not unreasonably, may check him, from giving the sanction of his Opinion in disfavor of so trumpeted a Character; now present in England; & in contradiction to great & powerful Numbers,[74] Numbers!—to whom without a Grain of Talents or Feeling, some Demon has whispered—Numbers! have a Taste!—[75] But, ⌈God Damn her, Hetty,⌉ to tell one Gravely that Gabriel has a *very weak Voice*—or a *Weak Voice—but very sweet & Polished, &c &c*! & then compare her, or prefer to the Bastard,[76] | who besides

---

[73] This is perhaps a clumsy attempt at a jest. In any case, it reflects SC's deep male chauvinism.

[74] This cynical appraisal has some merit, but not with regard to Gabrielli. CB's unpublished memoirs reveal that in *Hist. Mus.* he played down his preference for the newer Neapolitan style in deference to the prevailing taste for Handel, whom the King himself admired extravagantly. He was also careful not to be offensive about living composers whom he did not particularly like. See K. Grant, *Dr Burney as Critic and Historian of Music* (Ann Arbor, 1983).

[75] Cf. Pope, *Epistle to Burlington (Moral Essay IV)*, l. 16.

[76] SC seems confused here. It was FB's opinion that Gabrielli 'has very *little* voice,

sweetness & Taste, has all the powers of Thunder & Lightning in her; who can *mark* at pleasure every passage with what degree of strength & softness, Light & shade she pleases; who can strike you speechless with majesty, or melt you with Tenderness in the Change of a moment!—I would recommend to such worthy Judges, the singsong & prettiness of Waller & Cowley,[77] in preference to the sublimity of Milton & Homer— I shall set my mark upon y^r *Harris's*—*Bromfeilds*—&c &c, with regard to music, however—Adiêu—I am far from well— write directly—All here whom You love, return it sincerely— mine to the aforesaid Rogue & all the Creatures—Adieu—y^r loving Daddy SC $^|$

32   [St Martin's Street, 21 November–11 December 1775]

To Samuel Crisp

ALS (Barrett), 21 Nov.–11 Dec. 1775
3 double sheets 4to, 12 pp., *pmk* 11 DE seal
Addressed: Saml Crisp Esqr, | at Mrs. Hamilton's, | Chesington near | Kingston | Surry
Annotated (by FBA): Concert with Prince Orloff finished. Concert with C^t de Guignes, Edgcumbes, Brudenl [*sic*], Rauzini, Bruce 11 Dec. 75 N° 17 N° 46
This letter parallels FB's Journal, fos. 47–53. Cf. also *Mem.* ii. 51–67.

Tuesday Evening [21 Nov.]

Dear Dada,

I have this moment received your Letter—& being most conveniently alone, the family being ⌜in City⌝ at the Symp- sons,[78] I obey your Commands of Writing immediately.

---

though *sweetly* toned, & *polished*⌉, while SC praises EBB above for her preference of Agujari.

[77] Edmund Waller (1606–87) and Abraham Cowley (1618–67), poets. SC is pre- sumably thinking of Cowley's love poems; Cowley also aimed at the sublime in his irregular Pindaric odes.

[78] Perhaps CB and EAB's friend James ('Jemmy') Simpson or Sympson (d. before 30 July 1796), of King's Lynn, and his wife Eleanor (d. 1797). See *JL* xii. 780 and n. 5; subscription list to *Hist. Mus.*

You speak of Agujari just as she deserves to be spoke of, with Enthusiasm; nay, you express yourself with such a *justness* & *feeling* at once; that as I read for an Instant you cheated my Ears into an imaginary attention to her, & my *mind's Ear* at least, was once more pleased, charmed, soothed, astonished & enraptured as when I actually heard her.

Why, why did not you grant yourself the delight of *really* feeling her incomparable Excellence? I can't imagine how you, who never heard her, can contrive to describe her more to the Life, than any one who *has*? but I impute it to the remembrance of those great singers of former Times whose Talents must have borne so near an affinity to hers. Indeed, from the moment I heard her, I was struck with ideas exactly similar to those which your accounts of Carestini, Farinelli, &c had given me.

However, I frankly own, I have no notion of being *unjust* to all other people's merit, because Agujari united in her single self *every thing*; I regarded her as a prodigy, (which M. Colla called her) & therefore by no means shut my Ears or my Heart from receiving pleasure from those who are *not* supernatural. Nevertheless, though not *against* her; I can never dispute that I was most abominably disappointed in Gabrielli, who is, notwithstanding, a singer of very ⌈great⌉ merit. ⌡

I have received your last Letter[79]—my dear Daddy you have really half shocked—& at the same Time half flattered me;—I had begun to Write the moment I received your first Letter, but was interrupted, & have had no opportunity since; for at this Cold season, when there is no Writing in a *Fireless* Room, it is by no means easy to find Times for Letter Writing, where 3 or 4 sheets are to be filled. I will not, now, however, rest till I have answered all my promise & your desire.

So now, back to our first Concert,—I must trace back the circumstances in my memory, to the best of my power.—I left off before the arrival of the Prince.—So now, Enter his Highness, attended by a Russian Nobleman,[80] & followed by General Bawr.[81]

---

[79] Missing.

[80] Demidov.

[81] Friedrich Wilhelm von Bauer (1731–83), German general in the service of

The Prince is another Mr Bruce, being immensely Tall, & stout in proportion.[82] He is a handsome & magnificent Figure. His Dress was very superb. Besides a Blue Garter, he had a star of Diamonds, of prodigious brilliancy; he had likewise a *shoulder knot* of the same *precious Jewels*, & a Picture of the Empress Hung from his Neck, which was set round with Diamonds of such magnitude & lustre that, when near the Candle, they were too dazzling for the Eye. His Jewels, Dr. King says, are Valued at above £100.000.[83]

He was extremely gracious & polite, & appeared to be *addicted to pleasantry*. He speaks very little English, but knows French perfectly. He was received by my Father in the Drawing Room. The Library, where the music was, was so Crowded he only shewed himself at the Door, where he Bowed to Mr Chamier, who had met with him elsewhere.

I felt myself so *Dwarfish* by his *high* Highness, that I could not forbear whispering Mr Chamier 'Lord, how I hate | those enormous Tall men!' 'He has been less unfortunate,' answered he, archly, elsewhere!—that objection has not been made to him by *all* Ladies.' I knew he meant the Empress, but by no means desired a Conversation on the subject, & told him, I only *hated* them, because they made *me*, & such *as* me look so very insignificant. You may be sure his gallantry would by no means subscribe to this speech, which was followed by the usual style of *small talk*.[84]

Catherine the Great. See *Allgemeine Deutsche Biographie* (Leipzig, 1875–1912), ii. 142–3; below, p. 183.

[82] In middle age he weighed over 300 pounds (V. Cronin, *Catherine: Empress of All the Russias* (New York, 1978), p. 126).

[83] 'Orlow the Great, or rather the Big, is here; and as proud of his infamous diamonds as the Duchess of Kingston herself' (Horace Walpole to Sir Horace Mann, 14 Nov. 1775, *YW* xxiv. 143). At his presentation at Court, Orlov 'was dressed in scarlet, faced with black velvet, gold buttons, and buff waistcoat, the uniform of the Russian Artillery ... he had on the blue ribbon, the order of St Andrew, his star, cross, and epaulet ... of most superb *brillants*; and the portrait of the Empress, which he wears as her Majesty's adjutant, is set round with *brillants*' (*London Chronicle*, 26–8 Oct., cited *YW* xxiv. 143 n. 14). During his visit to England Orlov was robbed of a snuff-box 'said to be of the value of £14,000' (*Daily Adv.*, 3 Nov.).

[84] 'Mr. Chamier's gallantry could by no means neglect such an opportunity for civil speeches; indeed his own size is so little superior to mine, that probably he might *think* what he said upon that subject. He asked me if I remembered the French Proverb?—no. He then repeated one, which I don't exactly recollect, but which was very galant *pour les petites femmes*.

Lord Bruce rose & bowed very respectfully to the Prince, & quitted his seat to make way for him, went to the further End of the Room. 'Ah!' cried Prince Orloff, '*milord me fuit!*'

Mr. Brudenal then offered *his* seat to his Highness, but he would not accept it, & declared that if he disturbed any body, he would immediately retire:—he desired him, therefore, to re-seat himself, & when Mr Brudenal *demurred*, he said, with a Laugh (in answer to Mr B.'s pressing him to take his seat) 'Non, non, Monsieur, je ne *veux* pas, *absolument*, je suis *opiniatre*, moi! je ne *veux* pas!—Je suis un peu comme messieurs les Anglois!'

He gained his point, & the Prince at last *squatted* himself on the corner of a Form, just by Sukey, who as he seemed to shut her in, he called his *petite prisonniere*.

Mr. Chamier, in a whisper, said that 'I wish Dr. Burney would have had *Omiah* here, instead of Prince Orloff!'

The Grand Duet, of Müthel, was then played.

Added to the applause given to the *music*, every body had something to say, upon the singularity of the performers being man & Wife.

Mr. Boone said, to me, 'See what a man & his Wife can do together, when they Live in *Harmony*!'

'O Dr. Burney,' cried Lady Edgecumbe, 'You have set me *a madding.* | I shall never bear any other music!'[85]

Lord Bruce, turning to Prince Orloff, told him that the performers of the Duet were *mari & femme*.

The Prince seemed surprised,[86] & Walking up to Hetty, made her many Compliments; & expressed his wonder that

---

'Mr C. was extremely curious to know which was the Room that *Sir Isaac* used to study in, & asked me whether it was not our Library? I assured him, with great truth, that our Library was quite *magnificent* [compared] to *Sir Isaac's* studying Room, which was, as we are informed, the same my Father makes use of, & which is within the Library, & a *meer lumber room*. There was no possibility of shewing it to him then, otherwise I am sure he would have been highly diverted at sight of so much *learned confusion*' (Journal, fo. 48).

[85] 'Lady Edgecumbe, in her animated way, declared she was set *a madding*; vowed she would Practice *Night* & *Day* to be able to perform in such a manner, & said she had rather hear such a Duet than 20 Operas' (ibid.).

[86] '"Ma foi!" cried his Highness, "s'ils sont ainsi ⌈heureux⌉ en tout autre chose qu'en la musique, ils [*sic*] faut qu'ils soient bien heureux!"' (Ibid.)

two such Performers should chance to be United: & added 'Mais, *qu'a produit tant d'Harmonie?*'

'*Rien, mon seigneur,*' answered Hetty; laughing, '*que trois Enfans.*'

She vows she was *irresistably* led to make this queer answer at the moment, but was sorry afterwards, for the Prince laughed immoderately; & went immediately to Lord Bruce, & repeated *ce que Madame avoit dit*—with many droll comments & observations, such as, that such an *harmonious* secret should be communicated to the foreign academies; that it was of consequence to Natural philosophy—&c &c

Mr. Harris said he rejoiced, in *these degenerate Days*, to see such *Harmony* in married People.

'Your Father,' said the Dean of Winchester to me, 'has been so obliging as to make *my* Girls[87] undertake something of this sort;—but it will never do for *sisters*, A *man* & his *Wife* cannot take too much pains to shine *together*; but as to my Girls, even if they succeed, they will, in a few years, be parted;—at least they hope so!'

Mr. Chamier joined warmly in the Chorus of praise; he got himself into a little *snug recess* behind a Book Case, &, as he & I were engaged in a very *witty confabulation*, my mother came up to us, & said 'So, Fanny, I see you have got Mr Chamier into a Corner!'

You must know I don't at all like these sort of Jokes, which are by no means the *ton*, so I walked away.—but Mr Chamier answered—'No, Ma'am, it is *I* that seek out a Corner near where the lady Inhabits.'

General Bawr is a Hessian by Birth, though now *Lieutenant General a sa S. M. L'Imperatrice de Russia.* He wears *two* stars; he was in England formerly with the Hessian Troops, & at Winchester, as the Dean informed Us. Mr. Harris told us that *he was a man to be looked at*, for that he had commanded during the

---

[87] 'my 2 Girls' (ibid). Susanna Ogle (1762–1825) and Elizabeth Catherine Ogle (d. 1801), m. (1782) Henry Streatfeild, Esq. (1757–1829), of Chiddingstone, Kent. A younger daughter, Hester Jane, became the 2nd wife of Richard Brinsley Sheridan. See *The Letters of Richard Brinsley Sheridan*, ed. C. Price (Oxford, 1966), ii. 23, 29; *JL* xi. 250.

Turkish War, with so much Courage, conduct & success, that his valour & spirit could not be too much admired.[88]

He is Tall & rather Thin, of a stern & martial Aspect; but very well bred, & very fond of music. He speaks pretty good English, but came in so late that he missed both Duets, which he much regretted.

The Baron de Demidoff was likewise extremely delighted with the music: he is very thin & long Nosed, & has a most *triste* & meager Countenance: when the Duet was over, he claped [*sic*] his Hand on his snuff Box, with great vehemence, & called out, with energy, 'dis is *so* pretty as ever I heard in my life!'

Lady Edgecumbe was Introduced to Prince Orloff, whom she had never met with before. She Entered into a flirtation with him; & was so Courteous, & made so many reverences, that the Dean of Winchester, (who is very satirical) observed afterwards, that his *Diamonds*, & his *Highness* together, had quite penetrated her Ladyship.

She Invited him, with great earnestness, & great humility, to Honour her with a Visit, saying that though she had but a *small House*, she had a *great ambition.* Indeed it must be owned that it was great presumption in *Lady Edgecumbe* to Invite any person she met with at *Dr. Burney's*!—Ha—Ha!

The Conversation turned again upon Gabriella. The Prince said she had by no means sung so well as in Russia.[89] General Bawr declared that if he had shut his Eyes—he should not have known the Gabriella! |

I forget whether I told you of Gabrielli's *Train* as she quits the Opera House of a Saturday Night? Take it now, however, as Lady Edgecumbe told it.

'First goes a running Foot man; then the sister, then the

---

[88] Bauer was born at Bieber near Hanau in Hesse. He was in England from 1755 to 1757 as a junior officer in the Hessian artillery, in the pay of George II. He distinguished himself during the Seven Years War, attaining the rank of Col., but retired at the War's end. In 1769 he came out of retirement to enter the service of Catherine the Great, with the rank of Maj.-Gen. For his contribution to the victory over the Turks at the River Pruth in 1770 he was awarded the Orders of St Anne and St George. In 1773 he was promoted to Lt.-Gen. and named a knight of the Order of Alexander Nevsky. See *Allgemeine Deutsche Biographie*, ii. 142–3.

[89] Gabrielli was engaged at St Petersburg from 1772 to 1775 (*New Grove*).

Gabrielli; then a page to hold up her Train; then a Foot man; & then a man out of Livery, with her Lap dog in her muff!'

'But,' cried Mr. Brudenal, very drily, 'where is *Lord March* all this time?'

'O,' answered Lady Edgecumbe, '*he*, you know, is *Lord of the Bedchamber*.'[90]

Lady Edgecumbe, being obliged to *shew herself* at Lady Harrington's, *retired* soon after the last Duet. Mrs. Brudenal was going with her, but as she looked very soft & good Natured, I ventured to ask her to favour us with another song; & though her Cloak was on, she was so obliging as to return. She sung much better than at first, &, for all Mr Chamier, is a very good lady singer, & such a one as is not very frequently heard.[91]

When the Room was a good deal *Thinned*, Mr Harris told me he wished some of *the ladies* would express a desire of seeing the *Empress's Picture* nearer; 'I, you know,' said he, 'as a *man*, cannot, but my Old Eyes can't see it at a distance.'[92]

I went up to Dr. King, & made the request to him. He hesitated some time, but afterwards assented the demand to General Bawr, who boldly made it to the Prince. His Highness laughed, & with great good humour, desired the General to untie the picture from his Neck, & present it to us; & he was very facetious upon the occasion, desiring to know if we wanted any thing *else*? & saying that, if they pleased, *the ladies* might *strip him entirely*! Not very elegant, methinks, his pleasantry![93]

---

[90] March was a patron of the Opera and in fact a Lord of the Bedchamber, but Lady Edgcumbe was joking about his rakish taste for prima donnas and dancers. Gabrielli herself was notorious for her numerous love affairs. Just at this time Horace Walpole wrote to Sir Horace Mann (8 Dec. 1775) that she was being 'kept by a Mr Piers', probably Henry Peirse (?1754–1824) of Bedale, Yorkshire, MP, and she was also linked romantically with the E. of Beaulieu. See Highfill; *YW* xxiv. 148–9.

[91] 'Prince Orloff enquired of Dr. King, very particularly who we all were; the Doctor (who told us afterwards) to save trouble, told his Highness that all who were in Black were Dr. Burney's Daughters; at which the Prince exclaimed he should have thought it impossible, for that my Father did not look above 30 years of age' (Journal, fo. 49). The Burneys were still in mourning for Grandmother Burney.

[92] Harris had an ulterior motive in making this request, as he wished to compare Orlov's picture of the Empress with his son's picture of the King of Spain. 'He had the Empress's picture in diamonds, but I think yours of the King of Spain far more magnificent' (Harris to James Harris, 14 Nov. 1775, cited *ED* ii. 113 n. 1). The younger Harris (the future Ld. Malmesbury), currently the British envoy to Prussia, became the ambassador to Russia in 1777.

[93] 'Mr Pogenpohl's gallantry was far more polished' (Journal, fo. 49).

When we got it, there was hardly any looking at the *Empress* for the glare of the Diamonds. Their size is almost incredible. One of them, I am sure, was as big as a *Nutmeg* at *least*.

When we were all satisfied, it was returned, & the Prince, who [*sic*] most graciously made a Bow to, & received a Curtsie from, every one who looked at it.[94]

Well—& now, my dear Daddy, I think I have told you enough of this Evening, which was indeed a most agreeable one, & replete with *matter*. Now as to the last Concert, which you desire an account of, I have not so much to say, but take it as it was.

It was given in Honour of his Excellency the Count de Guignes,[95] at the request of Lady Edgecumbe, who talked so much to him of the *Duet*, that he expressed a great desire to hear it. I think I will Introduce the Company, which was very select, in the same way as before, viz, as they Introduced themselves to Us. & first,

Enter the Earl of Ashburnham.[96]

He is just made Groom of the stole, & 1st Lord of the Bed-chamber, & has a gold key Hanging from his Pocket. He is a Thin, genteel man, perfectly well-bred, attentive & elegant in his manners. Next.

---

[94] 'They stayed & chatted some Time after all the music was over, & were extremely lively & agreeable.

'The Dean of Winchester & Dr. King supped with us. My father told them that, if there was any Crime in having *music on a Sunday*, he hoped for *Absolution* from them. The Dean said, he thought music was a very excellent thing, *any* & *every* Day; & Dr. King said "Have we not music at Church?"

'"Ay, answered my Father, & much *worse* music, too than, I hope, you have heard here!"' (Ibid.)

[95] Adrien-Louis de Bonnières (1735–1806), comte (later duc) de Guines, French ambassador to England, 1770–6 (*JL* v. 271). CB wrote to Thomas Twining, 15 Nov. 1775 (Osborn): 'We had all the great Volk here on Sunday to nothing but Harp^d Lessons & duets,—& a song or two by Mrs Brudenel. But all were so charmés that I shall be forced to sacrifice another blessed day to let some other great volk hear our rumbles. L^y Edgcumbe almost downed on her scraggy knees to me this morning to let M de Guignes, Mad Diaden, & Count Bruhl hear'em....' The letter reflects CB's frustration over the time these musical parties took away from his labours on *Hist. Mus.* The 2nd concert took place on Sunday, 26 Nov. (CB to Twining, 30 Nov. 1775, Osborn).

[96] John Ashburnham (1724–1812), 2nd E. of Ashburnham (1737); First Ld. of the Bedchamber and Groom of the Stole, 1775–82. He was appointed to these offices on 18 Nov. (*GM* xlv (1775), 549–50).

Enter Lord & Lady Edgecumbe.

Lord Edgecumbe is short & *squabby*; he is droll & facetious, & never easy but when Joking. Lady Edgecumbe expressed herself in the most civil terms of thanks for my Father's making this party at her desire.—'I am particularly obliged to you, Dr. Burney, for giving your Time to my friends—' &c

Enter *His Honour* Mr Brudenal.

Enough of him before.

Enter Signor Rauzzini.

Every Eye brightened at his Entrance. He looked like an angel,—nothing can be more beautiful than this youth: he has the Complection of our Dick,—the very finest White & Red I ever saw: his Eyes are the sweetest in the World, at once soft & spirited: All his Features are animated & charming. I am extremely pleased to find that he gains ground with the Public Daily; his friends encrease every opera Night. The more they hear, the more they like him, especially as ⌐ ⟨at⟩ his first appearance,[97] he had the disadvantage of a terrible Cold. Mr Burney & Hetty are grown, of late, quite enraptured with him.

'Avez vous une Assemblée chez vous tous les Dimanches.' cried he, to my Father, 'Je viendrai un autre fois quand je pourrai chanter.'

Only think how we were *let down*! 'un *autre fois*! cried Hetty,— 'un autre fois! echoed Sukey,—'un autre fois! still more pathetically echoed your humble servant.

Mr. Brudenal soon after took Rauzzini aside to concert measures relative to his Benefit.[98] After which, Lord Edgecumbe hurried, in a droll manner, up to Rauzzini to tell him of Gabrielli's *Ceremony* on leaving the opera House—though to be sure he must know most of that matter himself. Lord Edgecumbe speaks but indifferent French, & referred every now & then to Lord Ashburnham in English. When he had told the whole Parade, & came to 'après cela, un valet, &

---

[97] On 11 Nov. (*LS 4* iii. 1929).

[98] Rauzzini's benefit took place on 29 Feb. 1776 with a performance of *L'Ali d'Amore*, a new opera, libretto by Carlo Francesco Badini, with 'Music entirely New by Rauzzini' (ibid. 1956).

puis,—un autre avec le petit Chien,' Rauzzini called out, 'Et puis, un autre pour un *singe*, & un autre pour un perroquet!'

'But, added Lord Edgecumbe, to Lord Ash^m—'*last* Night the Dog was Carried—only think how horrid!—by a woman, in a Handkerchief, instead of a *Gentleman* in his Hat! Now, my Lord, was not that enough to put any singer out of humour?

Rauzzini said he had Dined with Gabrielli. 'Comment se porte-t-elle?' cried Lady Edgecumbe.

'Fort bien, Madame.' answered he.

'Fort bien?—je suis bien fachée!'

'Comment donc?' cried he, with some surprise. She answered that she was sorry Gabrielli should *be* well, & not *sing* better.

Enter his Excellency, Count de Guignes.

The Count, when he first came from France, was esteemed to be a remarkable handsome man: but he is now grown so monstrous fat, & looks so sleek, that he is by no means an *Adonis* to [*MS torn*]. He looks very *soft* in the most extensive meaning [of the] Word, c'est [à] dire, in Temper, Person, & Head; remember, I speak only of his *looks*. However, he was very civil, though silent & reserved.

Enter the Baron & Baronness de Deiden, the Danish Ambassadour & his Lady.

The Baronness is one of the sweetest creatures in this lower World, if she is not one of the most deceitful. We liked her extremely at a former Concert which she honoured with her presence, but we liked her now a thousand Times more. Her Face is beautifully expressive of sense & sensibility; her manners are truly elegant, she is mild, obliging, accomplished & modest. Her Figure is equal to her Face, being Tall & well made.

The Baron is sensible & polite: &, what most pleased me, he seems extremely well satisfied of the merit & charms of his sweet wife. They both speak English.

The Baron made his Compliments to my Father with great civility, & the Baronness said 'How good it was in you, Sir, to remember Us! We are very much *oblige* to you indeed!' Then, going up to my sister, she said

'I have heard *no music* since I was here last!'

'For me, Mrs Burney,' added Lady Edgecumbe, 'I think I have *shewn* how much *I* was pleased, by my eagerness to hear you again so soon.'

Mr. Burney then went into the Library, & seated himself at the Harpsichord. Every body followed.

Enter—Lord Viscount Barrington.[99]

To *look* at this Nobleman, you would swear he was a Tradesman,—& by no means superior to stand behind a Counter. He has by no means *the Air Noble*, nor would you Dream that he almost Lives at Court, & has a private Conference with the king every other Day. But, I suppose, he has 'that within that passeth *shew*!'[1]

This Evening party was closed by the En[trance] of the Earl of Sandwich—of famous Name & C[harac]ter.

I thought of *Jemmy Twitcher*[2] immediately! He is a Tall, stout man & looks *weather proof* as any sailor in the Navy. He has great good humour & joviality marked in his Countenance. He went up to mama, & said to her 'I have heard of your son, Madam, & expect him Home Daily.[3]

The Duets went off, with their usual Eclat. Lady Edgecumbe Vowed she had rather hear them than 20 Operas. The Baron & Baronness were unaffectedly delighted—The Ambassadour was *gently* pleased;—Lord Edgecumbe, who had a bad Cold, almost choaked himself with stifling a Cough, nevertheless, his Wife scolded him about it, & said 'What do you come here for, my Lord, *Coughing*?'

Rauzzini was attacked by my Father, to vary the Entertainment, by a Rondeau de sa façon. He *supplicated*, with up-lifted Hands, to be excused; declaring most solemnly that he had,

---

[99] William Wildman Barrington (1717–93), 2nd Visc. Barrington (1734); Secretary at War, 1765–78. He was the elder brother of CB's friend, Daines Barrington.

[1] Cf. *Hamlet*, I. ii. 85.

[2] The treacherous friend of Macheath in Gay's *The Beggar's Opera*. Sandwich was branded with this name after his hypocritical testimony against John Wilkes in the affair of the *North Briton*, No. 45 (in 1763). Sandwich, a former friend and associate of Wilkes in the infamous Brotherhood of Medmenham, produced in the House of Lords the pseudonymous and indecent *Essay on Woman*. Wilkes had printed this work privately, probably for distribution to his brother 'Monks' of Medmenham. He was accused of being the author, and the *Essay* was adjudged a libel on Bishop Warburton, to whom the 'Commentary' was ascribed. At the same time the Commons denounced the 'No. 45' as a seditious libel. See *YW* xxii. 184–5 and nn. 14–25.

[3] JB's ship the *Cerberus* had returned from Boston in late July. It set sail again for the colonies on 8 Aug., arriving back in Boston harbour on 26 Sept. (Manwaring, pp. 57–8). For JB's return to England, see below, p. 197.

having a dreadful Cold, been obliged, the preceding Evening,[4] to exert himself so as to *force* his Voice, in consequence of which his Throat was actually quite *raw & sore*. He protested that he should have the greatest pleasure in singing to a select party of musical people, if he was able, & added that he *came* meerly to shew his willingness, though he ought to have been in Bed. In short, he did not absolutely *refuse*, but with so much earnestness & seeming regret begged my Father not to press him⌐that he niether could teize him, or yet, though very sorry, be at all offended at his declining to sing.

Lord Barrington made up to him, after this, & hinted his Wish to hear him thus in private. He made the same apology, & complained of the managers for obliging him to sing whether well or Ill, which occasioned his being ⌐forc'd⌐ either to disgrace himself, or *force* his Voice to his great detriment, '*car, pour moi, Milord, Je respecte le publique* & l'on ne m'a pas accordé le tems de me remettre; ainsi, de jour en jour, au lieu de me guerir, *j'en pire*.'

Lady Edgecumbe was then applied to to play; but she absolutely refused, & declared the Baronness to be *la premiere Dame pour la musique*.

The Baronness was therefore solicited; but in vai[n;] her invincible modesty made her regard herself a meer *Miss player* by Mr Burney & my sister.

I longed irresistably to speak with Rauzzini, & so when I saw him *stealing* from the Library back to the ⌐Dining⌐ Room, I gathered Courage to say 'Eh, vous ne chanterez pas, Monsieur?' he turned to me with the prettiest air imaginable, & cried 'Ah! je suis au desespoir! mais je ne le puis pas!—'

Sukey joined us, & we had a very agreeable *Trio* of about a quarter of an Hour, in which he told us that nothing made him so miserable as *refusing*; that to be where there was a Harpsichord, & musical people, & to be idle, made him quite unhappy; he protested that he would come some other Time, with the greatest pleasure. 'Mais *quand*?' cried Sukey. 'Quand M. *Borni* voudra,' answered he, '& alors, Je chanterai toute la soirée.'

---

[4] In *Didone* (*LS 4* iii. 1933).

He said that he must retire, & immediately go to Bed; that he would not disturb my Father, but left his best Compliments for him with me. & so he went. Leaving [|] every body monstrously disappointed, & Nobody displeased.

⌐I am so afraid of losing another post, that I must make up this Letter, & what I have to add of this Evening I shall send, perhaps, tomorrow, otherwise very soon[5] & tomorrow I shall also send Kitty's Black Silk. My mother desires her best Comp^ts to you, & that a Hare will accompany the black silk. They will be sent to Epsom.⌐

My Father is in want of the phil. tran. & of Mr Twiss.[6] By the way, that Gentleman called here last week, but saw Nobody. He is just returned from Ireland, where he told my Father, he went to be Dipt in the Shannon, to take from him his too great mauvaise honte![7]

Have I made my peace with you or not?

After all, you write such *snaps* in return for my Volumes, that I own it sometimes discourages & mortifies me, to think that so many Pages of writing cannot afford any matter for Comment or Observation.[8]

---

[5] FB probably sent SC an account of the rest of the evening, but the letter is missing. For her Journal account of the evening's conclusion (fos. 52–53), see *ED* ii. 114–15; the Baroness von Diede was finally prevailed upon to play an overture by Abel and a minuet of Schobert, and Charles Rousseau Burney played a long lesson by Schobert.

See also *Mem.* ii. 64–5 for the 'pomposity' of the comte de Guines's exit, when, failing to find 'half a dozen of our lackeys waiting to anticipate his orders ... he indignantly ... called out aloud: "*Mes gens! où sont mes gens? Que sont ils donc devenu? Mes gens! Je dis! Mes gens!*"' These phrases became a permanent part of the Burneys' vocabulary (*JL* v. 271 and n. 7).

[6] Presumably CB had loaned SC a volume of the *Philosophical Transactions* of the Royal Society and his copy of Richard Twiss's *Travels through Portugal and Spain in 1772 and 1773*, published the previous Apr. (see *Lib.*, pp. 46, 60; *YW* xxviii. 191 n. 2). SC, in his reply to this letter, 14 Dec. (Barrett), notes that ⌐I this day send the Books requir'd⌐.

[7] An allusion, of course, to proverbial Irish boldness. Twiss was presumably being ironic about himself. Boswell, in his journal entry for 24 Mar. 1776, records Dr Johnson and himself being entertained by two Lichfield ladies 'with the absurd forwardness of Twiss, the traveller, who had been some days at Lichfield' (*Boswell: The Ominous Years, 1774–1776*, ed. C. Ryskamp and F. A. Pottle (New York, 1963), p. 293). Later in the new year, Twiss published an account of his visit to Ireland as *A Tour in Ireland, in 1775* (see *GM* xlvi (1776), 420–3).

[8] SC responded: 'Don't imagine, that, because my letters are (from necessity, & poverty of Matter) shorter than Yours, I am therefore insensible, that the Advantage

My love to Kitty, & believe me, most affectionately

& faithfully yours

F. Burney |

[*The Journal for 1775 resumes.*]

Decr 12th

Bessy Allen is gone to Paris, for the purpose of compleating her Education, & refining her manners.

She is gone under the care of Mrs Strange, who will, I am sure, be a mother to her, & who has more good Qualities joined to great Talents, than almost any Woman I know. Mr. Lumisden,[9] her worthy Brother, is gone with them, as is Miss Strange, who I parted with with regret, for though far from a shining Character, she is a very estimable one, & had improved much on acquaintance. Mr. Strange & Bell, the 2^d Daughter, went to Paris some months before. The whole Party Dined with us the Day before their departure, & set off in excellent spirits. We have had the satisfaction of hearing they are all safe arrived at Paris.

We miss Bessy very much, but still rejoice that she is gone, for we hope much from the improvement of 2 years residence in Paris, & she was unformed & backward to an uncommon degree.[10]

---

is all on my Side ... But pray Remember, that when my Lord condescends to visit the humble Curate in his Batterd Cottage, he does not expect a Dinner like his own; but contents himself with the Parson's Ale, & Matters & Turnips, & this too rather at short Allowance ...' On Rauzzini he writes: 'You appear ... to be somewhat touch'd with the Charms of the beautiful Rauzzini; & perhaps 'tis well for you he did not add the Magic of his Voice to ⌈compleat your ruin—⌉'. See *ED* ii. 127–8.

[9] Andrew Lumisden (1720–1801). An ardent Jacobite, he had followed Prince Charles Edward into exile after the Rising of 1745. He served successively as secretary to the Old and Young Pretender until dismissed in 1768 by the latter, whom he had refused to let attend an oratorio while intoxicated. He moved to Paris, but was allowed to return home to Scotland in 1773 after an influential petition was presented in his favour (a free pardon was granted in 1778). He continued, however, to make Paris his headquarters.

[10] MAR had communicated her fears about her sister Bessy in a letter to FB, 10 Sept. 1775 (Berg): 'what a thousand pities her manners are not more Formed and attended to.... I own I am very anxious about the success of this Paris Journey ... Rishton ... has the same [fears] and we often talk of her future welfare and never wth dry Eyes on my side ...' The family's worst apprehensions were realized when Bessy Allen eloped with the adventurer Samuel Meeke in Oct. 1777. See below, p. 289.

Before they went, the whole Strange Family recommended very strongly to our Acquaintance the two Miss Paynes, Daughters of Mr Payne[11] the Bookseller at the Meuse Gate, saying they were *pretty*, & *motherless*, & it would be benevolent to attend to them. ⌐

⌐Susan & I Drank Tea with them last Saturday, & spent a very agreeable afternoon. The mother is Dead, & they live with their Father, who is a worthy old man, & their Brother.⌐[12]

The Eldest is very pretty, & about 18 years of Age. She is modest, gentle & obliging. The younger has, I believe, a deeper understanding, but is niether so handsome or so pleasing as her sister. The ⌐Brother, who seems very attentively kind to them, appears to be a very worthy young man.⌐

Decr 14th

To our great surprise, who, late in the Evening, should Enter, but Omiah!

How he found out the House, I cannot tell, as it is a Twelve month since he was here before. But he now Walks every where quite alone, & has Lodgings in Warwick Street, where he lives by himself. The King allows him a Pension.

He has learnt a great deal of English since his last Visit, & can, with the assistance of signs, & Action, make himself tolerably well understood. He pronounces English in a manner quite different from other Foreigners, & sometimes unintelligibly. However, he has really made a great proficiency, considering the disadvantages he labours under, which render his

---

[11] Thomas Payne (1719–99), the well-known bookseller, whose shop, a favourite haunt of the literati, was at the Mews Gate, Castle St., Leicester Fields. He m. (1745) Elizabeth Taylor (d. 1767). He and his children became close friends of the Burneys. The elder daughter was Martha ('Patty') Payne (1757–1803). The younger daughter Sarah ('Sally') Payne (1759–1832), m. (1785), at Chessington, FB's brother JB. FB chose Thomas Payne to publish her 2nd novel *Cecilia* (in 1782), and he also published CB's *Commem.* (1785) and co-published vols. iii and iv of *Hist. Mus.* (1789). See IGI; Findley burial registers (GLRO); Sarah Harriet Burney to Charlotte Francis, 20 Mar. 1803 (Berg), in L. Clark, 'The Letters of Sarah Harriet Burney: An Edition' (Univ. of Toronto Ph.D. thesis, 1989), p. 61.

[12] Presumably the elder brother, Thomas Payne (1752–1831), who in 1776 became his father's partner and in 1790 succeeded to the business. The younger brother, James (b. 1765), also became a bookseller and died in France in 1809 (*GM* lxxix^l (1809), 389; IGI).

studying the Language so much more difficult to him, than to other strangers; for he knows nothing of *Letters*, & there are so very few Persons who are acquainted with his Language, that it must have been extremely difficult to have Instructed him at all.

He is lively & intelligent, & seems so open & Frank Hearted that he looks *every* one in the Face as his Friend & well wisher. Indeed, *to me*, he seems to have shewn no small share of real greatness of mind, in having thus thrown himself into the power of a Nation of strangers, & placing such entire confidence in their Honour & Benevolence. |

As we are totally unacquainted with his Country, Connections, & affairs, our Conversation was necessarily very confined, indeed it wholly consisted in Questions of what he had seen here, which he answered, when he understood, very *entertainingly*.

Making Words, now & then, in familiar Writing, is unavoidable, & saves the trouble of *thinking*, which, as Mr Adison [*sic*] observes, we Females are not much addicted to.[13]

He began immediately to talk of my Brother.

'Lord Sandwich write, one, two, three,' (counting on his Fingers) '*monts* ago—Mr Burney,—come Home.'

'He will be very happy,' cried I, 'to see *you*.'

He Bowed, & said 'Mr Burney very *dood* man!'

We asked if he had seen the King lately.

'Yes. King George *bid me*,—Omy, you go Home. O very *dood* man King George.'

He then, with our assisting him, made us understand that he was extremely rejoiced at the thought of seeing again his Native Land, but at the same Time, that he should much regret leaving his friends in England.

'Lord Sandwich,' he added, '*bid me*, Mr Omy, you two ships— you go Home—I say,' (making a fine Bow) 'very much *oblige*, my Lord.'

We asked if he had been to the Opera?

---

[13] FB evidently regards *entertainingly* as her own coinage, but *OED* gives an earlier example (in 1754), and a use of the form in an obsolete sense in 1621. The intellectual vapidity of women is an occasional theme in the writings of Joseph Addison (1672–1719), essayist. See, e.g., the *Spectator*, No. 265.

He immediately began a *squeak*, by way of *imitation*, which was very ridiculous; however, he told us he thought the music was *very fine*; which, when he *first* heard it, he thought *detestable*.

We then enquired how he liked the Theatres, but could not make him understand us; though, with a most astonishing politeness, he always endeavoured, by his Bows & smiles, to save us the trouble of knowing that he was not able to comprehend whatever we said.

When we spoke of Riding on Horse back, an idea entered his Head, which much diverted him, & which he endeavoured to explain, of riding double, which I suppose he has seen upon the Roads. [|]

'First goes man, so!' (making a motion of whipping a Horse) 'then *here*' (pointing behind him) '*here* goes Woman! Ha, Ha, Ha!'

Miss Lidderdale, of Lynn, who was with us, & was in a riding Habit, told him that *she* was prepared to go on Horseback.

He made her a very civil Bow, & said 'O you,—you *dood* woman, you *no man*;—dirty woman,—Beggar woman;—ride so;—not you.'

We mentioned Dick to him, who is now at Harrow School, as we told him. He recollected him, & enquired after him. When we said he was gone to school, He cried 'O! to learn his Book? so!' (putting his two Hands up to his Eyes in Imitation of holding a Book.) He then attempted to describe to us a school to which he had been taken to see the *humours*.

'Boys here,—Boys there,—Boys all over!—one Boy come up—do so,' (again imitating Reading) '*not well;—man* not like—man do so!' Then he shewed us how the master had hit the Boy a violent Blow with the Book on his shoulder.

Miss Lidderdale asked him if he had seen Lady Townshend[14] lately? 'Very pretty Woman, lady Townshend!' cried he,—'I drink Tea with lady Townshend in 1 : 2 : *tree* Days.—Lord Townshend, my friend: Lady Townshend, my friend: very pretty woman, Lady Townshend!—very pretty Woman, M^{rs}

---

[14] Anne Montgomery (d. 1819), m. (1773) George Townshend (1724–1807), 4th Visc. Townshend, cr. (1787) M. Townshend.

Crewe!—very pretty Woman Mrs Bouverie!—very pretty Woman Lady Craven![15]—'

We all approved his Taste, & he told us that when any of his acquaintance wished to see him, they 'write, & *bid me*, Mr Omy, you come,—Dinner—Tea—or supper,—then I go.'

My Father, who fortunately, came in during his visit, asked him very much to favour us with a song of his own Country, which he had heard him sing at Hinchinbrooke. He seemed to be quite ashamed,—but we all joined, & made the request so earnestly, that he could not refuse us: but he was either so modest that he blushed for his own performance, or his Residence here had made him so conscious of the ^l *barbarity* of the South Sea Islands' Music, that he could hardly prevail with himself to comply with our request. & when he did, he began two or three Times before he could acquire Voice or firmness to go on.

Nothing can be more *curious*, or less *pleasing*, than his singing Voice, he seems to have none, & *Tune*, or *air*, hardly seem to be *aimed* at; so queer, wild, strange a *rumbling of sounds* never did I before hear; & very contentedly can I go to the Grave if I never do again. His *song* is the only thing that is *savage* belonging to him.

The *story* that the Words told was laughable enough; for he took great pains to explain to us the *English* of the song. It appeared to be a sort of *Trio*, between an old Woman, a young Woman & a young man. The two latter are entertaining each other with praises of their merits, & protestations of their passions, when the old woman enters, & endeavours to *faire l'aimable* to the Youth; but, as she cannot boast of her *Charms*, she is very earnest in displaying her Dress, & making him observe & admire her taste & fancy; Omiah, who stood up to *Act* the Tune, was extremely droll & diverting by the Grimace,

---

[15] Henrietta (Harriet) Fawkener (*c.*1751–1824), m. 1 (1764) Hon. Edward Bouverie, m. 2 (1811) Ld. Robert Spencer; and Lady Elizabeth Berkeley (1750–1828), m. 1 (1767) William Craven, 6th B. Craven, m. 2 (1791) Christian Friedrich Karl Alexander, Margrave of Brandenburg-Ansbach. All the ladies named by Omai were noted beauties. During his stay in England he had acquired some reputation as a dandy, and his association with the 'goddesses' of London society was later satirized in the anonymous verse *Omiah's Farewell; inscribed to the Ladies of London*. See E. H. McCormick, *Omai: Pacific Envoy* (Auckland, 1977), pp. 183–5.

minauderies & affectation he assumed for this Character, examining & regarding himself & his Dress with the most conceited self-complacence. The Youth then avows his passion for the Nymph; the old Woman sends her away, &, to use Omiah's own words, coming forward to offer *herself*, says 'Come! *Marry* me!' The young man starts as if he had seen a Viper, then makes her a Bow, begs to be excused, & runs off.

Though the singing of Omy is so barbarous, his Actions & ^I the expression he gives to each Character, are so original & so diverting, that they did not fail to afford us very great entertainment, of the *risible* kind.[16]

Decr 18th

[xxxxx *5 lines*]

˹Yesterday, in Pall Mall, I met with Omiah, who, to my great surprise, knew me, though I had passed him without happening to see him. He turned back, & came up to me. He Bowed, & said '*How do do? Where you walk?*'

I told him that his friend Mr. Burney was not yet returned. 'No, no, answered he, he come by & by.'

Our Conversation, however, was not very long, as we were niether of us *quite* at our ease in *each other's* Language.˺

[xxxxx *9 lines*]

December 30th

My Brother James, to our great Joy & satisfaction, is returned Home safe from America, which he has left in most terrible disorder. He is extremely well in Health & spirits; &

---

[16] Omai's biographer suggests CB as the author of an anonymous review (in the *Monthly Review*, liv (Jan. 1776), 28–9) of 2 articles by Joshua Steele on musical instruments brought back from the South Seas (in the Royal Society's *Transactions* for 1775, pp. 67–78). The author cites 'the testimony of a sober and discreet person [*presumably CB himself*], who has a tolerable good ear, and has heard Omiah sing one of his country songs'. According to this witness, 'The melody ... seemed to be wholly *enharmonic*—slubbering and sliding from sound to sound by such minute intervals, as not to be found in any known scale, and which made it appear to him as music,—if it could be called music, of another world' (McCormick, p. 160). Another possible author is William Bewley, who would then be citing CB's impression of Omai sent in a missing letter. His portrait of the 'witness' would be a characteristic bit of humour aimed at CB (see Lonsdale, pp. 176–8).

has undergone great hardships, which he has, however, gained both Credit & Friends by.[17]

He has a Brave soul, & disdains all self applause, & Egotism; nevertheless, he has so honourably encreased his friends, & gained reputation, that it is not in the power of his forbearance or modesty to conceal it.

He is now in very good Time for his favourite Voyage for the South Seas, which We believe will take place in February.[18]

His Friend Omiah, whom he is to convey Home, called here again last week, in company with Dr. Andrews[19] a Gentleman who speaks his Language very well; which we had reason to regret, as it rendered Omiah far less entertaining than on his former visit, when he was obliged in despight of difficulties, to explain himself as well as he could, having no Assistant; but now, this Dr. Andrews being ready as an Interpreter, he gave himself very little trouble to speak English. Now that James is returned, I doubt not his visits will be repeated.

⌐I saw Barsanti a few Days since, who is in great raptures upon having the part of the Widow Belmour[20] ˥ given her to study. She told me that if the managers [xxxxx *½ line*] gave her good parts, she should with infinite Joy give up her Irish scheme.

I heartily hope that she will.

---

[17] JB had been promoted to 1st Lt. of the *Cerberus* on 27 Sept., the day after that ship's arrival in Boston Harbour. From 17 Oct. the frigate was engaged in intercepting rebel privateers along the Massachusetts coastline. The situation in America had, of course, deteriorated into a full-scale war. Ld. Sandwich had ordered JB's commander-in-chief, Adm. Graves, to allow him to return to England if he preferred sailing again with Capt. Cook, and on 2 Dec. Graves wrote to Sandwich: 'Lieutenant Burney wishes to go again to the South Seas, I have appointed Mr. Atkins in his stead' (*The Private Papers of John, Earl of Sandwich . . . 1771–1782*, ed. G. R. Barnes and J. H. Owen (1932–8), i. 81). JB sailed for England on the *Boyne* man-of-war, which left Boston on 5 Dec. and arrived at Portsmouth on 26 Dec. (ibid., p. 99; *Daily Adv.*, 29 Dec.; Manwaring, pp. 58–61; MS commission of JB, 27 Sept. 1775, PML; *Documents of the American Revolution, 1770–1783 (Colonial Office Series)*, ed. K. G. Davies (Shannon, 1972–81), xi. 141, 201).

[18] See below, p. 200.

[19] Presumably Thomas Andrews (*c.*1746–1813), who was surgeon on the ship which brought Omai to England and who served as his chaperone and interpreter in London (McCormick, pp. 102, 109, 135, 160; *GM* lxxxiv[1] (1814), 100).

[20] In Arthur Murphy's *The Way to Keep Him.*

She was, however, in some distress concerning the *song to be sung in character*, first because she has now so little ⟨voice left for⟩ singing at all; & secondly because the music of *Ye Fair married Dames*[21] is so very *English*, & ⟨unsuited to⟩ her Taste & Natural g⟨ifts.⟩ [xxxxx *2 lines*]

I ⟨communicated⟩ her ⟨plight⟩ to my Father who is now somewhat relieved from his great hurry as his 1st Volume is nearly finished;[22] [xxxxx *½ line*] he undertook to [xxxxx *2 words*] set the Words & wrote down the following Questions for her to answer, that ⟨his setting might⟩ particularly suit her [xxxxx *2 words*] abilities.

How *high* & how *low* she can go without Fright?

Whether any *shake* is left?

Whether she would wish for a symphony with a *piece of Execution?*

The dear Creature was so delighted at this mark of fond remembrance from my Father, whom she had not even seen for these last 3 or 4 Years, that she could scarse refrain from Tears. The Air is composed, & my dear Father called on her himself this evening, & played it to her. I shall certainly go to hear its effect & success in performance.⌐23 |

[*This concludes the Journal for 1775. There is no extant journal for 1776. In her 'List of Persons' FBA notes: 'The whole of what was written of This Year was upon Family matters or anecdotes, & I have destroyed it in totality'. She also destroyed most of her correspondence. One of the lost letters, written early in the year, was on the subject of 'Mr. Bruce' (presumably James Bruce) and 'masquerades' (FBA's note on a cover enclosing 'A Letter or two preserved From & To Mr. Crisp in 1776' (Barrett)).*]

---

[21] 'Ye fair married dames, who so often deplore' was written by Garrick (the setting by Dr Arne) for inclusion in Murphy's expanded 5-act version of his play (first staged in 1761). The widow sang this song in Act III. By 1785 Murphy had reverted to his own original song ('Attend all ye fair & I'll tell you the art'), which the widow had sung in Act II of his 3-act version (1760). See the editions of 1760, 1761, and 1785 and n. 23.

[22] On 25 Jan. 1776 CB presented the 1st vol. of *Hist. Mus.* to the Queen, to whom it was dedicated 'at St James's in full drawing room', and on 31 Jan. it was officially published (Lonsdale, p. 173, citing an unpublished fragment of CB's memoirs (Berg)).

[23] Barsanti played the widow Belmour at Covent Garden on 24 Jan. 1776 (*LS 4* iii. 1947). It is not clear whether CB used Garrick's or Murphy's words, and his setting has not been found.

[St Martin's Street,
post 10 February 1776]

To Unknown

AL fragment (Berg), Feb. 1776
Single sheet 4to, 2 pp.
Dated by the reference to JB's commission as 1st Lt. of the *Discovery*.

[xxxxx *4 lines*] My sister [EBB] has been very ill; she therefore intends to go shortly to Worcester [xxxxx *1 line*] & to pass the summer there, in hopes of restoring her Health & strength [xxxxx *2–3 words*] She has Commissioned my Barborne Cousins to take a small House for her, very near their own.[1] We are willing to look forward with pleasure to the success of this scheme, yet the Parting will give great pain to us all, especially to Mr Burney, who would never have consented to it, but from the hope that he may rejoice for years by way of payment for grieving for months.

My Brother James is appointed First Lieutenant on Board the Discovery, which ship, under Capt. Clarke,[2] will accompany the Resolution, Capt. Cooke, in a new Voyage round the World, which will take place in May, when they are to convoy Omai back to the South Sea.

We have seen Omai several Times since we came from Chesington.[3] He was invited ⌜here⌝ one Sunday Evening, when Mr Burney & my sister were here, & we had very good Diversion with him. He Wanted exceedingly to persuade us to play at Cards. We told him that we never did on Sunday; but he assured us it was very common, for he had [xxxxx *2 words*] ¦

---

[1] EBB's illness was probably connected with her latest pregnancy; in Jan. 1776 she gave birth to her 4th child Frances ('Fanny') (1776–1828), to whom FB presumably stood as godparent. She went with her children to Worcester in May or June and remained there until Sept. Her sister SEB stayed with her ('Worcester Mem.').

[2] Charles Clerke (1743–79) was commissioned Commander of the *Discovery* on 10 Feb. 1776, the same day that JB was commissioned 1st Lt. They both joined their ship on that date (J. C. Beaglehole, ed., *The Journals of Captain James Cook* (Cambridge, 1955–74), iii, pt. ii. 1471).

[3] SC had invited FB and JB to Chessington in Dec. (SC to FB, 14 Dec. 1775, Barrett). They presumably went in Jan. or early Feb.

[*The bottom of the page has been cut away. The next page contains a sample of the quaint conversation of Kitty Cooke, who complains about Mlle Rosat ('Rossiter'), one of her aunt's (Mrs Hamilton's) boarders at Chessington. FB has written* Edward. *at the top of the page, presumably referring to her cousin Edward Francesco Burney, who came to London in May of this year to study drawing at the Royal Academy ('Worcester Mem.').*]

'to tell you the truth, You must know we believe she's a little out of her Head sometimes, so that makes one take no Notice of some of her odd ways. But a little while ago, she took the most surprisingest fancy into her Head, that ever you heard of; for she had said that I Gaped at her! Now you know it's a thing one would not do upon no account; howsever, it happened to be about the change of the moon, & so I would not say much to her, so I only just said, "Miss Rossiter, said I, if you are so very mean as to think I would do such a thing as that, why it's your own fault, & I am sorry for you, & I pity you; for I can assure you, I never did so vulgar a thing since I can remember." But what was the most plaguingest, was, that she said that I set the maid a Gaping at her too! now she must have such an ungenerous opinion of me, that it's enough to provoke a saint: besides, I am no very *p*elite person, I own, & yet I never was a person of that sort, for to Gape at my Aunt's Boarders, would be absolutely scandalous; & I assure you I never had such a thought. Besides, other people Gape as well as me; however, she's so very particular, that do you know, when she is in these humours, I dare no more Gape than any thing; & nothing can be more provokinger than to Live in such a restraint.' |

[*The end of the letter is missing.*]

34   [St Martin's Street,
                                      1–4] April [1776]

To Samuel Crisp

ALS (Barrett), 5 April 1776
Double sheet 4to, 4 pp., *pmk* 5 AP wafer
Addressed: Sam⸢ Crisp Esq⸣ʳ, | at Mʳˢ Hamilton's, | Chesington, near King-ston, | Surry.

Annotated (by FBA): Dr. B.'s first visit to Mrs. Ord. Mrs Ord. Mr. Pepys. Dr. Russel. Mr. Burroughs. The Wrights. Mrs. Smith Duchess of Devonshire Nelly Beatson. Chiefly Inserted in Dr. Burney's Memoirs. ✳ ✖ N° 2. Monday 5 [*sic*] April 1776
     See *Mem.* i. 336–8.

Monday
My dear Daddy,
     I long to hear if you have got, & how you like the Books. I would have sent Montaigne,[4] but was afraid the parcel would have been too heavy to be safe only [packed][5] in paper. So they must wait till the next opportunity.
     Our visit to Mrs. Ord proved very agreeable. The party was small, but *select*, consisting of Dr. Russel, who I have mentioned at one of our Concerts; Mr. Pepys,[6] a man who, to a most fashionable air, Dress & Address, adds great shrewdness & drollery; Mr. Burrows,[7] a clergyman who is a Wit, in a peculiar style, chusing to aim all his Fire at *the Ton*, in which he sometimes succeeds very well; Mr Wright, a stupid man, but one who was so obliging as to be generally silent; his Wife, who did not make him blush by her superiority; Miss Wright,[8] who is rather pretty, & very sensible & agreeable; Mr Ord,[9] The *Eldest hope* of the Family, who is an exceeding handsome youth, & seems good natured & *all that*; Dr. M^{rs} & F. & S. Burney. O but I should have first mentioned Mrs Smith,[10] who you may perhaps formerly have known, as she was an

---

[4] Perhaps a copy of the *Journal du voyage de Michel de Montaigne en Italie . . . en 1580 et 1581*, ed. Anne-Gabriel Meusnier de Querlon, pub. at Rome and Paris in 1774 (reprinted 1775) from the MS discovered *c.*1770 at Montaigne's chateau (*YW* xxiv. 16 and nn. 29, 36).
[5] Inserted by FBA.
[6] William Weller Pepys (1741–1825), cr. (1801) Bt; a master in chancery, 1775–1825. A *habitué* of bluestocking parties, he became a close friend of FB. See *JL* xii. 607; *A Later Pepys: The Correspondence of Sir William Weller Pepys*, ed. A. C. C. Gaussen (1904).
[7] The Revd John Burrows (1733–86), rector of St Clement Danes and of Hadley, Middlesex; also a bluestocking *habitué* and a friend of Pepys (*JL* iv. 141).
[8] Perhaps the 'Miss Wright' who was CB's scholar in 1768 (CB's pocket memorandum book for 1768, Berg). She and her parents have not been further traced.
[9] Mrs Ord's eldest son, William Ord (*c.*1752–89) (*JL* i. 76 n. 1).
[10] Probably Burrows's sister Mary (d. 1782), m. Culling Smith (1731–1812) of Hadley, cr. (1802) Bt. (*GM* lii (1782), 206; *A Later Pepys . . .*, i. 377, 380, and *passim*). She is very possibly the same Mrs Smith who is listed next to Mrs Pepys in Mrs

intimate friend of Mrs Greville's. She is very little, ugly, &
terribly deformed; but she is quick, clever, & entertaining.

Mrs. Ord herself is almost the best mistress of a Family I
ever saw; she is so easy ⌐herself,¬ so chearfully polite, that it is
not possible for a Guest in her House to feel the least restraint.
She banishes all ceremony & formality, & made us all draw
our Chairs about a Table, which she kept in the [middle of
the]^11 Room, & called the best friend to sociable conversation.

We stayed till near 11 o'clock, & had neither Cards, music
or Dancing. It was a true *Conversatione*. Every body went away
well satisfied, & returning Thanks to Mrs. Ord for having
been ¦ admitted of the Party. My attention was given too
generally & indiscriminately to all sides, to enable me to write
you any of the conversation, which I would otherwise do.

Mr. Bruce had a bad cold, & was not there.

When we took leave, my Father told Mrs Ord that it gave
him great pleasure to say that he knew *2 or 3 Houses* even in
these Times, where Company could be entertained & got
together merely by conversation, unassisted by Cards, &c.
'Such Parties as Mrs *Ord* collects, said Mrs Smith, cannot *fail*
in regard to Entertainment.'

'And yet, answered Mr Pepys, I have known meetings
where equal pleasure has been proposed & expected, & where
the *ingredients* have been equally good, & yet the *Pudding* has
proved very bad.'

'True, returned my Father, for if the *Ingredients* are not *well
mixed*, their *separate* goodness does not signify; for if one is a
little too sour, & another a little too sweet, or too bitter, they
counter-act each other: but Mrs Ord is an excellent Cook, &
takes care not to put clashing materials into one mess.'

[xxxxx *5½ lines*]

Hetty & I took a walk in the Park on Sunday morning,
where, among others, we saw the young & handsome Duchess
of Devonshire,^12 walking in such an undressed & slaternly

Thrale's 'classification' of her friends (*Thraliana*, i. 331) and whom Mrs Thrale likens
to 'an Aspique' (ibid. i. 348).

^11 Inserted by FBA.

^12 Georgiana Spencer (1757–1806), m. (1774) William Cavendish (1748–1811),
5th D. of Devonshire. Her great unaffected charm and ebullience made her a leading

204 I-4 April 1776

manner as, in former Times, M^rs R[ishton] might have done in Chesington Garden. Two of her Curls came quite Un-pinned, & fell lank on One ¦ of her shoulders; one shoe was down at Heel, the Trimming of her Jacket & coat was in some places unsewn; her Cap was awry, & her cloak, which was . rusty & powdered, was flung half on & half off. Had she not had a servant in superb Livery behind her, she would cer-tainly have been affronted. Every creature turned back to stare at her. Indeed I think her very handsome, & she has a look of innocence & artlessness that made me quite sorry she should be so foolishly negligent of her Person. She had hold of the Duke's arm, who is the very reverse of herself, for he is ugly, tidy, & grave. He looks like a very mean shop keeper's Journey man.

Omai, who was in the Park, called here this morning, & says that he went to her Grace, & asked her why she let her Hair go in that manner? Ha, Ha, Ha,—don't you Laugh at her having a Lesson of Attention from ˹Omai?˺[13]

˹Nelly Beatson, Miss Reid's clever little Neice, called here on Thursday & made an appointment to accompany my mother & me to the oratorio on Friday.[14] Accordingly she came, with her Brother Robert,[15] who is a youth educated at the Woolwich Academy. We had two Box and two Pit Tickets, so as we went along Mama said, 'I shall try for us all to go into the Pit together but if they will not take the Box Tickets in there, why we must part company, & 2 go into the Upper Box, & 2 into the Pit, & so meet when the oratorio is over.'

You may have heard me frequently mention what a very

figure in London society, but her private life was singularly unhappy. She has been the subject of numerous biographies (see, most recently, B. Masters, *Georgiana Duchess of Devonshire* (1981)). For FB's opinion of her when she met her in 1791, see *JL* i. 47–8.

[13] This is FB's last mention of Omai before his departure from England with Capt. Cook in July.

[14] A performance of *The Messiah*, 'By Command of their Majesties', at Drury Lane on Friday, 29 Mar., with a concerto on organ by the Burneys' friend John Stanley (*LS 4* iii. 1964).

[15] Robert Beatson (b. 1758, living ?1804), son of Robert Beatson of Kilrie, Fife. A brand-new 2nd Lt. in the Royal Engineers (as of 17 Jan.), he was promoted to Lt. in 1784, resigned his commission in 1789, and m. (1790) Jean Campbell (d. 1813), daughter of Murdoch Campbell of Rossend (A. J. Beatson, *Genealogical Account of the Families of Beatson* (Edinburgh, p.p., 1860), pp. 4–5; *Scots Magazine*, lxxv (1813), 319; T. W. J. Conolly and R. F. Edwards, *Roll of Officers of the Corps of Engineers* (Chatham, 1898), p. 10).

easy young Lady Miss Beatson is, who has no Notion of doing any thing but what she likes, so, when she heard this, she whispered me, 'Well, if we part, you and *I* will go into the Boxes, & Mrs. Burney & Bob shall go into the Pit—though Bob won't like that.'

Accordingly, ⟨when we got⟩ to the Door, the man refused the Box Tickets. ⟨My mother then asked young Mr. Beatson where he would ¦ prefer to be, in⟩ the Boxes or the Pit?

'In the Boxes, Ma'am,' answered he, very composedly.

'Well then, ⟨said Mama to Nelly, 'you & Fanny will go into the Pit,⟩ & your Brother ⟨& I into the Boxes, & we will meet⟩ by & bye.'

'No, no,' said Nelly colouring, 'Not so, no, I shall go where ever Miss *Burney* chooses, myself.'

Did you ever hear such boldness in your Life? However, my mother persist'd, & walk'd off with young Beatson. Nelly & I were very angry with Bob ⟨for his selfishness⟩ [xxxxx ½ *line*] ⟨Miss Beatson is a clever & entertaining girl,⟩ but is unused to contradiction, & has no notion of ⟨yielding to the wishes of any one else.⟩

Thursday

I find it impossible to keep to any particular Day for writing —⟨I had⟩ only promised a Letter a Week, without further ⟨condit⟩ion [xxxxx 2 *lines*]

I have ⟨received⟩ the 2 last ⟨Letters⟩ of Kitty—but have now only Time ⟨to subscribe⟩ myself,⁊

My dearest Sir,
Your ever affect^te FB

35   [St Martin's Street,
post 16 June–27 July 1776]

To Samuel Crisp

AL fragment (Barrett), July 1776
Double sheet 4to, 4 pp.
Annotated (by FBA): C Barrett C Broome July—76
Charlotte (Francis) Barrett was the eldest daughter of FB's sister Charlotte, later Mrs Broome. FBA may have meant to call this letter to Mrs Barrett's

attention after Mrs Broome's death (in 1838) because of the early mention of her mother in it.

The first part of the letter is dated by FB's reference to her brother's ship being stopped in Portland Roads by contrary winds, which arose the evening of 16 June.

Now really, my dear Daddy, this is *prodigiously* curious!—Was it *me* or *you* who should first shew *signs of Life*?—Does the *Traveller*, or the *fixed* [*resident*][16] expect *reasonably* the first Letter?[17]—Besides, till you issue your orders, & give me a few hints, I don't know what to write about, further than a *Bill of Health*—which take as follows:

My Father is *charmingly*. My mother still very weak, but acknowledges herself to be *better*. She is now at Lynn.[18] As to the destination of the family for the rest of the summer, I am even yet in the Dark, & cannot give you any intelligence.

But the Great man'of men is your Friend James—who is now, in *Fact*, & in *power*, Captain of his ship, though, alas—not in *Honour* or *Profit*. The Case is, Captain Clarke has obtained permission to stay some Time longer in Town, to settle his affairs, &, in the hope of profiting by some Act—that I don't very well understand, concerning *Debtors*, he has surrendered himself, & is now actually in the King's Bench. An Order has been sent, *from the Admiralty*, To our Lieutenant, to carry the ship himself to Plymouth. And further of his affairs, I know not myself, nor whether he is yet sailed, nor any thing about him.[19] We have never seen his sweet Face since the last

[16] Inserted by FBA.

[17] SC's letter to FB, implied here, is missing.

[18] Where her mother, Mrs Mary (Maxy) Allen, had died on 6 June, and been buried 10 June in the Chapel of St Nicholas.

[19] Clerke had made himself security for debts to money-lenders incurred by his brother, Sir John Clerke (d. 1776), also a captain in the Royal Navy. Sir John sailed off to the East Indies (where he died the following Oct.). The announcement that Clerke himself was about to leave on a voyage seems to have brought the money-lenders down on him, and he was committed to the Rules of the King's Bench. In the meantime JB, as acting commander of the *Discovery*, received orders from Capt. Cook *c.*13 June to proceed to Plymouth, where he and his ship arrived on the 26th, after a long delay in Portland Roads caused by a storm that arose on the 16th (see below). Capt. Cook and the *Resolution* joined the *Discovery* at Plymouth on 30 June. The *Resolution* set out to sea on 12 July, but Clerke was unable to reach Plymouth until 30 July. The *Discovery*, commanded by Clerke, left England on 1 Aug., meeting up with

day that I saw [|] yours. & that glorious Confusion to which you was a Witness,[20] was, I presume, meant by way of a tender Farwell [*sic*] of the House. He was stopt in the Portland Road, by contrary Winds, & took that opportunity of writing to my Father.[21] In his Letter, though he *clumps* Compliments, &c, to *All*, the only person he mentions by Name is Yourself.

Saturday, July 27

O dear—oh dear—oh dear!—I was unfortunately interrupted after writing the above, which I began the moment I received your Letter—& after that, I had an inflammation in my Eyes, which has almost incapacitated me from using them,—& indeed they are still so weak, that any exertion of them gives me a good deal of pain—

But indeed I am now quite *ashamed* to write at all—& had I any reasonable hope of seeing you, I would defer my apologies & my pleadings till that Time—but things seem so ordered, that I believe I shall not be allowed that happiness for a long Time—& therefore, after some very serious *confabs* between me & my Conscience, I have taken courage, & resolved to try to make my peace with my dear, & I fear much displeased Daddy.

O that I could devise any means or ways or [|] methods by which to attone for my dilitariness!—will you accept from me *two* Letters every Week till I have made up for the lost time?— — I know I must not expect any answer as yet—& therefore I will promise *myself* your compliance with this condition, which to me is not a very pleasant one, as I must own—Letter Writing gives me no manner of Diversion, save merely as the means of procuring returns.

My mother came from Lynn & Stanhoe last Saturday [20 July] so well, *aparently*, that no *common* Eye could discern she

---

Capt. Cook's ship at the Cape of Good Hope in Nov. See Manwaring, pp. 68–71; J. C. Beaglehole, ed., *The Journals of Captain James Cook* (Cambridge, 1955–74), ii. 960–1; iii, pt. i., pp. lxxii, 4, 6–8; pt. ii. 1508–11, 1513–14; *GM* xlvii (1777), 247; D. B. Smith, *Commissioned Sea Officers in the Royal Navy* (1954), i. 174 (annotated copy at PRO, Kew).

[20] Unexplained.

[21] The letter is missing.

had been Ill. However, she did not give up her Bristol scheme, & this very afternoon, she & my Father set off for that place—& with them, went Charlotte: who is to accompany my mother on to Wales, where she proposes spending near 2 months. That dear little Girl went so much *à contre cœur*, that I was quite sorry & concerned for her. I believe she would willingly & literally have parted with a little finger, rather to have been left behind with me & no wonder!—for she is never spoke to, never noticed at all, except as an *errand runner*: in which capacity, I am apt to suspect, she now Travels, as she is by no means a favourite. However, while my *Father* is of the party, (who leaves them at Bristol) I hope she may be happy. | I should myself have gone, but for the difficulty of placing Charlotte & Sally any where properly.

And so I am now quite alone—at large & at liberty!—Hetty & Susy remain at Worcester till September. I have nobody but Sally for a companion. But I have no dread of *ennui*, nor fear of idleness or listlessness. I am going—(as soon as I have finished this Letter) to study *Italian*, which I can do alone at least as easily as I did French. However, I believe I shall be rather *more* engaged, than less; for since my intended situation has been known, I have received more invitations, &c, than I ever before did &, in particular, my good old friend Mr Hutton, no sooner heard my summer destination, than he made me a most earnest invite to visit his wife—which he never before did to any of the family. The Miss Paynes—who are really sweet Girls, & very great favourites with me—will almost Live with me, for they are so willing to come here, that they want Nothing but asking to be with me for ever, & they serve admirably to keep up my spirits, & excite all sort of nonsensical sport & jollity. Indeed, but for them, I believe I should be apt to confin[e] |

[*The remainder of the letter is missing. An AL or AJ fragment in the F. W. Hilles Collection, Yale University, dated 16 Oct. 1776, has been attributed to FB. It contains a description of the King and Queen attending a play at Covent Garden, with a pen and ink sketch of the royal box. This item is reproduced in* LS 5 i, *between pp. 102 and 103. The present editor has reluctantly concluded, however, on both orthographic and stylistic grounds, that the attribution to FB is incorrect.*]

In an ALS fragment (Barrett), probably written in Nov. 1776, SC thanks FB 'for your Conversation piece at Sr James Lake's—If Specimens of this kind had been preserv'd of the different Tons *that have succeeded one another for 20 Centuries last past, how interesting would they* ⌐have⌐ be⌐en⌐! *infinitely more so than Antique Statues, Bas-reliefs, & Intaglios—to compare the Vanities & Puppyisms of the Greek & Roman, & Gothic, & Moorish & Ecclesiastic reigning fine Gentlemen of the Day with one another, & the present Age must be a high entertainment, to a mind that has a turn for a mixture of Contemplation & Satire; & to do you Justice, Fanny, you paint well; therefore send me more, & more.' FB's letter is missing.*]

36   [St Martin's Street,
                  2 December 1776]

To Samuel Crisp

ALS (Barrett), 2 Dec. 1776
Double sheet 4to, 4 pp., *pmk* 2 DE seal
Addressed: Samuel Crisp Esqr, | at Mrs. Hamilton's, | Chesington, near Kingston, | Surry.
Annotated (by FBA): on Agujari at a private Concert at Dr Burney's. 2 Dec. 1776 ✳ ✖ N° 5

⌐I am extremely sorry, my dear Daddy, to acquaint you that I have had no success about the Books, though I have been to several Booksellers—viz. all from Charing Cross to Ludgate Hill—since I wrote last. Marianne & the paysan[22] are very scarce,—I could, indeed, have had the former in 4 very small Volumes at 2^s 6^d per vol. from Elmesly,[23] but thought it too dear, & I could no where else meet with either, except at one [*space left blank*] a *Foreign* Bookseller, but he asked 7^s for the paysan B[oun]d & 5^s in Blue Paper stiched, & the same for Marianne—⟨As⟩ to the Horace I believe I must wait till I can meet with one 2^d Hand, as it is very horribly dear[24] [xxxxx *1 word*] but I shall make Charles ⟨seek⟩ it for me at Christmas.

---

[22] *La Vie de Marianne* and *Le Paysan parvenu* by Marivaux (see *EJL* i. 47).
[23] Peter Elmsley (1736–1802), bookseller in the Strand (Maxted).
[24] SC had perhaps asked FB to find for him a copy of the elegant 1770 Baskerville 4to edn. of Horace's *opera*, with engravings by Gravelot.

As to the character which the new volumes of Pope & Swift[25] bear, I have not even heard of their existence. Money of yours I have in plenty, but will send you the Particulars of the account next Letter.

Now, as to the Pantheon,—in regard to the *Business* & *Main Chance* of the story, my Father has given you all the particulars, & so I say Nothing:[26]—Again, as to the Evening when we all went, Hetty has already ┃ made you master of all I could have said as to our Entertainment[27]—however, as, in regard to yesterday Evening, my Father has only given you the *Sum Total* of the performance, I shall enlarge a little upon that subject.┓

The Party consisted of—Signora Agujari,—invited without the least *thought* of her singing, & merely as an *Auditor* herself. She looked charmingly, though horribly ill Dressed, in old *Court Mourning*, by way of being quite in the Fashion.

Signor Colla, & his *triste* sister,[28] stupid as a post, & tired to Death, for she niether speaks French or English, & was condemned merely to look & be looked at all the Evening.

Mrs. Ord, a very charming Woman, of whom I have spoken more than once. Her Daughter,—of whom Ditto. Mr. Ord,[29] a near Relation, a most agreeable, well bred, lively young man, who is just returned from his travels, & talked French & Italian delightfully. He is an Enthusiast in music, & seemed to enjoy Agujari with a rapture little short of what *We* felt ourselves.

---

[25] Probably *Additions to the Works of Alexander Pope*, ed. William Warburton, 2 vols. 8vo, published by Henry Baldwin and advertised in *GM* xlvi (June 1776), 278; and vol. i of John Nichols's *A Supplement to Dr. Swift's Works*, also published this year.

[26] About this time the proprieters of the Pantheon voted CB a salary of £100 per year 'for carrying on their foreign Correspondence for 3 years'. CB's ambitions included becoming a proprieter himself and obtaining 'the management of the whole Band' there. On 20 Feb. 1777 he bought a 50th share of the Pantheon from John Wyatt for the sum of £700. See Lonsdale, pp. 227–8; *Survey of London*, xxxi. 273; T. Twining to CB, 29 Nov. 1776 (BL); SC to CB, 17 Dec. 1776 (Osborn, Berg); Middlesex Land Registers 1791/2/163 (GLRO).

[27] At the Pantheon, 18 or 25 Nov. Agujari sang both evenings (*Public Advertiser*, 18, 25 Nov.).

[28] Not further identified.

[29] Thomas Orde (1746–1807), later Orde-Powlett; cr. (1797) B. Bolton. A graduate of Eton and Cambridge and a lawyer by profession, he had travelled in France and Switzerland in 1772, and in 1774 in Flanders, Holland, and Germany. He later became a prominent politician, and in addition was a talented etcher and cartoonist. See Namier; *JL* i. 184–6.

Mr. Fitzgerald, a hard featured, Tall, hard voiced & hard mannered Irish man: fond of music, but fonder of *discussing* than of *listening*,—as are many other people who, shall be *nameless*. Miss *Fitzgerald*,[30] his Daughter, as droll a sort of piece of Goods, (to use your expression) as one might wish to know. She is Good Natured & sprightly, but so unlike other misses of the present Time, that she is really diverting, for she speaks her mind as freely & readily, before a Room full ¹ of Company, as if with only a single Friend; she laughs louder than a man, pokes her Head vehemently, Dresses shockingly, & has a carriage the most *ungain* that ever was seen.[31]

Keene Fitzgerald,[32] her Brother, is half a Coxcomb, & half a Man of Sense; now humble & diffident; now satisfied & conceited; & so much for him.—Mr. Nollekens, who is a[s] jolly, fat, lisping, Laughing, under bred, good humoured [a] man as Lives; his *merit* seems pretty much confined to his profession, & his Language is as vulgar, as his Works are elegant. Mrs. Nollekens,[33] his wife, a civil, obliging, gentle sort of woman; rather too complaisant.

Governor Devaynes,[34] & Mr. Dudley Long:[35]—with these two, as I had no Conversation, I can say nothing.

---

[30] Mary Fitzgerald (d. 1823), daughter of Keane Fitzgerald (d. 1782), who had been the Burneys' next-door neighbour and landlord in Poland St. (see *EJL* i. 218). She married (1779) John Fitzgerald (1760–1818), a friend of SEB's eventual husband, Molesworth Phillips (*JL* i. 186 n. 15; *GM* xciii² (1823), 380).

[31] CB, in a letter to Charlotte Burney Francis, 4 Nov. 1788 (Barrett), calls Mary Fitzgerald 'our old Friend & favourite . . . she has an original spirit & Character that wᵈ strike fire out of a Norfolk Turnip or Dumplin.'

[32] Keane Fitzgerald (*c.*1748–1831), MA (Oxon.), 1772; barrister-at-law, Inner Temple, 1773; bencher, 1808.

[33] Mary Welch (d. 1817), daughter of Saunders Welch (*c.*1711–84), who was Henry Fielding's successor as a justice of the peace; m. (1772) Joseph Nollekens, sculptor. Through her father she became a close friend of Dr Johnson, who gallantly claimed he would have been her suitor had not Nollekens beaten him to it. Her husband's biographer, who had been his pupil, accuses both her and Nollekens of unbounded parsimony (J. T. Smith, *Nollekens and His Times* (1829), *passim*).

[34] William Devaynes (*c.*1730–1809), MP; London banker; a wealthy government contractor; at various times director of the East India Co. (sometimes chairman); director of the Globe Insurance Co. and the French Hospital; in 1776 also Liverpool commissioner of the Africa Co. (Namier). Mrs Thrale also called him 'Governor' Devaynes (*Thraliana*, i. 436).

[35] Dudley Long (1748–1829), afterwards North and still later Long-North; MA (Cantab.), 1774; Lincoln's Inn, 1769; later MP (Namier). He was a subscriber to *Hist. Mus.*

Miss B—*something*, a sister in Law of Mr. Hayes[36] of the Pantheon: a young lady quite *à la mode*,—every part of her Dress, the very pink & extreme of the Fashion;—her He[ad] erect & stiff as any statue;—her voice low & delicate & mincing;—her ⌐Head¬ higher than 12 Wigs stuck one on the other,—her ⌐waste¬ Taper & pinched evidently,—her Eyes cast languishingly from one object to another, & her Conversation very much *the thing*. What was most pleasant, this fashionable lady came in with Miss Fitzgerald, who is so exactly her opposite, that they could never be looked at, without having the difference unmarked. Mr. Merlin, Mr. Burney & my sister.—

O how we all wished for our Daddy, when the Divine Agujari said she would sing!—she was all good humour & sweetness— she sung—O Sir!—what words can I use?—Could I write what she deserves, you *would* come to hear her, let what would be the consequence. O Mr Crisp, she would heal all your complaints,—her voice would restore you to Health & spirits,—I think it is almost greater than ever,—& then, when softened, so sweet, so mellow, so affecting!—she has every thing!—every requisite to accomplish a singer, in every style & manner!— the Sublime & the Beautiful, equally at command!—I tremble not lest she should not answer to you, for she cannot, cannot fail!—she astonishes & she affects at pleasure—O that you could come & hear her!—is it impossible?—I die to have you enjoy the greatest luxury the world can offer:—such, to me— such, I am sure to you, would be—the singing of Agujari! Adieu, dear sir, my love to Mrs. Hamilton & Kitty.

ever most fondly yours FB

37   [St Martin's Street,
                                      25 December 1776]

To Thomas Lowndes

AL (Comyn), Dec. 1776
Single sheet 4to, 2pp., *pmk* 7 o'clock wafer

---

[36] Presumably one of the managers of the Pantheon. He and Miss B. have not been further traced.

Addressed: [M]r. Lowndes, | Bookseller, | Fleet Street, [Wed]nesday morning

The MS is in vol. 1 of a grangerized copy of *DL*. An early draft of this letter, which differs markedly from the version actually sent, is given in Appendix 1 of this vol.

The letter inaugurates FB's correspondence, anonymous on her side, with Thomas Lowndes (1719–84), bookseller in Fleet St., which eventually led to the publication of *Evelina* in Jan. 1778. It, like its successors and the MS of *Evelina* sent to Lowndes, is written in a feigned hand; since FB was her father's amanuensis, she feared that her handwriting might be recognized and the novel ascribed to her or to CB. She may have begun work on it (in her imagination, at least) as early as 1767, when she burned its forerunner, 'The History of Caroline Evelyn'. Large stretches of free time in 1776 enabled her to bring to completion the first 2 vols. At this stage only her sisters SEB and Charlotte and her brother CB Jr. were in on the secret. Together, she and they decided on James Dodsley (1724–97) as the publisher to approach, but Dodsley refused to consider an anonymous work. 'Chance', then, 'fixed them upon the name of Mr. Lowndes' (*Mem.* ii. 128). FB's letter, sent in the morning, was presumably answered by Lowndes the same day. See *HFB*, pp. 53–4, 60–5; E. A. Bloom, ed., *Evelina* by Frances Burney (1968), 'Introduction', pp. vii–ix; Maxted, s.v. Dodsley, James, and Lowndes, Thomas; Nichols, *Lit. Anec.* iii. 646–7.

Sir, As Business, with those who understand it, makes its own apology, I will not take up your Time with reading Excuses for this address, but proceed immediately to the motives which have induced me to give you this trouble.

I have in my possession a M : S. novel,[37] which has never yet been seen but by myself; I am desirous of having the 2 first volumes printed immediately,—and the publication of the rest, shall depend wholly on their success.

But, sir, such is my situation in Life, that I have objections unconquerable to being known in this transaction;—I, therefore, must solicit the favour of you to answer me the following queries, which I hope you will not think impertinent.

1st whether you will give a candid and impartial Reading, to a Book that has no *recommendation* to previously prejudice you in its favour?

Secondly, whether, if, upon perusal, the work should meet | with your approbation, you will Buy the Copy, of a Friend

---

[37] An incomplete MS draft of *Evelina*, 104 fos., is in the Berg Collection. Only a single leaf of the fair copy survives (PML).

whom I shall commission to wait upon you, without ever seeing or knowing the Editor?[38]

I shall be obliged to you to direct your answer to Mr. King,[39] to be left at the Orange Coffee House till called for, in the Haymarket.

[Lowndes's reply (Barrett) follows. FB has annotated it: ✷ Nº 2. 1776]

Sir

I've not the least objection to what you propose & if you favour me with sight of your Ms I'll lay aside other Business to read it & tell you my thoughts of it at 2 Press's I can soon make it appear in print for now is the time for a Novel

Fleet Street   yr obed^t Servt

Decr 25   Thos Lowndes

38   [St Martin's Street,
                                    ?26 December 1776]

To Thomas Lowndes

AL (Comyn), Dec. 1776
Single sheet 4to, 2pp.
Addressed: Mr. Lowndes, | Bookseller, | Fleet Street
The MS is in vol. i of a grangerized copy of *DL*.

Sir,

The frankness, with which you favoured me with an answer to my Letter, induces me to send you the M : S. with the firmest reliance upon your candour.

---

[38] In her draft of this letter (see head-note), FB presents herself as the 'author'. Here, she may either be attempting to distance herself further from her work, or she may be signalling in advance that her work is an epistolary novel. (Authors of epistolary novels conventionally pretended to be the 'editor'.)

[39] 'Mr. King' was CB Jr., just graduated from the Charterhouse, who agreed to act as intermediary between FB and Lowndes. For the Orange Coffee House in the Haymarket, see B. Lillywhite, *London Coffee Houses* (1963), pp. 427–8.

The plan of the first Volume, is the Introduction of a well educated, but inexperienced young woman into public company, and a round of the most fashionable Spring Diversions of London. I believe it has not before been executed, though it seems a fair field open for the Novelist, as it offers a fund inexhaustible for Conversation, observations, and probable Incidents.

The characters of the Sea Captain,[40] and *would be* French woman,[41] are intended to draw out each the other; and the ignorance of the former, in regard to modern customs, and fashionable modes, assists in marking their absurdity and extravagance.

I shall send you the second volume with all the expedition in my power, if that which is now under your | examination, makes you desirous of seeing it,

I am,

S^r

Your most obd^t servant

———————

[*Lowndes's reply (Barrett) is addressed* To Mr King at the Orange Coffee House To be left till called for *and annotated (by FBA)* N° 3 ⁂ 1776]

Sir

I've read & like the Manuscript & if you'll send the rest I'll soon run it over

yr obed^t

T. Lowndes

Decr 29

———

[40] Capt. Mirvan.
[41] Madame Duval.

39 [St Martin's Street,
pre 17 January 1777]

To Thomas Lowndes

AL (Comyn), Jan. 1777
Single sheet 4to, 2 pp.
Addressed: Mr. Lowndes,
The MS is in vol. 1 of a grangerized copy of *DL*.

Sir, I have been much mortified that a multiplicity of perverse engagements prevented my sooner sending you the second volume of Evelina.[1]

When you have perused it, I must beg that, with the same frankness you have hitherto shewn, you will be so good as to send me your opinion of it, and whether, and upon what terms, you are willing to take the copy.

As to the future volumes, their publication will depend solely upon the fate of these first—but, if you print the work, I shall send you an advertisement to this effect, to prefix to the first Volume,—and also a Dedication.[2]

The Heroine, as you will find, descending into a lower circle, now partakes of a round of Summer *Diversions*, which, though of an inferior cast to those of the Spring, are not less productive of Incidents for a Novel. |

I beg you to direct your answer as before.

I am,
 S^r
  Yr most obed^t servant _____ _____

[*Lowndes's reply (Barrett) is annotated (by FBA)* N° 4 1777]

Sir

I have read your Novel and cant see any Reason why you shou'd not finish and publish it compleat   I'm sure it will be

---

[1] FB was delayed by having to copy the volume surreptitiously and in a feigned hand. See below, p. 231–2.

[2] Her dedication to the 'author of my being', CB.

your interest as well as the Booksellers, you may well add One Volume to these, & I shall more eagerly print it. I Returnd one in a singular[3] State to a Lady on Thursday [16 Jan.] who has before favour'd me with the Production of her Pen[4] I w^d Rather print in July than now to Publish an Unfinished book. This I submit to your Consideration and with wishes that you may come into my Way of thinking I'll restore the MS to the Gentleman[s] that brought it.

Fleetstreet

Jany 17th

Y^r Ob^t Servt

T. Lowndes

40

[St Martin's Street, *post* 17 January 1777]

To Thomas Lowndes

AL (Barrett), Jan. 1777
Single sheet 4to, 1 p.
Annotated (by FBA): To Mr *Lowndes.* N° 5 Jany 1777. N.B. This was the hand Writing in which F.B. copied all Evelina to have her own unseen.
Like all the early letters to Lowndes, written in a feigned hand (see illustration). A reduced facsimile of this letter is in vol. ii of a grangerized copy of *The Early Diary* in the National Portrait Gallery (London).

Sir

I am well contented with the openness of your proceedings, & obliged to you for your advice.

My original plan was, to publish 2 volumes now, & two more next year: I yield, however, to your Experience in these matters, & will defer the publication, till the Work is completed,—though I should have been better pleased to have *felt the pulse* of the public, before I had proceeded.

I will write to you again, when I am ready for the press. In the mean Time, I must beg the favour of a line, directed as before, to acquaint me how long I may delay printing the

---

[3] Presumably a slip for 'similar'.

[4] Perhaps the same anonymous lady whose epistolary novel, *The History of Miss Pamela Howard,* Lowndes had published in 1773.

[5] 'Mr. afterwards Dr. Charles Burney' (FBA's note). In a letter to CB, 5 Sept.

To Mr. Lowndes.   [No 5]   Jan 7. 1777.   8

N.B. This was the hand writing in which F.B. copied the Evelina to have her own unseen.

Sir

I am well contented with the openness of your proceedings, & obliged to you for your advice.

My original plan was, to publish 2 volumes now, & two more next year: I yield, however, to your experience in these matters, & will defer the publication, till the work is completed;—though I should have been better pleased to have felt the pulse of the public, before I had proceeded.

I will write to you again, when I am ready for the press. In the mean time, I must beg the favour of a line, directed as before, to acquaint me how long I may delay printing the Novel, without losing the proper season for its appearance. I am, Sir,
Yr. humble servt. — —

4. Fanny Burney's letter to Thomas Lowndes, *post* 17 January 1777, showing her disguised hand.

Novel, without losing the proper season for its appearance.[6]
I am, S[r]

Y[r] humble serv[t] _____ _____ |

41   [Chessington, 15 March 1777]
To Susanna Elizabeth Burney

AL (Berg, paginated 585–[8]), 15 Mar. 1777
Double sheet 4to, 4 pp., *pmk* 15 MR red wax seal
Addressed: Miss S. Burney, | S[t] Martin's Street, | Leicester Fields, |
London
Annotated (by FBA): Chessington ✳ 15th March 1777
The pagination indicates that this letter was formerly inserted in the
Journal for 1777.

Your Letter,[7] my dear Susy, was a most acceptable regale to
me.—but I wish you would remember my so often repeated
request & entreaty to give me *two* for one; which I could
plainly prove would be but Justice & Equity, according to the
situations we are in, but that I will not affront your Judgement,
by supposing you require my assistance for discovering what
is so obvious.[8] I think you can't much wonder that Miss C.[9] is
not fond of her morning's amusement at our House,—upon
my Word I am ashamed to think of it. I don't know which was
worse, the *Rasberry*, or the *Coffee*, but *nothing* of the *Refreshment*
kind seems palatable in S[t] Martin's. Pray when you see her
next, make my best Compliments to her. I die to hear the
Vauxhall Mad Song![10] I have an idea of it that makes *me*

1782, Lowndes claims to have advised FB that 'if the *Marybone* Scene was abridged,
and the City Visits lessened, the Work would appear more lively; and, if the Author
would write a third Volume, replete with Modern Characters, I should be glad to see
it when finished' (printed *DL* ii. 481–2; the MS is missing). Perhaps this additional
advice was carried back to FB verbally by CB Jr.

  [6] If Lowndes replied to this query, the letter is missing. See below, p. 285.
  [7] Missing.
  [8] As FB indicates below, she was pretending to write letters to SEB, when in fact
she was composing the 3rd vol. of *Evelina*.
  [9] Probably Catherine Coussmaker (*fl.* 1764–1803), daughter of CB's friend Lady
Hales by her 1st husband, Evert George Coussmaker, Esq. She became a particular
friend of SEB. She m. (1798) Charles Lindsay (1760–1846), Bishop of Kildare (1804)
(*JL* i. 164 n. 54).
  [10] Not found. A contemporary example of a 'mad song' is *Tom O'Bedlam*, the words

almost mad that I missed it: however, to recover my senses, I must think of that pretty Couplet which, you know, of Old, is always a consolation to me, namely,

> What is wishing?—wishing will not do;
> We cannot have a Cake,—& Eat it too![11]

A wise maxim, Miss Susan,—& altogether as new & instructive as it is wise: & more over & above, expressive with no small poignancy of Wit.—The turn at the End is truly Epigrammatic, & makes my mouth Water.

I can easily believe Rauzzini has behaved in the same way he looks, ie, like an Angel,—since *you* say so: but I long to know the particulars of a conduct sufficiently seraphic to have made *you* restore him to his place among the Cherubims & seraphims.[12] You say you have much *more* to say, *had you Paper*; —surely never before had any one the meanness to avow so stingy an excuse! However, if you can't afford to *Buy*,—why, *Beg*;—or if you are too modest for That, why, *steal*;—for stealing can never impeach your modesty,—& that, you know, is a female's first recommendation,—since the very action itself, far from discovering any boldness, manifests an internal diffidence of being welcome to what is taken.

Now, as I hope I have cleared up this point to your satisfaction, & to the utter extinction of all vulgar prejudices, I entreat that I may never again hear so shabby an Apology.

We pass our Time here very serenely, &, distant as you may think us from the Great World, I some times, find myself in the midst of it,—though nobody suspects the brilliancy of the Company I occasionally keep.[13] We Walk, Talk, Write, Read, Eat, Drink, Thrum, & sleep. These are our recreations, which, for your better conception, I will some what enlarge upon.

---

by George Alexander Stevens, published by Peter Hodgson *c.*1775 (BL G. 306. (202.); Maxted).

[11] The source of this couplet has not been found. It may be FB's own, perhaps written when she was a child.

[12] Perhaps an allusion to Rauzzini's altercation with Sacchini, whom he accused of stealing some of his arias. The date of this quarrel is unclear, though. See Mercer, ii. 894–5.

[13] Alluding to *Evelina*.

Imprimis;—*We Walk*: The brightness of the sun, invites us abroad,—the tranquility of the scene, promises all the pleasures of philosophic contemplation, which, *ever studious of rural amusement*, I eagerly pursue, mais, helas! scarse have I wandered over half a meadow, ere the *bleak Winds whistle round my Head*, off flies my faithless Hat,—my perfidious Cloak endeavours to follow,—even though it clings, with well acted fondness, to my Neck;—my Apron, my Gown,—all my habiliments, with rebellious emotion, wage a Civil War with the *mother Country*![14]—though there is not an Individual among them but has been indebted to me for the very existence by which they so treacherously betray me! My shoes, too, though they cannot, like the rest, brave me to my Teeth, are equally false & worthless; for, far from aiding me by springing forward, with the generous zeal they owe me, for having rescued them from the dark & dusty Warehouse in which they were pent,—they fail me in the very moment I require their assistance,—sink me in Bogs,—pop me into the mud,—&, attaching themselves rather to the mire, than to the Feet which guide them, threaten me perpetually with desertion: & I shall not be much surprised, if, some Day when I least think of it, they should give me the slip, & settle themselves by the way.

Secondly: *We Talk*: *That*, you can do yourself, so shall not enter into a minute discussion of this point.

Thirdly: *We Write*: *That is thus*; Mr. Crisp, writes to Miss Simmons; Mrs. Hamilton, to the Butcher; & Miss Cooke, a list of Cloaths for the Washerwoman: & as to *me*,—do you know I write to *you* every Evening,[15] while the family play at Cards? The folks here often marvel at your ingratitude in sending me so few returns in kind.

Fourthly: *We Read*: Mr. Crisp pores over Crit: Reviews to Sir John Hawkins;[16] Mrs. Hamilton, the Tradesmen's Bills;

---

[14] The newspapers at this time were filled with accounts of the American war.

[15] i.e., she was writing *Evelina*.

[16] Hawkins's 5-vol. *A General History of the Science and Practice of Music* had been published in Nov. 1776. Following favourable reviews in *GM*, the *Critical Review*, and other periodicals, CB, feeling his own *Hist.* threatened, instigated his friend Bewley to attack Hawkins in the *Monthly Review*. SC presumably read, *inter alia*, Bewley's first article in the Feb. issue (*Monthly Review*, lvi. 137–44). Two more articles followed, in Apr. and Aug. Bewley's satiric onslaught, more amusing than fair, had the effect of

Miss Cook, her own pocket Book, or *Ladies Memorandum*,[17] & I,—am studying, against I return to Town, Le Diable Boiteux,[18] which contains no few moral sentences, proper for those who dwell in a great *Methropolis* [*sic*]. | Fifthly, *We Eat*. There is something, in this part of our Daily occupation, too singular & uncommon to be passed over without some particular Notice & observation. Our method is as follows; We have certain substances, of various sorts, consisting *chiefly* of Beasts, Birds, & vegetables, which, being first Roasted, Boiled or Baked, (N.B. We shall not Eat Raw flesh, till Mr Bruce publishes his Travels,)[19] are put upon Dishes, either of Pewter, or Earthern ware, or China;—& then, being cut into small Divisions, every plate receives a part: after this, with the aid of a knife & fork, the Divisions are made still smaller; they are then (care being taken not to maim the mouth by the above offensive Weapons) put between the Lips, where, by the aid of the Teeth, the Divisions are made yet more delicate, till, diminishing almost insensibly they form a general *mash*, or *wad*, & are then swallowed.

I must continue my acc^t of our Lives in my next. ⌐I have just got y^r Letter[20]—pray write [xxxxx *1 word*] to tell me by *whom* I am expected, & all about it.[21] Mr. Crisp won't hear of my going, unless by actual ⟨command⟩—*pray* don't fail writing to morrow, & every post—

I have a message for ⟨?Hetty⟩ but not Room nor Time— direct by *agua*—'tis quicker, & *2* times cheaper than by Land [xxxxx *1 word*] my dear Father, my mama, & [xxxxx *1½ lines*] ⟨pray give my love to⟩ Hetty, Mr B. & to [xxxxx *1 line*]¬|

---

making Hawkins an object of ridicule in 'polite' circles. Bewley's authorship was kept a close secret, and SC was probably unaware of CB's complicity in the articles. This less than attractive phase of CB's career is treated at length in Lonsdale, pp. 189–225. See also B. H. Davis, *A Proof of Eminence: The Life of Sir John Hawkins* (Bloomington, 1973), pp. 125–51.

[17] *The Ladies' Own Memorandum Book, or Daily Pocket Journal*, by 'a Lady', was published annually.

[18] Alain René Le Sage (1668–1747), *Le Diable boiteux* (Amsterdam and Paris, 1707).

[19] An allusion to Bruce's claim that the Abyssinians ate raw or live flesh. His assertion was met with general scepticism and ridicule.

[20] Missing.

[21] FB's uncle Richard Burney was coming to town to bring her back with him to Barborne Lodge in Worcester. See below.

[St Martin's Street,
27–]8 March [1777]

To Samuel Crisp

ALS (Barrett), 28 Mar. 1777
2 double sheets 4to, 7 pp., *pmk* 28 MR seal
Addressed: Samuel Crisp Esq*ʳ*, | at Mrs. Hamilton's, | Chesington | near
Kingston | Surry.
Annotated (by FBA): From Miss F. Burney to Mʳ Crisp 1777 ✻ ✖ Nᵒ 2 FB
First sight of *Dr. Johnson* and Mrs. Thrale an⟨d Mi⟩ss Thrale before the
publication of Evelina
Endorsed: March 28. 1777
FBA retraced this letter because of the faintness of the original ink. As she
notes, it is especially interesting since it records her 'First sight' of Dr
Johnson and Mrs Thrale, who were to play such an important role in her life
over the next 7 years. Cf. her revision of the letter in *Mem.* ii. 86–100.

28 March

⌜My dear Daddy,
     I might still have ⟨remained⟩ at Chesington, for any thing
that concerns my Uncle, for he is not yet arrived, niether have
we heard a Word about or from him since I came. I am
abominably provoked at having been cheated of so much
Time, & so much comfort. We both ⟨have⟩, & do, expect
Daily to see him, yet I have lost a Week ⟨about it⟩, come
when he will—besides, I am in a most ⟨vexing⟩ uncertainty in
regard to my Journey,—Nothing has been said of it here, so
that I know not, yet, whether I shall ⟨be a *Worsted Stocking*,²² or
not.⌝
     My dear Father ⌜however,⌝ seemed well pleased at my re-
turning to my Time: & that is no small consolation & pleasure
to me. So now to our Thursday morning Party.²³

---

     ²² i.e., 'a-*Worcestering*', or taking a trip to Worcester. The reading is conjectural, but
FB makes a similar pun at the end of the letter. (Cf. also '*Worsted Stocking Knave*'.)
     ²³ This party evidently took place on 20 Mar., as on 19 Mar. Johnson wrote to
Mrs Thrale: 'I shift pretty well a-days, and so have at you all at Dr. Burney's
tomorrow' (Johnson, *Letters*, ii. 166).

Mrs[24] & Miss Thrale,[25] Miss Owen[26] & Mr. Seward[27] came long before *Lexaphanes*;[28]—Mrs. Thrale is a very pretty woman still,—she is extremely lively and chatty,—has no supercilious or pedantic airs, & is really gay and agreeable.[29] Her Daughter is about 12 years old, ⌜&,⌝ I believe, ⌜not all together so amiable as her mother.⌝[30] Miss Owen, who is a Relation, is good humoured & sensible *enough*; she is a sort of *Butt*, & as such, a general favourite:[31] for those sort of characters are prodigiously useful in drawing out the Wit & pleasantry of others: Mr. Seward is a very polite, agreeable young man:[32]

My sister [EBB] was invited to meet, ⌜& play, to⌝ them.

The Conversation was supported with a good deal of vivacity —(N.B. my Father being at Home) for about half an Hour, &

---

[24] Hester Lynch Salusbury (1741–1821), m. (1763) Henry Thrale (?1729–81), brewer and MP; m. 2 (1784) Gabriel Mario Piozzi (1740–1809), Italian musician. CB had first met the Thrales in 1776, and began weekly visits to Streatham Park on 12 Dec. of that year to give music lessons to Queeney (*Thraliana*, i. 136–7 and n. 5). This morning party was arranged at the request of Mrs Thrale, who wished to see CB's family and library. FB later recalled that, as was her custom at such gatherings, she spent the morning sitting quietly in a corner, observing but not speaking (*JL* vii. 523). Her real friendship with Mrs Thrale did not begin until after the publication of *Evelina*.

[25] Hester Maria ('Queeney') Thrale (1764–1857), eldest daughter of the Thrales; m. (1808) George Keith Elphinstone Keith (1746–1823), cr. (1797) B. Keith, (1814) Visc. Keith.

[26] Margaret Owen (1743–1816), daughter of the Revd Lewis Owen (d. 1746), rector of Barking, Essex, and Wexham, Bucks., a childhood friend and distant cousin of Mrs Thrale (*Thraliana*, i. 405 n. 1)

[27] William Seward (1747–99). Son of a prominent London brewer, he attached himself to the Thrales' literary circle and became known as an anecdotist, author of *Anecdotes of Some Distinguished Persons* (1795–7) and its sequel, *Biographiana* (1799).

[28] Archibald Campbell (?1726–80), a Scottish purser in the navy, gave this name to Johnson in a satiric little book by that title (*Lexiphanes*, 1767) attacking the style of *The Rambler* (*Life*, ii. 44).

[29] Cf. FBA's fuller descriptions in *Mem.* ii. 87–8 and *JL* vii. 522–4, where she criticizes Mrs Thrale's ostentatious dress and entrance on this occasion.

[30] Altered by FBA to 'stiffly proper, I believe, or else shy & reserved: I don't yet know which'. In *Mem.* ii. 88 she emends this to 'She is reckoned cold and proud; but I believe her to be merely shy and reserved'. Cf. *JL* i. 176.

[31] In her table of ratings of her friends, on a scale of 0 to 20 Mrs Thrale gave Miss Owen a 0 for 'Conversation Powers', a 2 for 'Useful Knowledge', and a 1 for 'Ornamental Knowledge' (*Thraliana*, i. 331). Johnson thought her 'empty-headed', and she was the butt of many family jests (M. Hyde, *The Thrales of Streatham Park* (Cambridge, Mass., 1977), p. 157).

[32] FBA wrote in 1798 that she had 'always retained a true esteem for him, though his singularities, & affectation of affectation always struck me. . . . his solid mind is all solid benevolence & worth' (*JL* iv. 110).

then Hetty, & *Suzette*, for the first Time *in public*, played a
Duet, &, in the midst of this performance, Dr. Johnson was
announced. ˺

He is, indeed, very ill favoured,—he is tall & stout, but
stoops terribly,—he is almost bent double. His mouth is ˹in
perpetual motion,˺[33] as if he was chewing;—he has a strange
method of frequently twirling his Fingers, & twisting his
Hands;—his Body is in continual agitation, *see sawing* up &
down; his Feet are never a moment quiet,—&, in short, his
whole person is in perpetual motion:

His Dress, too, considering the Times, & that he had meant
to put on his best becomes, being engaged to Dine in a large
Company, was as much out of the common Road as his Figure:
he had a large Wig, snuff colour coat, & Gold Buttons; but no
Ruffles to his ˹Wrist, & Black Worsted Stockings[34]—so, you
see, there is another *Worsted Stocking Knave*, besides me,—
that's my comfort.˺

He is shockingly near sighted, & did not, till she held out
her Hand to him, even know Mrs. Thrale. He *poked his Nose*
over the keys of the Harpsichord, till the Duet was finished, &
then, my Father introduced Hetty to him, as an old acquaintance, & he ˹instantly˺ kissed her.[35]

His attention, however, was not to be diverted five minutes
from the Books, as we were in the Library; he poured over
them, almost brushing the Backs of them, with his Eye lashes,
as he read their Titles; at last, having fixed upon one, he began,
without further ceremony, to Read, all the time standing at a
distance from the Company. We were very much provoked, as
we perfectly languished to hear him talk; but, it seems, he is
the most silent creature, when not particularly drawn out, in
the World.

My sister then played another Duet, with my Father: but
Dr. Johnson was so deep in the Encyclopedie,[36] that, as he is

---

[33] Altered by FBA to 'almost constantly opening and shutting'.

[34] Changed by FBA to 'no Ruffles to his Doughty Fists; and Black worsted stockings.'

[35] FBA adds: 'When she was a little Girl, he had made her a present of the Idler.'
This probably occurred in the early 1760s, and may have been done as a reward for
her achievements as a child prodigy.

[36] CB owned a 33-vol. set of Diderot's famous *Encyclopédie*, presumably the 1st 33
vols., published 1751–77, and lacking the concluding 2 index vols. (1780) (see *Lib.*,

very deaf, I question if he even knew what was going forward. When this was over, Mrs. Thrale, in a laughing manner, said 'Pray, Dr. Burney, can you tell me what that song was, & whose, which Savoi sung last night at Bach's[37] Concert, & which you did not hear?' My Father confessed ⎮ himself by no means so good a Diviner, not having had Time to consult the stars, though in the House of Sir Isaac Newton. However, wishing to draw Dr. Johnson into some Conversation, he told him the Question. The Doctor, seeing his drift, good naturedly put away his Book, & said very drolly 'And pray, Sir—*Who is Bach?*—is he a Piper?'—Many exclamations of surprise, you will believe, followed this Question. 'Why you have Read his name often in the papers,' said Mrs. Thrale; & then gave him some account of his Concert, & the number of fine performances she had heard at it.

'Pray,' said he, 'Madam, what is the Expence?'

'O,' answered she, 'much trouble & solicitation to get a subscriber's Ticket;—or else half a Guinea.'

'Trouble & solicitation,' said he, 'I will have nothing to do with;—but I would be willing to give Eighteen Pence.'

Chocolate being then brought, we adjourned to the ⌐Dining¬ Room. And here, Dr. Johnson, being taken from the Books, entered freely & most cleverly into conversation: though it is remarkable, that he never speaks at all, but when spoken to; nor does he ever *start*, though he so admirably *supports* any subject.

The whole party was engaged to Dine at Mrs. Montague's:[38] Dr. Johnson said he had received the most flattering note he had ever read, or any body else had ever Read, by way of invitation. 'Well, so have I, too,' cried Mrs. Thrale, 'so if a note from Mrs. Montague is to be boasted of, I beg mine may not be forgot.'

---

p. 27). Johnson seems to have owned only the 1st 7 vols. (1751–9). He was perhaps reading in one of the latest 5 vols., published as a supplement in 1776–7 (see D. Greene, *Samuel Johnson's Library: An Annotated Guide* (Victoria, 1975), p. 55).

[37] Johann (John) Christian Bach (1735–82), the so-called 'London Bach'. With Karl (Carl) Friedrich Abel he directed a popular Wednesday night subscription series that lasted from 1765 till his death (*New Grove*; Highfill). The concert of Wednesday night, 19 Mar. 1777, is advertised in the *Public Advertiser* of that date, but Savoi and his song are not mentioned.

[38] Elizabeth Robinson (1720–1800), m. (1742) Edward Montagu (1692–1775), MP; the noted bluestocking hostess.

'*Your* note,' cried Dr. Johnson, 'can bear no comparison with *mine*;—I am *at the Head of Philosophers*; she says.'

'And I,' cried Mrs. Thrale, '*have all the muses in my Train!*'

'A fair Battle,' said my Father; 'come, Compliment [|] for Compliment, & see who will hold out longest.'

'O, I am afraid for Mrs. Thrale!' cried Mr. Seward, 'for I know Mrs. Montague exerts all her forces when she attacks Dr. Johnson.'

'O yes,' said Mrs. Thrale, 'she has often, I know, flattered *him* till he has been ready to Faint.'

'Well, Ladies,' said my Father, 'You must get him between you to Day, & see which can lay on the paint thickest, Mrs. Thrale or Mrs. Montague.'

'I had rather,' cried the Doctor, 'go to Bach's Concert!'

After this, they talked of Mr. Garrick, & his late Exhibition before the King, to whom, & the Queen & Royal Family, he read Lethe, *in character, c'est à dire*, in different Voices, & Theatrically.[39] Mr. Seward gave us an account of a Fable,[40] which Mr. Garrick had written, by way of Prologue, or Introduction, upon the occasion: In this, he says, that a Black Bird, grown old & feeble, droops his Wings, &c, &c, & gives up singing; but, being called upon by the Eagle, his Voice recovers its powers, his spirits revive, he sets age at defiance, & sings better than ever. The application is obvious.

'There is not,' said Dr. Johnson, 'much of the spirit of *Fabulosity* in this Fable; for the call of an *Eagle* never yet had much tendency to restore the voice of a *Black Bird*! 'Tis true, the Fabulists frequently make the *Wolves* converse with the *Lambs*,—but, when the conversation is over, the *Lambs* are sure to be Eaten!—& so, the *Eagle* may entertain the *Black Bird*,—but the Entertainment always ends in a *Feast* for the Eagles!'

'They say,' cried Mrs. Thrale, 'that Garrick was extremely

---

[39] This performance took place at Windsor Castle on 15 Feb. For the occasion Garrick chose to adapt his 1-act farce, *Lethe, or, Aesop in the Shades*, the very first of his plays (1740). See Stone, pp. 203–7; M. E. Knapp, 'Garrick's Last Command Performance', *The Age of Johnson* (New Haven, 1949), pp. 61–71; C. Oman, *David Garrick* (1958), pp. 350–1; Garrick, *Letters*, iii. 1153 and n. 1, 1155; *YW* xxviii. 285–6.

[40] 'The Mimic Blackbird, a Fable'. See Knapp, pp. 68–9, 71; *YW* xxviii. 285 and n. 5; Garrick, *Letters* iii. 1168 and n. 2.

hurt at the coolness of the King's applause, & did not find his reception such as he expected.'

'He has been so long accustomed,' said Mr. Seward, 'to the Thundering approbation of the Theatre, that a ^l mere *very well*, must necessarily & naturally disappoint him.'

'Sir,' said Dr. Johnson, 'he should not, in a Royal apartment, expect the hallowing & clamour of the one shilling gallery. The King, I doubt not, gave him as much applause as was rationally his due: &, indeed, great & uncommon as is the merit of Mr. Garrick, no man will be bold enough to assert that he has not had his just proportion both of Fame & Profit: he has long reigned the unequaled favourite of the public,—& therefore, nobody will mourn his hard fate, if the King, & the Royal Family, were not transported into rapture, upon hearing him Read Lethe. Yet, Mr. Garrick will complain to his Friends, & his Friends will lament the King's want of feeling & taste;—& then, Mr. Garrick will *excuse* the King! he will say that ⌐he⌐ might be thinking of something else;—that the affairs of America might occur to him,— or some subject of more importance than Lethe;—but though he will say this himself, he will not forgive his Friends, if they do not contradict him!'[41]

But now, that I have written this *satire*, it is but just both to Mr. Garrick, & to Dr. Johnson, to tell you what he said of him afterwards, when he discriminated his character with equal candour & humour.

'Garrick,' said he, 'is accused of vanity;—but few men would have borne such unremitting prosperity with greater, if with

[41] Horace Walpole, giving a hearsay but quite circumstantial account of Garrick's performance in a letter to William Mason, 27 Feb. 1777, noted that 'all went off perfectly ill, with no exclamations of applause and two or three formal compliments at the end. Bayes [Garrick] is dying of chagrin . . .' (*YW* xxviii. 286). James Northcote described the scene to Hazlitt: 'Garrick complained that when he went to read before the court, not a look or a murmur testified approbation; there was a profound stillness— every one only watched to see what the King thought. It was like reading to a set of wax-work figures . . .' (Hazlitt, *Conversations of James Northcote*, ed. E. Gosse (1894), p. 216, cited by Knapp, p. 69). Garrick consoled himself for months afterwards by reading and sending copies of the fable to his friends; on 3 June he read it to Mrs Thrale (ibid., p. 71). In 1790 FB recalled Garrick's 'disappointment and mortification . . . when he read *Lethe* to a Royal audience', but having herself read Colman's *Polly Honeycombe* to the Queen, she understood that a profound silence was 'the settled etiquette' (*DL* iv. 360–1).

equal moderation: he is accused, too, of avarice,—but, were he not, he would be accused of just the contrary, for he now Lives rather as a *prince*, than as an Actor: but the frugality he practiced when he first appeared in the World, & which, even then, ⌜was⌝ perhaps beyond his necessity, has marked his character ever since; & now, though his Table, his Equipage, & manner of Living, are all the most expensive, and equal to those of a Nobleman, yet the original stain still blots his name,—⌜though,⌝ had he not fixed upon himself the charge of Avarice, he would, long since, have been reproached with *luxury*, & ⌜with⌝ living beyond his station in magnificence & splendour.'

Another Time, he said of him 'Garrick never enters a Room, but he regards himself as the object of general attention, ⌜&⌝ from whom the Entertainment of the Company is expected,—& true it is, that he seldom disappoints them; for he has infinite humour, a very just proportion of Wit, & more convivial pleasantry than almost any other man. But then, off, as well as *on* the stage, he is always an Actor! for he thinks it so incumbent upon him to be sportive, that his gaity becomes mechanical, ⌜as it is⌝ habitual, & [he][42] can exert his spirits at all Times alike, without consulting his real Disposition to hilarity.'

Friday [28 March].

I am very sorry that I cannot possibly finish this account, ⌜for I am *Bothered* to Death⌝—my Uncle is just come,—Cousins James & Becky[43] ⌜are with him⌝—& all bent upon my returning with them.

⌜I intended a very long Letter, but have not any Time.⌝

A thousand thanks for yours,[44] which I have just rec^d. ⌜I wish to Heaven I could answer it as I ought—but I foresee I shall have no leisure this Age.

Your letter diverted me highly for 'tis the most honest & un-

---

[42] Inserted by FBA.
[43] James Adolphus Burney, and Rebecca Burney (1758–1835), m. (1788) William Sandford (1759–1823), surgeon.
[44] SC to FB, 27 Mar. 1777 (Barrett).

guarded one you ever sent me—depend upon my ⟨discretion⟩, however, as to [xxxxx *½ line*]⸢45

Your kindness is more grateful to me, than I can express,— I am monstrous glad you missed me,⸢46—⸢if, indeed, you do not flatter me by saying so.⸣

Adieu, my dearest sir,—a thousand loves & Compliments to Mrs. H[amilton] & Kitty, & believe me, with all affection & gratitude

Yours ever   Frances Burney.

I am now writing with a Steel Pen, which Mr. Cutler,⸢47 a very agreeable ⸢man, has⸣48 just sent me, with a note, & these Lines

Va, petite Plume—va servir Ma'm'selle Burney;— Puisse tu surpasser la Volantè de Gurney!⸢49

⸢Pray write to me *To Town*, for Susy will have Friends in case I should be gone a Worsted Stocking hunting.⸣

⸢45 Part of SC's letter has been obliterated by FBA and mostly not deciphered. One sentence recovered, however, is 'how ⸢do you ⟨account⟩ for it, that People, who don't love you can't let you stay away⸣', probably written with special reference to EAB. He also calls Richard Burney 'yʳ Lordly Uncle'.

⸢46 SC opens his letter: 'You can't imagine how We miss'd you as soon as you were gone.—there was a Void which still continues, & will not easily be fill'd up—'.

⸢47 Samuel Cutler (*c.*1727–98), a native of Danzig, was a London banker in the firm of Sir George Colebrooke and Co. (*GM* lxviii² (1798), 999). His note, which accompanied the pen, is dated 22 Mar. and is in the Berg Collection.

⸢48 Altered by FBA to 'old friend of my Fathers'. In 1791 FB called him 'that most excentric of queer Epistolary Men' (*JL* i. 104). She later reveals (in *Mem.* i. 340–1) that Cutler became a pest to her father, writing him long and repetitious letters that finally forced him to an open rebuff. Cutler seems to have ended his life a misanthrope; his obituary notes that he withdrew to Worcester, where 'he was lately remarkable for a total seclusion from the world, and a disregard to all the intercourse and even comforts of society' (*GM* lxviii² (1798), 999). He had apparently been an acquaintance of the Worcester Burneys (*JL* i. 104 n. 17).

⸢49 A reference to the shorthand system of Thomas Gurney (1705–70), a dictionary of which appeared this year, and which he adapted from the system of William Mason (*fl.* 1672–1709), published under the title *La Plume Volante* (1707). Mrs Ellis notes that 'Gurney's Flying Pen' was 'one of the advertised pens of the day' (*ED* i. 159 n. 1). If there was indeed such a pen, it was presumably marketed in connection with Gurney's system. Steel pens were a novelty at this time, and they did not really begin to replace the goose-quill until the mid-19th c. (see *Encyclopædia Britannica* (11th edn., New York, 1910–11), s.v. Pen). FB's strokes with the steel pen are thinner than with the quill; she seems subsequently to have stayed with the earlier instrument.

AJ (Early Diary, ix, paginated 581–[630], foliated 1–[37], Berg), Journal for 1777.

Originally perhaps 37 or more double sheets. Now 14 double sheets and a single sheet, 58 pp., plus three fragments of leaves. The first page is *annotated (by FBA)*: 1777 I ⌗

Names in FBA's 'List' for this year but not in the extant journal are: 'Sir John Pechell', 'Mr. Pechell', 'Mi⟨ss⟩ Pechell', 'Miss Chamier & Miss Betty', and 'Miss Jones'. 'Sir John Pechell' was presumably the Revd John Pearsall (1718–78), a native of Halne or Hawne near Halesowen, Worcestershire, who *c*.1770 assumed (probably spuriously) the baronetcy of Peshall and changed his name to Peshall (sometimes erroneously spelled 'Pechell'). 'Mr. Pechell' then would be his eldest son, John Peshall (1759–1820), who assumed the baronetcy on his father's death; 'Mi⟨ss⟩ Pechell' would be his daughter Elizabetha-Maria Peshall (1763–1836), who m. (1798) Busick Harwood (*c*.1745–1814), MD, Kt. (1806), professor of anatomy at Cambridge (*GM* cvi^2 (1836), 107, 222). The Chamiber sisters, possibly relations of Anthony Chamier and possibly met on the trip to Worcester, have not been further traced. Neither has Miss Jones.

Oh Yes!

Be it known, to all whom it may concern,—c'est à dire, in the first place,—Nobody;—in the 2^d place, the same Person;—&, in the third place, *Ditto*;—that Frances Burney, spinster, of the Parish of St Martin's in the Fields, —————did keep no Journal this unhappy year till she wrote from Worcester to her sister Susan, of the same Parish, & likewise a spinster. There are, who may Live to mourn this,—for my part, I shall not here enumerate all the particular misfortunes which this Gap in Literature may occasion,—though I feel that they will be of a nature the most serious & melancholy;—but I shall merely scrawl down such matters of moment as will be requisite to mention, in order to make the Worcester Journal, which is a delicious morsel of Learning & profound reasoning,—intelligible,—to the 3 persons mentioned above.

When, with infinite toil & labour, I had transcribed the 2^d volume, [of *Evelina*] I sent it, by my Brother [CB Jr.] to Mr. Lowndes. The fear of Discovery, or of suspicion in the House, made the Copying extremely laborious to me; for, in the Day Time, I could only take odd moments, so that I was obliged to sit up the greatest part of many Nights, in order to get it ready. And,—after all this *fagging*, Mr. [|] Lowndes sent me Word that he approved of the Book, but could not think of printing it till it was finished; that it would be a great disadvantage to it, & that he would wait my Time, & hoped to see it again, as soon as it was completed.

Now this man, knowing nothing of my situation, supposed, in all probability, that I could seat myself quietly at my Bureau, & write on with all expedition & ease, till the work was finished: but so different was the case, that I had hardly Time to write half a page in a Day; & niether my Health, nor inclination, would allow me to continue my *Nocturnal* scribling for so long a Time as to write first, & then Copy, a whole volume. I was, therefore, obliged to give the attempt & affair entirely over for the present.

In March, I made a long & happy Visit to my ever-dear & ever-kind Mr. Crisp;—there is no place where I more really *enjoy myself* than at Chesington; all the Household are kind, hospitable & partial to me; there is no sort of restraint,—every body is disengaged, & at liberty to pursue their own inclinations,—& my Daddy, who is the soul of the place, is, at once, so flatteringly affectionate to *me*, & so infinitely, so beyond comparison clever in *himself*,—that, were I to be otherwise than happy [|] in his Company, I must either be wholly without feeling, & [*sic*] utterly destitute of understanding.

From this loved spot, I was suddenly hurried by intelligence that my uncle was coming to Town. & the fear that he would be displeased at finding I made a visit to Chesington, nearly at the Time I was invited to Barborne; made me not dare out stay the intelligence of his intended Journey. He brought with him his son James, & his Daughter Beckey.

James is a very manly, good natured, unaffected, & good Hearted young man: he has by no means the powers of entertainment that his Brother Richard possesses, but he is so well disposed, & so sweet Tempered, that it is hardly fair, & hardly possible to find fault with him.

Beckey is rather pretty in her Face, & perfectly elegant in her Person. She is extremely lively, gay as the morning of May, & wild as the Wind of March,—her Temper is very sweet, her Heart affectionate, & her Head mighty well laden with natural stores of good understanding & sense. Like Betsy, she Laughs *rather more than reason,*—but she is so young, & so good humoured, that, though she may sometimes appear foolishly giddy, it is not possible to entertain an idea of ⌜anger against⌝ her. She is, upon the whole, a most sweet Girl, & one that I loved much at first sight, & yet more afterwards.

My Uncle's professed intention in his Journey, was to carry me back to Barborne: & he would not be denied; nor let my Father rest till he obtained his leave.—And so, Escorted by my Uncle, & ⌜Cousin⌝ James, I set off for Worcester, the beginning of April. | ⌜Edward[50] & Beckey were left in Town, for another Week.⌝

But, before I made this Journey, [xxxxx *2 lines*] ⌜⟨I⟩ was obliged so much by my dear Father's goodness,⌝ that, in the fullness of my Heart ⌜at his ⟨kind⟩ indulgence,⌝ I could not forebear telling him ⌜my ⟨scheme⟩ in regard to Mr. Lowndes [xxxxx *1½ lines*] ⟨I expressed the wish that⟩ I might have managed my affairs without any ⟨disturbance⟩ to himself.⌝ He could not help Laughing; but I believe was much surprised at the communication: he desired me to acquaint him, from Time to Time, how *my work* went on, called himself the *Pere confident*, & kindly promised to guard my secret as cautiously as I could wish.

So much to prelude the Worcester Journal.

But when I told my dear Father I *never* wished or intended ⌜he⌝ should see my essay, he forbore to ask me its name, or make any enquiries. I believe he is not sorry to be saved the giving me the pain of his criticism. He made no sort of objection to my having my own way in total secrecy & silence to all the

---

[50] Edward Francesco Burney (1760–1848), another of FB's Worcester cousins, who had come to London in May 1776 to study drawing at the Royal Academy ('Worcester Mem.'). A talented artist whose work was praised by Reynolds, he later became a fashionable book illustrator, though extreme diffidence prevented him from making more of a mark in his profession. FB describes him below (p. 271) as her 'very best Friend' among the Worcester Burneys. Edward never married, but Julia Caroline Wauchope, in a letter to Annie Raine Ellis, 18 Aug. 1887 (Gloucestershire Record Office) claimed, on the authority of Mrs Kingston (SBP's granddaughter), that he was successively in love with FB herself, FB's niece, Charlotte Francis, later Mrs Barrett (1786–1870), and Charlotte's daughter Julia Charlotte Barrett, later Mrs Maitland (1808–64), Mrs Wauchope's mother. See P. D. Crown, 'Edward F. Burney: An Historical Study in English Romantic Art' (Univ. of California, Los Angeles, Ph.D. thesis 1977).

Brighton :: Published as the Act directs

5. Barborne Lodge, Worcestershire. From a drawing by Clement Francis. If the drawing was indeed engraved and published, no copy has been found.

World. Yet I am easier in not taking the step without his having this little knowledge of it. |

[*A leaf or leaves are missing. The 'Worcester Journal' was originally addressed to SEB back in London. In the following scene FB describes shy Edward's reluctance to speak a prologue to Arthur Murphy's 'The Way to Keep Him', to be performed by the family at Barborne Lodge.*]

ᴿ'Why, Ned, how can you be such a fool? cried Betsy. 'I'm sure he'll [Uncle Richard] be so affronted he'll be quite angry.'

'Well, then, if I must, answered he, I'll speak myself.'

My Uncle still pursued the subject, *jocosely*[51] saying 'Why do you look so sour, Ned? I sha'n't make you say it whether you will or not. I declare I have no desire to have the Prologue spoke on my own account, but I'm sorry Ned so little desires it.'[52]

'Speak, Ned, speak!' cried Betsy.

He could not, however, prevail with himself,—his reluctance overcame his sense of propriety, & he remained silent & serious.

'The Boy looks at me as if I had done him an injury, continued my Uncle, however, don't be angry, Ned, for I assure you I don't want to have it spoke.'

'Ned, how can you be such an oaf? cried Betsy, why don't you speak'?

'I can't,—I can't, I tell you,' answered he.

Again I offered my service. 'Well, said Betsy, you'll have him quite affronted,—shall Fanny speak?'

'Why—if,—if she'll be so kind—' was the reluctant assent. I then immediately enquired after the prologue, begged to see it, & said I was sure my Cousin would speak it if there was Time for him to learn it.

This brought him [Uncle Richard] into humour, & he promised to look for it early in the morning.

Then, having drunk success to the cause, we all retired.ᴿ

Monday April 7

The morning was ushered in—by a general disturbance. We were all inconceivably busy;—we contrived, however,

---

[51] Presumably meant ironically.
[52] The prologue in question was perhaps written by Uncle Richard himself. FB mentions below (p. 237) that he looked for it but was unable to find it.

for little Nancy's[53] sake, to Rehearse Tom Thumb,[54] & then |
we Bribed her to lay down: &, most fortunately, she slept
more than three Hours, which made her very wakeful all the
rest of the Day & Night.

At Dinner, we did not sit down above 3 at a Time,—one
was with the Hair Dresser,—another, finishing some Dress,—
another, some scenery,—& so on;—I was quite amazed to see
how my uncle submitted to all this confusion,—but he was the
first to promote our following our own affairs.

And, indeed, I cannot speak too highly of the good nature of
Nancy[55] upon this occasion, for she has given up all her Time
to general assistance.

Before 5 o'clock, while we were all in the midst of our disorder, Mrs. Bund & her Daughter[56] arrived. They did not
know what they came for, & my Uncle & Miss Humphries,[57]
who received them, said we were preparing for a droll sort of
Concert which we intended to give them.

Next came Dr. Johnson[58] & Mr. Russel:[59] &, soon after, the

---

[53] Hannah Maria Burney, EBB's daughter, not yet 5 years old.
[54] Henry Fielding's *The Tragedy of Tragedies; or the Life and Death of Tom Thumb the Great*, the 3-act version first staged in 1731.
[55] FB's cousin Ann Burney.
[56] Probably Catherine Dandridge, 3rd daughter of John Dandridge of Great Malvern, Worcestershire, m. (1763) William Bund (d. by 1787) of Wick near Pershore, Worcestershire and Grays Inn, London; and her elder daughter Mary Bund, m. (1787) Revd William Probyn (*c.*1763–1825), rector of Longhope, Gloucestershire, later (1797) vicar of St Andrew's, Pershore (*GM* xxxiii (1763), 414; lvii² (1787), 836).
[57] Uncle Richard's sister-in-law.
[58] Emended by FBA to 'Dr. R. Johnston'; 'Dr. Johnson of Worcester' in her 'List'. The Johnstones were a prominent family of physicians, who practiced in or near Worcester, but there seems to have been no 'R. Johnstone' among them. This doctor was probably James Johnstone (1754–83), MD (Edinburgh, 1773), physician to the Worcester Infirmary; or his father James Johnstone (1730–1802), MD (Edinburgh, 1750), physician at Kidderminster, who at his son's death succeeded him as physician to the Worcester Infirmary (J. R. Burton, *A History of Kidderminster* (1890), pp. 157–8; J. Chambers, *Biographical Illustrations of Worcestershire* (Wotcester, 1820), pp. 473–8, 563–6).
[59] Probably William Russell (1719–1801), surgeon to the Worcester Infirmary (Chambers, pp. 448–52); or his son William Russell (1750–1812) of Powick, barrister-at-law, who m. secondly (1793) Elizabeth (d. 1813), sister and ultimately sole heiress of Sir John Pakington, Bt. (H. S. Grazebrook, *The Heraldry of Worcestershire* (1873), pp. 480–1; *GM* lxiii¹ (1793), 184).

3 Lawsons:⁶⁰ & then Miss Bridget Harris⁶¹ & Miss Knowell.⁶²

You can have no idea what ⌐agitation⌐ every new comer gave me;—I could hardly Dress myself,—hardly knew where I was,—hardly could stand. Betsy, too, was very much flurried, & so afraid of being worse, that she forced wine & water, & punch, down her throat till she was almost tipsey. Richard & James gave all their thoughts to their own adornment; Tom⁶³ Capered about the House in great joy; little Nancy jumped & Laughed; Edward was tolerably Composed;—but Beckey— was in extacy of pleasure,—she felt no fright or palpitation, but Laughed, Danced & sung all Day long delightfully.

⌐But I should have mentioned, that my uncle could not find the Prologue, to Edward's great satisfaction.⌐ |

We were now quite ready,—when the 3 Miss Brookes'⁶⁴ came,—&, to my great relief, no Dr. Wall⁶⁵ or Capt. Coussmaker.⁶⁶

---

⁶⁰ Probably Francis Lawson (1737–1816), barrister (Inner Temple, 1758), 'many years an acting magistrate for the counties of Gloucester and Worcester'; his wife (m. 1763) Margaretta née Cox (living 1816); m. the Revd Charles Whatley (*c.*1757–1835), MA (Oxon.), 1779, vicar of Lower Guiting, Gloucester, 1797–1835 (*GM* lxxxvi² (1816), 283; IGI; will of Francis Lawson, PCC, prob. 23 Nov. 1816). The Lawsons were friends of the Brookes (below).

⁶¹ Perhaps a daughter of the Revd Talbot Harris (*c.*1718–92), MA (Oxon.), 1743, a native of Droitwich; rector of Upton Warren and vicar of Powick (*GM* lxii² (1792), 774; MI, St Michael's Church, Upton Warren).

⁶² Probably a relation of Walter Noel (d. 1794) of Bell Hall, Belbroughton, but not further traced (*GM* lxiv² (1794), 772).

⁶³ Thomas Frederick Burney (1765–85). Youngest of the Worcester Burneys, he later showed 'an uncommon genius for pen & ink drawings' but died of consumption at an early age ('Worcester Mem.').

⁶⁴ Daughters of the Revd James Brooke (*c.*1717–94) of Upton-on-Severn; MA (Oxon.), 1742; rector of Croome D'Abitot, Hill Croome, and Pirton. They were: Hannah Brooke (living 1794), m. James Skey (living 1804); Elizabeth Brooke (living 1794), m. (between 1783 and 1787) Francis Welles (b. *c.*1745, living 1798), MA (Oxon.), 1770, BD, 1781; and Susanna Brooke (living 1794) (will of Revd James Brooke, PCC, prob. 10 July 1794; *GM* lxiv¹ (1794), 385; *Vict. Co. Hist.* [*Worcs.*] ii. 245; subscribers' list to W. Dyde, *History and Antiquities of Tewkesbury*, 2nd edn. (Tewkesbury, 1798)).

⁶⁵ John Wall (*c.*1745–1808), of Tewkesbury Park, Gloucester; MA (Oxon.), 1767, B.Med., 1770; son of John Wall (1708–76), D.Med. (Oxon.), 1759, a native of Powick and a noted physician of Worcester (*GM* lxxviii² (1808), 855; Chambers, *Biographical Illustrations of Worcestershire*, pp. 384–93).

⁶⁶ George Kien Hayward Coussmaker (1759–1801), Ensign in the 1st Foot Guards; Lt. and Capt., 1778; later Lt.-Col.; brother of Miss Coussmaker (above, p. 219).

The Band was now got into order for the Overture, & the Company going to be summoned up stairs,—when another Chaise arrived,—& it proved from Gloucester, with the Doctor & the Captain!

I assure you this frightened me so much, that I most heartily wished myself 20 miles off;—I was quite sick, &, if I had dared, should have given up the part.

When I came to be Painted, my Cheeks were already of so high a Colour, that I could hardly bear to have any added: but, before I went on, I seemed siezed with an Ague fit, & was so extremely Cold, that my Uncle, upon taking my Hand, said he thought he had touched ice or marble.

At length, they all came up stairs: a Green Curtain was drawn before them, & the overture was played. Miss Humphries did all the Honours, for Nancy w[as] engaged as Prompter, & my Uncle one of the Band.

The Theatre looked extremely well, & was fitted up in a very Dramatic manner: with side scenes,—& 2 figures, of Tragedy & Comedy at each end, & a Head of Shakespear in the middle. We had 4 Change of scenes. [The play we acted was 'The Way to Keep Him.']⁶⁷

Now for a play Bill which, I think, you will own was stupid enough,—but we dared not be *jocular* after my Uncle's interference⁶⁸ |

As soon as the Overture was played,—which, you must know, was performed in the *passage*, for we had no Room for an Orchestra in the Theatre,—Edward & Tom were seated at Cards, & the Curtain Drawn.⁶⁹ Tom's part was very soon over, & then Betsy entered;⁷⁰ she was much flurried, & yet in very great spirits, & acquitted herself *greatly* beyond my expectations: Edward was, I believe, very little frightened, yet not quite so easy or so excellent as I had imagined he would have been. Indeed the part is extremely unworthy of him, & I fancy he was determined to let it take it's chance, without troubling himself with much exertion.

---

⁶⁷ Inserted by FBA. The family performed an adaptation of Murphy's original 3-act version, first staged in 1760.

⁶⁸ The rest of this page and half of the next are blank. Obviously FB meant to copy in the playbill but did not do it.

⁶⁹ Edward played William, a servant to Lovemore, and Tom, another servant.

⁷⁰ Playing Muslin, waiting-woman to Mrs Lovemore.

Take notice, that, from the beginning to the End, no *applause* was given to the play. The company judged that it would be inelegant, & therefore, as they all said, *forbore*;—but indeed it would have been very encouraging, & I heartily [|] wish they had not practiced such *self denial!*[71]

Next came *my* scene; I was discovered Drinking Tea;[72]—to tell you how *infinitely*, how *beyond measure* I was terrified at my situation, I really cannot,—but my fright was nearly such as I should have suffered had I made my appearance upon a public Theatre, since Miss Humphries & Captain Coussmaker were the only two of the Audience I had ever before seen.

The few Words I had to speak before Muslin came to me, I know not whether I spoke or not,—niether does any body else:—so you need not enquire of others, for the matter is, to this moment, unknown.

Fortunately for me, all the next scene gave me hardly 3 words in a speech, for Muslin has it almost to herself: so I had little else to do than to lean on the Table, & twirl my Thumbs, &, sometimes, bite my fingers:—which, indeed, I once or twice did very severely, without knowing why, or yet being able to help it.

I am sure, *without flattery*, I looked like a most egregious fool;—for I made no use of the Tea things,—I never tasted a drop,—once, indeed, I made an attempt, by way of passing the Time better, to drink a little, but my Hand shook so violently, I was fain to put down the Cup instantly, in order to save my Gown.

By the way, I have forgot to mention Dresses.

Edward had a Coat Trim'd to have the effect of a rich Lace Livery;—He had a Capital Bag, long Ruffles & so forth.

Tom much the same.

Betsy, as Muslin, had a very showy striped pink & white Manchester, pink shoes, red Ribbons in abundance & a short Apron. The Paint upon her very pale Cheeks set her off to the greatest advantage, & I never saw her look nearly so well.

Mrs. Lovemore wore her Green & Grey, which I have trimed [|]

---

[71] FBA has noted on this page: 'From 2 Burnt. to 18.', in fact, fos. 3–17, or 30 pp. The conclusion of this sentence was probably copied by her from the first of the destroyed leaves.

[72] In the role of Mrs Lovemore.

with Gause, white Ribbons, Gause Apron, Cuffs, Robin[g]s, &c.

The next who made his appearance, was Cousin James,[73]— he was most superbly Dressed, but, as you saw his cloaths at the music meeting, I will not describe them. His Hair, however, I must not pass unnoticed; for you never saw the most foppish stage Character better Dressed in the *macaroni* style. Indeed, all our Hairs were done to the astonishment of all the Company.

He entered with an air so immensely conceited & affected, &, at the same Time, so uncommonly bold, that I could scarse stand his *Abord*: &, through out the scene that followed, he acted with such a satisfied, nay, *insolent* assurance of success, that, I declare, had I been entirely myself, & free from fear, he would have wholly disconcerted me: as it was, my flurry hardly admitted of encrease: yet I felt myself glow most violently.

I must assure you, notwithstanding my embarrassment, I found he did the part *admirably*,—not merely *very much* beyond my expectations, but, I think, as well as it *could* be done. He looked very fashionable, very assured, very affected, & very *every way the thing*. Not one part in the piece was better or more properly done: nor did any give *more* entertainment.

We were, next, joined by Richard:[74] whose *non chalence*, indifference, half vacancy & half absence, excellently marked the careless, unfeeling husband which he represented. Between his extreme unconcern, & Sir Brilliant's extreme assurance, I had not much trouble in appearing the only languid & discontented person in the Company.

Richard was in a very genteel morning Dress.

A short scene next followed, between Betsy & me, which I made as little of as any body might desire—indeed, I would Challenge all my Acquaintance around, to go through an act more thoroughly to their own dissatisfaction. So, that is saying more than every body can, however.

The Act finished by a *solo* of Betsy, which I did not hear, for I ran into a Corner to recover Breath against next act.

My Uncle was very good natured, & spoke very comfortable things to me—which I did by no means expect, as at first, he

---

[73] As Sir Brilliant Fashion.   [74] As Lovemore.

seemed not delighted that Betsy had given me her part. He said I wanted *nothing but exertion*, & charged me to speak louder, & take courage.

'O! cried Edward, that this had but been Lady Betty Modish![75]

However, since I was so terribly Cowardly, I now rejoice that I had a part so serious & solemn, sad & sorrowful.

Cousin James was prodigiously ⌐facetious⌐ in comforting me, ⌐taking my Hand,⌐ & supporting his *tendresse* yet more strongly off than on the stage. The truth is, he is so very good natured, that the least idea of pity really softens him into down right tenderness.

Richard was entirely occupied in changing his Dress for Lord Etheridge.[76]

In the next Act, the widow Belmour made her appearance. Beckey's elegant Figure & ⌐*bred*⌐ Face were charmingly set off, for her Dress was fashionable & becoming: she had on a lilac Negligee, Gause Cuffs trimmed richly, with Flowers and spangles, spankled [*sic*] shoes, Bows of Gause & Flowers, & a Cap!—*quite the thing*, I assure you!—full of flowers, frivolete, spangles, Gause, & long Feathers;—immensely high, & [her Hair][77] delightfully well Dressed. She was in great spirits, & not at all frightened. Her Entrance, I am sure, must be striking, & I was surprised the folks could forbear giving her applause.

⌐I must, however, frankly own that she did not answer my too high raised expectations in her performance. I thought her unequal to the part, she wanted rather more *coquetry* & rather more *dignity*, to make it that first rate character it has always been reckoned. Yet she did it *very* prettily, & with infinitely more ease & moderation as to action & Gesture, than, from her general flightiness & gaiety, might be expected. Her appearance was perfectly genteel, nay elegant, & she committed nothing that the severest Judge, could, I believe, call a *fault*, though she did not act up to the full power of the part.⌐

Betsy changed her Dress entirely for Mignonet,[78] & did the Character very well; though the worse for having another in

---

[75] In Cibber's *The Careless Husband*.
[76] Lovemore's disguise, assumed for his affair with the Widow Bellmour.
[77] Inserted by FBA.
[78] Properly 'Mignionet': the Widow Bellmour's maid.

the same play, as she saved herself very much for Muslin, which she did admirably.

During my reprieve from Business, I thought I had entirely banished my fears, & assumed sufficient Courage to go through the rest of my part to the best of my capacity;—but far otherwise I found it, for, the moment I entered, I was again gone!—knew not where I stood, nor what I said,—a mist was before my Eyes, so strong that it almost blinded me, & my Voice faltered so cruelly, that, had they not all been particularly silent whenever I aimed at speaking, not a word the better would they have been for my presence!—

And all this for pleasure!—but indeed it was too much,—& I have not yet recovered from the ⌈most⌉ painful sensations I experienced that night,—sensations which will always make my recollection of the 'Way to keep him' disagreeable to me.

Fortunately for me, my part & my spirits, in this Act, had great simpathy;—for Mrs Lovemore is almost unhappy enough for a Tragedy Heroine:—&, I assure you, she lost none of her *pathos* by any giddiness of mine!—I gave her melancholy feelings very fair play, & *looked* her misfortunes with as much sadness as if I really experienced them.

In this Act, therefore, circumstances were so happily miserable for me, that I believe some of my auditors thought me a much better & more *arttificial* [*sic*] actress than I ⌈really was⌉ & I had the satisfaction of hearing some few *buzzes* of approbation which did me no harm.

But I would never have engaged in this scheme, had I not been persuaded that my fright would have ended with the first scene: I had not any idea of being so completely overcome by it.

The grand scene between the Widow & Lord Etheridge, Richard & Beckey acquitted themselves extremely well in. If Richard had a fault, it was being *too* easy,—he would have had more spirit, had he been *rather* less *at Home*. His Dress for this part was all elegance.

This Act concluded with the scene that I prevailed with Edward & Betsy to add,—they did it vastly well, & are both, I believe, well pleased that they listened to me.[79]

Again, my Uncle spoke the most flattering things to en-

---

[79] This additional scene was probably written by FB herself. It does not survive.

courage me, 'Only speak out, Miss Fanny, said he, & you leave nothing to wish;—it is impossible to do the part with greater propriety, or to speak with greater feeling, more sensibly,—every, the most insignificant thing you say, *comes Home* to me.'

You can't imagine how much this kindness from him Cheared me. In the third act I recovered myself very decently, *compared* to the 2 first,—but indeed I was very—, very far from being easy, or from doing the part according to my own ideas.

So that, in short, I am totally, wholly, & entirely—dissatisfied with myself in the whole performance. Not once could I command my voice to any steadiness,—or look about me otherwise than as a poltroon, either smelling something unsavoury, or expecting to be Bastinadoed.

In the most Capital scene of Mrs. Lovemore, with her Husband, in the third Act, when she is all *Air, alertness, pleasure and enjoyment*,[80] I endeavoured what I could to soften off the affectation of her sudden change of Disposition; & I *gagged*[81] the Gentleman with as much ease as my very little ease would allow me to assume. Richard was really charming in this scene; so thoroughly negligent, inattentive & sleepy, that he kept a continual *titter* among the young Ladies;—but, when he was roused from his indifference by Mrs. Lovemore's pretended alteration of Temper & Conduct,—he *sung small* indeed!—when *her* flightiness began, you can hardly suppose how *little* he looked,—how mortified!—astonished! & simple!—it was admirably in character, & yet he seemed as if he *really could not help it*,—& as if her unexpected gaity quite confounded him.

Betsy, Beckey & James were all of them very lively, and ⸢really⸣ very clever in all they had to do in this Act.

I am ⸢very,⸣ very sorry that Edward could not have more justice done to those talents which I know only want to be called forth.

At the End of all, there was a faint something in *imitation* of a Clap,—but very faint, indeed: yet, though applause would much have encouraged us, we have no reason to be mortified by it's omission, since they all repeatedly declared they *longed*

---

[80] FB is quoting Mrs Lovemore.
[81] i.e., deceived or imposed upon. *OED* cites this passage as containing the earliest instance of the verb used in this sense (s.v. Gag *V*.³).

to clap, but thought it would not be ⏐ approved: & since we have heard, from all quarters, nothing but praise & compliment.

Richard spoke the last speech [in a]⁸² very spirited manner: & he was very delicate & very comfortable to me in our reconciliation, when Mrs. Belmour says 'Come, kiss and Friends!'— & *he* adds 'it is in *your* power, Madam, to make a reclaimed libertine of me indeed,'—for he excused all the embracing part, & without making any fuss, only took my Hand, which, Bowing over, (*like Sir Charles Grandison*,) he most respectfully pressed to his Lips.⁸³

We now all hastened to Dress for Tom Thumb, and the Company went into the Dining Room for some refreshments. Little Nancy was led away by Miss Humphries, who made her take a formal leave of the Company, as if going to Bed, that they might not expect what followed.

The sweet little thing was quite in *mad spirits*, which we kept up by all sort of good things, both Drinking, Eating & flattery: for our only fear was lest she should grow shamefaced, & refuse to make her Entrance.

She flew up to me, 'Ay, Cousin Fanny, *I* saw you Drinking your Tea there!—what made you Drink Tea by yourself, before all the Company!—did you think they would not see you?'

You must know she always calls me *Cousin* Fanny, because, she says, every body else does, so she's sure I can't really be *an aunt*.

During the whole performance, she had not the least idea what we all meant, & wanted several Times to join us. Especially while I was *weeping*;—'pray what does Cousin Fanny cry for, aunt Hannah?⁸⁴—Does she cry really, *I say*?—'

But I must now, for your better information, tell you exactly how the Parts in Tom Thumb were cast. ⏐

| Lord Grizzle,
Noodle,
Bailiff, | } | Mr. Edward Burney. |

---

⁸² Inserted by FBA.

⁸³ Another instance of FB's prudishness.

⁸⁴ Presumably Miss Humphries. This mention seems to give us her forename, as 'Worcester Mem.' identifies her simply as 'Miss H. Humphries'.

Doodle,	Mr. Thomas Burney,
King, Bailiff's Follower, } A Fighting man,	Mr. Richard Burney
And Tom Thumb	by Miss Anna Maria Burney
Huncamun[c]a,[85]	Miss Fanny Burney
Cleora,	Miss Becky Burney
[Glumdalca, Queen,	Giantess, Mr. James Burney][86]
And Queen	by Miss Elizabeth Burney.

Noodle & Doodle, who opened the Farce, were both Dressed very fantastically, in the old English style, & were several minutes practising antics before they spoke. Edward disguised his voice in this part, & made the Burlesque doubly ludicrous by giving a foppish *twang* to every period: Tom did Doodle vastly well.

Then Entered the King,—which was performed by Richard most admirably, & with a *dignified drollery* that was highly diverting & exceeding clever. Betsy accompanied him; she was ⌈*very*⌉ well in the Queen, ⌈—no, she was *better* than *very well*, though by no means excellent.⌉ Their Dresses, though made of mere 'Tinsel, & all sort of gaudiness, had a charming & most Theatrical effect: their Crowns, Jewels, Trains, &c, were superb.

Next—entered,—Tom Thumb!
⌈But First,⌉ when the King says

But see! our Warrior comes!—the great Tom Thumb!—
The little Hero, Giant killing Boy!—

Then there was an immense *hub a dub*, with Drums & Trumpets, & a Clarionet, to proclaim his approach.

The sweet little Girl looked as beautiful as an Angel;—|She had an exceeding pretty & most becoming Dress.—made of pink persian, trimed with silver & spangles,—the form of it the same as that of the others, i.e. old English. Her mantle

---

85 Inserted by FBA.
86 Inserted by FBA.

was white,—she had a small Truncheon in her Hand, & a *Vandyke* Hat. Her own sweet Hair was left to itself.

When she was to appear, I took her Hand, to put her on; but she shrunk back, & seemed half afraid; however, a few promises of grand things, caresses & Flattery, gave her courage again, and she strutted on in a manner that astonished us all.

The Company, none of them expecting her, were delighted & amazed beyond measure: a general Laugh & exclammations of surprise went round: her first speech

> When I'm not thank'd at all,—I'm thank'd enough;
> I've done my duty, & I've done no more!

She spoke so loud, so articulately, & with such courage, that people could scarse credit their senses, when they looked at her Baby Face: I declare,—I could hardly help crying, I was so much charmed, &, at the same Time frightened for her: O how we all wished for Hetty!—it was with difficulty I restrained myself from running on with her,—& my Uncle was so agitated, that he began, involuntarily, a most vehement Clap—a sound to which we had hitherto been strangers:—but the hint was instantly taken, & it was echoed & re-echoed by the audience,—

This applause would have entirely disconcerted her, had it been unexpected; but, as we all imagined she could not fail meeting with it, we had accustommed her to it at all Rehearsals: so that she seemed very sensible of the reason of *the Noise*, as she calls it, & highly gratified by it.

The meaning & energy with which this sweet Child spoke, was really wonderful; we had all done our best in giving her instructions, & she had profitted with a facility & good sense that, at her age, I do indeed believe to be unequalled: when the *Ice* was once broken, in regard to Applause, it was not suffered to be again cemented,—but, while behind the scenes, I could not forbear myself leading a Clap to every one of Nance's speeches.

I wish I could give you any idea how sweetly she spoke

> Whisper ye Winds that Huncamunca's mine!
> Echoes repeat that Huncamunca's mine!

The dreadful Business of the War is o'er,
And Beauty, heavenly Beauty, crowns my toils!—

But it is impossible,—nor do I expect any body not present to do her the justice she deserves.

At the end of that speech, the Drums & Trumpets again made a racket, & the King, Queen & Tom Thumb marched off in triumph. I caught the dear little Hero in my arms, & almost devoured her. 'I wasn't afraid of the people, now, Cousin Fanny; cried she, was I?—no, I wasn't, nor I wasn't ashamed niether;—was I?—'

We gave her all sort of good things to keep up her spirits, & she was so well pleased, that she wanted to go on again immediately; & such was her innocence, that, without having any notion of connection in the piece, she begged me to accompany her directly. 'Do, now, Cousin Fanny, let's you & I do our scene now,—why won't you, *I say?*—'

After this, Lord Grizzle made his appearance. And here, Edward did shine indeed! he was Dressed very richly, though ridiculously, & in high spirits; indeed I must own I think he excelled them all, clever as Richard, his only possible Rival, was. He spoke with such solemnity, such tragic pomposity & energy, & gave us such fine & striking attitudes, while his Face preserved the most inviolable gravity, that to enter into the true spirit of Burlesque with greater humour or propriety would be impossible. Among his numerous talents, he has undoubtedly real abilities for the stage.

But I have neglected to mention the entrance of Glumdalca, from my eagerness to speak of little Nancy; yet can nothing in the piece be more worthy of mention, for nothing excited greater merriment.

James was Dressed in a strait Body with long sleeves, made of striped Lutestring, lapelled with Fur, & ornamented with small Bows of Green, Blue, Garnet & yellow; the Back was shaped with Red. His Coat was pompadour, trimmed with white persian; his shoes were ornamented with tinsel, he had a Fan in his Hand; a large Hoop on, & a Cap, made of every thing that could be devised that was Gaudy & extravagant,—Feathers, of an immense height, cut in paper;—streamers of ribbons of all Colours,—& old Earings & stone Buckles put in his Hair, for Jewels. We were obliged to keep the Hair Dresser, upon his account, for Sir Brilliant's Tête would by no means do for the Giantess,—no, he had the full Covering of a modern Barber's Block, Toupee, Chinon [*sic*], & Curls, all put on at once: the height of his Head, his Cap & Feathers, was prodigious: &, to make him still more violent, he had very high heeled shoes on. His Face was very delicately *rouged*, & his Eye Brows very finely arched;—so that his Face was not to be known. You cannot imagine how impossible it was to look at him thus transformed without laughing,—unless you recollect our infinite *Grinning* when we saw Aunt Nanny in Dr. Prattle.[87] Indeed, there was nothing but Laughter whenever he was on the stage.

The second Act I had myself the Honour of opening, attended by Beckey. My Dress was a good sort enough of Burlesque of Tragedy Dresses, but so made up as to be quite *indescribable*, though of no bad effect. Cleora's was of muslin & pink Gause, & really very pretty,—rather *too* pretty for the purpose. The Curtain was Drawn, & the love sick Huncamunca ⌐ was discovered, reclining on an easy Chair, & weeping: Cleora standing humbly by her side.

'Give me some music!—see that it be sad!—'

was followed by the *very* sad air of Two Black Birds sat upon a spray,[88]—in which Beckey was accompanied by the *passage Band*, & which gave high diversion to the audience, & great Benefit to *the princess*,—who had Time to become quite easy before she spoke any more.

Indeed, happily for me, my spirits were now entirely restored to me: The seeing the first act, & my being so much interested about Nance, made me quite forget my *self*, &, to my great satisfaction, I found myself forsaken by the Horrors. The extreme absurdity & queerness of my part contributed greatly to reviving me & I was really in high & happy spirits:— though I must own I had been fain to Drink ⌐a ⟨glass⟩ of ⟨punch⟩⌐ before I began.

[87] Presumably CB's sister Ann Burney playing the apothecary Prattle in a domestic performance (otherwise unrecorded) of George Colman's farce *The Deuce Is In Him*.
[88] The words are: 'Cupid, ease a Love-sick Maid, / Bring thy Quiver to her Aid;' etc. (1731 edn.).

The scene that followed went off far beyond my expectations: during Beckey's song, I put myself into all sort of affected attitudes of rapturous attention, & had the pleasure to find each of them produce a Laugh.

She then left me, & I had the Honour of a scene with the King,—in which I exerted myself to the utmost of my power, in Tragic pomp & greatness;—and I believe the folks hardly knew me again, for I could hear sundry expressions of surprise from different parts. Indeed, had my extreme terror lasted longer, I should have hated heartily the very thoughts of acting ever after.

The King had not gone a moment, ere I was visited by Lord Grizzle,—who, kneeling, began

Oh Huncamunca!—Huncamunca Oh![89]— |

to which came the most haughty of all my speeches,

'Ha! dost thou know me?—Princess that I am!
That thus of me you dare to make your Game?

&, I do assure you, it wanted no energy or imperiousness that I could give it. So that my transition to kindness afterwards, in proposing to be married in the Fleet, was ⌜so⌝ laughable & ridiculous ⌜that it hit the *general fancy*.⌝

When we had arranged our plan, & he quitted me to Buy a License, my other Lover, Tom Thumb, entered. O that you could have heard her say

Where is my Princess?—where's my Huncamunca?—

She spoke it with a *pathos* that was astonishing.

The tender Princess easily yields to the eloquence of her little Hero, & they are just coming to terms, when the appearance of Glumdalca interrupts them.

And this scene occasions more excess of Laughter than [any][90] other throughout the piece: Glumdalca's first speech,

---

[89] Grizzle's address continues with praise of Huncamunca's 'pouting breasts'. Such mild indecencies were no doubt omitted from the Barborne performance.

[90] Inserted by FBA.

> I need not ask if you are Huncamunca,
> Your Brandy Nose proclaims———

Caused almost a *roar*, & the scornful airs of the two Ladies, while deriding the charms of each other, kept it up as long as we continued together.—But, had you seen little Nancy, standing between James & me, & each of us taking a Hand, & courting her favour,—you would have Laughed ⌐yourself sick.⌐

I came off, however, victorious, & we left Glumdalca to mourn her slighted love. Little Nancy, who stood listening for some Time, heard some of them say that *this is Tom Thumb's wedding Day,*—'Am I married?' cried she,⌐ 'O Yes.' '*Who* am I married to then?' 'Why to *me*, my love.' 'O, I'm glad it isn't to Uncle James, then, 'cause he's such an ugly Woman.

The 3^d act had many alterations, in order to lengthen the part of Cleora. Beckey also put ⌐in a speech of her own, which was a pretty good one. She did the part very well, but I must own her acting abilities are not of that superior sort I had been made to expect.⌐

The Battle scene went off extremely well: but Edward [as Grizzle], while fighting with the Giantess, had his forehead, & the side of his Eye most terribly wounded.

The whole concluded with great spirit,—all the performers dying, & all the Audience Laughing.

The Curtain was then drawn, & we all ran into our Green Room. And here we remained till the Company went down stairs. They had refreshments in the Dining Room.

James changed his Dress, & went to pay his Compts to his acquaintance: Betsy & Beckey, after some hesitation, followed him: but I begged to be excused, as I knew none of the party, & had been pertly stared at enough. I would have persuaded Richard to make one among them, but he said he *looked so ugly,* (by ⟨means⟩ of Whiskers, & so forth) that he could not bear to be seen. ⌐He was gallantry itself to me, kissing my Hand, & pouring forth Compliments in abundance, declaring that I was Capital indeed—& that he had never seen Mrs. Yates so great—&c.⌐

While we were waiting at the stair's Head for the Companys retiring, a voice to which I was an utter stranger, &

speaking masquerade manner, called out 'Where's Miss Fanny? Why won't Miss Fanny shew herself?—' I could not imagine [who this was—but ⟨it was⟩ Dr. Wall][91] |

[*It would appear that 2 months of the journal have been destroyed here, since FB's visit to Gloucester, described next, can be dated 10–12 June. The next 12 surviving leaves have been enclosed in a cover entitled 'Visit to Gloucester circa 1777'. FBA herself has noted* visit to Gloucester *on fos. 26–28 and 31,* visit to Gloucester In Continuation *on fo. 29, and has marked* ✶ *or* ✢ *on fos. 26–31.*]

⸢*stag*, which was performed by Edward & James to admiration; —& others pretty good, which I cannot recollect.

I enquired of Richard if he had yet received *Mrs.* Wall's[92] present? No, he said, nor did he believe the Cloaths were yet sent from London. I then attacked him concerning a Lock of Hair which Miss Arrowsmith[93] told me she had found in his pocket Book, which she had stolen from him the last Time he was at the Rid,[94] & he asked *very*, very inquisitively, if I knew who, the *favourite Lady* was? 'But pray, continued my ladyship, how came it that you suffered the Lock of a Lady's Hair to be seen?' 'Why, said he, I never saw such people in my Life,—Miss Arrowsmith & Miss ⟨F⟩acton[95] got at my Pocket Book, &, while I was tuning the Harpsichord, there were they examining all my Papers & things!'

'I suppose one may not ask whose the Hair is?—but Miss Arrowsmith told me it was very ugly, & coarse, & bad coloured.'

'Phoo, nonsense,—what signifies what she says?—'tis nothing but Jealousy—'

'Jealousy, upon my Word!'

'No, no,—no,—you misunderstand—you—you don't comprehend—I don't mean *jealousy*,—but Envy,—that's all.'

And enough, too, thought I.⸥

---

[91] Inserted by FBA at the bottom of the page; probably copied from the 1st line of the next leaf, which is missing.

[92] Mary Brilliana Popham (d. by 1789), m. (by 1774) John Wall (*Vict. Co. Hist.* [*Glos.*] viii. 132; *GM* lix² (1789), 669; IGI).

[93] Perhaps of the family of Benjamin and Thomas Arrowsmith of Upton-on-Severn, cider merchants, who went bankrupt in 1784 (*GM* liv¹ (1784), 319). Not further traced.

[94] Presumably slang for *ridotto*.

[95] Not identified.

We arrived at Gloucester about 5 o'clock. Dr. Wall Handed us out of the Coach, with one shoe all over mud, & the other clean, but without any Buckle. He welcomed us very cordially, 'But how happened it,' cried he, 'that you did not come by Water?—I have been almost to Tewksbury[96] to meet you, & walked along the shore till I was covered with mud:—& here I would not wait to Dress before I came to you:—but there are two or three Barges gone up the River[97] to meet you. Captain Coussmaker returned from Bath Yesterday, & he should have gone to *escourt* you, if ¹ you would have fixed your Time for coming.'

He then went up to his Wife, & returned with her Compliments, & that she was extremely unhappy she could not wait upon us, but had all her Hair Combed out, & was waiting for the man to Dress it, who had disappointed her ever since 2 o'clock.

I think I never saw a more queerly droll Character than Dr. Wall's: he Lives just according to the whim of the moment, he is passionately fond of sports, of all sorts & kinds, & would purchase them at any trouble or Expence: he says every thing that occurs to him, whether of praise or Censure, Compliment or ridicule; he means to offend nobody, & never dreams of taking offence himself: &, *withall*, he has the most absurdly odd Face, & wears the most ridiculous Wig I ever saw.

He began immediately to talk of *the Play*, & said he could think of nothing else. 'I hope, Miss Fanny,' said he, 'you are now quite recovered from the fright of your first appearance in public:—though, upon my Word, I should never have found it out, if they had not told me of it,—it appeared so well in Character, that I took it for granted it belonged to the part.'

'It was very fortunate for me,' said I, 'that I had so serious & melancholy a part for I should totally have ruined any other.'

---

[96] Where he had his country seat. John Wall acquired Tewkesbury Place through his wife, who had inherited it in 1770 from her relation Mary née Popham, widow of Sir William Strahan (*Vict. Co. Hist.* [*Glos.*] viii. 132). His town residence was at 9 College Green (information courtesy of Miss Suzanne Eward, MA, FSA, ALA, Librarian and Keeper of the Muniments at Salisbury Cathedral, *per* Miss Olwen Hedley).

[97] The Severn. See *ED* ii. 180 n. 1.

'The Character, Ma'am,' returned he, seemed wrote on purpose for you! Captain Coussmaker says he went to the Way to keep him at Bath,—but it was so ill done, that, after all of you, he could not sit it,—so he came out before it was half over.'

We had then to explain the reasons of our not coming by Water. James, in a Whisper, asked me where I thought Richard was?—I could not possibly guess. 'Why,' said he, 'he is in the back Lane, leading to the House, standing in the Rain, without his Great Coat, & talking to Mrs. Wall, who is ⌐leaning out of her Window, to answer him, with all her Hair about her Ears!'—Thus, you see, there was no exaggeration,—ver prett:[98] n'est ce pas of Richard's favour with this fair lady.

Captain Coussmaker came soon after. Lord Berkeley[99] had promised to spend the Evening at Dr. Wall's, but afterwards sent an excuse, that he was so busy, mustering & examining men, that he could not possibly keep his Engagement.

Lord Berkeley, you must know, is Colonel of the militia of Gloucestershire, & makes it his Business to keep it upon a footing remarkably respectable.[1] He is so active & vigilant in the Direction of the affairs of the Corps, that the lowest soldier in the militia cannot have done more actual Business. He is a very handsome man, & looks remarkably sensible, penetrating & serious.[2]

Mrs. Wall did not make her appearance till Tea was half over; for the Doctor insisted that Nancy[3] should make Tea, & not wait for *Mrs. Brilly*, which, or *my Ladyship*, he always calls her. I think *you know* that Mrs. Wall's name is *Briliana*?

---

[98] FB is echoing Omai. See above, p. 195.

[99] Frederick Augustus Berkeley (1745–1810), 5th E. of Berkeley; Lord Lieutenant of Gloucester, 1766–1810.

[1] He had been Col. of the 1st (or South) Battalion of Gloucestershire Militia since 1768 (*List of the Officers of the Several Regiments and Corps of Militia* (1779), p. 24). The Battalion had assembled at Gloucester on 15 May to begin the 28 days of the annual exercise (*Gloucester Journal*, 14 Apr., 26 May).

[2] FB seems unaware of his appearance in 1773 with a Miss Bayley in one of the notorious tête-à-tête portraits in *Town and Country Magazine*. He later had a mistress, Mary Cole, whom he married in 1796; he subsequently forged a series of entries in the Berkeley parish register in an attempt to legitimate the 4 bastard sons he had by her before 1796 (GEC, *Peerage*, ii. 142–4).

[3] FB's cousin Ann Burney.

As she is in mourning,[4] her Dress did not shew to so much advantage as to pay us for Waiting so long to see it. And now, if you would have my opinion of Mrs. Wall, from what I saw of her in a visit of 3 Days, take it. I think her very plain, though very smart in Dress & appearance; she is clever, but very satirical; she makes it a rule never to look at a Woman, when she can see a man; she takes it in turn to be very natural, & very affected; she spends infinitely more than half her Time at her Toilette, to which she is an absolute slave; she is exceedingly fond of Laughing & making merry, but rather tiresome in *pointing out* that *penchant*, not leaving it to others to *discover*, &, in short, she has 3 ruling passions, each of them so strong, it would be difficult to say which predominates: & these are Dress, Admiration, & *Fun*—simple, honest, unrefined *Fun*.

I can believe any thing as to *the present* from her behaviour & looks: she is forever seeking Richard's Eyes, &, when they meet, they smile so significantly!—& look with such intelligence at each other! but, indeed, Mrs. Wall does not *confine* her smiles to him, any more than *he* does his gallantry to her: were I Dr. Wall, I should be infinitely miserable to have a Wife so apparently addicted to flirting, & seeking objects with whom to Coquet from morning to Night.

Dr. Wall, though a very indifferent performer, is really very fond of music, & he has so strange & mixed a Collection of musical Instruments as I never before saw: he brought them all out of a Closet in the parlour, which he appropriates to keeping them, one by one; & he drew out some tone, such as it was! from each before he changed. First came a French Horn,—then a Trumpet,—then a violin,—a Bass,—a Bassoon,—a macaroni fiddle,[5]—&, in short, I believe he produced 20 of different kinds.

An Overture was then attempted,—every body that possibly could, bore a part,—& I really would not wish to hear a much worse performance: & yet this music lasted to supper!—

Mr. Coussmaker stayed supper. He is a very pretty sort of

---

[4] For whom is not known, but presumably a relation.

[5] Presumably a small, highly decorated violin, suitable for a fop. *OED* cites FB (s.v. Macaroni 9), guessing at a definition.

young man, but rather too shy & silent, which, though infinitely preferable to forwardness & loquacity, nevertheless
may be carried too far, either for the comfort of the owner, or
pleasure of satisfaction of those with whom he converses. We
were, however, very jocose: though, unfortunately for me, I
had a very bad Head ach,—& could not contribute my mite
towards the general Cause. [|]

After supper, ⌜we all Drank⌝ about sentimental Toasts; We
were all mighty stupid at them, & he [Dr Wall] was obliged
to help every body. When my turn came, I told him that not
being able to think of a *sentiment*, I would give a *good wish*, &
then I Drank A Fair Day for the Review To-morrow.

Dr. Wall pretended to misunderstand me, & gave it out
Miss Fanny Burney's good Wishes, & a Fair Review,—that is
added he, *All* Miss Fanny Burney's Wishes,—for I dare say
they are All good.

When he called upon Mr. Coussmaker, he, too, said he
really could not recollect one; 'No? cried Dr. Wall, what,
don't you recollect any thing about *Full pay?*—O 'tis a most
excellent sentimental Toast!'

Nancy, Betsy & Beckey were all equally at a loss,—I know
not what bewitched all our memories, but not a soul could
recollect one when called upon,—'Well, cried Dr. Wall, don't
suppose, Gentlemen, that the Ladies *have* no sentiments,—the
only thing is, they are ashamed to own them,—that's all.'

Provoking enough,—but he says any thing: for example,
looking hard at Betsy, 'Pray, said he, did ever any body take
notice of your Eyes?'—'My Eyes, Sir?—Why?—' 'Because
they a'n't fellows,—one is Brown, & one Grey.'—&, indeed,
it is very true. And when he was helping Edward, to some
Duck, he bid him cut it very small, for he was afraid *his mouth
would hardly hold it.*

When he called upon Edward for his Toast, 'Come, Sir,
cried he, what do you Gentlemen of the Royal Academy give
for sentiments?—A model of Venus?—or what?—You, that
study from Nature, must certainly be very sentimental.' [|]

The next morning, before we were Dressed, Dr. Wall ser-
enaded us with sundry Instruments, one after another. When
we came down to Breakfast, Mrs. Wall, having slightly

enquired how we did, said 'Pray do you know why *Dickey* does not come!' for so she jocosely calls our Cousin Richard. All the Gentlemen, you must know, slept at some Inn, as Dr. Wall could only accomodate the Females with Beds.

Soon after we were seated, a party Entered who were invited to spend the Day, consisting of Miss Holcomb,[6] a most fright-ful & disagreeable Woman, Miss Hayward, an old maid, who is Deaf, & should have been *Mrs.* Hayward many years ago; her Brother, a fat Headed man,[7] & Miss Wall,[8] sister of the Doctor, who is ugly, but agreeable.

Our 3 youths & Mr. Gale[9] stroled in soon after. Richard seated himself, with his usual ease, at Mrs. Wall's Elbow, while she made Breakfast: & her Company was not the more attended to for his *vicinity*.

We had but just done, when the militia began to be drawn forth upon the College Green, where Dr. Wall Lives, & Lord Berkeley, who resides next Door but one to the Doctor, ap-peared before the Windows. We all flew to put on our Hats, & then went in a body to the Door, to see the Ceremony of preparing the men for marching to the Field. Here we were joined by Captain Coussmaker, Captain Snell,[10] Captain

---

[6] Perhaps a daughter of the Revd Samuel Holcombe (d. 1775), prebendary of Worcester and rector of Severn Stoke. Three daughters, Ann, Frances, and Judith, were christened at Severn Stoke between 1737 and 1742. One of these, still unmarried, apparently died at Powick in 1807. See *GM* xlv (1775), 255; lxxvii[2] (1807), 780; IGI.

[7] FB below calls the Haywards *'people of consequence'* (p. 259). The brother was perhaps Thomas Hayward (1706–81), of Quedgeley, near Gloucester, formerly an MP (Namier). His sons Charles (*c.*1741–1803) and William (*c.*1743–1818) were both contemporaries of Lord Berkeley at Eton. The spinster sister has not been further traced. The Haywards may also have been connections of George Coussmaker, whose mother was a Hayward.

[8] John Wall had two unmarried sisters at this time, Catherine and Elizabeth. This was probably the one described by Mrs Thrale in *Thraliana* (i. 28, s.v. 28 May 1777): 'Doctor Wall's Daughter was a fine straight Healthy Girl till 13 Years of age; She then accidentally swallowed a Brass Button which produced a Train of dreadful Symp-toms in Succession for 8 years after; among the rest her Bones were so soft'ned by the poyson, that they bent, and She grew extremely crooked. She recovered however.... She was 35 years old when I heard the story [*c.*?1775].' See also J. Chambers, *Biographical Illustrations of Worcestershire* (Worcester, 1820), pp. 385, 393; will of John Wall (d. 1776), PCC, prob. Nov. 1776.

[9] Perhaps John Gale (d. 1812) of Charlton Kings, Gloucestershire (*GM* lxxxii[1] (1812), 494).

[10] Powell Snell (*c.*1738–1804) of Guiting Grange, Gloucestershire; MA (Oxon.), 1759; Middle Temple, 1765; Capt., South Gloucestershire Militia, 1772; resigned,

Miers,[11] & heaven knows who,—for Dr. Wall is acquainted
with all the Corps,[12]—who are all men of fortune & family.
We were also joined by a Mr. Davis,[13] commonly, nay, uni-
versally, called Harry Davis; a young man, a Neighbour of the
Doctor, celebrated for flightiness, freedom, gallantry & rioting.
He is handsome & agreeable, though ⌐I should like him much
better were he less forward: for, not contented with renewing
an intimate acquaintance with Betsy & Beckey, he *began* one
with me upon the same free Terms at once!

We went to the Review in 2 Coaches; in one, the same party
that Travelled to Gloucester, & in another Miss Holcomb,
&c. But Mrs. Wall—stayed at Home lest she should miss a
Hair Dresser she wanted to *have to herself* against the Ball!—
Richard, Harry Davis & Mr. Gale Walked; for the Field of
action is but just out of the City.

⌐There were a great number of Carriages, & several Gentlemen [xxxxx *7–8 words*] looked very tidy & clear, & all the
officers remarkably neat but the militia is reckoned to be uncommonly well regulated.⌐

Our Coach was so placed as to give us the best view we
could have, from one spot, of the shew. James & Edward
immediately got out, as did all the men who came in Carriages.
When *the salute* was to be given to Lord Berkeley, most of the
Ladies, also, alighted: so did all our party, myself excepted, &
I was by no means well, & had silk shoes, & the Day was cold,
the Ground damp, ⌐I wished to save myself for the Ball at
Night,⌐—I determined to content myself with what I could
see from the Coach: & away went all the rest, except Edward,
⌐he stood by the Coach Door whether I would or not.⌐ Harry
Davis, also, insisted on keeping me Company: & he entertained
me with an account of the state of party affairs in Gloucester;

1793 (*List of the Officers of the* ... *Militia* (1779), p. 24; Gloucestershire Militia Lists,
1782–93, WO 13/834 (PRO)).

[11] Certainly John Meares, commissioned *lieutenant* in the South Gloucestershire
Militia, 24 Oct. 1775. He is last found in the militia lists in 1779. Not further traced
(*List of the* ... *Militia* (1779), p. 24).

[12] He later joined it and became its Lt.-Col.

[13] Possibly Henry Davies (b. *c.*1757), son of Thomas Davies, Esq., of Gloucester.
This Henry Davies matriculated at Trinity College, Oxford, in 1774 but did not
graduate.

& told me, that though he loved Dancing better than any thing under Heaven, & would give the World, yet he would not go to the Ball at Night for 50 Guineas, because it was a | *Berkeley* Ball,—& he & his Family were *Chesters!*[14]

Soon after, Dr. Wall paid me a Visit, &, assuring me Nobody took Cold at a Review, advised me, or, rather, *rioted* me, to get out, & go & see the salute: & so, though I was Cold & uncomfortable, rather than appear finical & fine ladyish, I got out, & was escorted across the Field to the rest of the party, who stood very near Lord Berkeley, the better to see the Ceremony.

Harry Davis, looking at my shoes, said I should certainly catch my Death if I did not take care (for it had rained all the morning,) & then put down his Handkerchief for me to stand upon: I was quite ashamed of being made such a fuss with, but he *compelled* me to comply: &, every Time we moved forwards or backwards, he picked it up, & every Time we stood still, he put it on the Ground, and insisted on my making use of it. ꜛI saw many Ladies look with a half Laugh at me:—& Edward, I am afraid, held me *rather cheap*, for at the Review [xxxxx *1–2 words*] he had most violently ridiculed Miss Holcomb's delicacy, for [xxxxx *3–4 words*] fear of the damp &, in imitation of Mr. Crisp, has called her *pretty Creature* ever since: indeed, I *would* not have accepted such an indulgence, but that I preferred *any* thing to straggling, which, with Harry Davis, was my only alternative.ꜛ The men were reckoned, by all the Judges, to go through their different manœuvres with great neatness, dexterity & spirit: but for the *Firing*, which always shakes my whole Frame, I should think a Review a sight as agreeable as it is undoubtedly grand & striking.[15] |

ꜛ[xxxxx *1 word*] however, I was so indifferent, that I was

---

[14] Politics in Gloucestershire were dominated at this time by the Beaufort and Berkeley families. When one of the MPs for the county, Edward Southwell (1738–77), was called to the Upper House in 1776, the Berkeleys decided to run George Cranfield Berkeley (see below), brother of Lord Berkeley, against the Beauforts' man, William Bromley Chester (1738–80), in the race for the vacant seat. Chester won the election by only 46 votes, and Berkeley petitioned against the result, charging that the sheriff was partial and had closed the polls when more of Berkeley's supporters were coming to vote. A committee of the Commons ruled in Apr. 1777 that Chester's election was valid. Feelings were still running high during FB's visit to Gloucester. See Namier.

[15] 'On Wednesday last [11 June] the South ... battalion ... of Militia of this

allowed, by general advice, to return to the Carriage, while the other Females paraded the Field. Edward accompanied me & would sit with me till the rest found us. I know not how it happens, but I am almost always so unlucky as to be Ill, or *unwell*, at least, upon these sort of occasions.⌐

When we returned Home, we found that Mrs. Wall was still at her Toilette! ⌐Mrs Yate, Miss Honeywood who was, called, —but she would not see her. That lady ⟨looked⟩ very hard at me, but did not recollect me, though she told Harry Davis afterwards that she thought she knew me & asked if I was not a Miss Burney? She is still very handsome, though much paler than when I knew her at Tingmouth.⌐16

Mrs. Wall is as Cavalier & easy in *actions*, as her Husband is in Words: for, though she had a House full of Company, ⌐& several of them *people of consequence*, such as the Haywards & Miss Holcomb,⌐ yet without the least hurry or discomposure, she gave the whole Day to the adornment of her person.

As we found we had our Time pretty much at our own disposal from the Review till Dinner, it was proposed to shew me the Town; & so we all went in a body, attended by Harry Davis, up & down the principal streets. The City is very little worth seeing,—indeed the Cathedral seems the only Building worthy notice; there are a few good Houses, & *no* good streets. We then strolled upon the *Parade* at the College Green, ⌐where Richard would not be contented without Handing me, as if I had been going into a Carriage.⌐ And here we met Dr. Wall, Mr. Coussmaker & Mr. Hayward, | who were going to Dine with Lord Berkeley & the Corps; & invited our Gentlemen to accompany them: only James accepted the offer. When we returned Home, poor Harry Davis looked *au desespoir*; for, though very intimate at Dr. Wall's, he was obliged not to Enter the House, because the Berkeley party, to which the Dr. belongs, were always popping in & out. When he left us, he said he was afraid he should Hang himself before Night: but he advised me repeatedly to see the College the next morning, to which he proposed attending us.

county . . . [was] reviewed [on the Town Ham] by the Lord Lieutenant [Lord Berkeley], and made a very fine appearance' (*Gloucester Journal*, 16 June 1777; see also 9 June).

16 See *EJL* i. 301 and n. 9.

Mrs. Wall was still invisible: & when, at last, she appeared, she had only her Hair Dressed, & very extravagantly, nay, preposterously, & no Cap on, or any other appearance of readiness. After slightly begging our pardons, 'Tell them, said she to the man, to bring in Dinner directly,—for it has been waiting for me this Hour.' Then, turning to Richard, with a smile of ineffable satisfaction, 'how came *you* not to Dine at the Booth,[17] with my Lord?'

'Ma'am I,—I rather thought,—that—as the other Gentlemen went—' affectedly stammered Richard,—

'Upon my Word, Sir, we are much obliged to you,—but I am afraid you *rather thought* you was not Dressed—hay?—M[r] Dickey?—was not that the case?—'

Dinner was then brought in, & Richard did the Honours for Dr. Wall; drinking with all the Ladies, helping them, & so forth. Mrs. Wall complained bitterly that she was very backward in her Dress, & feared she should not have Time to be ready: the Hair Dresser was appointed to be with her again by 4 o'Clock. As soon as we could with decency, we all separated to *beautify*.

When the man came, he was siezed by so many, one after another, that we almost feared we should have been obliged to give up the Ball, it was so very late ere he came near us: the affair became so serious, & the waiting so alarming, lest the minuets should be over, that the party was fain to separate, & go off in Chairs, as they were ready. ⌐This was mighty disagreeable to me, who was ⟨set⟩ about last, because I had taken all the Time I could for laying down, to ⟨per⟩mit again Dancing.⌐

Betsy & I were the last in the House;—& she went off about two minutes before me. When I went down, in the Hall I was met by *Harry Davis*,—who Handed me into the Chair, charging me not to over fatigue myself at the Ball, because he built upon accompanying me to the College next morning.

⌐As soon as I stoped at the Assembly Room,[18] I found Edward at the foot of the stairs, waiting for me which I was mighty

---

[17] The Booth Hall, on the south side of Westgate St.; since destroyed (see *ED* ii. 189 n. 1).

[18] The Ball was held in the Bell Inn (*Gloucester Journal*, 9 June).

glad of, for I should not have known what to do with myself. He hurried me up stairs, for he said, the next minuet was then Dancing.

James & Richard both waited for me at the Ball Room Door, & escorted me to the rest of the Party.⌐ The last ⌐minuet was⌐ by Lord Berkeley & Mrs. Yate.

James immediately engaged me for Country Dances.

Dr. Wall was so differently *Wigged*, that I really did not know him,—& when he came & said to me 'So, Ma'am, I'm glad to see you here,—why you like coming late to these places? —' I, at first, took him for a stranger: & he plagued me about it all the rest of the Time I remained | at Gloucester,—for Mr Coussmaker informed against me: 'So you did n't know me?—' made every 3^d sentence.

⌐I had now an opportunity of seeing, & to great advantage, the two sister Beauties Richard has talked so much of, Mrs. Lumley, & Miss ⟨Miers⟩;[19] they are, indeed, very handsome. The country Dances were begun by Mr. Berkeley,[20] my Lord's Brother, & Mrs. Wall. Betsy Danced with Mr. Coussmaker, Nancy with Mr. Gale. Dr. Wall, Richard, & Edward did not Dance at all.

Between the Dances, we had Tea & refreshments upon long Tables, at which only Ladies sat, for the men waited behind them & Lord Berkeley's militia Band who all came from London for the Review, surrounded us very agreeably during the Repast.

The Company was very well Dressed, & seemed to be very genteel. Captain Coussmaker was the most elegantly gay Dressed man in the Room. I shall cut short any amount of Description of any of the party, because they are unknown to you, but the Ball proved very lively & agreeable.

We did not break up till near 2 o'clock, & then we went Home in Chairs two ⟨abreast⟩, James & Edward ran by the side of mine.⌐ |

---

[19] Neither sister has been identified.

[20] George Cranfield Berkeley (1753–1818). An unsuccessful candidate in the recent by-election for Gloucestershire (see above, p. 258 n. 14), he stood unopposed in 1783 and represented the county in the Commons until 1810. He was also a career officer in the Navy, and eventually attained the rank of admiral (Namier).

I think I left off with the Ball at Gloucester?—you make no answer, so, I presume, silence *gives* Consent.

Eh bien. It was 2 o'clock in the morning ere we sat down to supper. Mr. Berkeley & Captain Coussmaker were of our party. We were all in prodigious spirits, & *kept it up* till near 5 in the morning.

Mr. Berkeley is a handsome man, & *very well*; but I think him affected, & therefore like him not.

Richard, who came in last, (because he waited for a Chair,) found no Room at the Table; & so he got behind me, & said he would *wait*: 'Not behind *my* Chair, however, cried I, for I can't bear it.' 'No, no, Dick, cried Dr. Wall, don't stand behind *her* Chair,—go to some *agreeable* lady.' Richard, upon my re-peating the desire, walked off, & got a seat behind Mrs. Wall's, & by degrees, & her assistance, wedged himself in between her & Nancy, at the Top of the Table;—where he Laughed & figured away very jocosely.

Dr. Wall, who sat next me, was mighty facetious: & he *stuffed* me all supper Time, saying he had '*given orders I should not be stinted*'; & conjecturing, when I refused any thing, that, 'I wanted *something I could niether Eat nor Drink*;—' indeed, he scarse ever spoke to me, but with a quotation from Tom Thumb, or an allusion to Huncamunca.

After supper, Richard, James, Betsy & Mrs. Wall sung some Catches:—┌indifferently enough, upon the whole, though I like┐ the Voice of Richard very much on these occasions. Mr. Berkeley some times joined the Treble part, & Dr. Wall, the *Bass*, but so ludicrously, as to make me Laugh immoderately. Richard gave himself a thousand droll airs, in the *Italian way*, squaring his Elbows, making faces, heightening his Eyebrows, & Acting profusely. |

┌'What a clever fellow that is!' (cried Dr. Wall, to me, for I sat between him & Mr. Coussmaker,) is he not?—don't you think him very Clever?'

'Yes, indeed,—answered I, & then asked him if he had ever heard him sing Fuggiam dove sicura?[21]

Yes, he said, & then called upon him to give it to us, im-mediately, that Mr. Berkeley might hear it. Richard, in too

---

[21] From Rauzzini's *Piramo e Tisbe*.

great spirits to make any hesitation, complied directly, &
Betsey accompanied him on the Harpsichord, while he stood
up, & taking a Book in his Hand, sung the song with all the
airs & graces & grimaces he could assume.

'That Dick Burney, cried Dr. Wall, is the drollest of men in
the World, is he not?—' 'Yes, indeed.' 'But is he not *very* droll,
very clever? tell me, now, don't you admire him vastly?'

I assented very readily, & then begged him to ask for é pur
bella la Cecchina[22]—he immediately complied, though he
Laughed, & cried he would *come upon me next*. Richard made no
fuss—Chairs & Tables were removed, a stage made, & on he
came to sing his best, & made the Caricature of Lovatini more
strong & diverting than ever.[23] Mr. Berkeley was quite delighted with him, repeatedly declaring he never saw so good
an Imitation.

'He's a charming fellow, upon my Honour! cried Dr. Wall,
always to me, & in a low voice, is not he a most charming
fellow?—isn't he droll? clever? humourous? don't you think
so?—don't you admire him extremely? don't you like him of
all things?'

In this manner, he absolutely insisted upon my praising
him most violently, & would not be contented without my
echoing every word he said in his favour.⌐ |

When we were all re-arranged, & Richard again took his
seat next to Mrs. Wall, the Doctor said to me 'Come, now for
a little of Tom Thumb;—come, Miss Fanny, what part will
you speak?—the Goose pie & half a pig?—come, you *must* give
us something.'

Upon my remonstrating, or, rather, absolutely refusing,
'But you *must*, cried he,—come, do,—else I'll set Dick Burney
upon you!'

'No, no, cried I,—*O spare my Blushes!*—' and, after a little
further fussation, & much jocularity, he gave it up: to my
great satisfaction, for, had he persisted, & made his request
public, I could never have consented.

---

[22] From Piccinni's *La Buona Figliuola*.

[23] Lovattini had sung *é pur bella* in the role of il Marchese della Conchiglia; the aria
concludes scene ii. See N. Piccinni, *La Buona Figliuola* (London: R. Bremner, [1767]),
pp. 13–18 and *passim*.

When, at length, we thought it Time to retire, Mrs. Wall rang for Candles,—but, upon opening the Parlour Door, for all us Females to decamp, we all burst into a general ⌐Chorus of⌐ Laughter at the call for Candles, for we found ourselves in *Broad Day Light!*—We therefore wished all the Gentlemen *good morning*, & left them to their Wine.

We were so little disposed for sleep, that we considered for some Time whether it would be worth while or not to go at all to Bed: & we all went into Mrs. Wall's Room, where we Chatted & Laughed & weighed this important point: which was at length determined, by our all agreeing that to change our Dresses being absolutely necessary, we might as well condescend to *take a Nap* into the Bargain: upon which consideration, we bid good Night to the morning, & sought to conceal ourselves from the bright glare of the obtruding sun, by softly reposing our Languid Heads | & wearried Limbs, on downy Pillows & enervating Feather Beds.—We ought, perhaps, to Blush at acknowledging such depravity & weakness of spirit,—yet, had you seen what Ghosts we looked,—you must, at least, have owned, that, from whatever Cause, the Effect of a Blush could never be more becoming.

The Gentlemen parted very soon.

⌐We did not rise very early the next morning:—a circumstance which I should not mention but that I think you must be very much surprised at it, & from the Time I began Journalising from Barborne, I made a solemn resolution, to which I have most strictly adhered, never to notice any thing that had not the recommendation of Novelty to make it worthy your attention.⌐

Dr. Wall gave us our usual serenade before we were Dressed, & *blew* to us all the Country Dances we had figured in the preceding Evening. We were down long before Mrs. Wall, whose Toilette is an affair of moment,—though only in *one* sense,—for, as to *Time*, 'tis an affair of much longer duration.

As soon as we entered the Room, the Doctor, siezing me, forced me to sit [xxxxx *3 words*] he was looking over Thicknesse's[24] Tour,—& we both went on with it, & made Com-

---

[24] Philip Thicknesse (1719–92), author of *A Year's Journey through France and Part of Spain* (2 vols., 1777). The reviewer for *GM* found the work 'amusing' and 'instructive',

ments which, had the Author heard, might have endangered our safety for the rest of his Life.

'Pray, Miss Fanny, cried he, how does the *Yellow lady* do?' '*Yellow lady?*—' 'Yes,—did n't you know your sister turned yellow while she was in Worcester?'[25]

There was never such a ⌐queer⌐ man, I believe, *before*, for making strange speeches. He says any & every thing: but he seems so good naturedly disposed to ⌐take, as well as *give*, that one has never any idea of being affronted by him.

Scarsely had Mrs. Wall entered the Room, ere she said 'But where's *Dickey?*—why does n't he come to Breakfast? Then, ringing the Bell, 'Tom, go to the Inn, & tell the Gentlemen we wait for them.'

An Answer was brought, that they were already at Breakfast at the Inn, but would attend us soon.

We then talked over the Ball & Review, & both the Doctor & his lady pressed us to stay some Time longer, in a very earnest manner,—but our going was absolutely indispensable, as my Uncle had charged us by no means to stay longer than the Thursday.

'Lord!—what shall we do, when you are all gone? cried Dr. Wall,—why you may as well stay,—Miss Humphries can amuse Mr. Burney, you know.'

'How dull shall we be! cried the *affectionate Wife*; I shall be ready to drown myself;—yesterday the Review & the Ball!—& to Night,—*nothing!*—only the Doctor & I!—do, Dr. Wall, let me go with the Ladies just to Gorse Lawn,[26] for a frolic!—'

The Doctor would not hear of this, 'No, Mrs. *Brilly*, no, *my ladyship*,—you'll fatigue yourself to Death,—besides, how will you get back?'

'O!—I'll manage that!—' However, the subject was waved

but criticized the author's misanthropy (*GM* xlvii (1777), 281; cf. Nichols, *Lit. Ill.* v. 737). Dr Johnson alludes to Thicknesse's complaining, but thought the book, on the whole, 'entertaining' (*Life*, iii. 235–6).

[25] SEB had suffered an attack of jaundice the preceding year. Her father 'commemorated' her illness in verses, 'To Sue on her recovery', beginning: 'When the Crocus & Snowdrop their *white* have display'd / Come the Primrose & Cowslip in *Yellow* array'd' (Berg).

[26] i.e., Corse Lawn, 6 miles NW of Gloucester; a stopping place on the road to Worcester.

for the present. As soon as Breakfast was over, a ⸢new Horse⸣ was brought to the Door, for the Doctor to *try*. He mounted it immediately, & Capered all round the College Green in a very Laughable manner, for he made his Horse Dance in & out of every other Tree, *Hay*[27] *Fashion.* |

We sauntered about the Hall & Parlour till near one o'clock, expecting in vain our Beaus: & Mrs. Wall perpetually exclaiming 'Lord, what can be become of *Dickey*?—I'm afraid the pretty Creature has lost himself!—'

Nancy, having a Visit to make to a Mrs. Barnes,[28] proposed our then going: & Mrs. Wall said she would take the opportunity to call upon a lady who was just going to quit Gloucester. 'And I hope, cried she, that when we return, the *sweet Dears* will have found their way to the House. I *must* tell you what a nice trick I served *Dickey* last Saturday!—ha, ha, ha!—it makes me Laugh to think of it!—you must know, when he was going to Cheltenham, as usual, on Saturday morning, I took it in my Head to try a new Horse the Doctor had bought me, & so make a visit at Cheltenham at the same Time: well, Mr. Dickey was to be my 'squire,—so off we set, & ⸢swift⸣ enough we were, you may be sure: well, we both Dined at Mr. Delebere's,[29]—& I saw that Mr. Dickey kept on his Boots,—but I did not know that he intended to return with me to Gloucester that Evening, for I thought it was all by Choice, or his custom: & he never said a Word to me of having any such design: so, after Dinner, he went to one of his schools:—&, in the Evening, I saw nothing of the Gentleman, so I set off without him!—Ha, Ha!—was it not a nice trick?—poor Dickey was so mad!—for he had intended all along seeing me Home,—but how should *I* know that?—I can't think why he could | not as well tell me so at once;—'

'Probably, said I, he concluded you would take it for granted.'

'Why I did call at the Swan, where he puts up,—but he was

[27] 'A country dance having a winding or serpentine movement, or being of the nature of a reel.' 'To dance the hay' is 'to perform winding or sinuous movements (around or among numerous objects)' (*OED*, s.v. Hay *sb.*[4] 1).

[28] Perhaps the same Mrs Barnes listed as one of the gentry residing in Gloucester city in 1790 (Bailey's *Universal British Directory* (1790–3), iii. 190). Not further traced.

[29] Probably John Delabere (d. 1793) of Cheltenham, a JP for Gloucestershire (*GM* lxiii[1] (1793), 93). FB met him in 1788 (*DL* iv. 47). See also J. Goding, *Norman's History of Cheltenham* (1863), pp. 109–11.

not there,—so I came away without him,—I have Laughed at
him about it ever since:—yet he might as well have let me
know his design,—indeed I can't think why he did not.'

A very nice trick indeed!—& not at all *by force*:—what folly
to talk, nay, *boast*, of a *trick*, when sh[e] took such pains as to
call at an Inn in ⟨order⟩ to have his Company!—

We then proceeded, Nan[cy,] Betsy, Beckey & myself, to
[Mrs.] B[a]rnes: & there, w[e] were scarse seated, [e]re we
were followed by Harry Davis, who Lives almost next Door to
her. 'Mrs. Barnes, cried he, I hope you will admit me, for I
must come to pay my Compliments to the Miss Burneys.'

[The] Ball & Review, you may be sure, furnished ma[tter]
sufficient for Conversation: Harry Davis asked me [how I]
liked the Assembly?—'I can tell you, cried he, who you Danced
with.' 'I'm glad of it, answered I, because it will be rare news
to me.' 'But I am sorry you were so late, returned he,—why
you lost all the minuets!—'

So this forlorn Beau, instead of *Hanging* himself, had been
enquiring into all the particulars of the Ball.

In a short Time, we were joined by Richard, James &
Edward. Harry Davis then asked me if I ⎮ would not go to see
the College? I was very ready to comply,—& so we all took
leave of Mrs. Barnes,—a person whose name to have mentioned has occasioned my writing *two* words too much.

We first took a stroll in the College Green, & then Harry
Davis ran to procure the keys, & get Doors open for us: ⌐Richard
absolutely *made* me hold by his arm all the morning, & whisked
me about with him, up & down the College, as if I had become
a part of his own person, & neither of us could move but by
mutual consent [xxxxx *1 line*]⌐

This ⌐*College*⌐ is extremely well worth seeing, for its antiquity. There are many curious old monuments in it, though it
by no means abounds with any of modern elegance: Cuthbert,
King of the Saxons,[30] is, I believe, the most ancient: it is a

---

[30] An error; FB perhaps means Cuthred (d. 754), King of the West Saxons. The
monument she refers to, though, is probably the one honouring Osric, King of the
Hwiccii, who founded the abbey at Gloucester *c.*681. This shrine dates from the reign
of Henry VIII. A stone effigy, thought to represent Abbot Serlo, dates from *c.*1280.
See D. Verey, *Gloucestershire: The Vale and the Forest of Dean* (*The Buildings of England*, ed.
N. Pevsner) (Harmondsworth, 1970), pp. 198, 216.

Figure cut in stone, & very entire. There is another Figure carved in Oak, & painted, of the Conqueror's Eldest son.[31] Edward the Second[32] has, also, a monument in this Cathedral. There is a good deal of Painted Glass remaining here, &, in particular, one whole & very larg[e] Window, which is reckoned extremely curious.[33]

We went up, by terrible old steps, & crooked stair case, to the Top of the Tower. ⌐[xxxxx ½ *line*] Mr. Davis invited us to see how many could stand under the great Bell, but I did not like *his looks*. He hauled Betsy under it &, as soon as she was there, most literally & truly paid himself for the Trouble of escorting her, & then, looking very foolish, she was Handed back, yet though *foolish, quiet,* for she held by his⌐ | Arm ⌐all the rest of the morning. But I have remarked, in many instances, that Girls in the Country, even the most modest, *think nothing of kissing*. It seems a *thing of Course*,—a gallantry not of the least consequence.—more ⟨cause⟩ of merriment, [& on]ly tending to promote Laughter.⌐

The Tower is very curious Gothic workmanship, & so high that, from the Ground, it has the appearance of fine *Net work*,[34] though, when we were close to it, we should have thought such Netting rather course, even had it come from Otaheite. We had a grand *Coup d'oeil*, from the Top, taking in the greatest part of the County, with some of Worcestershire. But I have seen many more beautiful views, as I think Gloucestershire a County by no means of the *first Class*: at least, the parts round the City are not of beauty incomparable.

We had a good deal of diversion, all together, while in the

---

[31] Robert (1054?–1134), D. of Normandy. One of the few existing wooden effigies made in Bristol in the 13th c., it was broken during the Civil War and restored after the Restoration (ibid., p. 216).

[32] Edward II (1284–1327), King of England. His effigy is made of alabaster, with a limestone canopy and a marble tomb chest; it dates from c.1330 (Verey, p. 217).

[33] FB refers to the choir east window, probably finished by 1350. The design is still considered to have been remarkable for its time: 'It is the first as well as the grandest example of the window filled with tiers of full-length figures which became characteristic of the following century' (Verey, p. 211).

[34] The Tower is 225 ft. high, and dates from about the middle of the 15th c. It is crowned by an open parapet and 4 openwork pinnacles of stone, and is 'patterned all over with tier upon tier of blank arcading' (Verey, pp. 202–3).

College,—but I have waited too long to recollect particulars. There is a *Whispering place* here;—Harry Davis stayed at one End, & Richard went to the other; the latter began with 'How Cursed mad Harry Davis was last Night, that he could not go to the Ball!—' & the other returned, 'I am afraid Mrs. Wall is a *turn Coat*, & that George Berkeley has *Danced her* to his party.'

We then took another stroll about the Town,—& I saw enough of it to die contented if I never should see it again;—& then we paraded upon the College Green, till we were obliged to return to Dinner, when Harry Davis was fain to go to his own Home.

Mrs. Wall was not returned; but we found the Doctor playing upon the Bassoon, &, as usual, surrounded with the Lord knows how many other Instruments. He presently flung them all away,—& what do you think for!—why to *Romp with me!*— I'm sure you would never have guessed that. But the less he found me inclined to this sort of sport, the more determined he seemed to pursue it, & we Danced round the Room, *Hayed* in & out with the Chairs, & *all that*, till it grew so late, that he ordered Dinner, saying 'Come, good folks, let's take care of ourselves,—*Mrs. Brilly* is certainly run away,—so we'll have our Dinner without further ceremony.'

We made some remonstrances, but they had no effect. In truth, I think he really did right, for she certainly *ought* to have been at Home sooner.

We had just done Dinner before she made her appearance. She was extremely surprised to find how late it was, & we were all rather ashamed of our Employment, & were forced to tell her that the Doctor had insisted upon our not Waiting any longer for her. 'Why, Mrs. Brilly, cried he, we thought you had forgot us,—& so, *my Ladyship*, we sat down to Dinner: but they have settled to fling all the fault upon *me*.' 'O, to be sure! cried I, you had Nothing in the World to do with it, in *reality*! —however, it may pass that we have but *just begun*,—only we've Eat *fast*.' 'Very well thought of; said he,—but, my *Ladyship*, what shall I help you to?—'

'Why—I don't know,—(looking about her,)—but I think here seems nothing *very* nice.'

What an Air!—I rejoiced in the Doctor's answer.

'Why then, Mrs. Brilly, why did not you provide us some-thing better?'

'Shall *I*, Ma'am, cried Richard, have the Honour of helping you?'

This was assented to; & she then began, in a low Voice, a Conversation with him which lasted till he left us to go to Business: I did not hear what passed, as my Neighbour, Dr. Wall, employed my attention: but Nancy told me that she acquainted him she had ^l met with George Berkeley, & *could not get away from him*,—& ran on with much stuff to that pur-pose, as if to *pique* Richard! but he is much too easy for her to succeed in any such attempt,—however *praise worthy* the endeavour.

When Richard was gone, she grew extremely sociable with the rest of the Party, particularly with James: & she was quite urgent to dissuade us from leaving Gloucester; and, when she found us inexorable, she grew mad to accompany us, on Horse back, as far as Gorse Lawn. When she pressed her Husband to consent, 'Mrs. Brilly, said he, it cannot be,—you will never be ready in Time,—you can't possibly get Dressed.'

To this, in our own minds, I believe we all agreed; for a greater slave to her Toilette never existed. She would not, however, give it up, but, in a low voice, desired James to *speak for her*;—James complied, but in a very slight manner, for he is extremely Cavalier with the *World in general*, & reserves his *politesse* pretty much for his favourites. The Doctor still refused his consent, & Mrs. Wall again exclaimed 'Lord, how mon-strous dull we shall be! only us two!—Lord, how stupid!'

Poor Woman! who could deny her *pity*,—a *Wife*, & the mother of *three Children*,[35] to be left at *Home*, & with her Family! — unhappy Creature!—what an Object of Compassion would she think our Hetty![36]—

However, I must do her the Justice to say, that her Children

[35] Two of the children were Robert Martin Popham Wall (1774–1847), who became a Lt.-Col. of the Oxfordshire militia, and John Wall (1775–1817), MA (Oxon.), 1800, later rector of Wollaston, Stoke St Milborough, and Quatt, Salop. The 3rd child was presumably the Miss Wall, 'daughter of Lieut.-Col. W. of the Lodge, near Tewkesbury', who m. (1803) Samuel Crane, Esq., of Worcester (*GM* lxxiii[1] (1803), 82; T. F. Kirby, *Winchester Scholars* (1888), p. 278; IGI).

[36] EBB was expecting her 5th child, born in Sept.

never occasioned the least trouble or disturbance;—for not once did they appear,—nor did we ever hear them mentioned: so that, but for previous information, I should not have had the slightest suspicion that [|] Mrs. Wall was a mother. I am sure it would be superfluous to tell you how infinitely a conduct so tender, so maternal, raised her in my esteem & regard.

Dr. Wall was so drolly troublesome to me during the rest of the Time we stayed, that I hardly knew whether to be ⌐jolly,¬ or *angry*,—& so, I was something *between both*;—a very agreeable mixture, you'll allow. But he ⌐Romped¬ most furiously & made so many attempts to be rather too facetious, that I was fain to struggle most violently, to free myself from him: yet there was such a Comic queerness in his manner all the time, that, as I *succeeded* in keeping off ⌐caresses,¬ I could not but be highly diverted with him. The Girls, Betsy & Beckey, were upon the *high Gig* all the Time, for they enjoyed seeing me thus whisked about of all things.

When, at last, we took leave, he said *he should often think of Miss Fanny*,—there was *something so Comical in her*.

We went in a Coach & Four, in the same manner as before. Harry Davis came to the Door as we left the House. I believe he was watching for our coming out. He kept us Talking as long as he could, & then,—off we went, extremely well pleased & satisfied with our Expedition.

⌐Richard we left behind, as his Gloucester Business obliged him to stay till Saturday. Mr. Gale attended us on Horseback.

In our Journey Home, we were rather *muzzy*,—& nothing happened,—unless I tell you of a foolish Quarrel I had with Edward,—which, indeed, was some what extraordinary, as I believe I may look upon him as my very best Friend in this House. But he did not seem to enjoy himself during the whole of our Expedition, & he had looked forlorn & out¬ [|] [?of sorts]

[*At this point at least 4 leaves have been cut away, as indicated by 4 detached stub fragments pinned together. At the top of the next page FBA has annotated*: ※ ※ visit to Westwood.]

[?We] ⌐⟨all⟩ sallied forth together, & strolled about the Field till supper was ready.

Nothing could be more ridiculous than the Conversation of Richard during this Walk: he hardly knew a Word he said, & told the same stories, & gave the same accounts, fifty Times over: & took such *extra good* care of me, that I had full employment in managing him.

During supper he was equally absurd, & *Bothered* himself so much, that he never knew what he was talking about: yet *talk* he would, & *Laugh*, too, though told to be silent a thousand Times both by my Uncle & Miss Humphries.

O sweet Effect of Intemperance!—how dearly do those who indulge it, pay the forfeit of their folly!⌐37

July—

My Visit to Westwood, which was to have taken place last Week, was pos[t]poned, *for* reasons, & *by* accidents which I shall not trouble you with relating,—for all the little in & out circumstances of these sort of affairs, have so little interest or importance to recommend them, that it is not one Time in a thousand they are worth mentioning. But on Tuesday Evening I had a Note from Nancy, who was there, to tell me that Sir Herbert Packington38 would call upon me in his chaise the next morning, if it would be *agreeable* to me to accompany him to Westwood, to stay a few Days. I ⌐graciously⌐ assented, &, accordingly, at about 1 o'clock, the Baronet arrived.

As you have the satisfaction of knowing him,39 I must deny myself the pleasure of describing his Person, which, otherwise, I should think well worth Description, for its excellent Ugliness. He is, however, very good natured, extremely civil, & uncommonly hospitable.

Our Journey proved very *yea* & *nayish*;—Beckey longed vastly to accompany us,—& I, for my part, extremely longed that she should,—but what *Argufied*40 that?—We might as ¦ well

37 This comment is the only direct evidence we have that Richard Gustavus Burney may have suffered from a chronic drinking problem. Alcoholism may account in part for his sometimes bizarre behaviour elsewhere in these journals.

38 Sir Herbert Perrot Pakington (d. 1795), 7th Bt (1762), of Westwood Park, Worcestershire. Westwood is 7½ m. NE of Worcester by way of Droitwich, the nearest town.

39 SEB had evidently met him during her visit to Worcester the previous year.

40 FB may be echoing Smollett; *OED* cites both *Peregrine Pickle* (the earliest example) and *Humphrey. Clinker*.

not have longed at all, for the good it did us,—but Beckey is a sweet open Hearted Girl, & totally free from pride,—she *owns* all her wishes with the utmost sincerity,—which, by the way, very few people condescend to do; for they always chuse to be thought to *despise* whatever they cannot obtain. Well, to return to Sir Herbert & my fair self,—why perhaps you will be glad to hear our Conversation,—for we had a Tête à Tête of full two Hours long,—& in that Time, much might be said,—I have known many a good thing hit upon in a quarter of the Time. I can't pretend to give you all the *particulars*, but for the *Heads* of the Discourse, they were as follow. Viz, the Weather,— The Hay,—& Dr. Dodd.[41]

Now you will allow, that to make those three subjects last 2 Hours, must require no small art of expatiating: & I hope you will honour us accordingly.

Now the reasons why I do not give you further particulars, are as follow:

Viz, *Imprimis*, as to the Weather, I have now forgot *clean & clear*, whether it was good or bad.

Secondus, as to the Hay,—it has been so often spoilt, that the subject is melancholy, & I am afraid it should give you the vapours.

Thirdly, as to Dr. Dodd, the poor man is Dead, & I would have his Name rest with his Ashes.

All these circumstances considered,—the Journey drops,— & you behold me safely arrived at Westwood.

Here, again, my Descriptive Talents are rendered useless;— for you have forestalled a most excellent account. What is to be done in this Affair of urgency?—must that venerable Castle,—its antique Towers,—it's formidable Turrets,—its Noble Wood,—its

> Windows—that exclude the Light
> And passages—that lead to Nothing,—[42]

must they all, all pass unnoticed?—why, ⌈Sukey,⌉ I protest to

[41] William Dodd (1729–77), LL. D, divine, hanged for forgery on 27 June. A popular preacher who had fallen into dissolute ways, he was executed despite the intercession of Samuel Johnson and a petition signed by 23,000 people.

[42] Thomas Gray, *A Long Story*, ll. 7–8. CB owned copies both of *Designs by Mr. R. Bentley, for Six Poems by Mr. T. Gray* (1753), in which *A Long Story* first appeared, and William Mason's edition of Gray's *Poems* (1775) (*Lib.*, pp. 26, 34).

you I have not had so good a subject since I left you,—& now, I might as well have none!—

Indeed, for the future, I must beg leave to visit places with which you are wholly unacquainted,—for here, my Genius is perpetually curbed,—my Fancy nipt in the Bud,—& the whole Train of my descriptive powers cast away, like a ship upon a desert Island!—

Very like a ship, indeed,[43]—a marvellous good simile! &, as to the Desert Island,—why, to be sure, Worcester is some-what Inhabited,—but what of that?—'tis a marvellous good simile,—because the *less* like, the *more marvellous*. So, you see, I have made it out, as clear as the sun at Noon Day,—but, now, I think of it, a string of similes will rather better suit the Taste of Mrs. Esther than yours, therefore I shall set about a flowery Epistle to her, by the first convenient opportunity this side Christmas, &, in the mean Time, I must descend to plain, vulgar matter of fact, from which I have, I know not *how*,— nor will *you* easily find *why*, thus long digressed.

I was very much pleased with the House & situation at Westwood: with the *House*, for its antiquity, & the singularity of its style; & with the *situation*, for its retirement, prospects.[44] Lady Packington[45] received me most ⌜graciously,⌝—& she shewed me the utmost civility & attention during my stay. I think her a rather fine Woman of her Age, & sensible & notable: but she is *parading*, & tolerably uncultivated as to Books, & Letters, & such little Branches of Learning: ǀ She is, also, so immoderately fond of her mansion, that she will scarse

---

[43] Probably an echo of Polonius's 'Very like a whale' (*Hamlet*, III. ii. 400).

[44] The house and its surroundings are illustrated in T. Nash, *Collections for the History of Worcestershire* (1781–2), i, facing p. 350. The house was built in the reign of Queen Elizabeth 'as a lodge or banquetting-house', and enlarged by the Pakington family after the Civil Wars. 'Westwood house consists of a square building, from each corner of which projects a wing in the form of a parallelogram, and turretted, in the stile of the Chateau de Madrid near Paris, or Holland-house. It is situated on a rising ground, and encircled with about two hundred acres of oak timber. The richness of the wood combining with the stateliness of the edifice forms a picture of ancient magnificence unequalled by any thing in this county. A lake designed to cover one hundred acres, and now extending itself over sixty, is a great ornament to the eastern side of the park' (ibid. i. 351).

[45] Elizabeth née Hawkins (d. 1783), daughter of Caesar Hawkins (1688–1752), sister of Sir Caesar Hawkins, 1st Bt. (1778), widow of Herbert Wylde of Ludlow, Salop; m. (1759) Sir Herbert Perrot Pakington.

suffer anybody to pass a *fly*, if it is upon one of her Windows or Tables, without remarking how well it stands, or how beautiful it looks. But I find she did not become mistress of this great House early in life, which accounts for that pride of possession that Time & early use might have diminished, but which her late arrival at makes her feel in all its Juvenile force & vivacity.

Miss Packington[46] & Miss Dolly[47] are both good sort of Girls,—but have nothing extraordinary, & consequently I can by no means presume to press your further acquaintance with them.

But the most agreeable circumstance of my Visit remains to be told,—namely, that *Miss Waldron*[48] was at Westwood the two first Days of my residence there. Now, as you know nothing of her but from Richard's Imitation, I shall take the liberty to enlarge upon her person, Character & behaviour. She is short, thick set, fat, clumsy, clunch & heavy: but her Face is very handsome; she has pretty blue Eyes, & a most brilliant Complection, with a Colour the finest that can be. She is very good natured, & is not *a natural*,—that is, not an absolute Ideot,—but she is the veriest *Booby* I ever knew: she cannot speak, without making some blunder; she is so *bothered* in every speech, that she is eternally contradicting herself; she never speaks without exciting mirth, yet seldom discovering the *cause*, she always joins in the *effect*, & Laughs as simply as she makes others do artfully: &, at the same Time that her ignorance invites pity, her happiness renders it ⌐superfluous.¬

She was, indeed, the very *quintessence* of sport during the Visit; every body Laughs at her with little or no ceremony, but Nobody affronts her: she takes all in good part, & if you do but *tell* her she is not the subject of your mirth, she is thoroughly satisfied, & Laughs on herself without further enquiry.

At Dinner Time, she was the general *Butt*, Sir Herbert piques himself upon *shewing her off*, & makes ridiculous Comments upon every thing she says; Lady Packington sneers, &

---

[46] Elizabeth Pakington (d. 1813), m. (1793) William Russell of Powick (see above, p. 236 n. 59).
[47] Dorothy Pakington (*c.*1763–1846) (*GM* cxvi¹ (1846), 334).
[48] Elizabeth or Hannah Waldron (b. 1756), daughter of the Revd John Waldron (see below, p. 280; IGI; Hartlebury registers (copy), Society of Genealogists).

exposes her to the strongest ridicule; the young Ladies titter unmercifully;—even Nancy's smiles border upon the full grin;—&, for my part, I Laughed most heartily; yet was nobody more merry than herself. I would fain give you a specimen of the Conversation, that *you* might Laugh too,—but, unless I could *paint* her, & shew you, at the same Time, the extreme vacancy of her Countenance,—& give you some idea of the *drone* of her Voice, & of her unmeaning manner,—I could hope for no success at all equal to my wishes, or to the subject.

When Dinner was over, Lady Packington took me a long Walk, to shew me the park, plantations, & various improvements which Sir Herbert has lately made; & they were extremely well worth seeing,—at which I rejoiced the more; because I found it extremely necessary to *say* so,—& that warmly, & repeatedly. No praise was too high,—nor could scarse any be sufficient to gratify her Ladyship's extreme greediness upon this subject. She then shewed me the spot upon which there was formerly ⌐a Chapel, belonging to a Nunnery: some fragments of Ruins are still left, & ancient Coins are frequently found when the Workmen are Digging. The Westwood House, she told me, was originally a monastery.[49]

My curiosity ⌐was⌐ a good deal excited to know some further more satisfactory particulars of this place, ⌐&⌐ I asked abundance of Questions, for I found her very ready to figure in the information way.

To my first enquiry, if she knew when the House was built, she said that it was began [*sic*] in the Time of the *Romans &* *Saxons*:—no difference, to be sure, *which*! But, when I came to more close Quarters, she told me that they had accounts of it so far back as *Henry the first*![50] this was a sad falling off, after naming the *Romans*: but, afterwards, she added: '&, indeed, I believe we have so late [*sic*] as Richard the first.'[51] Very in-

---

[49] See above, p. 274 n. 44. The Benedictine nunnery at Westwood dated back to the reign of Henry II (1154–89). 'The nunnery stood where the kitchen-garden now is; there are no remains, only in digging they sometimes find stone coffins, and foundations of buildings' (Nash, i. 350, 351).

[50] Henry I (1068–1135), King of England, 1100–35.

[51] Richard I (1157–99), King of England, 1189–99.

genious, was it not? to come *forward* in her Dates *4* Reigns, &
all the Time suppose she was going *back*? From this Intelligence, so accurate & satisfactory, I could not but regret that
she did not communicate her materials to some able Historian.

After Tea, the rest of the Evening was given to music: the
Performance of the Miss Packingtons exactly tallied with the
expectations your account of them had given me; &, ⌐really,
all their disadvantages considered, I think they do Nancy great
credit.¬[52]

At supper, Miss Waldron was requested to *sing*; she declined it for some Time, saying 'I don't sing at all well;—you'll
only think I'm a squalling,—for I don't know any thing of the
music,—so sometimes I'm *in* the Tune, & sometimes I'm out
of it,—but ⌐ I never know which. And so it's the same with my
Brother,[53] for he sings just as I do; we both squall, after a sort,
but it is n't very well.'

We all, however, pressed her very much, & Sir Herbert in
particular, 'Come, *Lillies* & *Roses*, (that is the name he gives
her,) come, give us *Guardian angels*,[54]—come, tune your pipe,
—now!—quick!'

'Ay, come, Miss Waldron, cried Lady Packington, give us a
fine Italian air,—I suppose, Miss Fanny, you are very fond of
Italian music?'

'Lord, my Lady, cried Miss Waldron, I really don't know
the music at all,—I'm sure I shall only frighten you.'

'O, we *know* you don't, returned she, but never mind, you
can let us hear your Voice.'

'Come, Lillies & Roses, said Sir Herbert, don't be too long,—
begin at once.' Chucking her under the Chin.

---

[52] Cousin Nancy was their musical tutor; see below, p. 279.

[53] Miss Waldron perhaps means her eldest brother Edward Waldron (1758–1813),
MA (Oxon.), 1782; rector of Hampton Lovett and Rushock, Worcs., 1807–13. Her
other brothers were John (1760–*post* 1794); Thomas (1762–?1813); and George
(1765–1829), MA (Oxon.), 1808, rector of Elmley Lovett, Worcs., 1800–23 (*GM*
lxxvii² (1807), 662; lxxxiii² (1813), 94; IGI; will of John Waldron (*c.*1725–94), PCC,
prob. 11 July 1794; Hartlebury registers).

[54] Probably the 'favourite' song of that title performed by Ann Catley (1745–89) in
The Golden Pippin, a burletta (by Kane O'Hara) first staged at Covent Garden in 1773
and most recently at the same theatre on 11 Mar. 1777. It was published as a single
sheet folio by Robert Falkener (copy, BL H. 1648. F.(21.); see also Highfill; Maxted;
LS 4 iii. 1692–3, 1858; *LS 5* i. 64).

'Ay, do, Miss Waldron, said Miss Packington, or else you'll make us expect too much.'

'Do you know no pretty new song? said her Ladyship.

'No, my Lady, I know hardly any songs,—that is to be sure. I dare say I know above a Hundred,—but I don't know the music of 'em.'

'Well, any thing,—just what you please, cried Lady Packington, only don't make us wait,—for that is not very well worth while.'

'Why then, if you please, my Lady, said she, I'll sing "before the Urchin well could go,"[55]—only I can't sing it very well,—so I tell you that before Hand.'

'Is *that* by way of something new, Miss Waldron?'

Regardless of this question, the poor Girl began:—and never before did I hear any thing so ludicrous: she has not even a natural good *voice* to excuse her miserable performance: on the contrary, it is a *Croak*, a *squeak*,—Nature has been as little her Friend as Art has been her Assistant.

For some Time, I sat in an Agony, almost killing myself by restraining my Laughter;—but finding that Nobody else took the same trouble, by degrees I began to excuse it myself, & very soon after took the general liberty which example gave me, & Laughed without controul or disguise.

She could not get on *3 words* at a Time, on account of the confusion, for she caught the Laugh, & stopped to join in it; & then, like a Noodle, the moment she recovered her own Countenance, with the utmost solemnity, she again began the song.

Nothing affected her, in the manner any other person would have been affected for the merriment she excited only served, occasionally, to *interrupt* her, but she never thought of stopping it by ceasing to sing,—the *only* way in her power. Nay, *Sir Herbert*, though the *most* desirous to hear her, took such methods to render her ridiculous, as must have most cruelly *affronted* any other character in the World: he burst out a Laughing in her Face; patted her Cheeks, slapped her shoulders, chucked her under the Chin, & exclaimed '*Brava*, Lillies & Roses!' perpetually:—but, it was *all one to her*, for whenever she could

---

[55] i.e., *The Fair Thief*, by John Worgan. The song dates back at least to 1758, when it appeared in *Clio and Euterpe, or British Harmony* (1758–9), i. 137.

conquer her own foolish tittering, she made up a Face of stupid composure, &, with the utmost indifference, began her song again.

Sir Herbert, determined to spare no pains to expose her, finding how well she ⌜took⌝ all he had ⏐ hither to offered, at length took up a large spoon, & fairly *entered it* down her Bosom, where the opening of her Handkerchief left a most inviting vacancy.

I expected that this stroke would have raised some spirit; but she *continued* her song with the same gravity, only, & with the utmost deliberation, taking the spoon out, & quietly putting it into it's place!

The interruptions, however, in spite of her own Tranquility, were so frequent, that, as she always *began again* upon any stop of her own, she could get no further than the two first Lines: & the case, now, appearing desperate, with regard to this song, Sir Herbert desired her to begin another.

'Come, Lillies & Roses, now try Guardian Angels.'

'Ay, do, Miss Waldron, said Lady Packington, and never mind the Girls,—don't stop for their Laughing.'

'No more I would, my Lady, said she, only that I can't help it,—for they make *me* Laugh too.'

Guardian Angels was then begun,—but so long was it in performing, that we all retired the moment it was sung: & really I was glad of a little *relaxation* from Laughter: though I did not obtain it immediately, for as Miss Waldron slept in the next Room to ours, she Undressed herself in company with us. & she was so entertaining the whole Time she stayed without having the least design or knowledge of being so, that when I went to Bed I was quite weak and exhausted.

Thursday morning she came to sit with me, till Lady Packington was ready for Breakfast, ⌜—as Nancy & the young Ladies were practicing down stairs.⌝

She then gave me a very circumstantial account of her Life & employments, & told me all her Affairs ⏐ with as much openess & unreserve as if she had known me many years. I will recollect what I can of her Relations. &, when you read what she says, you must suppose it spoken in a very *slow* & *slovenly* Voice.

As Richard teaches ⌜Dancing⌝ at the school which her

Father[56] keeps at Hartlebùry, the Conversation began by my enquiring if they did not *make very merry* when he was among them?

'Why, yes, he's merry enough, sometimes;—only he must n't be so with our young Gentlemen: but he makes fun enough with my Brother, sometimes, they two'll Laugh like any thing,—but it's mostly at my expense! but the thing is, I don't much mind 'em, for it's all one to me; for if I was to mind it, they do it as bad again.'

'Well, but, I hope *you* Laugh, too?'

'Yes, I Laugh enough, too, some times; but then when I do, my Brother says I'm just like a Jack ass in fits;—besides, I must n't Laugh much, when my papa's at Home, because if I do, he says, "come, let's have no more Noise; it's all Levity;—" but I talk enough, for all that, sometimes, for M[r] Smith & Mr Giles[57] say they can hear me at their House, I talk so loud,— & that's as far off as half a mile, almost, I believe;—but I've enough to do, some times, because of our young Gentlemen, for I've no Time to myself;—I'm always doing some odd Job or another,—yet you'd think I do nothing,—& no more I do,—only papa says I've a mind to make a fuss about it: but I never get up till past 9 o' | clock,—Lady Packington would be finely angry if she knew it, for she'd say it was all a whim,— but I never tell her about it, but I'm tired as any thing before Night,[58] for our young gentlemen will have their own way, & one has enough to do to content 'em all.'

'But I hope Mr. Waldron will leave off his school soon, or else that you will settle some where else,—for it must be a fatiguing Life to you—'

'No, he won't leave it off,—& indeed I like it very well,— we *both* like it, because the thing is we've found the profits of it. For before my Papa kept that school, he had but 60 pounds

---

[56] The Revd John Waldron (*c.*1725–94), BA (Oxon.), 1746, MA (Cantab.), 1768; rector of Hampton Lovett and of Rushock, 1768–94. He had been schoolmaster of Hartlebury Grammar School since 1751. Sir Herbert Perrot Pakington was his patron. He m. (1755) Mary Wilmot (d. 1766) of Bromsgrove (Hartlebury registers; Nash, i. 540; *Vict. Co. Hist.* [*Worcs.*], iv. 527).

[57] Neither has been identified.

[58] At this point the middle of the leaf has been cut away from the top. The middle fragment is in the Barrett Collection, BL Egerton 3690, fo. 143.

year;—& you know that would do nothing, to Live upon, with 8 children:[59] it wasn't half enough. And another thing is, I never get any Dinner,—so that's bad enough for me, when I'm at Home, & so I'm glad enough to get out, sometimes: I'm sure I'm never so happy as at Westwood, for I Eat what I like.'

'But how comes it about that you have no Dinner?'

'Why as soon as ever I sit down to Dinner, I'm forced to begin helping the young Gentlemen,—& so by the Time I have helped them all round, why[60] him as I helped first, is ready to begin again, & so then I can get none at all: for if I was to put myself a bit by, they'd think I took the best: so I only Eat a bit of Bread & Cheese.'

'Well, but that's very hard upon you: I wonder you don't make them wait a little?'

'Why there's nothing I love so well as Bread & Cheese;—I prefer it to meat a great deal. Sometimes I'm as dirty as can be,—& I hardly know how, for I do nothing: but one Day a Gentleman came to our House, he's one of my Cousins,[61] so he said to me very gravely, says he, do pray get me a wash Hands Bason, & a[62] Towel, & a piece of soap: so I went, & [?found] that I could not bring them all at once, so I'd two Journeys for my pain, never suspecting all the while what he meant: so when I'd brought 'em, he gets up, & he falls to scrubbing the Towel with the soap as hard as ever he could: & then, he comes up to me, & says, "Now you've taken the trouble to bring the things, I must have the pleasure to wash your Face, for it's as black as soot." So you can't think how angry I was, for I said, says I, could n't you as well have said to me at once,

---

[59] There seems to be some confusion here. Waldron's appointment to the Hartlebury School (in 1751) apparently antedated his marriage by 4 years (see above, p. 280 n. 56). He was ordained a deacon at Worcester in 1747, and priest in 1749. His windfall year was 1768, when he received his livings at Hampton Lovett and Rushock, besides being named chaplain to the E. of Coventry. Only 5 of the Waldron children have been identified, of whom only the 4 brothers named in p. 277 n. 53 are mentioned in the father's will.

[60] Here the bottom of the leaf has been cut away (middle fragment, Barrett, bottom fragment, Berg).

[61] Perhaps son of her aunt, Mrs Aubery, mentioned below. Not further identified.

[62] Top of leaf cut away from middle fragment here.

go & wash your Face; as to give me all this trouble to bring the things here for nothing?'

When we were summoned to Breakfast, 'I think, said she, I may as well put away my things this morning, because may be Lady Packington may take the whim to come in my Room, for perhaps she may have a mind to shew you the House herself: so I think I had best be before Hand with her,—for she's very particular, you must know.'[63]

We then descended: &, after Breakfast, Lady Packington was so civil as to go entirely over th[e] House with me: & it is so large, that she was quit[e] fatigued by the Time we returned to the Parlour.

The Weather was, unfortunately, very indifferent duri[ng] my stay at Westwood, which prevented my enjoying any Benefit from the beautiful Pool, which [|] is in the park, though Sir Herbert was so obliging as to plan a Water Excursion every Day, for he was very desirous to shew me his Barge, & to display all the beauty of his largest pool, which is reckoned the finest in England, being more than two miles long, & proportionably wide: however, the Weather never allowed of any such scheme being put in execution.

Not withstanding I Laughed so intolerably at Miss Waldron, I continued so well to satisfy her that *she* was not the Object of my mirth, that we were exceeding good Friends, and she invited me very cordially to make her a Visit at Hartlebury: ⌐'you know, said she, your Cousin Richard comes every week, —so do you *try to persuade* him to bring you along with him:⌐ & then we'll go together to Stour port: but you must let me know when you come, or else I sha'n't be Dressed, for I always go any how at Home,—you can't think what a Figure I am;— now if you come without telling me first, I'll tell you how you'll find me: I shall have on a Cotton Gown, & a muslin Handkerchief about my Neck, & a Cloth Apron, may be, & quite a close Cap;—for I never do my Hair up when I'm alone, for I don't much mind our young Gentlemen, & I shall have on a red stuff Coat; & now I'll lay you any thing you will that's the way you'll find me?—'

---

[63] Bottom of leaf cut away from middle fragment here.

I ventured not to lay *against* her, because I thought her rather too much in the secret.

While I Dressed for Dinner, she gave me her company & Conversation;—&, indeed, there was no person in the House I so much desired to have with me, for she was always as *good as a Comedy* to me.

She marvelled very much at the quantity of my Hair, &, bidding me look at hers, said 'See, what a little I have, & my Hairs as low as any thing,—& for all that, it's all a falsity!— only see:—one Day, one of the Curls ˡ came off, and Master Packington[64] tied it to the Bell;—I am often angry enough with Master Packington, for he was always doing something or other to me.'

I enquired of her whether she ever Danced ⌜Before⌝ when Richard was at her Father's at Hartlebury.

'Why, said she, I used, sometimes, when a new young Gentleman came, & Mr Richard Burney had no partner to Dance with him, because then he used to ask me. But he never does now.'

'Do you wish he did?'

'I like Dancing of all things,—only I don't Dance at all myself,—not well, I don't: for I'm always a falling down. & Lady Packington makes such Game of me for it, you can't think. But I've left off Dancing now, for one of our young Gentlemen affronted me.'

'Affronted you?—how was that?'

'Why he kicked me, here, upon the shin,—& you can't think how he hurt me,—so I said then I would never Dance with the young Gentlemen any more.'

I then asked her to sing to me: she immediately complied, & I *squeezed* in my Laughter with great decency.

When we came down, Lady Packington took her to task for not being Dressed herself: & the poor Girl looked so foolish, that nobody could refrain from *smiling*, at least.

When she was going, as her Journey was, for the present only to Droitwich, which is but two miles from Westwood, Lady Packington said she would take that opportunity to

---

[64] Presumably the eldest son, John Pakington (1760–1830), who succeeded his father as 8th Bt. in 1795.

shew me more of the Park, & to give me a drive round the pool: Accordingly, I attended her Ladyship in seeing Miss Waldron to Mrs. Aubery,[65] her aunt. I was very sorry to leave her, for I had, by no means the same entertainment after ⸢she was gone⸣: indeed I *told* her that I was sure we should not be *so merry* when she was gone—& she seemed extremely pleased at the Compliment. ❘

[*top of page cut away*]

The next Day, as it Rained all the morning, we could not Walk out: therefore Lady Packington produced some Coins she had had very lately dug out by the Nun's Chapel, & then got Rapin's History of England,[66] & we went to Work in viewing the Coins of the different Reigns, in order to discover the Age of those she had found. She is fond of figuring upon these subjects, but yet she shewed so much ignorance of History, as to render her researches truly ridiculous: for so little did she know of the matter, that she always took it for granted that every king of the same Name followed in regular succession;— and so, when we had examined the Coins of Henry the second, 'Now, said she, we'll come to Henry the third,'[67]—but happening, instead, to meet with Richard the first, with the same correctness, she looked for Richard the second:[68]— ❘

[*The bottom of this page and top of the next have been cut away. In the following passage FB seems to be describing a fair at Droitwich.*]

⸢we were told there was *a surprising little Woman*,[69]—at another, *Wild Beasts*, at another, the *learned Horse*, & at another very fine shows, we did not, however, chuse to regale ourselves at any of these places, but, when James had led me about to shew me the Town,—which, indeed, is not worth shewing, we had a charming stroll Through the Park, & then returned Home: though we found supper had waited for us near an Hour,—to our great *shockation*.[70]

---

[65] Not further identified.
[66] Paul de Rapin-Thoyras (1661–1725), *The History of England* (15 vols, 1725–31) and later edns., trans. by Nicholas Tindal (1687–1774) from *Histoire d'Angleterre* (10 vols., The Hague, 1724–7).
[67] Henry III (1207–72), King of England, 1216–72.
[68] Richard II (1367–1400), King of England, 1377–99.
[69] Presumably a dwarf or midget.
[70] This humorous formation is not in *OED*. Cf. '*fussation*', above, pp. 175, 263.

The next morning, there was to be a public Breakfast at Droitwich: & Nancy & I called again upon Miss Tayler,[71] & accompanied her & her party to the Green where it was held. James was obliged to return to Worcester.

I was never in any place where I saw so much unmixed ordinary Company before: a set of Apprentices stiff in new Cloaths, & a set of Farmers' Daughters vulgar in gay ones, formed almost all the Company.

There was, however, good diversion [xxxxx *2 words*] the Danc[ing]⌐

44   [St Martin's Street,
                                      *c.*15 September 1777]

To Thomas Lowndes

AL (Comyn), Sept. 1777
Single sheet folio, 1 p., wafer
Addressed: Mr Lowndes | Fleet Street
Annotation (in an unknown hand): Write to Dr Watson Longman for 1st Vol of Edinb ⟨Pope⟩ wch W. Davis left with him
The MS is in vol. i. of a grangerized copy of *DL*. It is dated by the reference to CB Jr.'s 'return to the university in a fortnight', i.e., on Michaelmas Day, 29 Sept.

Sir, The MS. concerning which I troubled you last winter, is at length finished, and if the perusal of the 2 first volumes has given you any desire to see the last, I will consign it to your care, whenever you are able to give it immediate examination.

I must, also, entreat you will be so good as to inform me what time of the year will be most expedient for [publish]ing the Work.

The Gentleman [CB Jr.] who is so kind as to be my Agent in this Business, will be obliged to return to the university in a fortnight,[72] and therefore, as it is my desire to transact this affair by no other Deputy, I shall be sorry to part with the

---

[71] Not identified, but perhaps related to the Taylers of Lynn (see *EJL* i. 9 and n. 28).

[72] CB Jr. had been admitted a pensioner at Caius College, Cambridge, the preceding Jan.

Copy, unless it will be convenient to you entirely and finally to settle this matter before that Time expires. If this should not, at present, be in your power, I will defer sending the M.S. till January, when I hope to again see my Friend in Town.

The uprightness and openness with which you have dealt determine me not to consult with any other of your Profession previous to being acquainted with your opinion and intention.

    I am,
      Sir,
         Your most obed^t h^{le} ser^t

—————————.

⟨Let me beg⟩ favour of you to direct for me, as before, [xxxxx *1 word*] to be left at the Orange Coffee House

45   [St Martin's Street,
                              pre 27 September 1777]

To Thomas Lowndes

AL (Comyn), late Sept. 1777
Single sheet 4to, 1 p.
Annotation (in an unknown hand): Porte Royale Greek Gram^r & Letter⟨s⟩
Directed to Mr Roberts at White Horse Fetter Lane
The MS is in vol i. of a grangerized copy of *DL*.

I am much ashamed, after having been myself so slow, to talk of haste to *you*; but as my young Friend acquaints me, his Time will not be at his disposal after next Saturday [27 Sept.], when it must be devoted to the pursuit of his studies, I am obliged, though very unwillingly, to beg a decisive answer with all the speed in your power and convenience, as to your opinion of the MS. now under your inspection, for I am so peculiarly situated, that I can by no means entrust the management, or even the knowledge of this affair to any other agent.[73]

---

[73] Lowndes did not reply until Nov. See below.

46 [St Martin's Street,
1 October 1777]

To Esther Burney Burney

ALS, in the possession of Professor Margaret Doody, Princeton University, Princeton, New Jersey.
Single sheet, 1 p.
Transcript kindly supplied by Professor Doody.

St. Martin's St: Oct\[r] 1 1777:

Sister Charles Burney,
Please to send me an Invitation to spend the Day with you to-morrow. When I come, I will give you sufficient Reason to rejoice & make glad.[74]

The excuse to be *fudged* up for this purpose, I leave to your own ingenuity.

Write a Note that I may make public.

Provide a very genteel Dinner, but don't get more than 2 Courses & a Dessert, as I hate a fuss. Specify in your Note that I must not get away early. If you fail, you will be ready to break your Heart when you know more.

Yrs. F.B.

[*The following is Lowndes's reply (Barrett) to FB's letter of* pre *27 Sept. FBA has annotated it* N° 6 1777]

Sir
I've read this 3\[d] Vol & think it better than 1 & 2\[d] If you please I'll give you Twenty Guineas for the Manuscript and without loss of time put it to Press

yr obed\[t] Serv\[t]
Tho\[s] Lowndes

Fleetstreet
Nov\[r] 11

[74] FB was probably planning to reveal to EBB her authorship of *Evelina*, and its imminent publication. The need to 'fudge up' an excuse in a 'public' note underscores the continuing tension between the Burney daughters and their stepmother. EBB was presumably regaining her strength at home after giving birth to her 5th child, Sophia Elizabeth, on 26 Sept. (CB's verses 'To my daughter Esther on the birth of her 5th child, Sept\[r] 26\[th] 1777', in his 'Poetical Notebook', Osborn shelves c 33, pp. 127–9).

[St Martin's Street,
                                       post 11 November 1777]

To Thomas Lowndes

AL (Comyn), Nov. 1777
Single sheet 4to, 2 pp.
Addressed: Mr Lowndes | Fleet Street
The MS is in vol. i of a grangerized copy of *DL*.

Sir, I am much gratified by your good opinion of the M.S.
with which I have troubled you; but I must acknowledge that,
though it was originally written merely for amusement, I
should not have taken the pains to Copy & Correct it for the
Press, had I imagined that 10 Guineas a Volume would have
been more than its worth.

As yet the work has been seen by no human Eye but your
own & mine; if, however, you think it's value inadequate to
this sum, I would by no means press an unreasonable Demand;
I shall, therefore, only beg the favour of you to deliver the 3^{d}
Volume to my Friend,[75] who will call for it to-morrow evening.
My intention is to submit it to the perusal of a Gentleman who
is much more experienced in authorship business than myself,
& to abide by his Decision.

Should his opinion coincide with yours as to the Value of
the MS, I will immediately & frankly return you the ^{l} three
volumes & upon your own terms;—but if this should not be
the case, I will give you no further trouble than that of begging
you to receive my apologies & thanks for what you have already
taken.[76]

    I am,
      Sir,
        Yr most obed^{t}
          & most h^{le} ser^{t}

———— ————

[75] By the time of this letter FB's cousin Edward Francesco Burney had taken CB
Jr.'s place as her courier. See *Mem.* ii. 131 and below.

[76] It is not known whether in fact the 3rd vol. was returned to FB and subsequently
shown to a 'Gentleman' friend. FB may have meant to show the MS to SC. In any
event, SC did not see *Evelina* until after its publication, and FB agreed to the lower
sum. See *EJL* iii.

[*The Burney family received a double blow in Oct. of this year. In the first place, Bessy Allen, who two years before had been sent with the Stranges to Paris in hopes that she would 'improve' there (see above, p. 192), rewarded her parents' good intentions by eloping to Ypres with an adventurer, Samuel Meeke. They were married in the Reformed Church there on 12 Oct. 1777 (extract in the St Margaret's Church baptismal registers, King's Lynn; HFB, pp. 70–2; Lonsdale, pp. 240–2). The event is reported in the following manner by Mrs Elizabeth Draper (1744–78), Laurence Sterne's 'Eliza', who was a friend both of EAB and of the Stranges. Writing from London on 20 Nov. to Mary Bruce Strange in Paris, she observed: 'poor Mrs. Burney a fatality seems to attend her, I think, with respect to the Establishment of her Children, but the little Gypsey, in question, must have been an Hypocrite in her Heart, for I remember, in the only tête a tête, I ever had with her, that she inveighed particularly against the impropriety of English Girls choosing for themselves without the Consent of their Parents, and instanced in her own case, as a piece of good fortune, her having been educated in Paris, where they inculcated very different Notions—I was pleased to hear her express herself so seriously on the Subject, as I thought it a kind of security for her never following the example of her Sister [MAR], and indeed, I do not remember that I was ever more taken with a Girl at first sight than I was with this little Simpleton, for that she has been such, in her choice, is most certain if the one half of what is said of her Man is true—Who by the way, seems to be a Bankrupt in fame as well as Fortune, in short my dear, the least said of him, I beleive, is the best, as every new light seems to throw an Additional Odium on his Character—Unhappy Girl I have no doubt but she is doomed to Experience Poverty and Wretchedness, in spite of her Ample fortune and former good Prospects—pray, is she Married? I am told, that even this is a doubt—poor Mrs. Burney—I have not seen her since her return from France [EAB had gone to Paris in Aug. with the intention of taking Bessy home with her to England], they tell me that she avoids Company, and is a prey to the most disquieting Apprehensions—who can wonder at this especially if she is kept in Suspence with regard to her Child's change of Name, or not—' (cited in W. L. Sclater, 'Letters Addressed by Eliza Draper to the Strange Family 1776–1778', Notes and Queries, clxxxvii (1944), 30–1; see also A. H. Cash, Laurence Sterne: The Later Years (1986), pp. 270–304, 343–7).*

The second blow fell about the last week of Oct. when CB Jr. was expelled from Cambridge for stealing books. Years later FBA suggested to his son, Charles Parr Burney, that the future classical scholar and collector committed the theft out of a 'MAD RAGE for possessing a library', and that he subsequently sold some of the purloined books to London booksellers only 'from the fear of discovery' (FBA to Charles Parr Burney, 26 Feb. 1818, JL x. 795 and n. 4). It is more probable, though, that his love of gaiety and lack of prudence as a young man caused him to incur heavy debts, possibly aggravated by gambling, and that he sold the books to avoid discovery, not of the theft, but of the debts (see R. S. Walker, 'Charles Burney's Theft of Books at Cambridge', Transactions of the Cambridge Bibliographical Society, *iii (1962), 323–4* and passim*). In any case, his hurt and furious father refused to let him come home to London, banishing him instead to the country (ibid., pp. 314–15).*

The wayward Bessy and her husband settled at Geneva, and in 1778 CB Jr. enrolled in King's College, Aberdeen, as the first step in his 'rehabilitation'. The thoughtless acts of the two children caused their family to begin the new year in an atmosphere of gloom. But that gloom would soon enough be dissipated by the publication of Evelina *and the fame this event brought to FB.]*

APPENDIX 1

FANNY BURNEY'S FIRST LETTER
TO THOMAS LOWNDES

THIS is an early draft, single sheet 4to, 1 p., of FB's first letter to the publisher. For the version actually sent, see above, p. 213. The draft is in the Barrett Collection, with *FBA's annotations*: ✳ Nº 1 To Mr. Lowndes | *Bookseller, Fleet Street.* | *Dec' 1776.*

Sir,

As an author has a kind of natural claim to a connexion with a Bookseller, I hope that, in the character of the former, you will pardon me, although a stranger, for the liberty I take of requesting You to favour me with an Answer to the following queries.

Whether You will take the trouble of candidly perusing a MS. Novel sent to You without any public Name, or private recommendation?

Whether it is now too late in the Year for printing the first volume of the above MS. this season?

And whether if, after reading, you should think it worth printing, you would buy the Copy without ever seeing, or knowing, the Author?

The singularity of this address, you may easily imagine, results from a singularity of situation.

I must beg you to direct your Answer to Mr. King, To be left at the Orange Coffee House till called for.

I am, Sir, your very humble Servt

——— ———

Mr. Lowndes.

APPENDIX 2

A LETTER OF MRS ELIZABETH ALLEN BURNEY TO FANNY BURNEY

ANNOTATED by FBA as 'in the style of a certain Lady—', this letter from her stepmother (2 single sheets 4to, 4 pp., Berg) is dated 11 July and was written in 1778. It is given here as probably an accurate reflection of EAB's eccentric conversation and manners. It recalls Kitty Cooke's assessment of her, as reported by FB: '. . . she's such a queer fish,—to be sure, for a sensible woman, as she is, she has a great many oddities . . . for, you know, for such a good soul as the Doctor to have such a Wife,—to be sure there's some thing very disagreeable in her,—Laughing so loud, & hooting, & clapping her Hands,—I can't love her, a nasty old Cat,—yet she's certainly a very sensible woman' (Journal for 1778 (Berg), p. 651; see *EJL* iii; *HFB*, p. 39). The letter is *addressed*: Miss Fanny Burney— | at Mrs Hamilton's | Chessington | near Kingston | Surry *and postmarked* 13 IY

A postscript by SEB is omitted here.

St. Martin's Street.

July 11th

I can tell you but this, Madam Fanny, whatever you may think on't, that now the little curled Devils have done tormenting & every thing is settled to Y^r fancy about them Morthers the Paynes, in such a sort o' way, I desire that you'l not take it into y^r fancy, to expect any more letters from me till I hear again from you!—do you hear that goody?—for before I began to write I was as tired as a Dog with towing out my hair—only I w^d write, that I was determined upon, merely to ask you to write me word in y^r next what Crisp thinks of the Dab Chick Patty Payne—& that big lord'ling girl her sister—& their brother,—dear cre'ter—Id have given worlds to have been present at the meeting—So pray dont forget—for as he may not take it into his fancy to come croaking up to Town for this age to come, I can't hear the acc^t thro' any other Channel.—I think Chessington air is very likely to be of g^t service to Patty P. if one may judge by you—Im sure I never saw such an alteration in my days in any human being, as in you the day before you left Town, when all your aunts & Cousins came to take leave of you, & when I saw you last.

I suppose Chess: must be divine at present—I dare say the fruit is in high perfection—ours is very plentiful, but we have strawberries so often that to be sure they put me in mind of Thompson's shoulder of Mutton.—That wretched creter Piozzi came in while we were eating some the other night, but he w^d n't chew any, for he had been eating a dinner at the Panton St. Hotel 'till he c^d n't see out of his eyes!—but says I 'stay & see us eat, we wont eat you'—He mullied something between his teeth in French that I c^d n't rightly hear 'what does the man say'? cried I—to wch Sukey or Susey, Susey or Sukey, its all one I suppose, answered 'He says he never eats any Ma'am' 'Why then my dear Man, says I, as madam Young said to old Mother Cooper *its time you sh^d.*'—but I c^d n't persuade him to it!—

That nibbetting yepping thing wretch stands gloring over my papers, & says she wonders what I am writing; but I tell $^|$ her wondring is n't good for her—& to stop her yep have sent her for a wafer—when Im as young as her, & she's as old as me, I'll do as much for her—tho' I believe I might as well have gone for it myself, for as Dean Swift says there's nobody's work so well done as those that do it themselves.—

You must know I'm a little out of yumer just now—for I've just been having a disputation with Madam Sukey—I can't for the life of me persuade her that Aguara's voice is not superior to Gabbrielli's—to be sure I'm no judge, [just] know what pleases me—I only say *I* dont [like] that violent furious style of singing—it goes thro' my head!—but Gabbrielli's is so round & so soft & so sweet, it runs quite warm down the marrow of my back!—

I suppose you may have heard that Madam Chas Burney has parted with that Stothering Creter Betty—to be sure she was the dirtiest of all human beings—I believe she said some little dirty things of me once—but keep never heeding she need n't put herself in trouble for if I was to meet her at Madam Burney's I sh^d say 'how d'ye do Betty?' nevertheless, I believe;—but she'l never be good for anything while her eyes are $^|$ open—the creter is to me aversion upon aversions—she was so rude the last time I drank tea with her mistress when I only wanted her to bring me up a glass of water—that tho' I went to the top of the Kitchen stairs & cried 'is this body here'? half a hundred times she never made me any answer! tho' I'll take my oath she heard me.—if you dont write soon, I shall Conclude that you re either sick or sulky—so pray do, & believe me to be &c &c—

I hear that little Dickey is now ascending the temple of Science in the art of drawing.

626-633   Appendix 2

APPENDIX 3

FANNY BURNEY'S LETTER TO ESTHER BURNEY, JULY 1770

THE MS of this letter, missing for a century, surfaced at auction in California after the first volume of *EJL* had gone to press. The letter is reprinted in *EJL* i. 136, 138 from *ED* i. 101–2. Mrs Ellis normalized the text and also introduced 3 minor verbal errors. The MS is an ALS, single sheet folio, 2 pp., *addressed* To | Miss Burney | Chesington
and annotated (by FBA) 1770

The annotation is in brown ink, not in pencil, as incorrectly noted by Mrs Ellis. The month, 'July', which she says was there, is now worn away. The MS now belongs to Miss Paula Peyraud of Chappaqua, New York, who has kindly supplied the editor with a photocopy for transcription here.

My dearest sister

With a very short Time to write, and a very great deal to say, I take up my Pen to thank you most heartily for your comfortable Letter—I had thought it very long on the Road. —We are now in Daily expectation of the important Letter from Papa—& let me say one thing—it seems to me not unlikely that immediately as Papa receives the last Pacquet, he will write to my Uncle—I hope therefore that you have ere now acquainted him with your affairs, or else that you directly will, as it would be shocking for him to hear of it first from abroad, & as he would then perhaps always believe that you intended to secret it from him.

How it can have got about, god knows, but every body here speaks of your marriage as a certain & speedy affair—So you will have it in Town—I fear mama cannot go—as for me, I am ready to break my Heart when I think of being absent from you—O that it were in my power to quit this place directly!—but I hope all for the best—indeed I cannot bear to *suppose* I shall be away from you.—Miss Allen goes to Snettisham to-morrow, is too busy to write, but will from thence, Susette's best love attends you—I have had a sensible & affectionate Letter from my Cousin which I beg you to thank him for in my name—

Sweet Chesington!—abominable Lynn!—

My dear Hetty I shall write myself in the vapours & then give them to you—or I will have done—but I must say how much I admire your Plan of Life—certainly it would seem very strange for you to have gone to the Coffee House ¹ for all his & your own acquaintance will be visiting you on the occasion. I will write to you the very instant we hear from Venice—my kindest & best love to my ever dear Mr Crisp & to dear Kitty—Let us know about the Barborne's when you can—Adieu my dearest dear sister—I am in much haste— my first wish is to be with you—God forbid I should not!— believe me ever with the utmost affection

Your   Frances Burney

INDEX

This is an index of all proper names in Fanny Burney's text and of selected names in the introduction, annotations, and appendices. In general, women are given under their married names unless they first appear under their maiden names. Similarly, peers are given under their titles unless they are first mentioned before their elevation. For the most part, works are cited under the author (translator, editor), composer, or artist. Main biographical notes are indicated in boldface.

Abel, Carl Friedrich (1723–87), composer 191 n.

Abington, Mrs Frances (1737–1815), actress 94

Abyssinia xii–xiii, 44

Addison, Joseph (1672–1719) 194 and **n.**

Admiralty, London 41, 105, 206

Adonis 188

Adventure (ship) xii, 41 nn.

Africa 10, 44

Aguiari (Agujari), Lucrezia (1743–83), singer xii, 73–80 and **nn.**, 93–4, 98–100, 115, 151, 154–6, 160, 167–8, 171–2, 175, 178–80, 209–10, 212, 293

Aikin, Miss *see* Barbauld, Mrs

Ailesbury, Charles, 3rd E. of (1682–1747) 175 and **n.**

Aleppo 100, 102

Alexandria 100

Allen, Elizabeth ('Bessie' *or* 'Bessy'), later Mrs Meeke (1761–*c.*1826), FB's stepsister xiii, xvi, 32, 36–7, 113, 127, 162, 167, 192, 289–90

Allen, Mrs Mary, née Maxy (*c.*1705–76), EAB's mother 11, 13–14, 17, 19, 23–4, 206 n.

Allen, Maxey (*c.*1730–1804), of King's Lynn, EAB's brother 41

Allen, Stephen (1724–63), King's Lynn merchant, EAB's 1st husband xvi

Allen, Revd Stephen (1755–1847), FB's stepbrother, xvi, 74

Allen, Mrs Susanna, née Sharpin (1755–1816), wife of above 74

Allen, William Maxey (1792–1865) xvi

Amazons 92–3

America 80, 105, 197, 228

Andrews, Thomas (*c.*1746–1813), ship's surgeon 198 and **n.**

Andromache 92–3

Anfossi, Pasquale (1727–97), composer: *La Marchese giardiniera* (opera) 67, 79

Anguish, Mrs Sarah, née Henley (d. 1807) 131 and **n.**

Apollo 101

Armstrong, Dr John (*c.*1709–79), physician, poet, essayist 7, 39

Arne, Dr Thomas (1710–78), composer 96 and **n.**

'Ye Fair Married Dames' (song) 199

Arrowsmith, Miss 251 and **n.**

Ashburnham, John, 2nd E. of (1724–1812) 186–8 and **n.**

Aubery, Mr ?281

Aubery, Mrs 284

Bach, Carl Philipp Emmanuel (1714–88), composer 77

Bach, Johann (John) Christian (1735–82), composer 226–7 and **n.**

Bagnall, Ann Maria, later Mrs Scott (*c.*1755–1809) 100, 102

Bagnall, John (d. 1802), of Erleigh Court 100, 102

Banks, Sir Joseph (1744–1820), Bt, naturalist 41, 59–60, 62, 92

Barbauld, Mrs Anna Laetitia, née Aikin (1743–1825), poet, writer 21 and **n.**

'Come Here Fond Youth' 21

Poems 21

Barborne Lodge, Worcester 40 n., 46, 200, 264

visit to 231–3, 235–51

Baretti, Giuseppe (1719–89), writer 17–18

Barlow, Thomas (b. *c.*1751), FB's would-be suitor xiv-xv and n., 115–29 and **n.**, 135–49, 151–4, 157–8, 163–4

letters of 117–18, 139–40

letter to 148

Barnes, Mrs, of Gloucester 266–7

Barrett, Mrs Charlotte, née Francis (1786–1870), FB's niece 205–6

Barrington, William Wildman, 2nd Visc. (1717–93) 189–90 and **n.**

Barsanti, Francesco (1690–1775), composer 114, 150

Barsanti, Jane ('Jenny') (d. 1795), singer, actress 3 n., 81, 94, 114, 135, 150, 161–2, 198–9

Barsanti, Mrs 81, 114

Barthélemon, François-Hippolyte (1741–1808), violinist, composer 37

Bartolozzi, Francesco (1727–1815), engraver 12 and **n.**

Bath 252–3

Bauer, Friedrich Wilhelm von (1731–83), German general 180 and **n.**, 183–5

Beatson, Helena ('Nelly'), later Lady Oakeley (1762–1839), artist 5 and **n.**, 8, 9, 70–1, 202, 204–5

Beatson, Robert (b. 1758, living ?1804) 204–5 and **n.**

Bell, Michael (c.1751–73), victim of Maori massacre 43 and **n.**

Bell Inn, Gloucester 260 n., 265

Berkeley, Frederick Augustus, 5th E. of (1745–1810) 253 and **n.**, 256–61

Berkeley, George Cranfield (1753–1818) 261–3 and **n.**, 269–70

Berriedale, John Sinclair, styled Ld. (c.1756–89), later 11th E. of Caithness 32 and **n.**, 37

Bewley, William (1726–83), surgeon, apothecary 38–9, 134

Blake, Anne 34–6 and **n.**

Blake, Diana 34–6 and **n.**

Blake, Elizabeth 34–6 and **n.**

Blake, Jane (d. 1798) 34–6 and **n.**

Blake, Rachel 34–6 and **n.**

Blake, Sarah 34–6 and **n.**

Blomefield, Sir Thomas (1744–1822), Bt, army officer 156

Boccherini, Luigi (1743–1805), composer 131 and **n.**

Bodville, Mr 93

Bodville, Mrs 93

Boone, Charles (c.1729–1819), MP 172 and **n.**, 177, 182

Booth Hall, Westgate Street, Gloucester 260

Boston, Massachusetts 91

Boswell, James (1740–95), journal-writer, biographer xiii, xiv n., 96 and **n.**

Life of Johnson xiii–xiv and n.

Bottarelli, Giovanni Gualberto, librettist: *Armida* 54

Bouverie, Mrs Henrietta (Harriet), née Fawkener (c.1751–1824) 196 and **n.**

Bradmore 37

Bristol 135, 150, 162, 208

Bristow, William (d. 1803), naval officer 105 and **n.**

British Museum 74

Broad Street, London 37, 103

Bromfield, William (1712–92), surgeon 98, 166, 169, 179

Brooke, Elizabeth, later Mrs Welles (living 1794) 237 and **n.**

Brooke, Mrs Frances, née Moore (1723/4–89), author 4–9, 54–6, 78, 94, 160, 163, 165

Lady Julia Mandeville 163

Brooke, Hannah, later Mrs Skey (living 1794) 237 and **n.**

Brooke, Revd Dr John (1709–89) 8, 55, 165

Brooke, Susanna (living 1794) 237 and **n.**

Brown, Thomas (1663–1704): 'I Do Not Love You, Dr. Fell' 126

Bruce, James ('Abyssinian') (1730–94), explorer xii–xiii, 44–5 and **n.**, 81–94, 98–102, 104, 108–11, 114–15, 179, 181, 199, 203, 222

Bruce, Thomas Bruce Brudenell, B., later E. of Ailesbury (1729–1814) 175 and **n.**, 182–3

Brudenell, Hon. Anne, née Legge, later Lady Brudenell (d. 1786) 172–3 and **n.**, 175–6, 179, 185

Brudenell, Hon. James, later 5th E. of Cardigan (1725–1811), MP, 172 and **n.**, 179, 182, 185, 187

Buckinghamshire, John Hobart, 2nd E. of (1723–93) 171 and **n.**

Bund, Mrs Catherine, née Dandridge 236 and **n.**

Bund, Mary, later Mrs Probyn 236 and **n.**

Burgoyne, Gen. John (1723–92) 105 and **n.**, 110

Burney, Mrs Ann, née Cooper (c.1690–

1775), FB's grandmother xiv, 116–17, 119, 123, 135–6 and n., 144, 157–9, 163

Burney, Ann (1722–94), FB's aunt xiv, 116–17, 119–20, 123–24, 135, 136 n., 157–8, 163–4, 248

Burney, Ann ('Nancy'), later Mrs Hawkins (1749–1819), FB's cousin 236, 238, 253, 255, 261–2, 266–7, 270, 272, 276–7, 279, 285

Burney, Dr Charles (1726–1814), music historian, FB's father 6–33 and *passim*

 FB's obedience to and love of xiv, 127, 137–8

 sterling character and qualities of xv–xvi, 16, 24, 26–7, 29, 36, 119, 138, 147, 149, 168, 224, 233

 health 4, 46–7, 52, 54, 66, 106, 112, 134, 159, 206

 condemns *La nouvelle Héloïse* 21

 youthful appearance of 28–9

 buys house in St Martin's Street 32

 industry and busyness of 36, 40, 99, 112, 161, 167, 177

 international fame 75

 speaks in favour of Barlow as FB's suitor 146, 152

 relents about Barlow 147, 164

 fear of offending general opinion 178

 low opinion of musical performances in church 186 n.

 becomes foreign correspondent for and buys a share of the Pantheon 210 n.

 his campaign against Hawkins's *History of Music* 221 n.

 told by FB of her approaching Lowndes with a novel 233

 his anger at CB Jr.'s dismissal from Cambridge 290

Sunday musical parties xi, 33 n., 87–91, 100–102, 129–34, 169–77, 180–91, 210–12   ,

 General History of Music xi, 30, 32–3, 81, 88, 96, 112, 159, 163, 174, 199

 German Tour ?7, 26, 55, 79

 'Lesson' by 133

 'Ye Fair Married Dames' (sets for Barsanti) 199

Burney, Revd Dr Charles (1757–1817), FB's brother xi, 96, 167, 209, 213–15 and n., 217, 231, 285–6, 289–91

Burney, Charles Crisp (1774–91), FB's nephew 54 **n.**

Burney, Charles Parr (1785–1864), FB's nephew 289

Burney, Charles Rousseau (1747–1819), musician, FB's cousin, EBB's husband xiv, 29, 40, 63, 68, 74, 78, 87–9, 94, 101–2, 116–17, 128, 131–3, 135 n., 144, 146, 152, 154, 155 n., 167–70, 174–5, 178, 182–3, 187, 189–90, 191 n., 200, 212, 222, 295

Burney, Charlotte Ann (1761–1838), FB's sister xvi n., 32, 36, 54, 95, 97, 103–4, 127, 153, 167, 205–6, 208, 213 n.

Burney, Edward Francesco (1760–1848), artist, FB's cousin 201, 233 and **n.**, 235, 237–9, 241–5, 247, 249–51, 255–61, 267, 271, 288

Burney, Mrs Elizabeth, née Allen (formerly Mrs Allen) (1728–96), FB's stepmother xii, xvi, 4 and n., 6–8, 11, 13, 19, 22–5, 28–9, 31–3, 35–7, 39, 42, 46–7, 54–5, 60–2, 66–7, 81, 83, 85, 90, 101, 103, 108–10, 112–13, 117–18, 120, 124, 127, 134, 136, 138, 140–1, 144, 151–2, 165, 167, 170, 177, 183, 189, 191, 202, 204–8, 222, 230 n., 287 n., 289, 295

 letter of 292–4

Burney, Elizabeth Warren ('Blue') (1755–1832), FB's cousin 233, 235, 237–43, 245, 247, 250, 255, 257, 260–3, 267–8, 271

Burney, Mrs Esther, née Sleepe (1725–62), FB's mother 104, 147

Burney, Mrs Esther ('Hetty'), née Burney (1749–1832), FB's sister xiv, 11, 28–9, 42, 46, 54, 63, 66, 74, 76–8, 87–8, 98–9, 101–3, ?115, 116, 119–21, 123, 126–8, 131–3, 135, 146, 148–50, 152–3, 166–70, 171 n., 172, 174–5, 178, 182–3, 187–8, 190, 200, 203, 208, 210, 212, 222, 224–5, 246, 271, 274, 293

 letter of 121

 letters to 287, 295–6

Burney, Frances ('Fanny') (1752–1840), journal-writer, novelist:

 her powers of observation and description xii and *passim*

 her shyness, propriety, prudishness

Burney, Frances ('Fanny') (*cont.*):
15–16, 20–22, 56, 81, 86, 153, 176, 181, 183, 185, 263 *see also* amateur performance (and stage fright)
her thoughts: on coquetry 3; on the general superiority of men 3; on the moral superiority of women 3; on the barbarity of bullfighting 14; on the levity of Continental women 24; on the civility of foreigners 34; on the melancholy of being a physician 39; on art and nature 63; on crayons and oil painting 68; on the need to cultivate great talents 78; on marriage and spinsterhood 119–20, 125–9, 138, 152, 164; on female modesty 220
her knowledge and study of Italian and Latin 11, 15, 17, 30 and n., 208
works as CB's amanuensis xi, 32–3, 213
amateur performance (and stage fright) in plays at Barborne 235–53, 262–3
illnesses 4, 58–9, 207, 255, 257–60
grief at death of mother and Grandmother Sleepe 104, 147
love of CB and SC and dislike of EAB xvi, 32, 127, 147, 232
rejection of Thomas Barlow xiv–xv, 115–29, 135–49, 151–4, 157–8, 163–4
first meeting with Dr Johnson and Mrs Thrale 223–29
visits: to Chessington 32–3, 45–52, 220–22, 232; to Barborne Lodge, Worcester 231–3, 235–51; to Gloucester and Gloucester Cathedral 251–71; to Westwood 271–84; to Droitwich 284–5
her journals and correspondence (qualities of, her thoughts on, etc.) xi, xiv, 1–4, 32, 45–6, 57–8, 64–6, 73–4, 104–5, 107–10, 115, 165, 180, 191, 199, 205–7, 219
'Caroline Evelyn' xi, 213 n.
Evelina (composition and publication of) xi, xv, 213–17, 219–21, 223, 231–3, 235, 285–8, 290–1
Teignmouth Journal (references to) 58, 65–6, 73–4, 105, 110
'*A Treatise upon politeness*' (proposes to write) 48–50

Burney, Hannah Maria (1772–1856), FB's niece 236–7, 244–50
Burney, James (1750–1821), naval officer, FB's brother xii, 41–6, 54, 59–63, 80, 91, 104–5, 108, 110, 163, 189, 194, 197–8, 200, 206–7
Burney, James Adolphus (1753–98), FB's cousin 229, 232–3, 237, 240–1, 243, 245, 247–51, 253, 256–7, 259, 261–2, 267, 270, 284–5
Burney, Rebecca (1724–1809), FB's aunt xiv, 116–17, 119–20, 123–24, 135–6 and n., 157–8, 163
Burney, Rebecca, later Mrs Sandford (1758–1835), FB's cousin 229 and **n.**, 232–3, 237, 241–3, 245, 248–50, 255, 257, 267, 271–3
Burney, Richard (1723–92), of Barborne Lodge, Worcester, FB's uncle 223, 229, 230 n., 232–3, 235–8, 240, 242–3, 246, 265, 272, 295
Burney, Richard Allen (1773–1836), FB's nephew ?40, 42
Burney, Richard Gustavus (1751–90), FB's cousin 232, 237, 240–5, 247, 249–51, 253–4, 256–7, 259–63, 265–7, 269–72, 275, 279–80, 282–3
Burney, Richard Thomas (1768–1808), FB's half-brother 32, 37, 40, 54, 61, 151, 162, 187, 195, 294
Burney, Sarah Harriet (1772–1844), FB's half-sister 97, 158, 163, 208
Burney, Susanna Elizabeth, later Mrs Phillips (1755–1800), FB's sister 6, 9, 11, 13, 21, 23–5, 27, 54–5, 59–60, 67, 76, 81, 94–5, 101, 112–14, ?115, 124, 127, 140, 145, 147, 150, 153, 167–8, 170, 172–3, 182, 187, 190, 193, 202, 208, 213 n., 225, 230–1, 265, 293, 295
letters to 40–2, 45–52, 219–22
Burney, Thomas Frederick (1765–85), FB's cousin 237–9 and **n.**, 245
Burrows, Revd John (1733–86) 202 and **n.**
Buxton, Derbyshire 159, 163

Caesar, (Gaius) Julius (100–44 BC) 172 n.
Cairo 100
Cambridge University 285, 289
Campbell, Archibald (?1726–80): *Lexiphanes* 224 n.

Carestini, Giovanni (*c*.1705–*c*.1760), singer 154 and **n.**, 180

Carlisle House, Soho Square, London 149

Carlton House 106

Caroline Matilda (1751–75), Queen of Denmark 147 and **n.**

Castell, Madame and Monsieur ?34, 39

Castle Street, London 94

Catherine II ('the Great') (1729–96), Empress of Russia xiii, 169, 170 **n.**, 181, 183, 185–6

Cavanagh, John (*c*.1742–73), victim of Maori massacre 43 and **n.**

Celestini, Eligio (1739–1812), violinist, composer 149

Cerberus (ship) 80, 105, 189 n.

Chads, Capt. James (d. 1781), naval officer 105 and **n.**, 110

Chamier, Anthony (1725–80), financier 173–4 and **n.**, 176, 181–3, 185

Chamier, Elizabeth ('Betty') 231 n.

Chamier, Miss 231 n.

Charing Cross Road, London 209

Charles Street, Covent Garden, London 94

Charlotte, Queen (1744–1818), consort of George III 163, 227

Chelsea 26, 30

Cheltenham 266

Chessington, Surrey xi, 1, 32–3, 45, 48, 52, 54, 57, 63–4, 73, 104, 107, 109, 117, 128, 134, 137, 154, 156–7, 163, 165, 176, 179, 200–1, 204, 209, 219, 223, 232, 292–3, 295–6

Chesterfield, Philip Dormer Stanhope, 4th E. of (1694–1773) xii, 33, 49, 62
Letters to His Son 33

Cholmondeley, Gen. James (1708–75) 56 and **n.**

Christian VII (1749–1808), King of Denmark 92 and **n.**

Cibber, Colley (1671–1757):
The Careless Husband 241
The Refusal 162

Cipriani, Giovanni Battista (1727–85), painter, draughtsman, engraver 12 and **n.**

Clarges, Sir Thomas (1751–82), 3rd Bt 129–30

Cleaveland, Lt.-Col. Samuel (*c*.1716–94), army officer 105 and **n.**

Cleland, John (1709–89):

The Dictionary of Love 22
Fanny Hill 22 n.

Clementi, Muzio (1752–1832), composer 68 and **n.**, 149

Clerke, Capt. Charles (1743–79) 200 and **n.**, 206

Clerke, Capt. Sir John (d. 1776) 206 n.

Cley, Norfolk 159

Clinton, Gen. Henry (1730–95) 80, ?105 and **n.**, 110

Coke, Thomas William, later E. of Leicester (1754–1842) 54 and **n.**

Colchester 79

Colla, Signorina 210

Colla, Giuseppe (1731–1806), composer 75–8 and **n.**, 154–5 n., 180, 210
Didone (opera) 155, 160, 165
Non hai ragione, Ingrato (aria) 155
Per salvare il mio Bene (aria) 76 n.
Son Regina e sono amante (aria) 155, 167–8

College Green, Gloucester 256, 259, 266, 269

Collins, Mr 91

Colman, George, the elder (1732–94), playwright 75, 114
The Clandestine Marriage 137
The Deuce is in Him 248

Constantinople 169

Cony, Carlos (*c*.1726–1806), attorney 38–9 and **n.**

Cook, Capt. James (1728–79), circum-navigator 42–4, 105, 200

Cooke, Papilian Catherine ('Kitty') (1730–97) 1 n., 47–52, 63, 98, 107, 156–7, 177, 191–2, 201, 205, 212, 221–2, 230, 292 n., 296

Cooper, Grey (*c*.1726–1801), MP ?172 and **n.**

Cooper, 'Mother' 293

Coram, Thomas (1668–1751) 20 **n.**

Correspondents, The (anonymous novel) 163

Corri, Domenico (1746–1825), composer 34, 149–50
Allessandro nell'Indie 34 n.

Corri, Signora, née Bachelli 34 n., 149–50

Corse Lawn, Gloucestershire 265, 270

Courvoisyois, Mademoiselle 46–9, 51

Coussmaker, Catherine, later Mrs Lindsay (*fl.* 1764–1803) 219 and **n.**

Coussmaker, George Kien Hayward (1759–1801), army officer 237–9 and **n.**, 252–6, 259, 261–2

Covent Garden Theatre 161

Coventry, Revd Francis (c.1725–59), writer: *Pompey the Little* ?172 n.

Cowley, Abraham (1618–67), poet 179 and **n.**

Craven, Elizabeth, Lady, née Berkeley, later Margravine of Brandenburg-Ansbach (1750–1828) 196 and **n.**

Crawford (Craufurd), Miss 103–4

Crawford (Craufurd), Mr 103–4

Crewe, Mrs Frances, née Greville (1748–1818) 196

Crisp, Ann (c.1696–1776), SC's sister 64–5 and **n.**, 73, 78, 81, 92, 107, 110, 142, 146

Crisp, Samuel ('Daddy') (c.1707–83) xi–xiv, xv n., xvi n., 32–3, 47, 49–52, 57, 98, 103, 117, 120, 152, 221–2, 232, 258, 288 n., 292, 296
  letters of 107–8, 121–4, 178–9
  letters to 1–3, 57–66, 73–8, 98–100, 104–7, 109–15, 125–38, 154–6, 158–77, 179–92, 201–12, 223–30

Cumberland, Henry Frederick, D. of (1745–90) 30 n.

Cumberland, Richard (1732–1811), playwight:
  The West Indian 161

Cupid 139

Cuthred (d. 754), King of the West Saxons ?267 and **n.**

Cutler, Samuel (c.1727–98), banker 230 and **n.**

Dagge, Henry (d. 1795), theatre manager 161 and **n.**

Davies, Cecilia ('l'Inglesina') (?1753–1836), singer 24 and **n.**, 25, 39, 74, 79–80, 94, 104, 106–8, 150, 156, 168

Davies, Henry ('Harry') (b. c.1757) ?257–60 and **n.**, 267–9, 271

Davies, Marianne (c.1743–?1816), glass harmonica player 24 and **n.**, 25, 79, 106

Davies, Thomas (c.1712–85), bookseller, author 22

Davies, Mrs (fl. 1744–86), mother of Cecilia Davies 24 and **n.**, 79, 106

Debbieg, Clement (d. 1819) 37

Debbieg, Hugh (c.1732–1810), army

officer 37, 103

Delabere, John (d. 1793) 266 and **n.**

Demidov, Pavel Grigor'evich (1738–1821), Russian aristocrate 174 and **n.**, 180, 184

Denmark 14

Devaynes, William (c.1730–1809), MP, banker 211 and **n.**

Devonshire, Georgiana, Duchess of, née Spencer (1757–1806) 202–4 and **n.**

Devonshire, William Cavendish, 5th D. of (1748–1811) 203 **n.**, 204

Dickenson, Miss xiv, 116–17, 123, 145, 157

Diderot, Denis (1713–84):
  Encyclopédie 225

Diede, Ursula Margrethe Constantia Louisa von, née von Callenberg of Huset Muskau (1752–1803) 128–9 and **n.**, 131–4, 188–90, 191 n.

Diede, Wilhelm Christopher von (1732–1807), Danish envoy to England 129 and **n.**, 132, 134, 188–9

Difesa d'Amore, La (pasticcio) 140 n.

Discovery (ship) 200, 206–7 n.

Docking, Norfolk 41

Dodd, Revd Dr William (1729–77), divine, writer, forger 273 and **n.**

Dodsley, James (1724–97), bookseller, publisher 213 n.

Donaldson, Mr (alleged lover of Mrs Yates) 55 n.

Dormer, Sir Clement Cottrell (1686–1758) 177 and **n.**

Dorset, John Frederick Sackville, 3rd D. of (1745–99) 67 and **n.**

Draper, Mrs Elizabeth (1744–78) 289

Droitwich 283–5

Drury Lane Theatre 40, 59

Dublin 162

Earle, William Benson (1740–96), philanthropist 130 and **n.**

Eckard, Johann Gottfried (1735–1809), composer 132 and **n.**

Edgcumbe, Emma, Lady, née Gilbert (1729–1807) 106 and **n.**, 171–5, 179, 182, 184–90

Edgcumbe, George, 3rd B. Edgcumbe of Mount Edgcumbe, later E. of (1721–95) 106 **n.**, 179, 187–9

Edward II (1284–1327), King of England 268 and **n.**

Egypt 85

Eichner, Ernst (1741–77), bassoonist, composer 131

Elmsley, Peter (1736–1802), bookseller 209 and **n.**

England 10, 42, 110–11, 155, 166, 169, 178, 183, 194, 282, 289

Epsom, Surrey 191

Europe 10

Facey, William (*c.*1747–73), victim of Maori massacre 43 and **n.**

Facton?, Miss 251

Farinelli (Carlo Broschi) (1705–82), singer 154 and **n.**, 180

Fell, Dr John (1625–86), Dean of Christ Church, Oxford 126 and **n.**

Fetherstonhaugh, Robert (*fl.* 1771–4), boarder at Chessington 52

Fielding, Henry (1707–54):
  Tom Thumb 164, 262–3
    performance of, at Barborne Lodge 236, 244–50

'Fiera in Mascherata' (masquerade) 113

Fisher, Mrs Elizabeth (d. 1780), theatre manager 161 and **n.**

Fitzgerald, Keane (*c.*1748–1831) 211 and **n.**

Fitzgerald, Keane (d. 1782) 211

Fitzgerald, Mary, later Mrs Fitzgerald (d. 1823) 211–12 and **n.**

Fleet Street, London 213–14, 217, 249, 285, 287–8, 291

Folkes, Sir Martin Browne (1749–1821), 1st Bt 156

Foote, Samuel (1721–77), playwright 98

Fordyce, Lady Margaret, née Lindsay (1753–1814) 85

Foundling Hospital Oratorio 20

France 188, 289

Frederick II ('the Great') (1712–86), King of Prussia 27 and **n.**

Furneaux, Capt. Tobias (1735–81) 41–3 and **n.**

Fydell, Elizabeth, later Mrs Betts ?151–2 and **n.**

Fydell, Frances ('Fanny'), later Mrs Rogers ?151–2 and **n.**

Gabrielli, Caterina (1730–96), singer xii, 74 and **n.**, 77, 155–6, 159–61, 165–9, 171–4, 177–8, 180, 184–5, 187–8, 293

Gabrielli, Francesca (b. *c.*1735), singer 160 and **n.**, 167, 169 n., 184

Gale, John (d. 1812) ?256–7 and **n.**, 261, 271

Galli, Caterina Ruini (*c.*1723–1804), singer, composer 160

Gallucci, Signora, singer 77 and **n.**

Gardner, Capt. Henry (d. 1792), army officer 110 and **n.**

Garrick, Arabella ('Bell'), later Mrs Schaw (1753–1819) 56

Garrick, Carrington (1751–87) ?56 and **n.**

Garrick, Catherine ('Kitty'), later Mrs Payne (1756–*post* 1822) 56

Garrick, David (1717–79), actor 40, 80, 94–7, 100, 227–9
  The Clandestine Marriage 137
  Isabella 59
  Lethe; or, Aesop in the Shades 227–8
  'The Mimic Blackbird, a Fable' 227
  'Ye Fair Married Dames' (song) 199

Garrick, David (?1754–95) ?56 and **n.**

Garrick, Nathan (1755–88) ?56 and **n.**

Gast, Philip (d. by 1748), Dutch merchant 64 **n.**

Gast, Mrs Sophia, née Crisp (*c.*1706–91) 64–5 and **n.**, 73, 104, 107, 110

Gay, John (1685–1732):
  The Beggar's Opera 189

Geneva 290

George III (1738–1820), King of England 31, 33, 59–61, 189, 193–4, 227–8

George IV (as Prince of Wales) (1726–1830) 31 and **n.**

Germany 26–7, 39

Giardini, Felice de (1716–96), violinist, composer 12–13, 25
  Ruth (oratorio) 20

Giles, Mr 280

Giordiani, Nicolina, singer 149 and **n.**

Gloucester, William Henry, D. of (1743–1805) 30 n.

Gloucester (city) xii, 238
  visit to 251–71

Gloucester Cathedral 259–60, 267–9

Gloucestershire 267

Golden Square, London 103, 159

Goldsmith, Oliver (*c.*1730–74):
  'Essay on the Theatre' 50 n.
  She Stoops to Conquer 50 n.

Grass Cove, New Zealand 43

Gray, Thomas (1716–71), poet:
A Long Story 273
Great Russell Street, London xii
Greville, Mrs Frances, née Macartney (c.1730–89), FB's godmother 203
Guines, Adrien-Louis de Bonnières, comte (later duc) de (1735–1806), French ambassador to England 179, 186 and **n.**, 188–9, 191 n.
Gurney, Thomas (1705–70), shorthand system deviser 230 and **n.**

Haller, Albrecht von (1708–77) 29 n.
Hamilton, Sarah (c.1705–97) 1, 47, 51, 57, 64, 66, 73, 104, 107, 109, 123, 128, 137, 154, 156, 165, 179, 201, 209, 212, 221–2, 230, 292
Hammersmith, London 16
Handel, George Frideric (1685–1759), composer:
The Messiah 20 n.
Harrington, Caroline, Lady, née Fitzroy (1722–84) 171 and **n.**, 174, 185
Harris, Bridget 237 and **n.**
Harris, Mrs Elizabeth, née Clarke (d. 1781) 130 and **n.**
Harris, James (1709–80), of Salisbury 128, 130–1, 133, 149, 174–5, 177, 179, 183, 185
Philosophical Arrangements 130
Three Treatises 130
Harris, Louisa Margaret (1753–1826) 128, 130 and **n.**, 133–4, 149
Harris, Thomas (d. 1820), theatre manager 161 and **n.**
Harrison, Capt. Thomas (d. 1768), naval officer 131 and **n.**
Harrison, Miss, later ?Mrs Hatton 131 and **n.**
Harrow School 163, 195
Hartlebury, Worcestershire 280, 282–3
Hartlebury Grammar School 279–80
Hatton, John Emilius Daniel Edward Finch (1775–1841) 13 and **n.**
Hawkesworth, John (1720–73), writer 26–7
Hawkins, Sir John (1719–89) 96
General History of the Science and Practice of Music 96, 221
Hayes, John (c.1708–92) 59–61
Hayes, Mr, of the Pantheon 212
Haymarket, London 167, 214
Hayward, Thomas (1706–81), MP ?256

and **n.**, ?259
Hayward, Miss 256 and **n.**, 259
Heidegger, John James (Johann Jakob) (1666–1749), impressario 55 and **n.**
Heinel, Anne Frédérique (1753–1808), French dancer 132 and **n.**
Henley, Mrs Catherine, née Hare (d. 1778) 41 and **n.**
Henry I (1068–1135), King of England 276 and **n.**
Henry II (1134–89), King of England 284
Henry III (1207–72), King of England 284 and **n.**
Hill, Thomas (c.1745–73), victim of Maori massacre 43 and **n.**
Hinchingbrooke (seat) 45, 59, 63, 196
History of Miss Pamela Howard, The (anonymous novel) ?217
Hoadly, Benjamin (1706–57), playwright:
The Suspicious Husband 114
Hodges, Sir James (d. 1774), publisher 9 and **n.**
Holcombe, Miss 256–9 and **n.**
Holkham, Norfolk 54
Holyland, Mary, later Mrs Smyth (d. 1806) ?110–11 and **n.**
Homer 179
The Iliad see under Pope, Alexander
Hoole, John (1727–1803), translator 3 **n.**
Horace (Quintus Horatius Flaccus) (65–8 BC), poet:
Opera (1770 edn.) ?209
Howe, Gen. William, later 5th Visc. Howe (1729–1814) 80, ?105 and **n.**, 110
Hoxton, London xiv, 125–6, 135–7, 140
Hull, Thomas (1728–1808), theatre manager 161 and **n.**
Humphreys (Humphries), Hannah (c.1724–96) 236, 238–9, 244, 265, 272
Hunter, John (1728–93), anatomist, surgeon 111 and **n.**, 114
Hunter, Dr William (1718–83), physician 94
Huntingdon, Francis Hastings, 10th E. of (1729–89) 55 n.
Hutton, Mrs Elizabeth (Betty) (c.1719–post 1780), cook ?293–4
Hutton, James (1715–95), Moravian Churchman xii, 26–33 and **n.**,

109–10, 114–15, 163, 165, 208
letter from 28–30
Hutton, John, footman 114, 124, 126, 140
Hutton, Mrs Louise, née Brandt (1709–78) 30 **n.**, 165, 208

India 103
Ireland 18–19, 191
Italy 39, 77, 99, 129

Jenner, Charles (1736–74), novelist:
The Placid Man 44
Johns, Edward (d. 1773), boatswain, victim of Maori massacre 43 and **n.**
Johnson, Dr Samuel (1709–84) xiii–xiv and n., 7, 18, 74, 96–7, 135, 159 n., 223–9
The Idler 225 n.
A Journey to the Western Islands of Scotland 135
Johnstone, Dr James (1730–1802), physician ?236 and **n.**
Johnstone, Dr James (1754–83), physician ?236 and **n.**
Jones, Edward (1752–1824), Welsh harper, historian, composer 131 and **n.**, 134, 149
Jones, Miss 231 n.
Jonson, Ben (c.1572–1637):
The Alchemist 95
Every Man in His Humour 143
Joseph II (1741–90), Holy Roman Emperor 25 and **n.**
Justamond, Mrs Ann, née Maty (b. 1748) 76 and **n.**

Keate, George (1730–97), writer xii, 34–6
'Burlesque Ode' 35–6
Ferney 34
Poetical Works 36 n.
A Short Account of Geneva 34
King, Revd Dr John Glen (1731–87) xii, 109, 112–14, 169–71, 181, 185, 186 n.
King's Bench, 206
King's College, Aberdeen 290
King's Lynn, Norfolk xvi, 24, 38, 41, 82, 195, 206–7, 296
King's Theatre, Haymarket (the Opera) 24, 55–6, 67–8, 101, 155, 160, 165–7, 171–2, 174, 184, 187, 194

Kingston-upon-Thames, Surrey 1, 52, 57, 64, 73, 104, 109, 128, 137, 154, 165, 179, 201, 209, 223, 292
Kinnaird, Margaret, later Mrs Wiggens (d. 1800) 34

Ladbroke, Ann, later Mrs Littler (d. 1791) ?20 and **n.**
Ladies' Own Memorandum Book, The 222
Lake, Sir James Winter (c.1742–1807), 3rd Bt, antiquary, collector 129 and **n.**, 133, 209
Lake, Joyce, Lady, née Crowther (c.1747–1834) 129 and **n.**, 133
Lake, Mary, later Mrs Webb 129 and **n.**
Lalauze, Charles (d. 1775), dancer, actor 16, 127
Lalauze, Miss, later 'Mrs Masters' (c.1754–?post 1809), dancer, actress, singer 153
Lawson, Francis (1737–1816), barrister 237 and **n.**
Lawson, Mrs Margaretta, née Cox (living 1816) 237 and **n.**
Lawson; Margaretta Ann Elizabeth, later Mrs Whatley 237 and **n.**
Leake, James (1724–c.1790), theatre manager 161 and **n.**
Leicester Fields 32, 52, 94, 148, 219
Le Sage, Alain René (1668–1747):
Le Diable boiteux 222
Lidderdale, Maria Georgina ('Liddy') (1742–87) 138, 151–2, 195
Lindsay, Lady Anne (1750–1825) 85 and **n.**
'Auld Robin Gray' 85 n.
Lindsey House, Chelsea 26, 30
Lock Hospital Oratorio 20
London 98–9, 103, 150, 219, 251, 261, 289–90
Long, Dudley, afterwards North, later Long-North (1748–1829) 211 and **n.**
Lovattini, Giovanni (fl. 1760–82), singer 79 and **n.**, 263
Lowndes, Thomas (1719–84), bookseller, publisher xi, 213 **n.**, 231–3
letters of 214–17, 287
letters to 212–17, 219, 285–6, 288, 291
Ludgate Hill, London 209
Lumisden, Andrew (1720–1801) 70 n., 192 and **n.**
Lumley, Mrs 261

Lyttelton, Apphia, Lady, née Witts (1743–1840) 163 and **n.**
Lyttelton, George, B. Lyttelton of Frankley (1709–73), poet 163 and **n.**
Lyttelton, Thomas, 2nd B. Lyttelton (1744–79) 163 and **n.**

Madan, Martin (*c.*1725–90), writer, composer 20 **n.**
Madras 94
Madrid 14
Mann, Revd Daniel (d. 1788) ?32–3 and **n.**
Manzuoli, Giovanni (*c.*1720–82), singer 171 and **n.**
March, Ld. *see* Queensberry, 4th D. of
March, Miss 94
Marivaux, Pierre Carlet de Chamberlain de (1688–1763), novelist, playwright:
  La Vie de Marianne 209
  Le Paysan parvenu 209
Market Lane, London 54–5, 94
Mars (god) 139
Martin, Dr Raymond Paul xvi
Martinelli, Vincenzio (1702–85), writer, adventurer 34
Mason, William (*fl.* 1672–1709), shorthand system deviser:
  La Plume Volante 230 n.
Maty, Louisa, later Mrs Jortin (1746–1809) 76 and **n.**
Maty, Martha (b. 1758, living 1812) 76 and **n.**
Maty, Mrs Mary, née Deners (*c.*1716–1802) 76 and **n.**
Maty, Dr Matthew (1718–76), librarian, writer 74–7
Meares, John (*fl.* 1775–9), militia officer 256–7 and **n.**
Meeke, Samuel (d. 1802) 289
Melville, Gen. Robert (1723–1809), army officer, antiquary 84 and **n.**, 87, 89
Merlin, John Joseph (1735–1803), instrument maker, inventor 68, 77, 87, 130–2, 134, 149, 212
Metastasio, Pietro Trapassi, called (1698–1782), poet:
  Didone 155, 160, 165
Mews Gate, Castle Street, Leicester Fields, London 193
Miers, Miss 261

Miller, Miss (*fl.* 1769–74), actress 75 and **n.**
Millico, Giuseppe (1737–1802), singer, composer 78, 155 n.
Milton, John (1608–74) 179
  Paradise Lost 101
Milton, William (*c.*1753–73), victim of Maori massacre 43 and **n.**
Minerva (goddess) 47
Mingotti, Regina, née Valentin (1722–1808), singer 171 and **n.**, 173
Molière (Jean-Baptiste Poquelin) (1622–73):
  Les Précieuses ridicules 121–2
Montagu, Mrs Elizabeth, née Robinson (1720–1800) 226–7 and **n.**
Montagu, George Brudenell, 1st D. of (1712–90) 172 and **n.**
Montaigne, Michel Eyquem de (1533–92), philosopher, essayist:
  Journal du voyage de Michel de Montaigne en Italie ?202
Monticelli, Angelo Maria (*c.*1710–64), singer 171 and **n.**
Montreal xvi
Moon (Moone), Mrs 47–50
Morning Chronicle 161–2
Mulgrave, Constantine Phipps, 1st B. (1722–75) 129
Mulgrave, Constantine Phipps, 2nd B. (1744–92), naval officer 44, 129
Murphy, Arthur (1727–1805), playwright:
  The Citizen 3 n.
  The Way to Keep Him 198
  performance of, at Barborne Lodge 238–44, 252–3
Murphy, Francis (*c.*1740–73), quartermaster, victim of Maori massacre 43 and **n.**
Müthel, Johann Gottfried (1728–88), composer 88 and **n.**
  Duetto 88 n., 133, 175, 182, 186

Naples 14
Newfoundland 103
New Orleans xvi
Newton, Sir Isaac (1642–1727) 32, 52, 176–7, 182 n., 226
New Zealand 42–3
Niceron, Jean Pierre (1685–1738):
  Mémoires pour servir à l'histoire des hommes illustres dans la république des lettres ?95

Nisbet, William (1747–1822) 98–102 and **n.**, 104

Noel, Miss 237 and **n.**

Nollekens, Joseph (1737–1823), sculptor 211

Nollekens, Mrs Mary, née Welch (d. 1817) 211 and **n.**

Normandy, Robert, D. of (1054?–1134) 268 and **n.**

Oberea *see* Purea

O'Connor, Mrs (*fl.* 1775–8) xiv, xv, 116–17, 119, 123–24, 136 n., 145–6, 157–8, 163–4

Ogle, Elizabeth Catherine, later Mrs Streatfeild (d. 1801) 183 and **n.**

Ogle, Revd Dr Newton (1726–1804), Dean of Winchester 170 and **n.**, 172, 183–4, 186 n.

Ogle, Susanna (1762–1825) 183 and **n.**

O'Hara, Kane, composer: *Guardian Angels* (song) 277, 279

Omai (*c.*1753–80) of Tahiti xii, 40 **n.**, 41, 44–5, 57–63, 91–2, 106, 182, 193–8, 200, 204

Onofrio (Onofreo), Signor (d. 1776), singer 165 and **n.**

Orange Coffee House, Haymarket, London 214–15, 286, 291

Ord, Mrs Anna, née Dillingham (*c.*1726–1808), bluestocking 130 and **n.**, 202–3, 210

Ord, Charlotte (1753–95) 130 and **n.**, 210

Ord, William (*c.*1752–89) 202 and **n.**

Orde, Thomas, later Orde-Powlett, later B. Bolton (1746–1807) 210 and **n.**

Orford, George, 3rd E. of (1730–91) 45

Orlov, Alekseï Grigor'evich, Count (1737–1808) xiii, 165, 169–71 and **n.**, 174, 177, 179–86

Orlov, Grigoriï Grigor'evich, Count (1734–83) xiii, 170 **n.**

Owen, Margaret (1743–1816) 224 and **n.**

Oxford University 111

Pakington, Dorothy (*c.*1763–1846) 275–7 and **n.**, 279

Pakington, Elizabeth, later Mrs Russell (d. 1813) 275–9 and **n.**

Pakington, Elizabeth, Lady, née Hawkins (d. 1783) 274–80, 282–4 and **n.**

Pakington, Sir Herbert Perrot (d. 1795), 7th Bt 272–3 and **n.**, 275–9, 282

Pakington, John, later 8th Bt (1760–1830) 283 and **n.**

Pall Mall, London 94, 106, 197

Pantheon 75, 77, 115, 155, 160, 172, 210

Panton Street Hotel, London 293

Paris 111, 162, 192, 289

Parma 74

Parma, Ferdinand, D. of (1751–1802) 74 and **n.**

Payne, Mrs Elizabeth, née Taylor (d. 1767) 193 and **n.**

Payne, James (1765–1809), bookseller 193 n.

Payne, Martha ('Patty') (1757–1803) 193 and **n.**, 208, 292

Payne, Sarah ('Sally'), later Mrs Burney (1759–1832) 158, 193 and **n.**, 208, 292

Payne, Thomas (1719–99), bookseller 193 and **n.**

Payne, Thomas (1752–1831), bookseller 193 and **n.**, 292

Penneck, Revd Richard (*c.*1728–1803) 75 and **n.**

Pepys, William Weller (1741–1825), later Bt 202–3 and **n.**

Peshall, Elizabetha-Maria, later Mrs Harwood (1763–1836) 231 **n.**

Peshall (formerly Pearsall), Revd 'Sir' John (1718–78) 231 **n.**

Peshall, John (1759–1820) 231 **n.**

Peter III (1728–62), Czar of Russia xiii, 169

Petrarch, Francesco (1304–74), poet 97

Phipps, Henrietta Maria (d. 1782) 44, 128–9, 132, 134

Piccinni, Niccolò (1728–1800), composer: 'É pur bella la Cecchina' (aria) 263

Piozzi, Gabriel Mario (1740–1809), singer, composer 293

Plymouth 206

Poggenpohl, William Henry (d. by 1814) xiii, 185 n.

Pompey (Gnaeus Pompeius) (106–48 BC) 172 n.

Pope, Alexander (1688–1744), poet: *Additions to the Works of Alexander Pope* 210

Epistle to Dr Arbuthnot 36

Epistle to Burlington 178

Iliad, trans. by 93

Portland Roads 206–7

Portsmouth 91, 105
Portugal 10, 14
Powel, Mrs 136 n.
Pringle, Andrew (d. 1803) 103
Pringle, Sir John (1707–82), 3rd Bt, PRS 114 and n.
Pringle, Robert (d. 1793), army officer 103
Pringle, Mrs Veronica, née Rennie (d. by 1791) 37, 102–4, 150, 153
Purea (Oberea) (d. 1775/6) of Tahiti 91–2 and n.

Queen Charlotte Sound, New Zealand 43
'Queen of Scots' (masquerade character) 92
'Queen of the Amazons' (masquerade character) 92
Queen Square, London xi, 1, 2, 27, 30, 38, 40, 52 n., 110
Queen Street, Golden Square, London 81 n., 94
Queensberry, William Douglas, 4th D. of ('Old Q.') (1725–1810) 185

Radier, Jean-François du (1714–80): *Dictionnaire d'amour* 22 n.
Rapin-Thoyras, Paul de (1661–1725): *History of England* 284
Rauzzini, Venanzio (1746–1810), singer, composer, harpsichordist 8 and n., 55, 77–8, .133, 159–60, 165, 167, 172, 179, 187–91, 192 n., 220
Piramo e Tisbè (opera) 133, 140 n., 176
'Fuggiam dove sicura' (aria) 133, 262–3
Read, Catherine (1723–78), painter 4 and n., 5, 6, 9, 68, 70–2, 94, 204
Reddish, Samuel (1735–85), actor, manager 135 and n.
Resolution (ship) 200, 206–7 n.
Reynolds, Sir Joshua (1723–92), painter 67–8
Richard I (1157–99), King of England 276 and n., 284
Richard II (1367–1400), King of England 284 and n.
Richardson, Samuel (1689–1761): *Sir Charles Grandison* 244
Rishton, Mrs Maria, née Allen (1751–1820), FB's stepsister xvi, 65, 92, 109, 134–5, 150, 204, 289, 295

Geneva journal of 58, 65
Rishton, Martin Folkes (c.1747–1820) 54, 134–5, 150, 156
Romans, the 276
Rosat, Mademoiselle 47–51, 201
Rosebery, Neil Primrose, 3rd E. of (1729–1814) 85 and n.
Rousseau, Jean-Jacques (1712–78): *Julie ou la nouvelle Héloïse* 21
Rowe, John (c.1745–73), master's mate 43 and n.
Royal Academy, London 112, 255
Royal Society, London 10, 59
Philosophical Transactions 191
Russell, Dr Patrick (1727–1805), physician, naturalist 100–102 and n., 202
Russell, William (1719–1801), surgeon ?236 and n.
Russell, William (1750–1812), barrister ?236 and n.
Russia 14, 169–70, 174, 184
Russo-Turkish War 184
Ryder, Thomas (1735–90), theatre manager 162 and n.

Sacchini, Antonio (1730–86), composer 67–8, 130, 133–4, 160
Armida (opera) 54
Motezuma (opera) 78
St Cecilia 68
St James's Park, London 203–4
St Martin-in-the-Fields, London 231
St Martin's Lane, London 175
St Martin's Street, London xi, xii, xiii, 32, 52, 57, 64, 73, 98–9, 104, 109, 125, 128, 137, 148, 154, 158, 165, 179, 200–1, 212, 214, 216–17, 219, 223, 285–8, 292
Salgas, Charles Jean de (c.1729–95) 31 and n.
Salisbury 130, 174
Sandwich, John Montagu, 4th E. of (1718–92) 45, 62, 98, 189, 194
Savoi, Gasparo (*fl.* 1765–77), singer, 160, 226
Saxons, the 276
Schindlerin, Signora, singer 80 and n.
Schobert, Johann (c.1735–67), composer 132 and n., 191 n.
Scotland 19, 32, 34, 84, 111, 149, 162
Scott, John (*fl.* 1748–76), publisher 9n.
Senesino (Francesco Bernardi) (d. by 1759), singer 154 and n.

Sestini, Giovanna (*fl.* 1774–91), singer 67 and **n.**, 79, 167

Seton, Alexander (1743–1801), of Edinburgh 103

Seven Years War 26–7

Severn River 252

Seward, William (1747–99), anecdotist 224 and **n.**, 227–8

Shakespeare, William (1564–1616) 238
Hamlet 189, 274
Julius Caesar 123
Macbeth 27
Much Ado About Nothing 164
Othello 113

Shannon (river) 191

Shebbeare, John (1709–88), writer 5–9 and **n.**
Letter to the People of England 5
Lydia (novel) 9
The Marriage Act (novel) 9

Shebbeare, Mrs Susannah, née Cornhigh (d. 1779) 7–8 and **n.**

Sheeles, Mrs Anne Elizabeth, née Irwin (*fl.* 1735–75) 104

Shepherd, Revd Dr Antony (1721–96) 13–15, 19–20, 23

Sheridan, Mrs Elizabeth Anne, née Linley (1754–92), singer 68, 130

Sicily 77

Simmons *see* Symons

Simpson (Sympson), Mrs Eleanor (d. 1797) ?179 and **n.**

Simpson (Sympson), James ('Jemmy') (d. by 1796), of King's Lynn ?179 and **n.**

Sleepe, Mrs Frances, née Dubois (d. by 1775), FB's grandmother 147

Smith, Mrs Mary, née Burrows (d. 1782) 202–3 and **n.**

Smith, Mr 280

Smollett, Tobias (1721–71):
Humphry Clinker 177

Smyth, Dr James Carmichael (1742–1821), physician, medical writer 37, 110–11

Snell, Powell (*c.*1738–1804), militia officer 256 and **n.**

Snettisham, Norfolk 295

Society Isles 43

Solander, Dr Daniel Carl (1736–82), botanist 59–62

Solly, Samuel (*c.*1724–1807), merchant 100–101 and **n.**

Southampton Street, London 94

Spain 10, 11, 14, 19, 22

Spring Garden Gate, St James's Park 153

Stanhoe, Norfolk 207

Stanhope, Mrs Eugenia, née Peters (d. 1783) 33 **n.**

Stanhope, Hon. Philip (1732–68), diplomatist xii, 33 and **n.**, 62–3

Stanley, John (1712–86), composer, organist 3 n., 4 n.

Stanley, Mrs Sarah, née Arlond (d. by 1786) 3 n., 4 n.

Steele, Sir Richard (1672–1729):
The Funeral 3 n.

Sterne, Laurence (1713–68), novelist 289

Stevenson, Mrs, school of ?110

Stourport 282

Strand, London 94

Strange, Mrs Isabella, née Lumisden, later Lady Strange (1719–1806) 8, 32, 81–93, 98–102, 111, 162, 192

Strange, Isabella Katherina (1759–1849) 82 and **n.**, 84–6, 91, 110, 192

Strange, Mary Bruce (1748–84) 44, 82–7, 90–3, 100–101, 111, 153, 192, 289

Strange, Sir Robert (1721–92), engraver 5–6, 7, 8, 59–60, 62, 81, 88, 108, 111, 192

Strange, Thomas Andrew Lumisden (1756–1841) 111 and **n.**

Stranges, the 44, 78, 89, 94, 108–9, 111, 193, 289

Surrey 1, 64, 73, 104, 109, 128, 137, 154, 165, 179, 201, 209, 223, 292

Swan Inn, Cheltenham 266

Swift, Jonathan (1667–1745) 293
The Furniture of a Woman's Mind 5
Polite Conversation 49
A Supplement to Dr. Swift's Works 210

Swilley, James Tobias (d. 1773), captain's servant, victim of Maori massacre 43 and **n.**

Switzerland 46

Symons, Mrs Elizabeth (d. 1794) 47–8 and **n.**, ?51, 58, 107, 157

Symons, Capt. John (*c.*1733–99), later Admiral 47 **n.**

Symons, Miss 48, ?51, 107, 157, 221

Tahiti (Otaheite) 91, 268

Tavistock Street, London 94
Tayler, Miss 285
Teignmouth 259
Tewkesbury 252
Thebes 81
Thicknesse, Philip (1719–92) 264–5 and **n.**
  A Year's Journey through France and Part of Spain 264
Thompson, Mr 293
Thrale, Mrs Hester Lynch, née Salusbury (1741–1821) xiii, 223–7 and **n.**
Thrale, Hester Maria ('Queeney'), later Lady Keith (1764–1857) xiii, 223–4 and **n.**
Tindal, Nicholas (1687–1774), translator:
  History of England by Rapin 284
Tolfrey, Mrs Margaret ?92–3 and **n.**
Tom (servant) 265
Tomkin (Tomkins), Mr, FB's admirer 127–8
Torre, Giovanni Battista (d. 1780), pyrotechnist 14 n.
Townshend, Anne, Lady, née Montgomery (d. 1819) 195 and **n.**
Townshend, George, 4th Visc. (1724–1807) 195 and **n.**
Turner, Mrs Catharine (Catherine), née Allen (d. 1796) 82–3
Turner, Charles (d. 1792) of King's Lynn 82–4
Turner, Frances ('Fanny'), later Lady Folkes (d. 1813) 37, 156
Turner, Sir John (1712–80), 3rd Bt, MP 37 and **n.**, 42 n.
Twining, Mrs Elizabeth, née Smythies (1739–96) 87 and **n.**, 89
Twining, Mrs Mary, née Little (1726–1804) 72 and **n.**
Twining, Thomas (1734–1804), divine, linguist, classicist 67–8 and **n.**, 70–3, 78–9, 87–9, 98–9, 106
Twiss, Richard (1747–1821), traveller, author xii, 9–26 and **n.**, 96, 135, 191
  A Tour in Ireland 191 n.
  Travels through Portugal and Spain 12 nn., 14, 17 n., 135, 191
Twiss, Miss (b. *c.*1757), sister of above 21
'Two Black Birds Sat upon a Spray' (song) 248

Vasil'chikov, Alexander Semenovich (b. *c.*1745), favourite of Catherine II of Russia 169, 170 **n.**
Vauxhall Gardens, London 36–7
'Vauxhall Mad Song' 219
Venice 296
Venus (goddess) 255

Waldron, Edward (1758–1813) ?277 and **n.**, 280
Waldron, Elizabeth (or Hannah) (b. 1756) 275–84 and **n.**
Waldron, George (1765–1829) ?277 and **n.**
Waldron, John (1760-*post* 1794) ?277 and **n.**
Waldron, Revd John (*c.*1725–94) 280 and **n.**, 283
Waldron, Thomas (1762–?1813) ?277 and **n.**
Wales 135, 151, 208
Wall, Catherine ?256 and **n.**
Wall, Elizabeth ?256 and **n.**
Wall, John (*c.*1745–1808), physician xii, 237–8 and **n.**, 251–66, 269–71
Wall, John (1775–1817) 70–1 and **n.**
Wall, Mrs Mary Brilliana, née Popham (d. by 1789) xii, 251–7 and **n.**, 259–66, 269–71
Wall, Robert Martin Popham (1774–1847) 270–1 and **n.**
Wall, Miss, later Mrs Crane 270–1 and **n.**
Waller, Edmund (1606–87), poet 179 and **n.**
Warwick Street, London 193
Westwood House, Worcestershire: visit to 271–84
Winchester 183
Windmill Street, London 94
Woodhouse, Thomas (d. 1773), midshipman, victim of Maori massacre 43 and **n.**
Woolf, Robert, agent 110 and **n.**
Woolwich Academy 204
Worcester (city) 200, 208, 231, 233, 265, 274, 285
Worcestershire 268
Worgan, John (1724–90):
  The Fair Thief (song) 278 and n.
Wright, Miss 202
Wright, Mr 202
Wright, Mrs 202

Yate, Mrs Annabella, née Honywood (*c.* 1755–1808) 259, 261

Yates, Mrs Mary Ann, née Graham (1728–87), actress, Opera manager 55–6 and **n.**, 160–1, 172, 250

Yates, Richard (*c.*1706–96), actor, Opera manager 55–6 and **n.**, 160, 166

York Street, Covent Garden, London 126

Young, Arthur (1741–1820), agriculturalist 4 n., 12–13, 18, 36–7

Young, Elizabeth (*c.*1744–97), actress 161–2 and n.

Young, Mrs Martha, née Allen (1741–1815), EAB's sister 4 n., 12–13, 15, 18, 21, 23, 36–7, 117, ?293

Ypres 289

Zinzendorf, Nicolaus Ludwig (1700–60), Count of Zinzendorf and Pottendorf 30 **n.**